ANDRZEJ WAJDA

ANDRZEJ WAJDA

History, Politics, and Nostalgia in Polish Cinema

Janina Falkowska

Berghahn Books
New York • Oxford

First published in 2007 by

Berghahn Books

www.berghahnbooks.com

©2007, 2008 Janina Falkowska
First paperback edition published in 2008

Library of Congress Cataloging-in-Publication Data

Falkowska, Janina, 1951-
  Andrzej Wajda : history, politics, and nostolgia in Polish cinema / Janina
Falkowska.
    p.cm.
  Includes bibliographical references and index.
  ISBN 1-84545-225-9 (hbk: alk. paper)
1. Andrzej Wajda, 1926---Criticism and interpretation. I. Title.

PN1998.3W34F34 2006
791.43023'3092--dc22
[B]

2006019288

British Library Cataloguing in Publication Data
A catalogue record for this book is available from the British Library
Printed in the United States on acid-free paper

ISBN 978-1-84545-225-4 hardback, 978-1-84545-508-8 paperback

�CONTENTS

🧷 Acknowledgments

In acknowledging the help and support from friends, acquaintances, and colleagues throughout the long process of writing and editing a book, one always risks omitting some. I hope that those of you who are omitted will forgive me for any oversight.

First of all, I would like to thank Andrzej Wajda himself, who knew about my project from its inception in 1998 and who fully supported my efforts, providing access to his archives, explaining to me details of his life, and offering many useful comments regarding the production aspects of his films.

Second, I would like to thank Scott Holden for his patient examination of the text for cohesiveness, accuracy, and stylistic consistency.

Third, I would like to thank the Social Sciences and Humanities Research Council of Canada and the Dean of Arts at the University of Western Ontario for supporting this work with generous grants.

During the preliminary planning stages of this project, I encountered a great deal of enthusiasm on part of both English- and Polish-speaking film academics. Leading film academics in Poland or those of Polish descent in Canada and the United States were instrumental in my completion of this book. In particular, Prof. Alicja Helman from the Jagiellonian University in Kraków and Prof. Marek Haltof at Northern Michigan University, both authors of numerous books and scholarly articles on Polish and world cinemas, greatly inspired me with their work and with their enormous knowledge of the subject. They approached my texts and my methods critically and were helpful in the final edition of this text. Other prominent scholars and experts on East-Central European film studies who have been invaluably supportive include Prof. Paul Coates at the Department of English, University of Aberdeen (Scotland), and Prof. Graham Petrie, formerly of MacMaster University in Hamilton, Ontario. Thanks to their unflinching support and professional advice, this project has come to a successful end.

I would also like to thank my dear colleagues for their emotional support and for their assistance in the tedious process of researching data and verifying historical facts for this book. First and foremost, I would like to thank Prof. Wojciech Tomasik (Akademia Bydgoska) for his help with Polish resources; Prof. Marek Haltof (Northern Michigan University), for his invaluable suggestions after a first reading of the draft; Christopher Gittings (The University of Western Ontario); Wacław Osadnik (The University of Alberta); and many others in Poland, Canada, and the United States for their unfailing support for this work.

My thanks also go to my husband for his patience and understanding during the difficult process of gathering data and the countless long hours working on drafts and revisions; to my friends and family who were often abandoned when I decided to spend my time writing instead of socializing with them; and to family members and friends in Poland who provided accommodation in Konin, Kraków, Szczyrk, Bydgoszcz, and Katowice when I needed to work in those cities.

Finally, I would like to thank both colleagues and students at the University of Western Ontario, whose intellectual motivation provided inspiration and challenge. Profs. Allan Gedalof, Richard Green, Nandi Bhatia, Diana Brydon, and Angela Esterhammer; and students Nicolas Muzzin, Kyle Tabbernor, Chris Girvan, Bryan Atkinson, Jennifer Thomson, and Aimee Mitchell are only some of those who should be included in these acknowledgments.

I am also grateful to the staff of the National Film Archives in Warsaw, in particular Grzegorz Balski and Adam Wyżyński, for their generous assistance with the photographs reproduced in this book. Other photographs come from the fabrykaobrazu.com website of Piotr Bujnowicz. I would also like to thank Perspektywa, Kadr, Oko, and Tor film studios for granting permission to use the photos from their films. Special thanks go to Wendy Pearson for the design of the book cover.

A final note: Parts of this book are based loosely on works published elsewhere. The following publishers have granted permission for the use of their texts: Berghahn Books, for permission to use some fragments from *The Political Films of Andrzej Wajda. Dialogism in Man of Marble, Man of Iron and Danton;* Universitas, for permission to use some fragments of the chapter "Głosy z zewnątrz. Recepcja filmów Andrzeja Wajdy w krajach anglosaskich," from *Filmowy Świat Andrzeja Wajdy;* and Wallflower Press, for permission to use fragments of the chapter "Ashes and Diamonds," which appeared in *24 Frames: Central Europe.*

❀ Introduction

ANDRZEJ WAJDA
His Words and His Archives

On 6 June 1998, all eyes in the Novorol Café in Kraków turn toward a man with gray hair and lively eyes. Andrzej Wajda, the best-known film-maker in Poland, approaches me with a smile. Still active and healthy in his seventies, he cracks political jokes, painstakingly explains the organization of the Andrzej Wajda Archives at the Manggha Center[1] in Kraków (on a piece of paper he draws the floor plan of his archives, a big room filled with countless materials related to his films' production and reception), and asks questions about my project, a film biography about Wajda.

Clearly accustomed to the admiration of strangers, Wajda listens politely to my plans. Now and then, he adds some remarks that open new vistas for my work. Later, Wajda's suggestions concerning his archives help enormously in approaching the filmmaking materials. These are materials of unsurpassed value, which contain preproduction, production, and postproduction notes encompassing his life's work from the earliest études he made at the Łódź Film School to his latest films. From notes regarding his choices of actors, camera operators, and production crews to film reviews about his works, each film file opens like a separate treasury.

The months I spent in these archives from 1998 to 2000 were among the most fascinating of my life. Like a detective, I examined every piece of paper and traced the filmmaking process, from rough notes on paper to complete works. Sometimes, the making of a film seemed a painful and difficult operation, as shown in the production papers for the film *Bramy raju* (*The Gates to Paradise*, 1968). At other times, a film was produced in a hasty effort to overcome significant time constraints, as in the case of Człowiek z żelaza (*Man of Iron*, 1981). The process of production varies from film to film due to a variety of circumstances.

Out of our conversations and my archival research, Wajda emerges as a collaborator who knows intuitively how and when to employ the expertise of other people. His relationship with actress Krystyna Zachwatowicz, the film wife of Mateusz Birkut in Człowiek z marmuru (*Man of Marble*, 1977) and Wajda's real-life wife and confidante, exemplifies this kind of collaboration. On one occasion, I participated in a conversation with the two of them in which they discussed the choice of the actress who would play Zosia, the main female protagonist for Wajda's film *Pan Tadeusz* (*Mr. Thadeus,* 1999). Zachwatowicz seems to have a good deal of influence on her husband's work; Wajda listens patiently, but offers his own suggestions. He wants someone very young and fresh, a quintessential beautiful Polish maiden with blonde hair and blue eyes, someone who appears naïve and innocent. I listen in silence at the table in the Novorol Café, quiet witness to production talk that may lead to yet another great film. Wajda, always sensitive to the reactions of others, notices my silence and comments briefly, "You see how difficult it is to make the right decision."

These quiet conversations in June 1998 started my collaboration with Andrzej Wajda, a filmmaker whose work I have studied for many years and whose films I have shown repeatedly to students at McGill University in Montreal, Quebec, and at the University of Western Ontario in London, Ontario, as well as to the Canadian public at large. Wajda, thought of as the "mythical romantic" of the Polish cinema, a producer of historic panoramas who incorporates Polish national mythology in his films, comes across in person as a highly practical man, clearly aware of all the complications to be encountered in the processes of both filmmaking and writing.

As I found during my visits to the Manggha Center, Wajda organized his archives as meticulously as he did his huge, elaborate film productions. On neatly arranged shelves are posters, notebooks, prizes, and reviews related to the production of his thirty-seven films; perhaps the most interesting shelf is the one filled with unrealized screenplays. On the right side of the room as one enters, there is a small desk with books about Wajda. All of these publications, written in Polish, German, French, Italian, Japanese, English, and other languages as well, include critical assessments of the director and of his film and theater productions. On the left side of the desk is a bookshelf full of materials that Wajda wants to include in his autobiography. Another particularly interesting section of the room is occupied by Wajda's longtime fascination: Japan and its art.

As Wajda has explained to me, each large cardboard box, specially produced for this purpose by a bookbinder, contains three kinds of materials: preproduction documents and screenplays; film realization materials, including photographs and drawings; and, finally, press reviews from the films. During my many long hours in this archive, I contemplated elements of the preproduction stage of film production— an arduous, painstaking process—including detailed correspondence with set organizers, actors, and crew, as well as financial considerations of the film, including bills, balance sheets, and receipts. The insight gained from my examination of these mundane processes, frustrations, and successes contributes to a fuller understanding of the artist's work.

The final section of each film's file contains film reviews and audience responses from critics, colleagues, and, most touching, from the public. In their letters, spectators thank Wajda for the emotions his films evoke and for the actions they inspire. Some of these letters are very earnest, clearly showing that Wajda can touch the nerves of Poles when he presents his dilemmas in various social and historical circumstances. From these letters, Wajda is revealed as an artist who truly loves people. While Krzysztof Kieślowski, another Polish filmmaker, claimed to be at his best in the editing studio, Wajda is happiest when surrounded by his actors, technicians, and producers. In his book *Podwójne spojrzenie (Double Vision),*[2] Wajda explains the importance of cooperating with actors and technicians, of the process of borrowing their skills and bringing out their best work while assisting in their development as artists.

Following the painter's tradition, Wajda illustrates by hand his ideas for his films, a method developed while he was a student at the Academy of Fine Arts in Kraków. Thus, the first version of a film always appears on paper as drawings, often quite precise. Some of these drawings are on hotel stationery, on restaurant napkins, in old notebooks and the like, as if he were always and everywhere planning his next film. Many of these drawings are small pieces of art in themselves; others are playful, even erotic, and at times unabashedly voyeuristic. (His drawings for *Kronika wypadków miłosnych* [*A Chronicle of Amorous Incidents,* 1986] are prime examples of the lattermost.) Like Sergei Eisenstein, Wajda clearly takes pleasure in drawing, as if the very act itself organized and described the world for him. Wajda's roots as a former student of the Academy of Fine Arts plainly show through here.

In my analysis of Wajda's life and films, I devote some attention to the director's formative years spent at the Łódź Film School. These years were important not only for the formation of his general outlook on life, but also for the development of his technical abilities. During their first year, Łódź students get a thorough training in photography; they are taught how to build a frame, center images, and utilize light and shadow. At this period of his career, one sees in Wajda's early artistic works great attention to detail and composition, which is also important in the photographic art. As I began my research for this book, I scrutinized with amazement Wajda's early photographs of the figures of the saints (e.g., Saint Stanislas), the close-ups of faces, and the setups of elaborate historical scenes.

Later, during my research on some of his films, I saw the same meticulous approach to imagery in Wajda's drawings for the films and in the photographs illustrating the process of film production, from the photos of actors and of scenes to whole series of elaborate photograms documenting full sequences. Aside from his painterly style, other aspects of Wajda's directorial work also merit attention. He seems to enjoy the physical aspect of the whole endeavor of filmmaking. In one of the photographs in his autobiography, *Kino i reszta świata*,[3] he is shown lifting a heavy table used in one of his theatrical productions (Wajda is also a noted theater director). For me, this captured moment of physical effort epitomizes the work of a director who, at one time in his life, used to commute between Kraków and Warszawa every week to direct plays in the former city and, simultaneously, films in the latter city.

In my research, I was forced to give much thought to the way in which I should address this enormous body of material, yet build a consistent picture of the artist and his films in the context of political and social developments in Poland. As often happens, the simplest answer seemed the best: My final decision was to analyze the films in chronological order, decade by decade, chapter by chapter, and to make similarly chronological references to the historical, social, and political phenomena of each era that were especially visible in particular sequences or films. I treat all of Wajda's films as one discourse through which the political, the historical, the cultural, and the aesthetic weave a complex network of references to Polish realities. The personality of the director, who carefully exposes all these traits, is a binding agent guaranteeing the artistic and semantic cohesion of the discourse. The films constitute fragments of a complex tapestry that presents various strata of Polish society with its diverse properties and problems.

In approaching this rich discourse from the theoretical point of view, I have generally adopted a variety of theories, among which Mikhail Bakhtin's polymorphism, heteroglossia, and polyphony, as applied to the literary studies, are supplemented by some approaches to nostalgia. The most important theories, however, refer to the broadly understood concepts of intertextuality and of multiplicities of discourses, which explain the diversity of cultural and historical traditions in Wajda's films. These traditions emerge in various films and reappear in the form of a semantic continuum, providing a wholeness and consistency to the artistic output of the director. This intertextuality explains why so many traits present in Polish paintings and sculptures appear in Wajda's films and why, transformed by his artistic and directorial talent, they begin to function in their own way.

One of the crucial theoretical assumptions I had to make when I started to work with this material was to decide on the idea of film authorship. Who is Andrzej Wajda as a filmmaker, I asked myself, and what films do I consider "Wajda films"? Following my earlier theoretical findings,[4] I consider Andrzej Wajda a Foucaldian embodiment of the discursive function,[5] but also its centering source, the commander of what he considers important in this discourse. He forms both the narrative and the visual structure of the film in a dictatorial manner, imposing one consistent vision of the portrayed reality. He rigorously executes his directorial command over all the aspects of the film, and thus each of his films can be called a "Wajda film," an artistic work with a specific ideological thesis and a consistent aesthetics. Each is a work the director carefully planned from its initial idea, through the screenplay, the choice of actors and artistic directors, and the music and sound. A "Wajda film" literally exudes "Wajdaesqueness" in both its ideas and its aesthetics. Unlike a filmmaker functioning in the context of a complex system of command in a Hollywood studio, Wajda is both master and commander, and he has the absolute last word in his choice of every set designer, director of photography, camera operator, actor, and composer. In this sense, he can be also seen as one of the greatest independent filmmakers in the world.

In addition to presenting Wajda's films in chronological order, I tend to designate his work along two paths: *time* and *theme*. Overlapping and sometimes running parallel to the temporal plane is the thematic plane, which presents the major thematic preoccupations of the director in each decade. The concluding remarks at the end of each chapter, organized by decade, summarize the overlapping themes within that particular decade. In the conclusion, I discuss the thematic trajectory of the director's entire creative output. This temporal-thematic mode corresponds to real political events taking place in each decade, which, in turn, triggered their interpretation in particular films produced by Wajda. The historical trajectory in themes is paralleled by that in aesthetics, which in turn matches the aesthetic developments in chronology (e.g., the emergence of the French New Wave in the 1960s) or the dynamic style of the films in the 1990s. These thematic and aesthetic preoccupations are revealed in the discussion of film narratives, sequence after sequence. The narratives, the protagonists, and the images all speak of the director, who is ultimately responsible for the film's narrative and ideological content.

There are many reasons why my film analyses are presented in this fashion. First, each of the films has a fascinating story to tell. Furthermore, each unfolds with its own rhythm and, as it does so, reveals layers of meaning whose interpretations rely heavily on a knowledge of Polish history, society, and culture. These layers of meaning are not always revealed in a film's basic plot, but rather in individual sequences or even in singular images that require an informed analysis to reveal the film's ideological and visual complexities. Wajda's films have been produced over a span of fifty years. In approaching this work, I have decided to place it within the historical and cultural developments of East-Central Europe and Poland. For instance, cultural movements that developed (often at Polish universities) to counter the "official" culture propagated by the government are clearly present in many of his films. One of his films, for instance, *Polowanie na muchy* (*Hunting Flies*, 1969), has innumerable references to student life in the 1960s and includes quotations from the songs of well-known student singers such as Marek Grechuta.

The most fascinating document I encountered while undertaking this project is Wajda's *Kalendarium*, a detailed description of the major events in his life starting from 1926 and ending in 1996. When I asked Wajda in 1998 whether he was planning to finish this document, he said that he had lost interest in documenting his own life, and would rather concentrate on living than on his own "stale legend," as he put it. However, every year in his life is painstakingly documented in three distinct parts: personal life, films, and ideas. Starting in 1959, another part is added: the theater. At this point, instead of making only films, Wajda chooses the difficult double path of a film/theater director. In 1959, he began his theatrical directorial career with *Kapelusz pełen deszczu* at the Dramatic Theater in Gdynia. From that time, his theatrical career has been an important part of his artistic life, and he has been invited to direct plays in Kraków, Warszawa, and other major Polish cities. From this point forward, then, I have thought of the director dialogically, comparing the better-known of his theater productions with his activities on the film set and imagining how one artistic path influenced the other.

In *Kalendarium*, the entry for each year is full of factual and anecdotal riches. For instance, in 1957, Wajda starts his work on *Popiół i diament* (*Ashes and Diamonds*, 1958) and a moving story precedes this entry. Wajda went to a Polish spa called Krynica Morska for treatment of an ulcer (which, as he states, his body generated after he had produced *Kanał* [*Kanal*, 1957]). There, he met one of the greatest personalities of Polish theater, Tadeusz Janczar. One day, while they were walking in the mountains, Janczar told Wajda of Jerzy Andrzejewski's book *Popiół i diament*, which Janczar had just read. A month later, Wajda wrote a letter to Andrzejewski, asking whether they might collaborate on the screenplay.

So it goes, year after year, a wonderful screenplay for the unique film that shows the life of the great director in its human complexity, with all its passions and frustrations. Following the archival materials and the information in the *Kalendarium*, the life and work of the director opens rather like a storybook. The archival work has its high and low points, however. The highest is definitely the organization of the archive itself, a scrupulous division into parts, some of them rarely explored by any academic. (I am thinking here about a special shelf mentioned earlier, one full of unrealized screenplays. Wajda himself pointed it out to me: "Please, have a look at this. There are so many brilliant scripts. I was not allowed to [due to censorship restrictions] or did not have the money to produce these films. I would have loved to make these films.") Another high point is Wajda's private letters to his fans, friends, lovers, and wives. From all these letters, he emerges as a truly altruistic and kind person, personally responding to fans in small villages. A letter from the famed director undoubtedly made the day for many of these fans.

The low point, without a doubt, is the sheer volume of the material to be explored. I looked carefully at every piece of paper, be it telegram, fax, handwritten letter, review, drawing (on a restaurant serviette), or glossy press release photograph. One thing I knew: In this voyeuristic process of archival work, I was enthralled, recognizing from new perspectives the intense emotions each film had provoked in me in the past. I cherished the opportunity to get to know the man behind these words and images. The biography that emerges from the archives, my meetings with the director, and my own responses to Wajda's films (whether recent or from memory) constitute a polyphonic mosaic of research and findings interspersed with my own emotional reactions to his films.

Of course, in this complex process of researching the archives and dealing with the director in person, I was also forced to define myself as a biographer. First, as a Pole, I am intimately aware of the complexities of social and historical circumstances displayed in Wajda's work, but also of the complex ethical situation of the director who functioned successfully under such circumstances. Second, I am aware of Wajda's iconic status both in Poland and abroad, and of his role as a symbolic "father of the nation." In my attempts to analyze his work, I try to combine the elements of history, politics, and personality to explain the incredible phenomenon of Wajda the artist, the thinker, and the interpreter of the fortunes of Polish society.

Wajda's massive film corpus (thirty-seven fiction films to date) is artistically homogeneous, though composed of diverse genres: historical melodramas, comedies, and heritage films (generally based upon well-known literary texts that refer to the nation's past), among others. Thematically, these films relate the times of World War II, the period of social consciousness in the 1960s, the rise of political opposition in the 1970s, the disillusionment of the 1980s (after martial law had been introduced), and the social changes that took place after the onset of capitalism in the 1990s. All of his works share a compassionate attitude toward people: Wajda shows people fighting against concrete historical reality or being destroyed by it. While guarding the rights to subjecthood and independence, he raises issues of loyalty and duty—whether personal or national—in the face of adversity. In his depiction of powerful and conflicting emotions triggered by historical events, of various social groups in Poland and their ambivalent interests, Wajda's cinema is political on many levels. His strong sense of history and politics, the two being inseparable, is present not only in his famous early films of the 1950s (*Pokolenie* [*A Generation*, 1955], *Kanal,* and *Ashes and Diamonds*), but also in films of the 1970s (*Krajobraz po bitwie* [*Landscape After Battle*, 1970] and *Man of Marble*), films of the 1980s (*Man of Iron* and *Danton* [*Danton*, 1983], a film from the 1990s (*Korczak* [*Korczak*, 1990]), and, most recently, a film from the 21st century (*Zemsta* [*Revenge*, 2002]). Taking into consideration the many aspects of Wajda's filmography, I seek to investigate the historical perspectives present in his work (e.g., regarding the Solidarity strike in Gdańsk); its social implications (e.g., regarding the treatment of Jews in Poland); its aesthetic impact (e.g., his brilliant use of classical paintings in the design of mise-en-scène); its political impact (e.g., various political actions triggered by *Man of Marble* and *Man of Iron*); and, finally, the nationalistic intentions of his cinema.

Wajda has had great success with most of his films, but he has produced some weaker works as well that were not so persuasive in their presentation of social and emotional conflicts. My personal dissatisfaction with some of these films is clearly reflected in this book. Although I discuss all fiction films made by Wajda, with the exception of some films made for Polish television (e.g., *Z biegiem lat, z biegiem dni...* [*As the Years Pass, As the Days Pass...*, 1980]), I devote less attention to some of them than to others: Wajda's greatest films, generally the ones that garnered many international awards, are covered extensively, while other films, such as *Panna Nikt* (*Miss Nobody*, 1996) or *Hunting Flies*, are less fully addressed. This does not mean that the latter films were unimportant, but rather that they were less strikingly meaningful, both aesthetically and politically, than their more famous counterparts.

In general, not many Polish or Eastern European filmmakers (except perhaps Miklos Jancso and Andrei Tarkovsky) triggered such intense emotions—ranging from absolute reverence for the director to outright physical attacks—as Wajda. In particular, those films he produced in the 1970s and 1980s polarized audiences and triggered discussions on the restoration or the demise of Poland. Of all Polish filmmakers, Wajda has addressed issues of national identity most explicitly, articulating matters important to national tradition, and has deliberated the essence of Polish culture and history in most of his films.

In his films, Wajda has depicted virtually all of the social groups in Poland and the traditions they have represented: For instance, from a representation of the intelligentsia in *Wesele* (*The Wedding*, 1973) and *Panny z Wilka* (*The Young Ladies of Wilko*, 1979), he turns to the depiction of socialist workers in *Man of Marble* and *Man of Iron*. In an insightful manner, Wajda has approached crucial historical movements in his adaptations of literary works and in his historical films. Moreover, he has used his talent and influence to champion momentous political movements in Poland; for instance, he actively supported the protest of the young filmmakers against the totalitarian practices of Socialist Realism, and later he backed the political movement of Solidarity.

Wajda has not only received many national and international prizes for his films, but he is also a political activist and the recipient of numerous Polish orders and distinctions. It is worth noting, however, that despite producing his sometimes thought-provoking, contentious, and volatile films, and despite his outward opposition to the government, he has often enjoyed privileges and perks rarely granted to other filmmakers in Poland. Wajda has had an enormous influence not only on Polish film production, but on the creation of the political and artistic movements in Poland, such as the Polish Film School in the 1950s, the Cinema of Moral Concern in the 1970s, war films throughout his career, and the "cinema of nostalgia" in the 1980s and 1990s, and from 2000 to 2006. He has both inspired and provoked both young and old in Poland and in all the countries of the former Socialist bloc in Eastern Europe. Wajda's films were widely discussed in cinemas, student clubs and cafés, and in the district film clubs popular in Eastern Europe, especially in the 1960s and 1970s. Always surrounded by young filmmakers dreaming about making films under his supervision, he was often found in the company of those who were interested in what he had to say on particular issues, and among those friends who inspired him and whom he inspired in return. Many of them wrote about these meetings. In the early 1960s, Wajda stirred spectators' emotions only via films and theater productions; later, encouraged by film critics and journalists, he gave many interviews. These interviews and the many stories of his colleagues and fans, published only in Polish, are a rich source of information about Wajda the man, but also about his work methods and solutions to production problems. (I have carefully examined these sources, and some are used in this book.)

Andrzej Wajda: History, Politics, and Nostalgia in Polish Cinema has emerged from a research project sponsored by the Social Sciences and Humanities Research Council in Canada; the Faculty of Arts, the Department of English, and the Department of Film Studies at the University of Western Ontario; and the Film Studies Association of Canada. My research for this project was conducted primarily in Poland, Germany, and France between the years 1994 and 1999, among various Polish archives and libraries (including the Andrzej Wajda Archives at the Manggha Center in Kraków).

I hope *Andrzej Wajda: History, Politics, and Nostalgia in Polish Cinema* will be a valuable source of information about the director, his films, and the historical circumstances in which he worked.

1

THE LIFE AND TIMES OF ANDRZEJ WAJDA

There are many ways in which an author can approach the biography of a filmmaker. One can use commonly accessible sources like books, articles, and press releases, or one can go directly to the source: the filmmaker's diaries, personal notes and kalendaria. I chose to do the latter and tried to reconstruct Andrzej Wajda's personal story from these sources. Additionally, I used material from conversations with Wajda and from his personal letters to me. All these sources were laconic and concise, however; only in conversations did Wajda sometimes reveal his private thoughts. What the reader has below is my attempt at the reconstruction of the fascinating collection of facts and thoughts which, both in content and style, reflect on the "down-to-earth" nature of the director himself.

Andrzej Wajda was born on 6 March 1926, in Suwałki, Poland. His mother, Aniela-Zofia Białowąs, was a teacher and a voracious reader. Her favorite book was a well-known saga about gentry and intelligentsia by Maria Dąbrowska, *Noce i dnie*,[1] which describes the life of a noble family in the late nineteenth and early twentieth centuries. Herself a daughter of the middle-class family, Aniela-Zofia provided an informed and intelligent environment for her two sons, Andrzej and Leszek. Jakób Wajda, Andrzej's father, was an aide-de-camp in the Polish army, posted fulltime in Radom. Wajda's younger brother Leszek, who studied interior design at the Academy of Fine Arts in Kraków, designed the set interiors for *Ashes and Diamonds* in 1958 and for *Samson (Samson*, 1961) in 1960. Leszek remained at the Academy of Fine Arts in Kraków, Department of the Art of Arranging Exhibitions, where he was a professor. He still lives in Kraków.[2]

Andrzej Wajda describes Suwałki, where he spent his childhood, as a military town whose whole existence followed the rhythm of the army. In many interviews, he refers repeatedly to the influence this town had on the formation of his artistic interests. For instance, marches, elaborate scenes involving soldiers, or scenes referring to army life are present in ten of his thrity-seven films; many of these scenes are drawn directly from Wajda's memories of Suwałki's May 3rd Parade, the most important annual event in the life of the town, enjoyed by all the town's inhabitants—and especially by the children. On this day each year, several thousand soldiers marched to commemorate the anniversary of the first constitution of an independent Poland; these exuberant marches were performed to the tunes of army songs praising patriotism and bravery. The ardent nationalism often depicted so overwhelmingly in Wajda's films, presented in the context of army life, takes its humble origin in his memories of his childhood town.

The rich army life of the garrison town surrounded Wajda's family. The parades, army uniforms, battles, and horses that fueled so many of the patriotic paintings hanging in every Polish museum were eagerly copied or lovingly imitated by Andrzej's father, who was an amateur painter. Thanks to Jakób's great interest in painting and in historical art, Andrzej became well acquainted with these works of art. Reproductions of paintings by Jan Matejko, Jacek Malczewski, Artur Grottger, and Michał Elwiro Andriolli, all well-known Polish artists,[3] hung in the Wajda home. Aniela-Zofia was also open to such new inventions as film; among the very first films Andrzej saw as a twelve-year-old boy was *King Kong* (1933).

This peaceful and comfortable life was disrupted by the events of World War II. The impact of the war on the Wajdas' lives were disastrous, as for so many families. When the war broke out on 1 September 1939, Wajda's father was immediately sent to the front. The family lost contact with him for many years; they fled from the enemy, destitute and in constant fear of the Germans. They thought that Jakób had died either during the September campaign or in 1940 in Katyń, near Charków, where many Polish officers were executed. On 28 September 1939, at the order of Polish Army commander Juliusz Rommel, Jakób was awarded, in absentia, the highest distinction of the Polish Army, the Virtuti Militari Cross of the 5th Grade. In 1940, Wajda's mother received two letters and some money from her husband, who was alive and living in Kozielsk. They learned from one of these letters that he had been imprisoned by the Soviets. Thereafter, again, there was no word from him; this time Jakób was later presumed dead.

Thirteen-year-old Andrzej suffered greatly, so early in his life, from these two tragic events: Hitler's invasion of Poland and his father's disappearance. As he writes in *Kalendarium*,[4] Wajda looked with despair upon column after column of Polish army officers all marching to German prisons. This was Wajda's first meeting with history, which for him and for countless other Poles meant defeat and disaster for their country as well as personal tragedy for their families. These war experiences are later replayed in half of Wajda's films, and clearly constitute an important theme in his oeuvre.

Several weeks after the war erupted in 1939, Wajda experienced the Germans' brutality for the first time during his family's panicked flight first to Puławy and then to Kazimierz. This event left lasting memories in the young boy. Later, the fleeing family found refuge in Radom, where Wajda started his secondary education in a local high school (or rather a gymnasium). He continued this education throughout the war at the *tajna szkoła średnia* (secret high school): During the war and the German occupation, Polish teachers organized clandestine meetings for children and conducted regular lessons in private apartments and houses of teachers and co-workers. As a result, young Andrzej not only received a thorough primary and secondary education, but also developed his artistic interests in painting, both watercolors and oil, and in sculpture; this interest in art later shaped his entire artistic output in both film and theater productions. He studied under Prof. Wacław Dobrowolski[5] and later worked as an apprentice for the three artists who painted the polychrome at the Bernardin Catholic Church in Radom: Adam Stalony-Dobrzański, Eugeniusz Pisarek, and Wiktor Langer. In 1942, Wajda started producing portraits, landscapes, and historical paintings.

Also in 1942, Wajda joined the Home Army,[6] in which he performed the function of a liaison officer (courier), a duty customary for boys of his age. He was nearly arrested by the Germans for these activities, and as a result was forced to flee Radom for Kraków, where he lived for some time; there he continued his involvement in Home Army activities and was again nearly arrested by the Germans. He returned to Radom, where he finished high school. When the war ended in 1945, Wajda was nineteen years old. One of the most enduring memories he retains from that time is that of Warszawa, the capital of Poland, completely ruined by German bombardment. This highly visual memory later found its way into such films as *Kanal* and *Pierścionek z orłem w koronie* (*The Crowned-Eagle Ring*, a.k.a. *The Horse-Hair Ring*, 1993).

At the end of the war, Radom was, as Wajda calls it, a "cultural backwater," yet it managed to maintain contacts with leading literary figures of the time. Writers and poets from nearby Warszawa visited to present their literary works. Among the best-known of the cultural figures visiting Radom were poets Julian Przyboś, Julian Tuwim, Antoni Słonimski, Leopold Staff, and Władysław Broniewski and writers Jerzy Andrzejewski and Jan Parandowski. This short-lived but rich intellectual life in Radom contributed greatly to young Andrzej's development. His skills at argumentation were sharpened as a result of witnessing these debates and discussions, and his eyes were opened to means of expression other than the visual. Also born of these meetings was Wajda's long friendship with Jerzy Andrzejewski, a friendship that later produced their brilliant collaboration on the screenplay for *Ashes and Diamonds*. The year 1945 was important for Wajda in another sense, as well: While visiting certain Kraków museums, he chanced upon a collection of Japanese woodcuts by the artist Feliks Jasieński. Wajda remembers this moment very clearly, for it represents his first exposure to Japanese culture; this experience evolved into a significant area of artistic expression in his life, culminating in the cooperative film effort with Japanese artists that produced the film *Nastasja* (*Nastasja*, 1994) and, more recently, in the construction of the Manggha Japanese Culture Center in Kraków.

Moving further in the direction of visual arts in 1946, Wajda began his studies at Akademia Sztuk Pięknych (the Kraków Academy of Fine Arts). At the academy, he joined the *grupa samokształceniowa* (self-education group), the ideologue and leader of which was Andrzej Wróblewski,[7] one of the most talented artists of the post-war era. Later, Wajda audited the lectures of Prof. Zygmunt Rudnicki and also studied with Hanna Rudzka-Cybisowa, a post-Impressionist painter. Wajda soon came to believe, though, that his artistic inclinations, however profound, did not make him an accomplished painter. Despite the fact that he received awards for drawings and paintings at the academy, he felt that he was not particularly talented and humbly left the art school in 1949. The academy nonetheless played several important roles in Wajda's life. First, he received his artistic education there; second, he got to know Wróblewski; and, third, he met Konrad Nałęcki, who assisted Wajda in his early films.

At the academy Wajda also received his first bitter lesson in postwar politics, which he later recounted in his films dealing with Stalinist times. Wajda studied art during what is generally considered one of the worst periods in modern Polish history, when the totalitarian Stalinist regime dictated affairs in Poland. This political system made its inroad in Poland in 1945–56, when Stalin introduced Bolesław Bierut as his representative to Poland. Bierut governed the one-party state following directions from Stalin himself. The system espoused by Stalin demanded the complete ideological, psychological, and social subjugation of Soviet citizens in all areas of life. Bierut attempted to introduce this totalitarian ideology in Poland, but his efforts were undermined there by the intellectual resistance of the artists.

At that time, Polish citizens suffered many economic and social hardships, the worst of which were the lack of food and of political liberties. Freedom of speech was nonexistent, so many artists were deprived of the possibility of leading an active artistic life. Instead, they had to conform to the dictates of Socialist Realism,[8] the main purpose of which was to present an unrealistically positive picture of society. Those who did not obey official ideology were the targets of an unprecedented attack by the Ministry of Culture.[9] One such artist was Prof. Eugeniusz Eisbich, the rector of the Kraków Academy of Fine Arts, who was expelled from his own academy in 1948 because of his unorthodox views. This unfortunate event was followed by an outright attack on other artists in a futile attempt to apply punitive measures to curb independent thinking and creativity. This early experience gave Wajda an insight into the officially sanctioned Socialist Realism, which he later recalled in *Man of Marble* and other films. As Wajda comments in *Kalendarium*, "with the expulsion of Professor Eisbich, the regimen of Socialist Realist painting was fully implemented."

When Wajda learned about the opening of a school that would teach students how to make films, he decided to apply. In July of 1949, he was accepted to the Państwowa Wyższa Szkoła Filmowa w Łodzi (State Higher Film School in Łódź, or Łódź Film School), where he studied until 1952. The school was founded on 2 November 1948; two months later, Jerzy Toeplitz, a well-known film historian, became its director. The school was located on Targowa Street in the palatial mansion of a prewar factory owner. In the first stages of its existence, the few filmmakers and cinematographers in Poland joined the faculty to become lecturers; these included directors Wanda Jakubowska, Alexander Ford, Edmund Cękalski, Adam Bohdziewicz and cinematographers Stanisław Wohl, Adolf Forbert, and Andrzej Ancuta. The school also invited film experts from other countries. Thus, students had an opportunity to attend lectures by Bela Balazs, Georges Sadoul, Joris Ivens, Giuseppe de Santis, Basil Wright, Umberto Barbarro, Mary Seaton, Vsevolod Pudovkin, and Grigori Alexandrov, among others.[10]

The Łódź Film School had a rigorous curriculum with a predominantly theoretical component. The students had few practical classes and felt constrained by the intrusions of the instructors. For this very reason, Wajda was not very happy with his stay at the school—he considered the instruction to be too confining and dictatorial. As he comments in *Kalendarium*, "The stay at the school was disastrous for me; I was [extremely] disappointed."[11] The students were expected to produce short film études, and Wajda's are still accessible in the school's archives: "Zły chłopiec" ("A Bad Boy," 1951) and "Kiedy ty śpisz" ("When You Sleep," 1953). The first one is a narrative exercise based on Anton Czechow's short story by the same title, and the second a documentary impression based on the poem "Kiedy ty śpisz" by Tadeusz Kubiak. Wajda also started another film at the Łódź Film School: "Idę do słońca" ("I Go to the Sun," 1955)[12] is a paradocumentary about celebrated Polish sculptor Xawery Dunikowski, who specialized in making huge sculptures similar to those of Henry Moore. In 1951, Wajda also made his first documentary film, "Ceramika iłżecka" ("Ilsa Ceramic," 1951) and considered making films about the painters Jan Matejko, Aleksander Gierymski, and Harmensz van Rijn Rembrandt. The four films he produced as a student reveal Wajda's talent and his meticulous organizational skills. As Wanda Wertenstein suggests in the introduction to her book *Wajda Tells about Himself* (1991), Wajda's early credits should also include coauthorship of the screenplay for the narrative film *Trzy opowieści* (*Three Stories*, 1952) made by fellow students Konrad Nałęcki, Ewa Poleska (later Petelska), and Czesław Petelski.[13]

In 1953, Wajda received a certificate of completion from the Łódź Film School with, but not a graduation diploma—he left the school to become an assistant to director Alexander Ford. Wajda considers it a stroke of unprecedented luck that Ford asked him to join his film crew. Ford's film with Wajda under his wing was *Piątka z ulicy Barskiej* (*The Five from Barska Street*, 1954), a film about five young boys convicted of robbery and assault; this film signaled new sociorealist themes and aesthetics in Polish cinema. Ford used realistic set designs and muted color to mark the brutality and cynicism of the postwar years. The film won an award at the Cannes International Film Festival for Ford's directorial work. Even though as an apprentice on Ford's film he had very little to do on the set, Wajda admits that this was a great opportunity for him to see the experienced and well-known Polish director at work. What he saw and experienced on the set of this film led him directly to a similar choice of themes in his first fiction film, *A Generation*.

A Generation, his first important film, received a state award for his effort and clearly introduces the two major preoccupations of Wajda's early work: World War II and the predicament of young people in Poland. This film not only established Wajda as a prominent filmmaker, but also had an immediate impact upon other Polish filmmakers in the 1950s. *A Generation* and Andrzej Munk's *Człowiek na torze* (*Man on the Railway Track*, 1956), with their unique combination of themes and aesthetics, are generally considered to have formed the basis of the Polish School.[14] In October 1956, Wajda was given his first official directorial work assignment at the Zespoły Autorów Filmowych (The Film Authors' Unit), obtaining permission to make the film *Kanal*. In the autumn of 1957, he began work on *Ashes and Diamonds*.

The three war films, *A Generation*, *Kanal*, and *Ashes and Diamonds*, made Wajda famous both in Poland and abroad. These three films restate his interest in historical themes of World War II, the painterly tradition in the construction of mise-en-scène, and his skillful use of literary works for film adaptation. Thanks to the early success of these films, Wajda earned wide recognition and quickly accepted subsequent screenplays, starting work on several films simultaneously in 1959: *Lotna* (*Lotna*, 1959), *Samson*, *Sibirska leidi Makbet* (*Siberian Lady Macbeth*, a.k.a. *Fury Is a Woman*, 1962), and *Niewinni czarodzieje* (*Innocent Sorcerers*, 1960).[15] The first three continue the themes originally presented in his first masterpieces: *Lotna* deals with the events of World War II; *Samson* is the first of Wajda's films to describe the fate of Jews in contemporary Poland, a subject Wajda later presents in three subsequent films, *Ziemia obiecana* (*Promised Land*, 1975), *Korczak*, and *Wielki tydzień* (*Holy Week*, 1995); finally, *Siberian Lady Macbeth*, based on Nikolai Leskov's story, "Sibirska leidi Makbet" (itself based on Shakespeare's play), relates the events of a brutal murder in distant Siberia. *Innocent Sorcerers*, shot in the impressionist mode, portrays the emotions and unfulfilled desires of young people in post-World War II Poland, a refreshing diversion from Wajda's major historical films. Despite Wajda's and some critics' dissatisfaction with these films, they mark Wajda's progression from an immature, albeit enthusiastic and energetic young filmmaker into an auteur able to present complex philosophical questions on screen.

In 1959, Wajda also began his theatrical career. The first play he directed was *Kapelusz pełen deszczu* (*A Hatful of Rain*) by Michael Gazzo, a realistic, psychological American drama about drug addiction that had premiered in New York in 1955. From this point on, the paths of his creative work in both theater and film intersect, and specific parallels may be observed in the development of his work in both areas. (Wajda's theatrical career has been dealt with extensively in Maciej Karpiński's book, *The Theater of Andrzej Wajda*.[16]) At this point in his career, Wajda was fully recognized by the authorities as a filmmaker and an artist. In December 1960, he signed an official contract with Zjednoczone Zespoły Realizatorów Filmowych (Units of Film Producers), thus starting his full-time film career.

In 1962, Wajda produced a twenty-minute contribution to *Miłość dwudziestolatków* (*Love at Twenty*, 1962), an internationally produced collection of short films on the same theme. Other directors taking part in this collaboration were François Truffaut, Renzo Rossellini, Marcel Ophuls, and Shintaro Ishihara. Wajda's contribution was a short film about unrequited love, presented in the context of World War II memories, with the lead role brilliantly executed by actor Zbigniew Cybulski. The film is memorable for another reason, as well. It was on the set of this film that Wajda met Barbara Pec-Ślesicka, then assistant production manager, who later became his collaborator on the set of many films.[17]

In 1963, Wajda directed John Whiting's *Demons* at the Ateneum Theater in Warszawa; however, the play was poorly received.[18] After that time, Wajda stopped working on plays for seven years. From 1962 to 1965, he tried to have several screenplay projects accepted by the Censorship Board for *Promised Land, Man of Marble,* and *The Gates to Paradise.* His lack of success at this endeavor can be explained by the controversial political nature of these projects: *Man of Marble* deals with the issues of Socialist work in a highly critical manner, and *Promised Land* is equally controversial in its exploration of the beginnings of the industrialization of Poland. *The Gates to Paradise,* a film about children's martyrdom in the Middle Ages, offers a controversial interpretation of Christian preoccupations with martyrdom and suffering.

Undeterred by these rejections, Wajda began work in mid-1964 on his next film, *Popioły* (*Ashes*, 1965). The film's screenplay is based on Stefan Żeromski's novel by the same title; it tells the story of Prince Gintult and the noblemen Rafał Olbromski and Krzysztof Cedro, all fighting under Napoleon. The film's action takes place around the turn of the eighteenth century, at a time when Poland was partitioned by three occupiers: Austria, Germany, and Russia. Unorthodox and controversial, the film questions Poles' nationalist feelings and their allegiance to Napoleon, who promised the Poles freedom if they participated in his many battles. *Ashes* brought Wajda enormous success in Poland and stimulated fervent discussions in the press concerning its treatment of the concept of national identity and its appraisal of Polish history and national tradition.

In 1965, Wajda worked as a film director with the United Film Realization Unit in Warszawa and as a film professor at the Łódź Film School, his alma mater. During that year, Wajda also started work on what would prove to be his most troublesome film to date, *The Gates to Paradise*, for which he at last had received final approval from the authorities. The entire year of 1966 was devoted to the realization of this film about a children's crusade in the Middle Ages. However, an inappropriate choice of actors (and Wajda's lack of rapport with them) doomed the film to failure. Despite the beauty of the film's images, it simply proved unconvincing. Full of doubt and hesitation, Wajda feared he had been too ambitious with a project that, in hindsight, may not have been ideally suited to him. In the end, this difficult film, shot in Yugoslavia with German-speaking actors, brought the director much grief. It is considered one of his few failures, and it has never been shown in public cinemas in Poland.

Active on both filmmaking and educational fronts in 1965–66, the director was at this time invited to serve on the editorial board of the monthly periodical *Kino*,[19] the first issue of which appeared in 1966. His difficulties in attaining official sanction were exacerbated by the artist's personal problems. He was negotiating his divorce proceedings from his second wife, painter Zofia Wajda,[20] and had become involved in a romantic relationship with actress Beata Tyszkiewicz, who was playing the leading female role in *Ashes*. More or less at the same time, in 1966, Wajda purchased a house in Głuchy, which quickly became a refuge for the director, who was often exhausted from carrying out several projects at the same time.

In 1967, Wajda and Beata Tyszkiewicz were married and had a daughter, Karolina. In the same year, Wajda started work on one of his most startling films, *Wszystko na sprzedaż* (*Everything for Sale*, 1969), an aesthetic marvel of a film about Zbigniew Cybulski, the actor who had made *Ashes and Diamonds* so memorable. Shot in the mode of the French New Wave, *Everything for Sale* is a study of grieving and despair among Polish audiences as well as colleagues and friends of the deceased Cybulski; it is based on Wajda's own screenplay and combines elements of fiction and reality. With this film, Wajda secured his position in the world cinema as an auteur, not merely a brilliant filmmaker. It is worth noting that Barbara Pec-Ślesicka became Wajda's production manager on *Everything for Sale;* at that time, a fruitful cooperation that would span many years started between two talented film professionals.[21]

The 1960s were a time of political turmoil in Wajda's country, and might also be considered a time of great uncertainty in the director's private life; despite this, Wajda produced an impressive number of diverse films in that decade. Beside those films mentioned previously, he also produced films with issues that had not appeared in his earlier productions: *Przekładaniec* (*Roly Poly,* 1968), a humorous science-fiction novella about organ transplants, and *Hunting Flies,* a thoroughly misogynist portrayal of women. In these two films, the personal and the impersonal merge: the impartial adaptations of the stories written by others turn into accounts of Wajda's own feelings. *Roly Poly* is an amusing film based on a Stanisław Lem novella describing the lives of two brothers, Richard and Thomas, both avid car racers. When Thomas dies in a car accident, his various body parts are transplanted into or onto other people, including his brother, Richard (both parts are played by the excellent comedic actor Bogumił Kobiela). *Hunting Flies,* on the other hand, based on Janusz Głowacki's short story by that name, describes the life of Włodek, a "thirty-something" university graduate who majored in Russian Philology and who is dominated by his wife, his mother-in-law, and his young, ambitious lover. Manipulated and circumscribed by all these women, Włodek looks desperately for a way out.

While *Roly Poly* relates in a humorous way the feelings of fear evoked by the impersonal nature of scientific discovery, *Hunting Flies* presumably projects to the screen Wajda's own feelings of helplessness related to his personal conflicts with his recently divorced second wife, Zofia, and his troubled marriage with his third wife, Beata Tyszkiewicz. The ambivalent and at times bitter depiction of women on this film is painfully vivid. Amid his travels to London and to other European cities at this time, Wajda often thought about his marital problems and considered divorcing Beata. As he admitted in private conversation (in Kraków, 1999), his failing marriage with the young actress, whom he had gotten to know during the production of *Ashes,* was at least partly his own fault; Wajda confided that he was too preoccupied with his artistic dilemmas to pay sufficient attention to his young wife. Active on many fronts—including the professional, the artistic, and the political—during 1968 and in the following years, he finally divorced her and remained married only to his work for a number of years; during this time he became a member of the Association of Polish Filmmakers, and the next fifteen years constitute his consummate creative period, during which his most mature and most widely celebrated accomplishments to date were conceived and born.

In 1970, Wajda started work on *Krajobraz po bitwie* (*Landscape after Battle,* 1970), *Brzezina* (*The Birchwood,* 1970), and *Pilatus und Andere* (*Pilate and Others,* 1972) in a rapid succession of projects, and also began thinking about making *Promised Land.*[22] *Landscape after Battle* is a subtle portrayal of a young man coming to terms with himself after the end of World War II. *The Birchwood* garnered highest praise both in Poland and abroad for its mature treatment of death and the aesthetically beautiful way in which this theme is presented. The third film, *Pilate and Others*, presents the Passion of Christ in a contemporary context.

During the 1970s, Wajda came to be fully appreciated by Polish authorities as an artist important not only to Poles, but to audiences outside Poland as well. In 1972, he became the director of the film production unit, "Unit X,"[23] which employed, among others,[24] director Agnieszka Holland. A year later, Wajda was offered (and accepted) the position of artistic director at the Old Theater in Kraków. He soon turned the Old Theater into the most ambitious and exciting theater in Poland, home to the most ambitious theatrical performances in Poland during the 1970s and 1980s, yet it became his refuge from the hasty life of Warszawa. Among the most famous productions there during this time were Fyodor Dostoevsky's *Biesy* (*The Possessed*, 1971), adapted from Albert Camus's earlier work by the same name, and *Noc listopadowa* (*November Night*, 1974). Wajda considers *The Possessed* to be his most important theatrical achievement, for it signaled the beginning of a new poetics in Wajda's theater productions, an approach he called "total theater." Later, he returned to this theatrical production in the film realization of the same theme in his film *Biesy* (*The Possessed*, 1988). This period in the director's career also brought changes in his personal life. Having been divorced since 1969, he married Krystyna Zachwatowicz in 1975; they remain together to this day. In that year he also bought his first car, a Yugoslav-made Zastawa. As he has explained in several interviews, the filmmaking occupation virtually guaranteed a decent lifestyle for him and his family. Still, the purchase of his first car was a great personal accomplishment.

Later in the 1970s, Wajda returned to his earlier practice of using well-known literary texts as the basis for his films in works such as *The Wedding, Promised Land*, and *Smuga cienia* (*The Shadow Line*, 1976). These three films were all honored in Poland and abroad, and *Promised Land* won an Oscar nomination. However, the latter film's uncompromising portrayal of Poles as morally corrupt and opportunistic opened a hornet's nest of attacks and accusations. The director was criticized for his presentation of minorities in Poland, his cynicism regarding Poland's strengths and weaknesses, and a generally hypercritical treatment of his compatriots. Given this harsh and often unreasonable criticism, Wajda engaged in other artistic activities, such as directing Stanisława Przybyszewska's *Sprawa Dantona* at Teatr Powszechny in Warszawa in 1975. This last play serves as the basis for the film *Danton*, shot six years later. In 1977, at the Old Theater, Wajda directed *Nastassja Filipowna*, based on Dostoevsky's *Idiot* and later forming the basis for Wajda's film effort *Nastasja*.

In the latter half of the 1970s, the political and social situation in Poland changed drastically. First Party Secretary Edward Gierek, initially eager to accommodate Poles with huge loans from the West, tightened his rule. A society that had been enjoying a period of relative prosperity experienced a sudden deterioration in its standard of living. A time of great social unrest began in Poland. While strikes in the 1970s had brought Gierek into office, the end of the decade witnessed his fall. A series of incidents in 1976 involving striking workers in Warszawa, Poznań, and Radom revealed to both the authorities and the Polish society the decline in living conditions and democratic freedoms. Socialism's failings were exclaimed in underground political writings and in subversive cultural statements. With the emergence of Komitet Obrony Robotników (The Workers' Defense Committee), Polish society became openly politicized.[25] This growing concern was reflected in the films of the latter part of the decade. Wajda and his contemporaries brought to life a Polish film movement called the School of Moral Concern (a.k.a. the School of Moral Distrust, c. 1976–80), with Wajda as one of the movement's initiators.

Karol Wojtyła's appointment as pope and his visit to Poland were important events during this time, creating a proper climate for the Solidarity movement. The films produced during this period generally present the fights of individuals against the Communist system. Wajda's three films of the School of Moral Concern are generally considered to be *Man of Marble, Bez znieczulenia* (*Without Anesthetic*, a.k.a. *Rough Treatment*, 1978), and *Dyrygent* (*The Orchestra Conductor*, 1980).[26] In *Man of Marble,* Wajda depicts major political events in Poland during the 1950s and 1960s, ending with the momentous wave of strikes that signaled an era of uncertainty and political struggle for years to come. (These same events are later alluded to in *Man of Iron* as well.) Although officially criticized and banned at public screenings, the film enjoyed unsurpassed popularity. It responded to Poles' dissatisfaction with Socialism and was enthusiastically received as the first open settlement of political accounts. *Without Anesthetic* dissects many of the inner mechanisms of the totalitarian system, showing previously untold discriminations and repressions. *The Conductor* is a study of human nature, the story of a leader who understands and respects the people with whom he works. In it, Wajda makes clear reference to narrow-minded Polish political leaders, clearly contrasting them with the conductor—the understanding and benevolent figure that Poland needs at this time of political uncertainty, a persona created and winningly portrayed by Sir John Gielgud. Some critics postulate that the film is an eulogy to Pope John Paul II, a man of great political importance and moral authority among the majority of Poles. Wajda's most beautiful film of the 1970s is *The Young Ladies of Wilko,* with its stunning depiction of the Polish landscape in all its tranquility and quiet grandeur. The film constitutes Wajda's subdued response to the turmoil in his and his compatriots' lives caused by political events of that decade.

Despite the fact that Wajda co-created the School of Moral Concern, he was decidedly ambivalent in expressing political opinions during the mid-1970s. Although he noted his society's growing dissatisfaction with Socialist corruption, he did not openly protest that corruption by joining opposition movements. He knew that, as a filmmaker, he was dependent upon the whims of the authorities. Thus, because he considered filmmaking to be his primary calling, he decided to downplay his political commitments. He was well aware of the fact that his fellow citizens had started the KOR,[27] but he decided that his films were his children, so he could not openly confront the authorities, being fearful that his projects would be taken away from him. In any case, he believed that by making politically controversial films, he could undermine the system more effectively than by openly joining its detractors.

In this ambiguous dance between collusion and insurgence, he was sometimes placed in impossible situations. For instance, in July 1975, First Secretary Edward Gierek asked Wajda, whom the secretary considered to be an important cultural activist, to present his ideas on film and culture. Wajda complied. This ambiguity in political position was further expressed in Wajda's decision not to sign a petition of intellectuals and opposition activists who protested the 1976 changes to the Constitution (these changes concerned a proposal to write the Communist Party's leadership into the Polish Constitution). Amid production of *Man of Marble* at the time, Wajda realized that signing the petition would jeopardize the release of the film. Several years later he made the following comment on this momentous decision: "I didn't sign, but I was wrong. I think that regardless of what I thought at the time, I should have signed, and I can never forgive myself."[28]

In 1979, Wajda moved to his present house in the district of Żoliborz in Warszawa. Around that time, at the beginning of the 1980s during the Solidarity strike at the Gdańsk Shipyard, Wajda finally decided to take a decisive political stance. Until that time, he had always considered political events to be separate from his personal life, wishing to comment upon, but not to participate fully in them. However, with the production of *Man of Marble* and *Without Anesthetic*, this personal distance began to diminish and, with the momentous strikes in 1980, disappeared completely. In April 1980, Wajda was awarded a special one-year pass to the shipyard where the Solidarity strike took place. In that year, he appealed to the Solidarity Strike Committee for permission to film the strike in the shipyard. With some reluctance, the committee complied. Thanks to Wajda's intervention at the Polish Ministry of Culture and Art in Warszawa, official permission was given to documentary filmmakers and camera operators to document to strike in Gdańsk. Filmmakers Andrzej Chodakowski and Andrzej Zajączkowski and camera operators Michal Bukojemski and Jacek Petrycki left immediately for Gdańsk. The result of this intervention is the now famous documentary film by Chodakowski and Zajączkowski, *Robotnicy 80 (The Workers 80,* 1981).[29]

As Wajda has noted in numerous interviews and personal statements in books and articles, he fully supported the Solidarity movement from its inception. In the second part of the film *Moje notatki z historii (My Notes from History),* he states that he identified very closely and personally with the movement.[30] He became fully involved in its activities and supported it in his films. Wajda's new involvement in politics included his full support for Lech Wałęsa, the movement's leader. The filmmaker first met Wałęsa in August 1980 at the Gdańsk Shipyard, and only a short time later Wajda added his name to the petition of thirty-five intellectuals and activists demanding to reduce social tensions in Poland. He participated in many meetings and events, entering into what he has called "a love affair with Lech Wałęsa."[31] It should be stated here that Wajda contributed greatly to the creation of Wałęsa's revolutionary image by supporting him and Solidarity; in fact, Wałęsa is often shown after the strike wearing a *Man of Iron* T-shirt.

This period of political awareness is reflected in two plainly political films created by Wajda after the Solidarity strike, *Man of Iron* and *Danton.* From his criticism of Polish society in earlier films, Wajda now moves to scathing condemnations of socialism and its representatives. In *Man of Iron,* he presents the struggle of the working class, who seek only dignity and decent working conditions. The historical events leading up to the abolition of the Socialist government in Poland and the creation of the Solidarity movement, using documentary footage from the Gdańsk Shipyard, constitute the film canvas on which Wajda portrays the worker activists. *Danton* depicts the implementation of martial law in Poland, framed within the historical context of the French Revolution. *Man of Marble, Without Anesthetic, Man of Iron,* and *Danton* each won awards, lauded for their denouncing ways, their openness in their treatment of political subjects, and their audacity in challenging the political status quo. These films constitute the peak of Wajda's creative output, and are those most commonly associated with his name.

The months between August 1980 and December 1981 are considered by many to be the most turbulent yet exciting times in Polish post-World War II history. In social, cultural, and political spheres, this was a time of great change in many aspects of Polish life. Artists and intellectuals contributed enthusiastically to these changes, and Wajda was one of them. He was actively engaged in many political groups and activities, among which were the Nadzwyczajny Walny Zjazd Stowarzyszenia Filmowców Polskich (The Special Convention of the Polish Filmmakers' Association) in October 1980, at which Wajda addressed colleagues with a paper on the autonomous nature of film units; the

Komitet Obrony Uwięzionych (Committee for the Protection of Prisoners); the Kongres Kultury Polskiej (Congress of Polish Culture); and the Komitet Ocalenia Kinematografii (Committee for the Protection of Cinematography), the purpose of which was to support ambitious and unorthodox film and other artistic productions.[32]

During this period, Wajda was harassed constantly by the authorities as a result of his participation in Solidarity activities and opposition movements. In 1980, for instance, a total of forty-four filmmakers, journalists, historians, and activists (the so-called patriotic left) approached the central authorities to ban "mass presentations of Mrożek and Gombrowicz"[33] and to redeem awards for such films as *Man of Marble* and *Without Anesthetic*. Moreover, in the Polish press, the entire School of Moral Concern, with Wajda as one of its leaders, was under constant attack.[34] Seemingly unperturbed by these unprecedented attacks, Wajda continued his political activities, accepting invitations to politically provocative meetings such as the 25th Anniversary of June 1956 in Poznań.[35] Ironically, at the same time, Wajda was being honored for his achievements in film all over the world.

The period of exuberant freedom of expression and political thought came to an abrupt end with the introduction of martial law on 13 December 1981 (lasting until 22 July 1983); Solidarity leaders were arrested, many of them spending time in internment camps, Polish citizens lost basic democratic rights, and the military government introduced a number of strict military measures, including curfews and constant invigilation.[36] Martial law introduced military control into nearly every sphere of life, administrative, industrial, and cultural. Military presence was evident at universities, offices, and hospitals. Cultural life was greatly affected, so that many artists were forced to emigrate or to accept lesser positions.

Wajda's life was altered as well; the authorities attempted to silence the director and his famous charges, and in 1983, on the pretext of his frequent travels, Wajda was denied his directorship of Unit X. The filmmaking unit was dissolved. This fact was mentioned only briefly in the press. For instance, the weekly *Fakty* reported only that, "At the Unit X, Andrzej Wajda, Bolesław Michałek, and Barbara Pec-Ślesicka [were] released from their functions."[37] The dissolution of Unit X was an important moment in the director's life, after which he felt bitter and jaded. Certainly, the authorities intended to diminish the role of the now famous filmmaker and his peers in forming public opinion. Unit X was instrumental in the opposition's ascent at the end of 1970s, so the new military regime was pleased to see it dissolved. The unit's most famous younger filmmakers (e.g., Agnieszka Holland and Ryszard Bugajski) went abroad, and Wajda, who remained, suffered both personally and artistically. As he states, "The martial law was a dramatic event for me which I deeply deplore. It unsettled me at the time when I was in my best form. It created a horrifying emptiness which I could not easily penetrate."[38]

Despite this depressing situation, Wajda worked on other film projects. After all, he had not been totally silenced by the authorities, and filmmaking was his profession and his passion; without his work, he could not function as a human being. Despite his obvious support for Lech Wałęsa and his movement, Wajda was given permission to go to Paris to shoot *Danton*. In the meantime, the situation in Poland deteriorated under martial law. Wajda has admitted to feeling guilt during this period: While he played at making films, other less fortunate Poles suffered deeply. Yet he remained deeply pessimistic about the future of cultural life in Poland and feared that he would never again be able to do anything significant in Poland. After producing *Danton*, Wajda returned to the themes linked to World War II that had always interested him. *Eine Liebe in Deutschland* (*A Love in Germany*, 1983) transports viewers back to World War II, but this time through a story in which a young German woman and a young Polish man fall in love and are brutally punished for their transgression by the Nazi regime. Wajda here revisits the most painful of subjects in Polish history: war's inhumanity and the bitterness of Polish-German relations.

By the 1980s, despite the political controversies in which he had been (and remained) involved, Wajda was freely able to choose his film projects, and he produced them with a master's sure stroke. He was also highly respected among his colleagues, who awarded him another honor, the presidency of the Polish Film Association, which he held until 1983. After martial law ended in July 1983, Wajda once more became increasingly engaged in political life. He participated in many political opposition meetings and events despite his busy film and theater schedules. He maintained close ties with opposition member Jacek Kuroń, an advocate of the Solidarity union. In 1983, Wajda witnessed premieres of his films *Danton* and *A Love in Germany* and submitted new film projects to the film unit Perspektywa, where he worked after the dissolution of Unit X. In 1984, Wałęsa asked Wajda to participate in a meeting at St. Brygida Church in Gdańsk, where a group of forty intellectuals formed an advisory committee under the direction of Bronisław Gieremek; in November of the same year, he took part in the funeral of Jerzy Popiełuszko, who had been murdered by security police; and in 1986, he participated in the meeting between Jacek Kuroń and the newly released Solidarity activists, among whom was Wałęsa.

The government authorities were not quick to forget Wajda's political position, however. The director continued his political involvement with Solidarity activists and, because of his ardent political activism, remained in a kind of official hiatus. He made films but for years was not invited to official functions by government authorities. As in the 1950s, early in his career, he was sometimes unexpectedly harassed by government officials, as if those in power wished to remind him who was in charge. For instance, in 1984, he experienced problems with security officials and was denied his passport to go to Amsterdam with the troupe of actors performing the play *The Possessed*. In similar events, Wajda suffered all kinds of minor harassments at the whim of the authorities. Only in 1986, five years after the end of martial law, did Wajda receive his first official invitation, this from the Minister of Art, inviting Wajda to the New Year's meeting at the Royal Palace in Warszawa. A short time afterward, he was invited by the official film authorities to participate in government meetings concerning the film industry—he did not accept this latter invitation.[39]

Around this time, Wajda worked on the new films *A Chronicle of Amorous Incidents* and *The Possessed*, as well as a number of stage plays such as Ernest Bryll's *Wieczernik (The Night Vigil)* and Dostoevsky's *Nastasja Filipowna* and *Zbrodnia i kara (Crime and Punishment)*. In general, the late 1980s were witness to some excellent and some less remarkable films from the respected director. In my opinion, the relative weakness of the first two films, *A Chronicle of Amorous Incidents* and *The Possessed*, may have resulted from Wajda's reaction to martial law, about which he has repeatedly expressed his resentment and anger. His disillusionment proved detrimental to both his physical health and his art, a fact that was apparent in the weaker films of this period and the next few periods as well. In *A Chronicle of Amorous Incidents*, a nostalgic, slightly naive portrayal of prewar youth, Wajda returns to the events preceding World War II. *The Possessed*, although an ambitious adaptation of Dostoevsky's work, is laden with heavy dialogue and is not completely clear in its explanation of characters' motives or in its complex plot; this film was poorly received by both critics and general audiences. Undoubtedly the best of Wajda's films produced in the 1990s is *Korczak*, based on the true story of a Jewish doctor, revered by Jewish and non-Jewish Poles alike, who died among Jewish children on their way to Auschwitz. Wajda's Dr. Korczak is imbued with understanding, compassion, and honesty; the director is again in top form with this black-and-white film, creating a striking account of wartime suffering.

Already in the 1980s, Wajda began to direct his attention toward another country: Japan. Moving away from Polish themes in favor of a very different culture, Wajda traveled to Japan, where he concentrated on the production of the theater performance of *Nastasja*, which later materialized in his film of the same name. Around 1986, he also began to work on the documents related to his life's work, which roughly a decade later he gathered in the archives at the newly built Manggha Center in Kraków. The center is the direct result of the generosity of the director, who donated his City of Kyoto Award, given him by his Japanese admirers in 1987, to the construction of this Japanese Art and Technology Center, the execution of which he personally supervised.

In 1988, Wajda was personally invited by Wałęsa to participate in the activities of the newly emerging political force under Wałęsa's mandate. As Wałęsa wrote in a private letter to the director, "I hope that in this specific situation in which we find ourselves now, we will be able to define a political program to introduce necessary changes for improving the situation in our country."[40] The year 1989 marked a vital period in Polish political and artistic life, marking the official abolition of the Socialist system.[41] Wajda embraced these political changes enthusiastically and worked closely with Wałęsa's government in a number of capacities. He was elected senator and fulfilled this duty from 1989–91. Then, from 1992 to 1994, he chaired the Culture Council for the President of the Polish Republic.

Polish cinema also underwent radical changes in 1989, especially in the system of production.[42] In Maria Kornatowska's opinion, the new production model proved workable: "Since its implementation in 1989, an average of thirty films per year have been produced. In November 1992, thirty-three features were shown, including nine debuts, at the Polish Film Festival in Gdynia. This, no doubt, is proof of vitality."[43] The financing system also changed extensively, from one generously providing automatic subsidies to film studios to one providing grants on a competitive basis. The new system of production created a difficult situation for Wajda, who was forced to compete on the same footing with younger, innovative filmmakers. Because his privileged position had ended, he was forced to rethink his strategies. He also had to consider new techniques and new audience sensibilities. Movie-going audiences shifted their attention to cable, video, and television. The Polish-produced "mafia" film, produced in the fashion of American thrillers, had gained dramatically in popularity, and politics became much less important. As Kornatowska states, "Everyone stresses the fact that a certain era in Polish cinema is over. It has lost its privileged position and does not know how to make use of its recently acquired freedom. Censorship indeed disappeared but the rule of the market and the producer appeared.... Polish cinema has ceased to be the instrument of social and political critique it once was. It has lost its role as moral leader and conscience of the nation."[44]

Wajda was all too aware of the changing realities of Polish film. In an interview with *Cineaste*, he admitted that it was more difficult to make films after 1990 than before that time.

We have to remember that when I was making my political films, the public could not learn about the realities of politics, about the truth, from newspapers, television or radio. So they had to rely on what content we managed to smuggle into our films. But now it's completely different. Anybody can learn everything about history and contemporary issues from newspapers or television. In the past, an artist or director or filmmaker was kind of a voice of society or the nation. Today the political tensions are being solved in parliament, for instance, and this of course takes away all the prestige from the process of filmmaking, and all its social expectations, which were there when I made political films in the past.[45]

In view of these radical changes in audience sensibilities and production modes, Wajda looked once again to his well-tried themes, those of World War II. *Holy Week*, a film about Polish-Jewish relations, and *The Crowned-Eagle Ring* both represent a return to this subject matter. On the other hand, Wajda also tries to satisfy the tastes of younger audiences in *Panna Nikt* (*Miss Nobody*, 1996). However, each of these attempts is barely noticed by audiences interested in other matters. Nevertheless, the first two films are clearly recognizable as having been produced by the great master of the camera. In the first, Wajda tells the story of Poles who offer to help Jews about to be exterminated by the Germans; in the second, he presents young people struggling to adapt to life in a new capitalist Poland. Both films present difficult personal choices in an honest manner. *Miss Nobody*, however, attests to the director's poor choice of scripts, a rare occurrence in his long film and theater career. The film tells the story of three girls living in contemporary Poland. One of them, Marysia, comes from a poor family; her social climb is portrayed in a way similar to that of Birkut in *Man of Marble*, but this film lacks the power and honesty of its famous predecessor.

There is one film, however, produced during this period, that takes a separate place in the director's oeuvre. *Nastasja*, produced during this otherwise diminished period in Wajda's career, is an exciting experiment carried out with the famous Kabuki actor Tamasaburo Bando. One of the world's greatest *onnagata*, an actor trained to play both female and male parts, Bando plays both Prince Miskhin and Nastasja Filipovna in this film adaptation of Dostoevsky's *Idiot*. *Nastasja* is one of Wajda's most original films and is his most excellent adaptation of a literary work; sadly, it is generally appreciated only by connoisseurs of theater or of Wajda's, Bando's, or Dostoevsky's works.

During the late 1980s and into the 1990s, Wajda began to suffer from extreme fatigue due to managing his film, theater, and political careers simultaneously. At the end of the 1980s, his health visibly deteriorated. He seemed tired and weak. In October 1990 in Prague, Wajda suddenly fainted and was taken to the hospital to be treated for heart problems. Despite his failing health, he continued to perform many official functions. He also worked with the Committee for Radio and Television. In an interview with *Cineaste*, Wajda comments on this period in his life in the following way:[46]

> *Cineaste:* You had a term in the Senate. Was your experience as a politician a happy one?
> *Wajda:* As someone who made films that set certain political demands, society in turn could demand that I follow the same path and take this

responsibility upon myself. I believe that both myself and other parliamentarians of the previous term fulfilled our responsibility and our duty. We did exactly what was expected of us. We created a basis for Polish democracy, and now the others can take up on that level and go on.

Cineaste: It doesn't sound like something you liked well enough to do again, though.

Wajda: It's indeed a very interesting and very demanding and exciting vocation for a man to be a politician, perhaps the most exciting there is. But, as for myself, it should have happened to me much earlier, when I could see the results of my political action.

In 1993, Wajda oversaw the initial construction of the Manggha Japanese Cultural Center in Kraków. The Manggha Center, partly financed by the Kyoto Foundation, would later become a refuge for Wajda. He spent a lot of time working in his archives there and collaborating on various cultural exchange projects with Japan. In 1994, disappointed with the direction the Solidarity-led government had taken, Wajda resigned from his position as chair of the Culture Council. In 1995, he began work on *Mr. Thadeus* and saw his daughter Karolina married to Artur Nowakowski. In 1996, he worked on the autobiographical *Andrzej Wajda—My Notes from History*, a documentary film for Polish television.

In his most recent films, Wajda has concentrated on bringing to screen the greatest and best-known Polish patriotic literary works, such as *Mr. Thadeus*, a noble saga based on Adam Mickiewicz's poem of the same title. It epitomizes the main traits of Wajda's oeuvre: his dexterous choice of texts for adaptation; his preoccupation with grand historical themes (here, Napoleon's invasion of Russia); his deep understanding of Poland's collective psyche and national destiny; his attention to historical detail; his meticulous construction of mise-en-scène; his beautiful use of imagery in elaborate scenes and sequences; his subtle depiction of personal problems; and, finally, his mastery of pace and intensity in presenting events. As well, all of the general themes characteristic of Wajda's films are present: the literary origins of the script, the influence of his painting background, the national themes, historical dilemmas, and political issues.

After undergoing a triple bypass in 2000, Wajda regained his health and embarked on a series of new projects. On 9 May 2002, he opened a private film school, the Andrzej Wajda Master School of Film Directing, in Warszawa and also made another film, *Revenge*. He is constantly invited to social functions in Poland and abroad, and is present everywhere on the Polish cultural stage: Although he is now in his eighties, he is clearly aware of new directions and cultural movements in both Polish and international cinemas.

2

THE BIRTH OF A MASTER
Films of the Fifties

In the first part of this chapter, I concentrate on Wajda's early attempts at filmmaking. The three student études he produced at the Łódź Film School—"When You Sleep," "Bad Boy," "Ilsa Ceramic," and a short film produced after *A Generation*, "I Go to the Sun"—already reveal his talent and the meticulousness with which he plans and organizes his projects. Particularly in the last two of these four films, Wajda reveals his painter's eye in his lighting technique and careful construction of mise-en-scène.

In the second part of this chapter, I examine the historical conditions leading to the production of Wajda's war films (*A Generation, Kanal, Ashes and Diamonds,* and *Lotna*), which made Wajda famous both in Poland and abroad. These four films introduce some of the major themes and conventions in Wajda's oeuvre: historical themes of World War II, painterly tradition in the construction of mise-en-scène, and a skillful use of literary works for film adaptation.

The four early films produced by Wajda are at the archives of the Łódź Film School. The school's extensive archives contain many such treasures: for instance, the early études of other major Polish filmmakers such as Roman Polański and Jerzy Skolimowski. In October 1999, a special screening of Wajda's four student études was organized by the school's vice-rector, Prof. Jolanta Lemann. In the screening room—which faculty and students there affectionately refer to as *ogiernia* (stud farm)— I had the privilege of watching these four rarely screened Wajda films.

Although Wajda remains skeptical of the role the Łódź Film School has played in his career, the early films he produced there are interesting in many respects. "When You Sleep" is a poetic illustration of the poems of Tadeusz Kubiak,[1] one of the major propagators of Socialist ideology at that time. Narrated by Kubiak himself and filmed by Jerzy Lipman (the camera operator who later worked on both *A Generation* and *Kanal*), "When You Sleep" is a perfect example of the propaganda film techniques taught and applied in the 1950s. Illustrating Kubiak's pompous passages, the film follows the poetic descriptions of everyday life shot in tableaux-like scenes. As in Dziga Vertov's school of film, *Kino-Glaz* (Kino-Eye), the images of mundane events follow one another in a rapid succession of shots, starting with a mother bent over her sleeping child in the evening and then following the actions of night-shift workers. Optimistic in tone, the film tells the story of machine operators, bakers, and bus drivers as they prepare for the morning rush.

Despite its conventional mode of filming, "When You Sleep" is worth seeing for its superimpositions, its close-ups, and its pace—at times matching that of the images in Vertov's *Man with a Movie Camera* (1929). Moreover, Wajda's feeling for a film's rhythm is apparent in his careful harmonization of the length of the takes with the pace of the accompanying music: the brisker the music, the shorter the takes, while longer takes are complemented by perfectly coordinated music. Already in this early film, Wajda chooses various positions for the camera, low and high angles, as well as pans and various close-ups. To make this conventional film as interesting as possible, he concentrates on the creation of beautiful images that will later become his forte. Two images in particular are very memorable: the huge troughs in which dough is kneaded for the morning bread, and a tram being checked by maintenance workers from below as it moves. The first image startles the viewer with surreal rolls of slowly swirling dough; the second one resembles the early film images of approaching trains in the Brothers Lumieres' and in Vertov's films. This early film clearly demonstrates that Wajda understands film material intuitively and, even at that early time, could skillfully compose its various elements.

"Bad Boy," produced on 35 mm film, is a narrative based on a short story by the same title. Shot by Zdzisław Parylak, it already signals Wajda's future preoccupations: his preference for adaptations of literary pieces over original screenplays and his excellent narrative skills. Adapted from a story by Anton Czekhov, one of the most prominent of Russian writers, it is well narrated in short, interesting sequences, each quickly following the previous one. Here as well, Wajda reveals his penchant for interesting mise-en-scène and camera positions.

"Bad Boy" is the story of a young couple constantly harassed by a young boy; obviously in love and wanting to be alone, they try to escape the boy, only to be approached by him once again at the end of the film. Admittedly, the film's action is not entirely clear: Wajda's interpretation is, perhaps, somewhat too academic and literal, and the explanation of the boy's behavior seems ambiguous, occurring only at the end of the film. Yet, imperfect as it is, the film reveals excellent positioning of the camera, well-chosen close-ups, and good lighting. Despite the simplicity of narration, the film shows a great deal of action, with numerous setting and subject positions. Like "When You Sleep," "Bad Boy" contains many scenes that indicate a young director with a great deal of natural talent, a knack for the proper application of lighting, and an interesting sense of composition of the structure of an image.

The third early film is a propagandist paradocumentary with rigid voice-over narration. "Ilsa Ceramic" is devoted to the production of ceramic pieces (pots, clay toys, etc.) in the town of Ilsa. The film is composed of sequences featuring the products, the process, the people, and the places through which Ilsa's ceramics are produced. Wajda obediently applies the principles of a 1950s documentary with the didactic voice-over narration and an unrealistically optimistic interpretation of every scene, yet he enriches each with varying shot compositions, fast-paced scenes, and multiple camera positions. The film's positive points include well-designed lighting, excellent panning movements of the camera, interesting mise-en-scène (e.g., clay figures shot against a real landscape), and often centrally constructed shots, usually ideally framed.

Highly propagandistic, "Ilsa Ceramic" presents an idealized picture of the small town of Ilsa, in which the lives of whole families revolve around designing, making, and distributing ceramic products. The obvious discrepancy between the dismal living and working conditions clearly seen in every sequence and the optimistic voice-over commentary seem to escape Wajda's attention. Or perhaps Wajda demonstrates the typical (propagandistic) method of the 1950s documentary style, which each director was expected to learn at the school. As a school étude, the film was to demonstrate various film techniques within the Social Realist style taught rigorously there: perhaps it is merely another mark of Wajda's mastery that he adheres to these rules so perfectly. This is not idle conjecture, for the "incidental irony" of the Socialist scenario apparent in "Ilsa Ceramic" reappears later—and mockingly—in Wajda's propagandistic film about Birkut, a "Socialist hero," in his masterpiece *Man of Marble.*

In the early 1950s, Wajda found himself in a difficult position while making this particular film. On the one hand, Socialist ideology was officially taught and propagated at the school. On the other hand, it was sneered at and treated with an amused disinterest by both the instructors and by the students. Students *had* to learn how to make films according to the propagandist doctrines because they would fail their studies if they did not, but they were rarely convinced of the ideology's validity. In "Ilsa Ceramic," the irony of this situation is fully revealed. On the one hand, the film has a propagandistic tone, but on the other, it portrays the living and working conditions of the ceramic producers with documentary precision.

In Wajda's original notes illustrating the process of the film's production, one detects an uncertainty in the young filmmaker as to how to negotiate the political requirements of the school (i.e., producing an overwhelmingly positive presentation of the small town famous for its ceramics production) and the specific, naturalistic outcome of the documentary. In Wajda's own words, "There is no rigorous screenplay for a documentary film."[2] At this stage, Wajda also realizes his own shortcomings as a filmmaker and enumerates them in his notes. He writes that he must be both an organizer and an artist while producing a film; he has acknowledged problems when building particular scenes with his camera operator, and he is at this time deficient in editing and sound montage skills. These frank admissions signify a highly critical young man trying hard to perfect his craft and having difficulty traversing the narrow stretch of ground that lies between artist and reporter.

The fourth early film, "I Go to the Sun," is the director's early great accomplishment: a unique, innovative film showing the work of one of the greatest Polish sculptors, Xawery Dunikowski, in honor of the artist's eightieth birthday. As Wajda recalls, in making this film he concentrated mainly on the most expressive way to show Dunikowski's huge sculptures. The unique character of this biographical documentary consists not only in the director's innovative technique (e.g., he sets the sculptures against the background of the Baltic Sea), but also in using the sculptor himself as a commentator: Dunikowski is both the subject and the object of presentation in Wajda's film. Shot by Stefan Matyjaszkiewicz, with the voice-over narration of Aleksander Bardini, the film shows Dunikowski at work in his study and quietly contemplating his works while seated among them. The slow-moving camera seems a voyeur, a mysterious visitor—perhaps Wajda himself, fascinated by the aesthetic beauty of the sculptor's work—entering the artist's study and approaching Dunikowski's sculptures.

Most of Dunikowski's sculptures are figures of women, primarily pregnant women. Wajda lights them softly and shows them in low-angle camera positions. Delicate superimpositions gently lead the viewer from one sculpture to the next one. The most striking sequence in the film is shot at the sea bank, where several huge sculptures of pregnant women are loosely displayed. The women form a group, facing each other as if engaged in casual conversation, perhaps regarding their future children. A small boy with a shell in his hand approaches them and looks up at their enormous bellies. A countershot coming from one of the women's faces responds to his look, as if the motherly figure looks tenderly at the boy. This sequence poignantly reveals Dunikowski's fascination with women—especially pregnant women—and his love for people in general.

The final sequences of this short (fourteen-minute) but touching film are less appealing than the earlier ones; however, they are intended to show Dunikowski as a propagandist and crafter of Socialist monuments, not as a creator of humanistic, beautiful portrayals of simple people. A prominent artist within the Socialist system, Dunikowski was engaged in many official projects such as the erection of war monuments: Wajda again turns propagandist in showing Dunikowski's monuments and accompanying them with magnificent music. In the end, the grandiose monuments constitute a background against which Dunikowski himself climbs the stairs. As if wanting to highlight the importance of the sculptor to Polish culture, Wajda makes Dunikowski seem stupendous and lordly—at the great age of eighty, Dunikowski looks silently at the huge stones prostrate below him, each ready to become his next polished sculpture. Still, despite its propaganda, "I Go to the Sun" shows a glimmer of Wajda's future greatness, already discernible especially in his warm and tolerant presentation of people. Whether living and breathing or merely presented in sculpture, people are affectionately portrayed in this film using warm lighting and complimentary takes.

Wajda's three short Łódź études are the productions of a beginner. Aside from some moments of artistic intuition, the films are palpably amateurish. But Socialist Realist influences, didacticism, and the rather crude film techniques taught at the Łódź Film School at that time were mere stepping stones on the way to greater works. Wajda's attention to the artistic composition of the frame, his careful use of lighting techniques, and his sensitivity to people and to their feelings are clearly discernible even in these early films. Wajda himself is especially critical of his own films and almost completely disregards the role played by the Łódź Film School.

> What did I learn at the School in Targowa Street? This is a good question. It depends on how you look at it. When I think about lectures and classes, I must admit I did not learn much. We got no instruction on the principles of set design or on the technique of directing actors. There was a lot of talk about the art of film in general, but in fact I saw the director's workshop for the first time only when I worked for [Alexander] Ford. Also, I learned something by making innumerable mistakes during the production of my études. (These mistakes were always pointed out to me by my own film students whom I later taught at the same school; they deftly included my small films among their own student works, so I had no other choice but see them again.) The value of the Łódź Film School lies for me in these imperfect études. Later in my career, I not only understood the films' mistakes but also lamented them when I repeatedly returned to them in an effort to understand how these films should have been done.[3]

Yet despite the fact that Wajda has never been particularly happy with his experiences at the Łódź Film School, the études he produced there as diploma films not only reveal his mastery of basic film techniques, but also point to future greatness. Perhaps the most persuasive evidence of their influence in his growth as a filmmaker is the fact that the études are followed almost immediately by Wajda's greatest early fiction films.

All four war films, *A Generation, Kanal, Ashes and Diamonds,* and *Lotna,* belong to the artistic formation called the Polish School.[4] Alexander Jackiewicz, Antoni Bohdziewicz, Stanisław Ozimek, Tadeusz Miczka, and other Polish scholars situate these films within the context of the Polish Romantic tradition of this school. In an enlightening discussion of this artistic phenomenon, Marek Haltof summarizes several theoretical approaches to the school and delineates several important characteristics of this historical and artistic phenomenon. The Polish School can be temporally divided into four periods, of which Wajda's four films belong to the so-called proper period of the school (1957–59), "during which filmmakers focus mostly on the themes of war and occupation and situate their works within the context of the Polish romantic tradition."[5] (Miczka considers Wajda's films to be the "true" Polish School representatives.) Whether we apply the specific requirements of Ozimek and Miczka, the broad suggestions of Marek Hendrykowski and Ewelina Nurczyńska-Fidelska, or the generalizing approach of Marek Haltof, we can summarize the principles of the Polish School in the following way:[6]

> 1. It embraced the artistic activities of such well-known directors as Andrzej Wajda, Andrzej Munk, Wojciech J. Has, and Kazimierz Kutz. These directors are noted as the most important representatives of the classical trends of the school in the years 1955–62.
> 2. It is difficult to define as an artistic phenomenon. Within this school, a number of thematic and stylistic areas can be distinguished with a multiplicity of aesthetic tendencies and authorial expressions.
> 3. The majority of filmmakers within this school produced honest and brave films that openly challenged the themes and aesthetics of Socialist Realism. Most filmmakers of this formation dealt with the recent events of World War II and "deeply influenced the social consciousness since they helped to free the national mythology from mystifications and lies, permeating the socialist realist aesthetics."
> 4. Wajda is considered (by Ozimek, at least) to be the creator of the "Romantic-expressive" tendency and, by some, of the Polish School itself.

In this understanding of the Polish School, the following four films engage in a serious artistic and intellectual dialogue with their viewers, and deal with World War II events. These particular films' greatness arises from the fact that their specific idiosyncratically Polish contexts are somehow able to translate into universal human dramas, and are thus accepted enthusiastically all over the world. Of course, as noted elsewhere, Wajda's remarkable addition to the Polish School's greatness is in the creation of beautiful images, which function in these films like independent tableaux.

The three full-length fiction films made subsequent to the études, *A Generation*, *Kanal*, and *Ashes and Diamonds*, reveal Wajda not only as a promising and skilled director, but also as a passionate assessor of Polish history. These three films are considered a trilogy, although, as Dennis de Nitto argues, they were never intended as such by Wajda.[7] They are utterly genuine films in which Wajda presents the passions, feelings, and desires of young people, sentiments with which young spectators, in particular, could easily identify. These three films are representative of Wajda's personal Romantic period, in the sense of a passionate presentation of historical events, people, and ideas.[8] Moreover, the films are very well made in the narrative and aesthetic senses—especially *Ashes and Diamonds*, which has become one of Wajda's best known and most beloved films. The director himself cites *Ashes and Diamonds* as an example of his best filmmaking ideas in the book *Double Vision*,[9] and, as late as 1998, he repeated that he still considers *Ashes* to be one of his best films ever.[10]

A Generation (1955)

The screenplay for *A Generation*, written by Bohdan Czeszko, is based upon his own novel *A Generation*, although the screenplay was originally entitled *Candidate Term*. An examination of this film's production history reveals the sometimes accidental nature of the director's success. Skeptics observing Wajda's career have contended that, in the case of this particular film, fate or perhaps even luck was the decisive factor. As a very young filmmaker, Wajda was allowed to produce this film only for two reasons: first, because Alexander Ford, a celebrated and highly experienced Polish filmmaker, did not want to do it, and second, because a portion of this film was to function as Wajda's diploma work.[11] Regardless, the film heralds the dawn of a master who, in part intuitively and in part due to his early experience as a painter, is able to communicate complex political and historical messages in an aesthetically elaborate manner.

Shot in black and white, the film resembles both a documentary and an Italian neo-Realist film. It tells the story of a group of young people who, under German occupation, join the ranks of the Gwardia Ludowa (People's Army), a leftist clandestine military organization that regularly conducted acts of sabotage against the Germans.[12] The film opens with a crane shot, panning across the tattered landscape of the Warszawa suburb of Budy (in the Ochota district). Throughout the film, Wajda pays close attention to detail in his meticulous re-creation of Warszawa's climate and of the interiors of the run-down and dirty buildings in the poor suburb. The language of the characters matches the buildings' interiors—it is rough, bordering on the offensive. Yet the language is perfectly appropriate to the kind of landscape in which Wajda situates his film. As he states in *Wajda Films*,

> "*A Generation* features craftsmen's workshops like those with which I had become so familiar when working in them during the German occupation years, and council houses and poverty-stricken suburban streets like those where my wartime life was spent. I tried my best to transfer

the burden of great issues onto the characters of my film, boys from the suburbs and their working class families from Warszawa's Wola and Koło districts."[13]

The film's protagonists, the young men Stach, Kostka, and Zyzik, play a game with a knife, which they throw on the ground. They are lively, happy, and worry-free despite the war around them. Shortly, the youths hear an oncoming train filled with coal being transported for the German occupiers, and they decide to steal some for themselves. One of the most brilliant and well-known sequences in Polish cinema ensues, portraying the three young men jumping on the train. Shot in both medium and long shots and later edited in a rapid succession of quick snips, the sequence dazzles the spectator with its intensity and rapidity, as if forecasting the quick-paced action films of the Polish cinema in the1990s. The camera is ideally positioned in every shot, centrally embracing the youths as they jump on the train, push the coal from the freight cars, and try to avoid the gunshots of ruthless German guards. The sequence is exceptionally dynamic, and contrasts strikingly with many of the more static sequences later in the film.

As a result of the youths' bravado, Zyzik is shot by a German soldier and left on a pile of coal on the freight car. Kostka jumps off the train only to disappear from the screen entirely and from the film's diegesis as well. (Remarkably, the fate of Kostka, played by Wajda's favorite actor Zbigniew Cybulski, is repeated horribly a dozen years later when Cybulski himself dies jumping on the train at Wrocław Station in 1967; Wajda re-creates the actor's death in his film *Everything for Sale* in 1969.) Stach is the only one of the three youths who finds his way to safety as he runs to a nearby bridge. He hopes to find Kostka hiding under the bridge. Instead he meets a drunk, who, seeing that Stach is hurt, leads him to an old tap bar. There Stach meets Sekuła, a carpenter from a nearby shop who eventually arranges a job for Stach at his workplace, Berg Brothers Machinery.

After working there for a time, Stach befriends Jasio Krone, another inexperienced youth, and is supervised by the older and kindly Sekuła, who later leads Stach into the underground activities of the People's Army. Although inexperienced and uneducated, Stach is eager to work and to participate in the shop's activities, and he soon gains the respect of the other workers. Furthermore, he gets a basic economic education from Sekuła, who becomes a surrogate for the father missing from Stach's life; Sekuła explains the exploitation practiced by the unscrupulous and cynical shop owner, Berg, who engages in "double-play": he does business with the Germans and, at the same time, reluctantly helps the partisans by hiding their weapons on his premises.

Stach's advancement from miscreant to enlightened young man is aided by his enrollment in evening classes where he meets Dorota, a young activist of the Związek Walki Młodych (Fighting Youth Union).

Stach first notices Dorota as she distributes leaflets on campus calling for action, and he quickly falls in love with her. This potent combination of love and politics appears in some form in almost all of Wajda's films.[14] Under the influence of Dorota, and in anticipation of possible future involvement in resistance fighting, Stach steals a revolver from the workshop. Later, he actively seeks admission into the circles of the secret People's Army and, in doing so, realizes that Sekuła is also a member of that militant organization. Sekuła organizes an official meeting for Stach with his People's Army officer, who turns out to be none other than Dorota.

A love scene ensues, the amusing and delicate presentation of which will become a trademark in Wajda's later films. Shot in a medium take, the scene presents the two young people engaging in an innocent conversation, with only a present inkling of a future love. They talk and smile, and Dorota asks Stach to choose a nickname for himself; when he hesitates, she proposes the alias "Bartek," a name typical of peasant boys. She compares his look to that of a boy from a village, identifying Stach with the simple working-class folk of rural background who generally comprised the People's Army. Later, the two walk slowly toward the town and happen upon an old-fashioned photographer with a huge placard showing a heart with a head-size opening cut out of it. Stach's head soon appears in the opening as if he were posing for a sentimental photo. Accompanied by an emotional French song (performed by Edith Piaf), the scene recalls the sentimental films of the pre-World War II era, but also the heartrending images abundant in Polish visual art, literature, and poetry, portraying love as sentimental and passionate.

Dorota takes Stach to a clandestine meeting of young people pledging their loyalty to the cause of the underground fighters. Wajda shows these "warriors" passing a cigarette in a ritual of connection and integration, perhaps resembling the passing of the peace pipe among Native Americans. Dorota is not visible, but her impassioned words resonate over the scene. Were the sequence shot statically, with the camera on the face of the speaker, the pathos and sentimentality would no doubt undermine its novelty. Instead, the young people are more interested in the sparse cigarette they share than in Dorota's inspired patriotism. Wajda clearly and profoundly inhabits the minds of these freedom fighters, who cover their uncertainty and fear with bravado and nonchalance. This sequence leads to a more telling and significant ritual: a pledge made over a lit candle. All the participants stand in a circle over a single candle and pledge allegiance to Poland, with a promise to fight the German oppressor. This scene alludes plainly to Adam Mickiewicz's play *Dziady*,[15] a drama about Russian oppression in Poland, political dissidence, and insurrection, which today is taught in every Polish secondary school as representative of Poland's incessant struggles for freedom.

Two prominent sequences depicting the horrors of war provide the historical context and moral justification for the underground activities of the People's Army. The first sequence shows Jasio, who has been reluctant to join the fighters, pass through a gallows filled with fresh corpses of Poles hanged by the Germans. Stanisław Grzelecki describes this scene as illustrating "the passion of visual portrayal";[16] it is a scene in which

> every element is saturated with the truth[;] it stimulates ... unburied memories and recalls recent personal events.... In many scenes of the film, the intensity of vision, reinforced by the contrasting editing, is striking. Editing, characterized by rapid cuts in this film, serves to reveal the atmosphere of the days of the German occupation. During those days, the immediacy of the events startled people as so many life events took place in the short, tense moments of continual fights with the occupier.[17]

In this emotionally understated sequence, no gory details are shown; only the legs of the deceased are pictured, dangling ominously above the faces of the distressed onlookers. The camera focuses on Jasio's eyes, flicking rapidly back and forth from the hanging corpses to the German soldiers standing with their backs turned to the sullen passersby.

Another sequence shows Stach and an older worker from the shop leaving the German work camp. On their way out, they are searched and questioned by German guards; Stach is physically and verbally abused by one of the German officers, and they accuse him of theft. The young Pole cannot stand this humiliation and decides to avenge himself. A short time later, in the Aunt Valeria tap bar—the same one in which he was recruited to fight the Germans—Stach approaches the abusive guard with his friends Jasio, Jacek, and Mundek. Although the plan was only to give the German a thorough beating, things get out of hand very quickly. In a moment of surprising audacity, Jasio shoots the German. Surprised and frightened by this development, the youths run away to hide under the bridge, where Jasio brags about the killing as if he were a little boy playing with a wooden gun and the dead soldier a mere figment of his imagination. The others realize that the killing was a mistake, though, and in a moment of mature reflection, they blame Jasio for his unnecessary and savage act. They know they must now go into hiding to avoid a German reprisal.

Dorota, in her official role as commanding officer, is not happy with the outcome of the events at the tap bar, of course. She meets the young men under the bridge and reprimands them for the killing. Still, she does understand their desire to fight, and she even smiles discreetly when Stach, acting mature beyond his age, describes the event to her. Then, unexpectedly, Sekuła joins them and tells them about an uprising in the Jewish ghetto. With a remarkable newfound political sagacity, Stach responds to Sekuła's call for vigilance and alacrity—the boys will be needed to help their Jewish comrades. Sekuła's direct, urgent address is juxtaposed with images of fires in the ghetto. There is no understatement here: The fires are threatening and huge, their impact reinforced by orchestral music, creating an alarming if slightly melodramatic effect.

Later, at Jasio's home, the Jewish messenger Abram approaches Jasio for help in the ghetto uprising. After a moment of hesitation, Jasio decides to join the other members of his clandestine group in their efforts to liberate the ghetto. The youths meet at an amusement park near the ghetto to discuss their options (this scene will be replicated forty years later in Wajda's *Holy Week*). They decide to steal a car from the Germans to get to the ghetto and to help the Jewish fighters to escape. They drive carelessly, exultantly, as if they were merely playing truant. Wajda's presents the fighters as young, carefree, and careless youths—they enjoy their momentary immortality and give little thought to the war and possible death ahead of them.

The youths stop outside the ghetto fence to pick up some Jewish fighters they know to be hiding in the canals. Jasio stands guard nearby as the others go to find the hiding soldiers. However, their sortie is frustrated by the approach of a group of unknowing German soldiers. The other youths manage to escape to the car, but Jasio is flanked by the Germans and cannot escape. In the ensuing chase scene (another one that is brilliantly reworked in a later film, this time *Ashes and Diamonds*), Jasio flees, hides among some empty wooden crates, and then runs toward a steel grate enclosing the ghetto; he quickly realizes that he has run into a trap (in a scene reminiscent of the final scene in *Kanal*) and escapes into a nearby tenement. Finally, in a spectacular scene shot against the backdrop of a huge staircase, Jasio, in a white coat, shoots at the Germans but then, seeing no way to escape, jumps several floors to his death.

Together with the discovery of the missing gun in the carpenter's workshop (the gun that had been used by Jasio in the bar shooting), which prompts an internal investigation, the failed sortie forces Stach to seek a hiding place from the Germans. Dorota offers Stach refuge in her own apartment and, now clearly attracted to him, plants a kiss on his cheek. She now reveals to him her true name, Ewa—for "Dorota" is merely her nickname in the People's Army. By giving the film's female protagonist the name of the biblical first woman, Wajda makes Stach, by extension, into Adam, the archetypal man, who will now be initiated into the act of love. Furthermore, before the intimate scenario, Ewa tells Stach that she has nominated him platoon commander over a group of young fighters. With this symbolic transferal of power from female to male, Stach is granted the final stamp of manhood.

In the morning, a happy Stach ties his shoelaces on the stairs leading to Dorota's apartment. (A delicate fade only implies their lovemaking.) He carries on a casual conversation with the owner of a small shop in the same building when, suddenly, they are interrupted by the seemingly omniscient housekeeper, who warns Stach that Gestapo agents have entered Dorota's apartment. Stach hides behind the stairs and witnesses Dorota's capture by the Gestapo; contrary to typical representations of such soldiers as brutal and abusive monsters (especially in Polish and Soviet films), Wajda shows them quietly leading the young resistance officer to their car. Seen by Stach only from a distance, Dorota seems to accept her fate resignedly, as if she knew all along that her clandestine activities would end in her death. This romantic blend of traits so characteristic of revolutionary activities represented in all Polish art—love, politics, and death—finds its embodiment in this understated, short sequence.[18] Seen through the serious, newly matured eyes of Stach, Dorota's capture brings into question all clandestine activities in occupied Poland and evokes the memories of the many thousands of young, idealistic Poles who over the centuries have lost their lives in the numerous revolutions and battles leading to Poland's liberation.

In the last sequence of the film, Stach sits on a log on the outskirts of Warszawa, tears falling down his cheeks, no longer an idealistic, naive boy but now an experienced and aggrieved man. Suddenly, young people appear out of nowhere and silently await his orders. Stach is bound by his pledge to continue the fight. In a scene shot against the clear sky, the youngsters raise their eyes to their new leader with anticipation and trust. Stach, well aware of the perils and excitements of underground fighting, turns to take command of his platoon. He is now a mature man, a leader trusted by his younger subordinates. In this ending, Wajda adheres to Czeszko's version of the story in that, as Derek Hill of London's *Tribune* notes, *A Generation* is a documentation of "Stach's development from the casual, instinctive anarchy of near-delinquency to political awareness."[19]

A Generation is a pivotal achievement in Wajda's career, establishing him as a promising young film director who passionately presented the dilemmas of his generation and who did not shun controversy. The film immediately attracted a great deal of critical response, both positive and negative. Czeszko himself, the author of *A Generation*, expressed his criticism immediately. Instead of following his suggestions, Czeszko complains, Wajda decided to concentrate fully on the personal story of Stach, who slowly changes from a careless youth to a mature resistance fighter. The young filmmaker, in his own defense, wanted to produce a nonconventional film using unconventional aesthetics to reinforce the fighters' youthful bravado and immaturity. Czeszko, on the other hand, wanted to stress the moment of Stach's coming of age, his maturity, and the process of growth that ends with Stach's joining the Communist Party. As Czeszko notes, "I chose the title *Candidate Term* not without reason: I wanted to suggest to the youth of People's Poland that joining the Party is an extremely serious matter. People here treat too lightly the fact that the road to the Party is often paved with heroism. Nowadays there are new challenges to heroism and if one can rise to them, one will be worthy of becoming a Party member."[20]

Wajda realized that if he followed Czeszko to the letter, he would undoubtedly produce a Stalinist propaganda piece not much different from other Socialist Realist films at the time. His intention, instead, was to concentrate on the presentation of young fighters as people hopelessly embroiled in the makings of history, uncertain about their ideological preferences. This honesty in the presentation of their dilemmas is also visible in the film's paradocumentary look. Clearly influenced by Italian neo-Realism and documentary techniques, Wajda advised Jerzy Lipman, his director of photography, to take shots only on gray, rainy days, ignoring the sensitivity of the film. To suggest a certain cynicism regarding the events in the film, Wajda decided to use unorthodox music as well; Andrzej Markowski's score provides precisely the desired measure of irony to the entire film. Markowski, at the time a young composer, was a student in his last year at the conservatory when the film was being produced. Wajda was not interested in the kind of pomp usually required of war films; he was interested in the irony of the whole situation, the contrast between the exuberant young warriors and their desperate situation. As Wajda points out,[21] Markowski based his music on the works of Igor Strawiński, a fact that aptly illustrates the tragedy of the events unfolding in the film, from the youthful engagement of the protagonists to the arrest and/or death of three of them.

Although superficially a typical resistance film, *A Generation* defies the norms of similar war films produced at the time:[22] It is a gritty and unconventional film. As Roman Polański states in his autobiography, "The film encountered serious obstacles before its distribution. The censor's approval was not easily attained. Certain sequences had to be re-taken by Wajda to strengthen their ideological message, while others—the spectacular scene of my fight with Cybulski among them—were cut entirely. The universally screened and acclaimed version of *A Generation* was but a pale reflection of Wajda's original version."[23] At the time of the film's production, its fate was uncertain. During those Stalinist times, every screenplay had to undergo a detailed screening process by the Film and Screenplay Qualification Committee before its production was allowed.[24] The committee was extremely critical, in particular, of the scenes presenting Stach's political involvement and the practical matters of fighting, arms handling, shootings, and deaths because, as Andrzej Ważyk stated in 1953, these matters in the film took precedence over political education. In Poland in the early 1950s, with the influx of heavily ideological Soviet and Polish films about World War II, Wajda's presentation of the young fighters offended the sensibilities of many Poles who still remembered vividly the horrors of German occupation.

The members of the screening committee had some objection to almost every element in the film, from its composition, its cast, and its music to its ideological implications and points of view. The opinion of Ważyk is not surprising, then: "The lack of the definite point in the conclusion cannot be supported. The images suggesting an ongoing battle cannot compensate on screen for the painful message of a personal drama of the individual characters—Dorota and Stach. In my opinion, such an ending might create an ineradicably pessimistic impression."[25] After the film's release in 1955, official criticism became, if possible, even fiercer. Other critics, however, expressed their open admiration for the film.[26] Wilhelm Mach, an influential critic from *Przegląd Kulturalny*, writes of this film that it is "honest and painfully philosophical about the price that has been paid more than once by youth for its will to live. It portrays heroism without exaggeration or pride; it is not ashamed of confessions induced by fear, or of childish tears; it does not sculpt granite monuments to its warriors."[27]

Stanisław Grzelecki from *Życie Warszawy* underlines the film's intensity of vision: "In many scenes, there is an intensity of vision reinforced by the contrasting editing. Editing incorporating rapid crosscutting is used as one of the instruments to display the atmosphere of the days of occupation. During those days the sudden reality of events shocked people; many events took place in short, tense moments, during incessant fights which made every street corner an unknown territory."[28] Hill notes that the strength of the film lies in its honest presentation of the protagonists; Stach especially, in Hill's opinion, is genuine in his naïveté and in his playful desire to fight the aggressor: "the nucleus is not so much the heroism of its young Communist hero (an exceptionally honest performance by Tadeusz Łomnicki) but his development from the casual, instinctive anarchy of near-delinquency to political awareness."[29]

Ważyk's opinion was representative of the official party line when he states that "the political content of the fight should grow (in Stach) as he matured politically."[30] However, had Wajda followed the official suggestions, he would likely have been forced to create yet another war film replete with political monologues and saturated with ostentatious music, thereby seeking to construct the war effort as glorious and noble. Instead, by provoking the spectators with rough dialogue, with Markowski's thoughtful music, and with quick-paced sequences depicting the war as being almost playful, Wajda jarred audiences with the freshness of his vision. With this film, Wajda made his mark on the cinematic landscape of Poland. "Wajda alluded to documentary technique; he also did not resist the influence of the Italian Neorealism in his work. And yet, *A Generation* had something peculiarly Polish, thanks to—among other things—characters who did not quite fit into propaganda stereotypes. Wajda's creation did not resemble any of the films that had so far been made in People's Poland.... For us, it is a film of the highest importance. The entire Polish cinema can trace its roots to it."[31]

In producing his first major film, Wajda reveals one of his most interesting characteristics as a director, namely, his strong negotiating skills, as seen in both production and postproduction collaborations. He collected a group of friends early in the process of filmmaking, during the writing of the screenplay. Wajda has often repeated in interviews that the production of any film is a collaborative effort, and this approach is clearly visible in all his films and in photographs that document the process of his filmmaking. As Jerzy Wilmański notes, Wajda somehow managed to gather the best actors and technical crew available, most of whom later garnered their own success in the Polish film industry: "If we talk about the genius of Wajda the director, we see that in this first film the signs of this genius are already present. How much of the sensitive intuition is needed to faultlessly choose among a mass of debutantes the ones who will later constitute the core of the contemporary acting force?"[32] Kazimierz Kutz, who would himself become a well-known Polish film director, was Wajda's assistant on the film, and the actors Zbigniew Cybulski, Tadeusz Łomnicki, Tadeusz Janczar, and Roman Polański all became famous for their acting and directorial work. More interestingly, in some way or another, Polański, Cybulski, and Łomnicki, among others, have all at one time or another related their own personal success to the film *A Generation* and to its director.

This first fiction film gave Wajda an opportunity to hone his directorial skills and to present its issues in an engaging and passionate manner. Although naive and simplistic to the minds of many contemporary viewers, *A Generation* contains a remarkable energy, as Adam Michnik notes,[33] and generations of Poles have enjoyed its originality and vigor. This film also provides a glimpse into the possibility of greater films to come from this talented young filmmaker—such as the celebrated *Kanal*, a much more mature treatment of World War II than the enthusiastic yet admittedly somewhat naïve film, *A Generation*.

Kanal (1957)

From the most preliminary stages of *Kanal's* archival preproduction notes, this film emerges as a product of Wajda's unfailing imagination: a painstaking aesthetic vision the director had in his head long before shooting started. He produced many drawings for the film and concentrated especially on the carefully designed takes. The screenplay of *Kanal* was written by Jerzy Stawiński, adapted from his earlier novel of the same title. It is based on the true story of Armia Krajowa (Home

Army) platoon soldiers in Warszawa who attempted an escape through the underground sewage system just before the end of the Warszawa Uprising (on 2 October 1944). From the initial voice-over commentary, the spectator learns that the film is set at the end of September, and that the Warszawa Insurrection fighters are still struggling with the overwhelming German forces. The platoon soldiers of Lieutenant Zadra decide to escape German troops by going down into Warszawa's canals to reach the town center, there to help the few remaining fighting insurgents. The film follows the last hours in the life of the Third Platoon. The director obviates any mystery or suspense by stating in the beginning of the film that all the protagonists will die.

The film opens with a dynamic, continuous pan showing wartime Warszawa; smoldering ruins dot the deserted landscape amid dying fires. The following shots show the doomed platoon traveling in a ragged line toward an old garbage dump, obviously exhausted from fighting, their clothing ripped and filthy. The commanding officer, Zadra, confides in the second officer that he feels personally responsible for the soldiers, whom he himself recruited. In one of the most spectacular long uninterrupted takes in the whole film, the platoon slowly marches through the ruined city. The camera follows their movements and from time to time closes on one of the soldiers. When the platoon finally reaches a resting place already inhabited by other survivors, Zadra and his fellow commander acknowledge their impending deaths, and agree that they cannot show any weakness nor any sign of this knowledge to the soldiers under their command. This feeling of inescapable disaster looms large over the entire film and haunts the spectator to the very end.

In the meantime, however, the soldiers are happy to have a little rest, and they sit on the ground talking with soldiers from other platoons, exchanging jokes and greetings. One member of the platoon is Michał, an erstwhile composer. One of the officers notices an old piano in the corner of the room and asks Michał to play something. In contrast to the distant machine-gun fire, this haunting piano tune is a reminder of a remote past in which life bore some semblance of normalcy. Amid the general destruction and the filth, Michał's music is ethereal, like an intrusion from another world—yet also, cunningly, it accompanies appropriately small romances unfolding among the tired soldiers. The men and women flirt, talk, laugh, exchange innocuous sexual jokes, and behave as if their situation were pedestrian. In one such conversation, a young officer, Smukły, engages in flirtatious and deceptively lighthearted banter with a wounded young woman lying on a stretcher. Smukły asks the nonchalant woman about her wound and she replies that it is nothing serious. However, when bearers lift her stretcher, the officer sees that she has lost a leg.

The surrealism of these scenes recalls that of *Viridiana* and other films by Luis Bunuel, whom Wajda deeply admired. Although they were unable to see Bunuel's films as students in Stalinist Poland, Wajda and his friends, especially Polański, were aware of, and enthusiastic about, Bunuel's surrealist aesthetics. Wajda refers to *Kanal*'s surrealism when he writes of a press conference that took place after the film's screening in Cannes:

> "I was asked who I regarded as my master. I answered without hesitation, 'Luis Bunuel ... that is, he would be, if I knew his films.' And this was true. At film school I had only had the opportunity to view short fragments of *The Andalusian Dog* and *The Golden Age* [as the films were banned in Poland for their western and bourgeois content—my addition]. It was only after the festival that the film archives in Paris, moved by my admission, organized a screening of most of Bunuel's films for me. Roman Polański also took advantage of the offer and accompanied me to these showings."[34]

Kanal's scene with the tired soldiers in the opulent but ruined drawing room is rife with detail, rich in its display of light and shade, with a refined depth of focus. It looks like an extravagant black-and-white painting: elegant curtains hang over broken windows, juxtaposed in the same shot with the injured men and women. The short, dynamic takes in this scene contribute further to its intensity—the nervous soldiers in no way anticipate their doom. The scene concludes with a phone conversation between Michał and his family in the ghetto; they confirm that the uprising is over, crushed by the Germans. The soldiers now know that they have no way out: either they have to fight the Germans openly in a hopeless last stand, or they go down into the canals, trying to survive.

The following scenes show officers engaged in romantic encounters, Mądry with Halinka and Korab with Stokrotka. The remainder of the film concentrates on the latter two, however. Against the backdrop of death or capture, the lovers' scenario unfolds: They flirt, playing an emotional game of hide-and-seek, and suffer pangs of intermingled jealousy, love, and despair. These romances exemplify the love-politics blend Wajda has already introduced in *A Generation* and that he will continue in his other war films. Quickly, brutally, the love scene is interrupted by machine-gun fire. The lovers run out of the room to shoot at the approaching Germans. Korab scoffs cruelly at Stokrotka, telling her to get away from the field of battle. As in *A Generation*, Wajda introduces the motif of the conventional treatment of women by men, according to which women are to be both protected and commanded by men. (In some of his later films, such as *Man of Marble* and *The Young Ladies of Wilko*, women defy these roles with their strength and courage.)

The insurgents are soon overwhelmed by the well-armed Germans with their artillery and tanks, and the Polish soldiers shoot one last salvo and then retire from the fighting. Korab, however, decides to go on a suicide mission. In a desperate attempt to stop the approaching *go-liat* (a miniature, remotely guided tank with explosives in it), he runs out with a spade and cuts the cable that steers the device. A naive young man in a white shirt running desperately toward the death-machine, Korab personifies a childish but indomitable will to fight, a sheer passion and strength of will that, while spiritually superior, remains inferior to the Germans' tanks and artillery. This exalted model of the young, headstrong fighter is reiterated by Wajda in his later film, *Lotna,* where a young officer on a white horse symbolizes the same ingenuousness and helplessness that Korab does in this film—he succeeds in cutting the cord, but (inevitably) is shot in the chest on his retreat to the villa.

Rescued by a comrade, Korab is placed in the care of the weakest in the group, Michał the composer, and of course is also attended by Stokrotka. The long night is spent in silence, with the partisans waiting and humming songs while the scribbler, Kula, collects personal data from the injured soldiers. The following day, Zadra orders everyone into the canals. That night, all of them—two lieutenants, five lesser officers, and twenty soldiers—go to the canal inlets, and Stokrotka gets permission to take care of the injured Korab herself. Yet before they descend into the hellish sewers and the silence and horror of the canals, the platoon has to go through the purgatory of witnessing the expulsion from the ghetto: shouts, mayhem, people attacked by German soldiers, and mothers and children running through the fires.

These scenes are intercut with the tableaux of a young Polish soldier on the barricades, quietly emptying his shoes of the rubbish they have gathered; and of a distressed mother, clad in black, desperately imploring the soldiers around her to tell of her daughter's whereabouts. Surrealist and expressionist at the same time, these scenes recall Sergei Eisenstein's famous takes from *Potemkin* and *Strike.* Shots of high intensity interspersed with those of low intensity create an emotional contrast and heighten the sense of impending disaster. As the platoon enters the canals, one of the officers sums up their despair and their situation: "We have let so much of our blood, and now we have to scurry like rats."[35]

Although many reviewers have argued that the scenes in the canals overpower the rest of the film, these gruesome sequences in fact take up only half of its entire length: The film is ideally balanced between the scenes set above- and below-ground. Furthermore, the events in the canals are not merely gruesome wanderings in the dark; they are carefully structured scenes placed around moments of hope and despair. The platoon splits into three groups, the main one led by Zadra; the second one composed of Michał, Halinka, and Mądry; and the third one composed of Korab and Stokrotka. The spectator is made to identify with the last group, and, though the camera traverses periodically between each of the groups, the film largely follows Korab and Sto-krotka to the end.

Throughout the canal scenes, horror mixes with the grotesque, hope with despair. All of the soldiers are trapped by the claustrophobic space of the canals, by the German soldiers above, and by the vile smell of fermenting excrement. They begin to weaken as oxygen becomes scarce; the three groups slow down, but they trudge on regardless. Along the way, they experience moments of horror—they see corpses submerged in the feces; they nearly drown in fresh excrement; and, weakened, they are nearly trampled by civilians on their way out of the canals. Michał, reeling, recites lines from Dante Alighieri's *Divine Comedy* when he sees these developments, and later, unable to cope with his present reality, he wanders away from Mądry and Halinka playing an *okaryna*, a type of old-fashioned flute. The organ music off-screen blends with Michał's tune until both he and it disappear into the film's periphery.

Despite all the horrific events, the disjoined platoon squelches on, trying to find the exit on the outskirts of the town's center. All are look-ing for a sign indicating Wilcza Street, supposedly the exit from the canals; unable to find it, though, they go on, one by one fainting from exhaustion and asphyxiation. Stokrotka repeatedly coaxes the injured Korab to go on, pushing him, leading him, and, finally, dragging him to the exit only to find that it has been sealed with an iron grate. Their physical journey, quite apart from the narrative of war and defeat, sig-nifies a transformation of their budding romance into a mature love that endures beyond any temporal obstacle. Wajda's romanticism, only barely implied in *A Generation*, is fully realized in this film. Yet in *Kanal*, love—a source of strength and the wellspring of life—is also betrayed in the relationship between Halinka and Mądry, when the latter sud-denly announces to his young lover that he has a wife and children. Crushed and mortified, Halinka shoots herself. The other soldiers feel similarly disenchanted by his duplicity, and they are rendered powerless by the combined weight of hardship, the German oppressor's cunning, and this final internal betrayal. The hopelessness of their situation is beautifully, horribly, and stunningly encapsulated by one of the film's final shots: Stokrotka's despairing face pressed against the iron grid that blocks their escape to freedom.

Stokrotka's desperate look across to the houses on the other side of the Vistula River symbolizes, of course, the desire for liberation from the canals—but it also represents the freedom fighters' unfulfilled hopes for the support of the Soviet forces waiting on the other side of the river. The Soviets were expected to aid the Polish insurgents, but in-stead waited patiently on the other side of the Vistula until the city of Warszawa bled to death. Of course, Wajda could allude only met-onymically to the Soviet betrayal: "I could not show that Soviet troops were waiting on the other side of the Vistula River while the Warszawa insurrection died on this side. It was enough that I led the protagonists of my film to the canal's outlet, from which they could see the other side of the river. The audience knew what I was going to say—we communicated without words, using a symbolic, almost magical language."[36] Thus, the camera lingers on Stokrotka's longing look through the grate as she talks about the green grass on the far riverbank, clearly alluding to the notions of freedom and hope that this color would evoke in the national consciousness.

The film ends with two telling sequences showing the soldiers leaving the canals. In the first sequence, Mądry climbs out alone only to see other members of his platoon surrendering to the Germans, and he weeps hopelessly as he waits for the shots announcing their execution by the Germans. The second sequence shows Zadra and Kula leaving the canal in another part of the city amid desolate ruins, a sequence that has been preceded by a scene in which Smukły, who had earlier accompanied the two lieutenants, tries to remove an elaborate trap set by the Germans in the entry to the canal. A deadly mine composed of three hand-grenades is hung there, set to block the entry and prevent escapees from getting outside. Smukły carefully removes the grenades from the entrance, but he then slips and is killed by the grenades' explosion.

The shocking image of Smukły's torn body is juxtaposed with that of crisscrossed metal rods, clearly alluding to Christ's crucifixion, an iconic presentation found in many other Wajda films. (*Ashes and Diamonds, Samson, Pilate and Others,* and *The Gates to Paradise* come to mind immediately.) In fact, it is only through the newly blasted opening—both literally and figuratively through Smukły's death—that Zadra and Kula are able to escape their doom. The themes of Christian sacrifice and of senseless carnage emerge from this shocking scene, only to be reinforced by the ensuing dialogue: Zadra learns that Kula had deceived him when he reported to him regarding the missing fighters in the canal. Earlier in the canals, Kula had informed Zadra that their soldiers still followed them, knowing full well that they stayed behind. In a fit of disconsolate rage, Zadra kills his comrade and goes back into the canals to find the missing soldiers. The final sequence and the film end thus, with swelling musical accompaniment and a shot of tiny white pieces of paper scattering in the wind.

Predictably, the film provoked very strong reactions from party officials. Wajda presented the brutal truth of the Warszawa Uprising: the futility and hopelessness of the fight against the huge German army and the betrayal of the Red Army, which stood by and simply waited for the outcome of the fight.

> "I knew that a condition of producing this film was, in fact, to bury this truth as deeply as possible beneath the human drama of the uprising ... Was I consciously lying? What was I hoping for? I think that I believed the same thing that opponents to the film from the Assessment Commission,

who had correctly predicted the audience's reaction, believed. They were afraid of the audience's memory; I was counting on that very memory."[37]

The president of the Assessment Commission for Films and Screenplays, Leonard Borkowicz, was extremely critical of the film, even at the preproduction stage during the assessment of the screenplay. He accused Wajda of accepting an ahistorical and even libelous screenplay with "weak" ideological content. He criticized Wajda for his concentration on the love affair between Korab and Stokrotka rather than on the real meaning of the uprising. During the meeting of the Assessment Commission for Films and Screenplays, Borkowicz stressed that the heroism of that time is not sufficiently played out:

> "This screenplay, in some way, does not sufficiently address the problem of heroism. Comrade Konwicki [another member of the Assessment Commission] has said that there isn't a family which hasn't lost someone dear to them, but in the film, our good intentions are not good enough. We are in a very difficult political situation: the nature of the uprising is perfectly clear; none of those people who died were fighting against us; they were fighting against foreign invaders, and we are not questioning this."[38]

What Borkowicz meant by "difficult political situation" was the fact that due to its politically superior position, the former Soviet Union could not be overtly criticized for their abandonment of the Polish insurgents during World War II. Soviets were the de facto rulers of Poland, and their authority could not be undermined by any filmmaker. The ending of the insurgents' flight to freedom on such a negative note was seen by official reviewers as too accusatory. However, sensing the integrity and the power of the film itself, it was Borkowicz himself who, as the head of cinematography, made the final decision to show the film at Cannes. The film premiered in Warszawa on 20 April 1957, and immediately garnered the highest praise from both Polish and international critics. That same year, the film also received the Jury's Special "Silver Palm" Award at the 10th IFF (International Film Festival) in Cannes.[39]

Despite the awards and praise abroad, the film's unprecedented criticism in Poland continued on many fronts. This relentless criticism may have its source in Wajda's undermining of the Polish romantic tradition in the presentation of dirty and unkempt soldier in *Kanal*. In poetry, art, and war films, Poles have almost always been presented as heroic figures, bravely struggling with the enemy. The powerful *uhlan* tradition, which implied a romantic approach to a military effort, corroborated this heroic myth. An uhlan, a "mounted officer," has always represented in the Polish tradition an absurdly romantic warrior who would rather die for his country than surrender to the enemy. In the aesthetic sense, an uhlan is an impeccably dressed, handsome young man on horseback, attractive to women and heroic in stature. This romantic tradition of the immaculately dressed and impeccably well-kept warrior has been completely subverted by Wajda, whose soldiers are dirty, weak, and petty, preoccupied with mundane personal affairs and conflicts.[40] Wajda's formulation is quite important in light of the conventional, romanticized view of the uprising, which the film seemingly abrogates.

Wajda had predicted such responses, however, being aware of the enormous ideological and psychological importance of the Uprising to the defeated Poles. He was not surprised by the bitterness of some of the remarks.

> "The Jury's Award, or as it was then called, the 'Silver Palm,' did not protect my film from the Polish critics and audience. It was difficult to be surprised at the latter—to an enormous degree it was made up of participants in the uprising or families who had lost their loved ones in Warszawa. This film could not satisfy them. They had licked their wounds, mourned their dead, and now they wanted to see their moral and spiritual victory and not death in the sewers."[41]

Most reviewers, also aware of the ideological and psychological importance of the film, were extremely critical. Władysław Bartoszewski from *Stolica* declared, "*Kanał* is not a historical film about the Warszawa Uprising, nor is it a psychological film about the uprising";[42] Bolesław Michałek criticizes the film as one in which "the Warszawa Uprising remains an enigmatic creation in which unknown forces destroy human beings."[43] Other Polish critics recognize the film's narrative shortcomings, which Jerzy Płażewski summarizes in the following statement: "All with whom I spoke underlined the errors of the screenplay (its lack of culmination), the exaggerated and unnecessarily prolonged role of the composer (especially in the canals), and a lack of consistency in the tone of the narrative."[44]

However, the tone of criticism offered against this film is different than that voiced three years previous, immediately following the release of *A Generation*. In 1957, critics are more receptive to the work's political content and aesthetic merit; more attention is paid by the members of the commission who are writers and directors,[45] as opposed to faceless bureaucrats. This change was undoubtedly caused at least in part by "the thaw," a new political situation in the countries of the Eastern Bloc brought about by the sudden death of Stalin in 1953. The political atmosphere in Poland near the end of the 1950s became much more relaxed, and party bureaucrats ceased to apply the same stringent political standards to artistic endeavors that they had at the beginning of the 1950s. The late 1950s and early 1960s were times of optimism in Polish social life and of unsurpassed activity in Polish art.

The making of *Kanal* also marks an important period of artistic development in Wajda's film career, during which he became more preoccupied with the aesthetic impression that his film would make on its spectators than with the political implications of showing the War-szawa Uprising as a doomed enterprise. As half of the film was to take place in the sewers, Wajda searched for the best means to make the scenes convincing and aesthetically interesting. In specially built studios in Łódź, actors waded in water and artificial muck devised by his reliable partners; "the camera floated just over the surface of the slime, looked into the black depths of the dead-end corridors, or showed the open manholes high above, from which the harsh light of day poured into the interior."[46]

Yet the film's particular aesthetics mystified many foreign critics; in particular, the notably expressionist aspects of the film were not universally admired. Jean de Boroncelli writes of Wajda's "romanticism of horror,"[47] while Wolfgang Ebert comments on its romantic, neo-realist aspects,[48] and Bosley Crowther remarks upon "the hideous, stinking cesspool" that acquires Dantaesque proportions in Michał's mind.[49] Andre Bazin regards this aspect of the film as follows: "The weak side of *Kanał* is what links it with *Five from Barska Street:* expressionistic use of complicated, realistic sets, an artistic, dramatic, and psychological concept of action when the subject demands just the opposite style."[50] The film was heavily criticized—especially by Polish critics—because it dared to show the Warszawa Uprising as senseless and futile, yet *Kanał* clearly demonstrates Wajda's emotional approach to the subject and to filmmaking. His protagonists are courageous but believable, simply, desperately trying to survive. The film is aesthetically consistent from the beginning to end: its neorealism and surrealism intensify the human drama, but do not transcend the horror of the presented events as in Wajda's later film *Lotna*.

Already these two early films, *A Generation* and *Kanał*, reveal the director's attitude toward the spiritual treatment of the issues of nationhood and national identity. Wajda sees Polish identity as linked to the spiritual perception of the nation's essence and to its heroic past. He introduces the issues of responsibility, of the fight for freedom and honor, each important for the ultimate defining of national identity. Unlike Ernest Renan, who stresses only the spiritual essence of the nation, as exposed in his fundamental writings on the subject,[51] Wajda sees national identity as also defined by the geographic territory of Poland, for which one *must* fight. In a country ravaged by partitions, annexations, and wars, the demonstration of national feelings has historically been related to the fight for the country's independence. In the case of Poland, national identity has always had a specific territorial link—after all, Poland has not existed (geographically, at least) for over two hundred years. But like Renan, Wajda ascribes a large role to the nation's heroic past, which the former sees as "the social capital upon which one bases a national idea."[52] The territorial, spiritual, and heroic approaches to the issues of nation and national identity characterize all Wajda's films in a more or less explicit manner with the seed of this approach, present already in *A Generation*. Wajda becomes the interpreter of this complex amalgam of approaches to nationhood, their propagator and ardent supporter, and, as we shall see in the following chapters, the emotional and visual creator of national mythology.

Ashes and Diamonds (1958)

Ashes and Diamonds concludes the early period of professional growth in Wajda's career. This film is generally considered not only the highlight of his early period, but his best film altogether. Due to its universal appeal, *Ashes and Diamonds* has provoked intense emotional and intellectual response both in Poland and abroad. The film's action takes place on 8 May 1945, at the end of World War II; the story encompasses a one-day period, ending with the dawn of the following day. As Wajda comments, he considers the film almost a personal story that he had to relive:

> "To live further, one has to forget; in order to forget, one has to reinforce one's experience, one's life history, the whole past which is left behind. The fate of the boys from the canals, Tadeusz from *Landscape after Battle*, Marcin from *The Crowned-Eagle Ring* and Maciek Chełmicki from *Ashes and Diamonds,* could be my life story. I was simply luckier than they were. It was merely coincidence that I was not in their situation, so I considered it my duty to tell their story as skillfully and truthfully as I could."[53]

Jerzy Andrzejewski describes the process of scriptwriting in the following way:

> "I planned to film my novel a long time ago, in 1948–49. There were other directors, Erwin Axer and Antonioni Bohdziewicz, who thought about making such a film as well. For many reasons, their plans did not materialize. In autumn last year, Andrzej Wajda came to me to discuss the possibility of making a screenplay based on my novel. For a month we worked on the screenplay in Obory. We decided to limit some subplots and confine the film's action to twenty-four hours, thus maintaining the classical unity of time."[54]

Ashes and Diamonds starts with a bucolic scene set near a small country church, with birds chirping and the sun shining brightly. Maciek and Andrzej, officers in the Narodowe Siły Zbrojne (a unit of the Home Army),[55] wait for the car of Konrad Szczuka, a political opponent, to arrive; Drewnowski, a third Home Army member, stands guard nearby. The three young men plan to assassinate Szczuka, the district secretary of the regional party committee of Polska Partia Robotnicza (Polish United Workers Party), along with his assistant Podgórski. The Home Army and the Polish United Workers Party represent two opposing factions that fought for power in Poland once World War II ended. The latter group, and thus Szczuka, represents the communist regime force-fully implemented by Poland's liberator (and invader), the former Soviet Union.

The historical context of the film is of course dictated by the specific situation of Poland after World War II, when the country became one of Russia's satellites. During the war, the entire country was embroiled in the doomed effort to fight the Nazi invaders, with members of all political parties united. After the war, however, these same factions fought each other in ideologically grounded guerrilla wars. There were many individual guerrilla units comprised of the former Home Army soldiers, who bitterly fought the pro-Communist, Russian-trained People's Army. "After the victory of the Communists, the most recalcitrant of the opposition were executed during the Stalinist purges of the late 1940s and early 1950s."[56]

The very first scene in the film plunges the spectator, especially a Polish spectator familiar with the situation, into the middle of the ideological conflict. The scene begins from an idealistic and, in this context, surrealistic series of images. A ploughman works the field in a scene reminiscent of a well-known painting by Ferdynand Ruszczyc, called *Ziemia (The Earth)*. A little girl approaches the men and asks them to open the church. Standing against the pristine birch trees overlooking the scene, she embodies the innocence of youth, unaware of any political tensions. Meanwhile, Maciek and Andrzej engage in small talk, but they are soon interrupted by Drewnowski, who whistles to them as a car approaches. Rapid shooting ensues, during which the older man in the car is killed instantly. The young driver tries to escape but, after a short run, is killed mercilessly by Maciek in the church, with the Madonna ironically looking on. However, the attackers realize, after checking the documents of their victims, that they have mistakenly killed two innocents, a fact later corroborated by their superior, Major Waga. This first sequence introduces several elements that will reappear throughout the film: the youthful, reckless behavior of the assassin Maciek; the contrast between the pastoral, innocent character of the mise-en-scène and the ominous and terrible events that occur; and the iconoclasm of the scenes in the Catholic church.

Appalled by their fateful mistake, the young men flee; almost immediately, another car approaches the scene. Comrade Szczuka gets out of the car and quickly realizes what has happened. Approaching workers also witness the scene and hear Szczuka mourning the fallen comrades in a propagandist monologue redolent of the Socialist-Realist "newspeak." Szczuka informs the workers that the real fight for Poland has only recently begun and that it will necessitate the elimination of their (read: *his*) political opponents. The scene is surprisingly bold in its ideological tone, ostensibly condemnatory of the Home Army; it alludes to similarly styled scenes in well-known propaganda films, with Szczuka appearing against the open sky in the background, shot with a low-angled camera.

This characterization, however, is plainly out of place in the context of the rest of the film, which generally neither supports nor condemns the official ideologies but attempts rather honestly to present the political arguments of both the Communist Party and the Home Army. By presenting Szczuka in this somewhat overly zealous and thereby mocking manner, Wajda undermines the character's otherwise objective presentation. The scene simply strikes a wrong chord, which is somehow *wrong* within the larger film, unnecessarily parodying the newspeak of the new regime. Here Wajda may have been referring to the mode of Socialist Realism, an artistic trend introduced and enforced by Stalin in the early 1930s in Soviet Russia and forcefully implemented in Poland in 1940s and 1950s, in a self-parodying manner, as if commenting on this remnant from the past. At the same time, he directs the knowing spectator's attention to the context of the film's production, post-1953, at the beginning of "the political and artistic thaw" enthusiastically embraced by Wajda and by other artists in Poland.

After Szczuka's speech, the film shifts to the Hotel Monopol Restaurant in the nearby small town of Ostrowiec, near Warszawa, where the end of the war is being celebrated at a special banquet. The film's brief love affair between Maciek and Krystyna, a waitress, also starts here. Initially playful, their flirtatious exchanges quickly change into more serious dialogue. In this first scene of a charming subplot, Maciek plays at hide-and-seek with a vodka glass, finally taking out the military mug he would have used during the underground fighting. The *menażka*, a "soldier's mug," is a potent symbol of the perils and hardships of the warrior's life. By putting his mug on the bar in this way, Maciek symbolically acknowledges the end of the war but also signals that he is still deeply entrenched within it.

Another important sequence shows the bourgeois apartment of the Staniewicz family, who are Home Army sympathizers; Mrs. Staniewicz is also Szczuka's sister-in-law. Szczuka, it turns out, has a son approximately Maciek's age, Marek, who was brought up during the war by Mrs. Staniewicz. To further complicate matters, the Staniewicz household currently harbors Maciek's and Andrzej's Home Army superior, Waga, who is in hiding. Waga receives a telephone call from Andrzej, who informs him that the attack on Szczuka was botched. The major orders that the execution should be attempted a second time. Then, before going to the bar, Szczuka himself comes to the Staniewicz home seeking to reestablish contact with his son, but Marek is not there. Unhappy and unwelcome in the Staniewicz's bourgeois home,[57] Szczuka leaves the apartment without having taken his coat off.

Shortly, Maciek sees his quarry entering the hotel and, moving in, overhears a conversation between Szczuka and his assistant about the botched assassination attempt. Maciek realizes that, though the war may be over, he will have to kill again. Wajda introduces a fascinating psychological subplot here not present in the novel: the vaguely father-son relationship that develops between Szczuka and Maciek, who has no father of his own. Over the course of several cunningly shot exchanges of looks, the spectator senses that Maciek begins to see Szczuka as if he were his own father while Szczuka, unaware of Maciek's intentions and feeling the loss of his own son, treats the young partisan with warmth and interest. (Arguably, this subplot may have arisen out of Wajda's own longing for a father, for he lost his at the tender age of fourteen; in many later films, such as *Lotna* and *The Young Ladies of Wilko*, he affectionately re-creates such father-son relationships.)

In the meantime, the banquet starts. The guests at this reception represent many spheres of Polish society: party officials, members of the underground army, official press, and members of the Soviet army. The multiplicity and heterogeneity of Polish society introduced in this film is recounted later in both *The Wedding* and *Mr. Thadeus*. Aristocrats and commoners, artists and intelligentsia, Polish, Russian, Jew, and Ukrainian all mingle in an evidently harmonious ceremony. As Marek Hendrykowski comments, "everybody participates in this historical drama *nolens volens* [whether one wants it or not]."[58] The complexity of Polish society and the Poles' relations with Ukrainians, Russians, and Jews are issues deeply imbedded in many of Wajda's films. Such a reluctantly idealistic portrayal would attest to Wajda's deep wish to see Poland as a tolerant and united country, a wish openly proclaimed in his two most recent films, *Mr. Thadeus* and *Revenge*, and cynically subverted in *The Wedding*.

As the banquet scene unfolds, Hanka Lewicka, a young singer, begins the song "The Red Poppies of Monte Casino," a moving lyric about the heroism of the Polish Second Corps soldiers who fought the Germans at the Battle of Monte Casino. Historians have recognized that this battle in Italy was won largely thanks to those Polish fighters who sacrificed themselves for the good of the cause. The pain and despair of this passionate song constitutes an apt background for the scene, in which Maciek and Andrzej stand at the bar listening and reminiscing about dead comrades. In a famous moment later repeated in *The Crowned-Eagle Ring*, Maciek lights numerous glasses of vodka on fire, each intended to represent one fallen comrade. Asking Andrzej, "Do you remember Halinka? Wilga? Kossobudzki? Rudy? Kajtek?" he moves from glass to glass, recalling the names of their deceased compatriots, lighting one glass for each new name. The camera moves with him, changing positions and points of view, as if identifying singly with each name in the list of the dead.

As if to counteract the morbidity of this scene and the actors' consequent conversation about Szczuka's assassination, Wajda introduces a long comic sequence presenting Drewnowski, who stood watch for Maciek and Andrzej in the opening scene, and Pieniążek, a representative of the democratic press. Straight from the assassination near the church, Drewnowski has come to the banquet hall. He is a mere caricature, a shady career opportunist who cooperates with the Home Army while at the same time acting as secretary to the Communist bureaucrat in Ostrowiec. He and Pieniążek get ridiculously drunk while cynically discussing career prospects, new positions, new money, and new influence in postwar Poland. Through comedy, Wajda is able to approach these sensitive issues of opportunism and careerism. Drewnowski characterizes the two dominant (and contradictory) views in Polish society at the end of the Second World War; uncertain as to which political orientation would prevail, many Polish citizens were virtually forced to cooperate with the winning party against their inner wishes. The humorous sequence is one of Wajda's modest attempts at comedy, an area into which he has rarely ventured.

Still, moving freely between comedy and tragedy, Wajda once again leads the spectator to a scene full of symbolic connotations. In this scene, Maciek goes to his hotel room to check his gun. In the process, he loses his eyeglasses: symbolically he has lost the clarity of vision required to assess properly his role in Szczuka's assassination. As he fumbles and drops a piece of his gun on the floor, Krystyna knocks on the door. Distracted and confused, yet trying to appear relaxed, Maciek invites her to his room while simultaneously looking for the piece of the gun and his glasses on the floor. His relief at finding the missing part is matched by his relief at finding that Krystyna will stay, culminating in a sudden burst of boyish, liberating laughter. In an amusing scene shot from above, the young protagonists realize that they have fallen in love. Their budding romance is contrasted by somber dialogue, though, in which Maciek tells her that his dark glasses symbolize his unfulfilled love for his motherland and, more practically, the darkness he experienced in his long wading through the canals.[59] This sequence is intercut by the banquet scenes in which Szczuka enters the reception and an inebriated Pieniążek interrupts the official proceedings with his slurred speech.

Maciek decides that he wants to leave the hotel, so he and Krystyna go for a walk. Soviet soldiers pass them on their way; it begins to rain, and Krystyna and Maciek decide to hide in a ruined church. Krystyna notices a poem inscribed on the wall (Cyprian Kamil Norwid's "Ashes and Diamonds," from which the title of the film is taken). Maciek recites the lines in a somber tone:

> So often are you as a blazing torch
> With flames of burning hemp falling about you.
> Flaming, you know not if flames freedom bring or death,
> Consuming all that you most cherish.

Or if cinders only will be left and want, chaos and tempest shall engulf.
Or will the cinders hold the glory of a starlight diamond,
The morning star of lasting triumph."[60]

Norwid's poetry is highly romantic and sophisticated, full of hidden meanings; it is the poetry of worldly intellectuals. The poet Norwid was a nationalist who believed in and categorically supported Poland's freedom. His words express the aspirations of Maciek himself and, by extension, the deep convictions of many young Polish people regarding their nation's fate. Here, Wajda's romanticism is almost palpable. In reading the poem, Maciek bears out his conviction that he must sacrifice his happiness to national duty. As Marek Haltof explains, "The Polish romantic protagonist always solves such a dilemma by considering national matters as having topmost priority.... Like other Polish romantic characters, Maciek is a prisoner of fate that he is powerless to escape."[61]

The young people now walk about the church full of debris, in which the figure of Christ hangs upside down, suspended from the ceiling. As she moves around, Krystyna breaks her high-heeled shoe, and Maciek decides to repair it. In search of a hammer, he goes to the altar and finds a small church bell. In one of the most startling scenes in the film, one broadly commented upon by reviewers, Maciek repairs the shoe on the altar. This blasphemy is interrupted by an older man who guards the corpses of the two men Maciek and Andrzej slew earlier. The guard, unaware of the irony of the situation, scolds Maciek, telling him that he offends the memory of the dead people with his recklessness and insensitivity. This scene signifies the young man's lack of respect, his apostasy, his cynicism, and his immorality, all of which may have been brought about by his immersion in the war.

On the way back to the hotel, Maciek passionately kisses Krystyna good-bye. In a surreal moment when he turns away from her, he is approached by a white horse running loose in the streets. In Polish art and literature, the horse—and particularly the white horse—is an enduring symbol of virginity, innocence, and chivalry used in many of Wajda's films: *Lotna, Everything for Sale, Landscape after Battle, The Wedding,* and others. The symbol of the white horse has multiple connotations, however, and here also represents the unfulfilled dreams of the young fighter; it signals a transformation in Maciek, who now, suddenly, feeling that he is in love, thinks of the future for perhaps the first time.

Back in the hotel, Maciek, now a reluctant assassin, questions Andrzej about the necessity of killing. The war is behind him; he wants to live, to study, and perhaps to start a family. But Andrzej is a man of resolute principle; he counters that they both have a duty that cannot be abandoned. Dennis de Nitto and William Herman describe Andrzej's postwar dilemma fittingly:

The predominant feeling of many viewers toward Andrzej may be one of waste. Here is an intelligent, efficient, sensitive, dedicated man who kills and, we have no doubt, will be killed because he has chained himself to an ideal that is slowly sinking beneath the wave of change.... Although we may censure a man who refuses to be vulnerable to human emotions and connections, we cannot help but feel pity for an individual trapped in a situation that will probably cost him his life. We may even admire the courage, dignity, and self-control with which he faces the end of himself and his values.[62]

In a crosscut to the party scene, Drewnowski, now completely drunk, makes mischief at the banquet: He makes a fool of himself by climbing onto the banquet table and covering the other guests with foam from a fire extinguisher. Career and reputation thus ruined, he leaves the hall in shame. In a chaotic barrage of quickly ensuing scenes, the spectator sees Szczuka approached in the main hall of the hotel by an officer who knows the whereabouts of his son, Marek.[63] Maciek overhears this conversation and waits under the staircase. In an elaborate sequence, the legs of Szczuka descend slowly down the ornate staircase, inversely reflecting the mounting tension, and we see as well the frightened face of Maciek, who is aware that his moment of duty has come.

When Szczuka leaves the hotel hurriedly, Maciek follows him and asks for a light, and then, when offered it, shoots the older man in the heart. Szczuka staggers and slumps against the immobile Maciek. Just then the fireworks celebrating the end of the war erupt, illuminating Maciek and Szczuka standing still, seemingly crucified—Maciek stands with the fireworks aureole behind his back while Szczuka grabs his arms desperately, his sliding body imitating the convoluted body of Christ on the cross. This scene clearly invokes the religious connotations and also ties with the scene of the crucified Christ in the church where Maciek had earlier tried to repair a shoe on the altar. At the same time, the two men seem to form a father-son embrace, thus binding the two politically "bad" sons, Marek and Maciek, in one symbolic overlap.[64]

When Maciek afterward washes the blood off his hands in the hotel room, we hear the banquet going on downstairs, uninterrupted by the tragic event. In fact, at this moment, Frederic Chopin's *polonaise A-dur (Polonaise in A-major)* leads the tired banquet participants in a solemn dance of celebration. (A similarly austere dance will later reappear, with a slightly different tone, in *The Wedding*.) The film concludes with Maciek's attempted escape and subsequent death. He plans to leave by train, but when he approaches the tracks, he sees Andrzej beating Drewnowski for betraying the principles of the Home Army and for playing to two masters. Drewnowski notices Maciek and calls his name. As the startled Maciek begins to flee in an effort to catch the train, he accidentally runs into some Polish soldiers who, alert for saboteurs and members of the outlawed Home Army, shoot at him and fatally wound him.

The famous "laundry scene" follows, during which the bleeding Maciek tries to hide among the hanging sheets, all the while unable to believe that he has been shot. He eventually lurches toward the railway, but his strength finally fails, and, slowly, reluctantly, kicking, he dies on a pile of dirt.

In the meantime, through brilliant crosscutting, the spectator is led back to the banquet at which the polonaise continues into the early hours of the morning. At this point, the music itself carries a double meaning. Chopin's *polonaise A-dur* eventually turns into *Pożegnanie ojczyzny* by Michał Kleofas Ogiński, an ironic rewriting of Chopin's piece. This is Wajda's declaration to his Polish audience that after 1945 the past had gone, never to be repeated, marking the dispelling of illusions about Poland's political future. In the final sequence, the death of the young fighter is juxtaposed with the old porter taking out the Polish flag and with the last accords of the polonaise, these two accents providing a bitter commentary to Maciek's death.

Ashes and Diamonds is without a doubt the defining film in Wajda's career. It is always associated with his name and understood as the one film that combines the most important characteristics of his personal style. Marek Hendrykowski also stresses the fact that *Ashes and Diamonds* is the highest accomplishment of the Polish School.[65] As Hendrykowski states, it is a quintessential Polish School film as it describes the events of World War II; it presents the director's concern for the fate of Poland, depicts the romantic treatment of Polish history in accordance with the "romantic-expressive" tradition of Polish School, and presents various segments of Polish society. However, Wajda adds some specific ingredients that make this film an auteurist endeavor: he portrays love in a romantic and old-fashioned way; he introduces pertinent national symbols such as the soldier's drinking mug, the polonaise, the white horse, the Christian symbolism, and Polish art; and, finally, he situates all these themes in a framework broad enough that spectators can easily identify with the main protagonist and his dilemmas despite the national or geographic differences.

Hendrykowski postulates that much of the film's strength lies in its mythical dimensions: The tale of the fate of young Maciek is a universal story experienced in some fashion by many young people during and after World War II, but it also resonates with tremendous strength across Poland's entire national consciousness:

> When telling the story of Maciek Chełmicki anew, Wajda gave it an interpretation at once concrete and mythical. He managed to provide a brilliant personification of the human drama that has been a taboo theme in our cinema for many years. The director did not create this myth to make it more pathetic, but rather to ascribe to it a tragic dimension, a dimension denied to thousands of young fighters like Maciek for many years before this film appeared.[66]

Ashes and Diamonds remains the most widely and most often analyzed of all Wajda's films. The following authors analyzed the film extensively: Paul Coates, Hendrykowski, Tadeusz Lubelski, Ewelina Nurczyńska-Fidelska, De Nitto, Herman, Haltof, and others. The film is universally understood as a story about internal conflicts, about the necessity of history and the irony of an unnecessary death of a young person. The mythos of Maciek has been compared to that of the actor James Dean, a young man who also died an unnecessary death. Likewise, the simple but intricate structure of the film has been compared to an elaborate mosaic in which every piece falls neatly into place. At the same time, the film and its semantic cracks and uncertainties leave plenty of space for ideological and psychological interpretation allowing for serious ponderings on the intricate dialogues with history, culture, and politics at the time of the film's production and of the film's diegesis.

Throughout the course of various conversations, Wajda has averred clearly that he considers this film his best work. When commenting on the film in his unpublished biography, the filmmaker notes that he especially likes its quick-paced rhythm—"healthy," he calls it—a rhythm that Hendrykowski calls "the device of maximum density of temporal and spatial areas in the film."[67] Wajda credits the pace of the film especially to actor Zbigniew Cybulski, who portrayed Maciek and fascinated audiences with his onscreen presence. Fortunately, Cybulski's brilliant performance shows more through gesture and facial expression than through words, thus saving Wajda from the damaging scissors of censorship. Wajda reminisces about the difficult censorship process: "One way to please the censor was to cut out whole scenes or dialogues."[68] According to the censorship officials in those times, ideology was situated especially in words. Luckily, as Wajda reminisces, a film is primarily composed of visuals or, as he says,

> "something ungraspable, between sound and picture, that constitutes the soul of film. Yes, it is possible to cut out some words from *Ashes and Diamonds*, but it is impossible to censor the acting of Zbigniew Cybulski. It was his behavior, his way of dealing with people which contained this 'something,' which was politically unacceptable. The freedom of the boy in the dark glasses in the context of the superimposed reality."[69]

Although Polish authorities officially condemned the romanticization and glorification of the protagonists' clandestine activities, most Poles, whether young or old, clearly identified with their fight for Poland's ultimate independence. Young people especially, both then and now, understand Maciek and his intense emotional entanglement in the war events. Maciek is the romantic warrior-hero, yet he also defines Poland's fighter not as a dirty, indoctrinated partisan—a mere peasant briefed by the representatives of Soviet Red Army[70]—but rather as an intelligent, rebellious hero entangled in the twin dilemmas of war and love. This appeal to human emotion and experience makes *Ashes and Diamonds* universally captivating, appreciated for its honesty in presenting the most fundamental human emotions.

During the official discussion of the film in July 1958, before its screening, most reviewers agreed that the film had many good points.[71] After the premiere in Warszawa, however, the film was almost universally praised. Yet the film remained a political entity. Just after the release of *Ashes and Diamonds*, Wajda was denied a passport and therefore could not go to Paris for the film's premiere. A letter to Wajda from the Minister of Culture indicates the official cause of this rejection as being the result of poor political relations between Poland and France. The actor Ewa Krzyżewska (who played Krystyna) went to the premiere in Wajda's place.[72] Wajda considered this incident an affront to his directorial abilities, and since then he has always been careful to present bureaucrats in the most deprecating manner in his films. Still, critics both in Poland and abroad realized immediately that they were dealing with a masterpiece. Even in official party papers, such as *Trybuna Ludu*, critics were generally positive. Prof. Aleksander Jackiewicz, then the official film critic of *Trybuna Ludu* and editor of the weekly *Film*, states, "It is rare indeed—and not only in film art—for a young artist like Andrzej Wajda, at the start of his creative life, almost at its inception, to undertake a work which well may be the most outstanding work in his life."[73]

Some other reviews were more critical, however. The debate centered largely on depictions of Maciek (as he represented the Home Army) and Szczuka, the communist (representing the Workers Party). This criticism focused on the positive and romanticized presentation of Maciek whom the authorities would treat as a rebellious and unnecessary remnant of the war rather than as a romantic warrior. Szczuka, on the other hand, was portrayed by Wajda as an ineffectual, nonthreatening father figure easily eliminated by the young rebel. The explosive nature of this ambivalence in presentation was so problematic that Alexander Ford, Wajda's mentor, suggested to Jackiewicz a pact to "subdue" the Polish School. As Jackiewicz recalls,

> "He did this because he was still a representative of the Stalinist mode of thinking. His object of attack was the film *Ashes and Diamonds,* as he considered this film too 'nationalistic' and 'patriotic.' The influential Communist Party members with whom Ford identified were so powerful at that time that the film was never officially sent to any important film competition. Moreover, the then chair of the General Cinematography Committee, Jerzy Lewiński, in all likelihood lost his job when he allowed *Ashes and Diamonds* to be screened at a special show at Cannes Festival."[74]

A review written by Wiktor Woroszylski was the most critical, stressing the absurdity of the Home Army representatives' actions in the film. Yet

Zbigniew Florczak, Bolesław Taborski, and Jackiewicz[75] all vehemently disagreed. Some party activists questioned the portrayal of Szczuka, who in their opinion was unconvincing. Meanwhile, some critics thought the film so controversial that they did not recommend it for any film competition.

Yet despite (at times heated) debate concerning the characters of Maciek and Szczuka and the overall hypercritical approach to the film, *Ashes and Diamonds* has never ceased to fascinate spectators of all ages. The film is considered a masterpiece for many reasons: Its construction and aesthetics appeal to wide audiences through its carefully chosen symbols, its clearly defined mise-en-scène, and its skillfully organized film space. At the same time, the film seems almost a documentary rendition of the time and its people. The film's rich characterization of Polish society is unsurpassed in its variety and warmth. Laden with literary, artistic, and religious references, *Ashes and Diamonds* established Wajda as an important film director not only in Poland but in all of Eastern Europe.

The film was almost universally praised by Western critics who appreciated both the plot and the film aesthetics. Of the prominent Western critics, Nevio Corich noted the film's lyrical and baroque tone. Others, such as Foumy Saisho, praised Wajda for his "screen poetry"; Georges Sadoul compared the film to the works of Erich von Stroheim. There were some critics like Peter John Dyer who considered the film's "baroque excesses" as detrimental to the film's generally realistic purity of style.[76] Hendrykowski, however, considered this criticism of aesthetic elements to be laziness on the part of the critics: "Some critics were so lazy that they ascribed to Wajda's film the deleterious adjective of 'mannerist baroque' and 'empty ornamentation.' They were not inquisitive enough to find some sense in what they considered devoid of any sense at all. Nor were they brave enough to admit that they were unable to find meanings in the images in which ornament and sense are intertwined."[77] Certain Western critics clearly did not understand the elaborate images, so they analyzed them as surface phenomena only, omitting completely the symbols' deeper connotations. They disregarded the complexity of aesthetic discourses that resulted directly from Poland's complex history, its rich art and politics, which made the Aesopian discourse a necessity, not a caprice. Each scene in *Ashes and Diamonds* is permeated with these complexities, as if the director wanted to communicate this enormous intricacy in a kind of a capsule in which he contained all the cultural traits simultaneously, in a similar vein to haiku poetry. Wajda, a product of the country's history and culture, found his own way into the audience's imagination in the form of these complex images.

Years later, Wajda returned to "the lessons of *Ashes*" in making *The Crowned-Eagle Ring*. He has stated that what he created in *Ashes and Diamonds* was not accidental: He remembers every detail, even the famous ornament in the hotel main stairs crucial to the rising tension that precedes Szczuka's death. In making *The Crowned-Eagle Ring,* Wajda wondered whether he could reawaken the enthusiasm he had had for cinema in 1958, during the production of *Ashes and Diamonds*—an enthusiasm for the presentation of historical truth that contributed to the creation of a remarkable film whose politics emerged fully only when it was shown on the screen.[78]

Wajda's brilliant war "trilogy" was immediately followed by what are generally considered to be weaker films, in which he planned to revisit World War II, but also to concentrate on the realities of postwar Poland. Although dealing with issues every bit as volatile and painful as those treated in the previous three films, the first film in this series, *Lotna,* is not as emotionally convincing as any of the war trilogy films. Still, it appeals to the spectator with its remarkable clarity of artistic vision and its beautiful, ethereal images, once again arising from the aesthetics of Bunuelian surrealism and Italian neo-Realism.

Lotna (1959)

The action of this film takes place at the beginning of World War II and once again depicts war events through the heroic-romantic tradition. The film's screenplay is based upon Wojciech Żukrowski's short story *Lotna.*[79] The title comes from the name of the horse, Lotna, a white, spotted mare ridden by the commanding officers (the uhlan) of the platoon in the film. The horse is a symbol of the recent yet remote past, the lost age of bourgeois Poland with its palaces, salons, and pianos. The film combines many traits of aristocratic iconography in its presentation of noble houses, customs, and mores. At the same time, the film gives an insight into Wajda's most prominent cinematic devices: the painterly design of the shots; the attention paid to detail; the excessive, kitschy beauty of all the scenes; and the Polish historical themes.

This film opens with a sequence portraying Polish uhlan upon their horses. The four riders, shot from various camera positions, reveal Wajda's fascination with the romanticized iconography of the traditional Polish warrior-hero. The protagonists—Captain Chodakiewicz, Lieutenant Wodnicki, Officer Cadet Jerzy Grabowski, and Sergeant Major Latoń—notice a white horse running wild, a proud and stunning thoroughbred. This sequence is followed closely by a shot of a sculpture of a nude female in the garden of a nearby manor. This juxtaposition of a nude female figure and a white horse introduces the main theme of the film: The intense love for horses shared by all the men of the regiment, a love that is later jeopardized by Jerzy's love for the village teacher Ewa, who expresses a passionate jealousy toward Lotna, treating the animal almost as a human rival for her new husband's love.

The soldiers approach the old manor hoping to stay there for the night. Inside, the three officers hear light steps. As they seek the manor's occupants, they pass another sculpture, this one of white horses standing on a small table in a salon. In the master bedroom, the protagonists find an old man lying in bed; strikingly, the white horse they have already seen is standing next to him and eating from his hand. The officers introduce themselves, and Chodakiewicz informs the elderly man that the war front is moving this way and that the Germans will be here at any time. The elderly man responds that he is too old and sick to move anywhere. The only consolation for him is the company of his beloved Lotna, the last remaining horse from his stable. Aware that the horse may be in danger, the old man begs the officers to take her with them: "Let the horse carry you to victory." National tradition, historical continuity, uhlan's pride, and love of horses are all plainly blended in this sequence.

These lyrical interpersonal sequences are intercut with shots in which masses of people flee from the Germans. Amid scattered luggage, retreating civilians run wildly with screaming children in a spectacular, moving mass scene that will later become one of Wajda's trademarks. The uhlan regiment walks steadily against the stream of fugitives, proud and tenacious heroes resolved to conquer the Germans. Suddenly, though, bombs begin to fall on the fleeing civilians (in a scene based on actual photographs of German forces unscrupulously bombing fleeing civilians). The frightened Lotna, ridden at first by Latoń, is passed on to Chodakiewicz; the captain saddles her himself. With almost sensual pleasure, he mounts and smiles at the horse affectionately. Later, having found a safe place to stay for the night, the soldiers talk only about Lotna. One of them draws a picture of her; another describes her as if she were a woman. The commanders are afraid that she will be lamed in battle. The touching conversation among the soldiers is followed by a scene of flirtation between a soldier and a local woman. In the meantime, Chodakiewicz has learned of their dubious situation: The regiment is surrounded by German forces, so they must leave the village immediately. In a symbolic act, the soldiers clean and sharpen their sabers as they declare war on the Germans but also gloomily consider their chances for survival.

As in *Kanal*, Wajda intersperses lyrical scenes depicting everyday events with scenes of premonition and doom. Also, a deeply ingrained patriarchal discourse shows itself in Wajda's presentation of the woman of the manor, who is only seen briefly kneeling and praying, and later bidding farewell to the departing soldiers. The captain promises her "a nice uhlan charge" when the soldiers leave the manor. In full gallop, the riders proudly pass in front of the manor, shouting "hurrah." This scene conforms perfectly to the Polish romantic tradition, whereby the riding soldiers are always presented as proud and heroic, beautiful objects on display for admiring female eyes. A short time later, in another cavalry charge, the uhlans attack the Germans, their light field guns killing many German soldiers. Filmed with a tracking camera, the sequence presenting the soldiers shows the figures of the riders in sharp silhouette against the sky. At the same time, this aesthetically beautiful depiction of galloping uhlans is pathetic—the figures of the riders seem small, insignificant against the huge and empty sky.[80]

Then, in what begins as another triumphant gallop, the riders come upon the German tanks. Faceless and inhuman, huge and overpowering, the tanks easily crush the defenseless riders and their steeds. This scene with the German tanks is one of the most striking sequences in the film. It is dynamic and spectacular, shot aggressively through various camera positions. The camera, on tracks, follows the charging horses galloping from right to left. When the horses are attacked from the left by the advancing tanks, the camera changes direction and follows the menacing tanks from left to right. Portrayed in medium shot, the tanks overpower the screen, rendering both horse and rider useless and insignificant. The charge turns into a grisly slaughter, with riderless horses and terrified soldiers running around the field. This deeply symbolic scene, signifying the contrast between the brute force of the tanks and the fragility of humans and animals, is followed by other similarly overpowering scenes, such as shots of a soldier wiping his saber after the carnage and village children taking a German cap left fallen in the field. Finally, Lotna is shown bearing the lifeless body of the captain in a striking and powerfully symbolic scene of the faithful horse returning her master to the waiting soldiers.

Chodakiewicz's body is brought back to the village where, in the following sequences, during a long, slow funeral procession, his body is taken to a peasant house for a ritual of mourning. Throughout this scene we see Wajda's devotion to the accurate portrayal of minute historical detail and his overall respect for the representatives of all social classes in Polish society. He pays meticulous attention to the ritual through the washing of the body and the placement of the coins on the corpse's closed eyes, the covering of the mirrors, and the lighting of candles. Following its own internal logic of contrasts, the film's somber funeral sequence is followed by a sunny, enjoyable one in which the three remaining protagonists admire the beauty of Lotna. The priest who oversaw the funeral joins them and later asks the lieutenant if he may ride the horse; a wonderful prolonged shot of the galloping horse ridden excellently by the older priest shows the sheer beauty and sensuality of the creature, who is clearly enjoying the gallop herself. The priest on horse is seen from the open window of the peasant's hut in which the captain's corpse is lying on the table, a fact that only adds to the symbolic and aesthetic complexities of a film in which death and life are inextricably linked.

Elsewhere in the same village, Jerzy encounters Ewa, who, we find, is also a former school friend of his. At first unaware of the officer, Ewa unselfconsciously repeats a lesson aloud to herself in her classroom. Suddenly she notices Jerzy, who almost immediately begins to flirt unabashedly with her. A sudden, brief German bombardment ensues— quite conveniently, for Ewa quickly finds herself in Jerzy's arms, clinging desperately to the tall, handsome officer. Then, realizing her weakness, she flees the classroom. Once the bombardment ends, Wodnicki approaches Jerzy and tells him that they will have to stay for the night since their regiment has been ordered to protect those soldiers retreating from the battlefront. Jerzy is enthusiastic since he will be able to stay in the village for another night, so that he may court Ewa. This improbable reaction, besides revealing the naïveté and innocence of a young man, also demonstrates the ignorance of Polish army officers regarding the sheer physical might of the German army. Of course, this sequence recapitulates the dominant theme of Wajda's war films—that of romance and war being closely intertwined.

Jerzy's and Ewa's romance continues in a stable among a symbolic setting of coffins full of ripe apples. The juxtaposition of coffins and apples signifies the continuation of romance on the one hand, and its end on the other. The choice of names and the setting of the scene in a stable full of apples links the romance with the quintessential human romance of Adam and Eve, with all its connotations of fertility and sin. The two engage in flirtation full of humorous lovers' squabbles. These encounters between Jerzy and Ewa and those between the battalion soldiers and village women are illustrated with typical soldiers' songs. Young soldiers are shown as unrelenting romancers, moving lightheartedly from funerals to weddings; in fact, an ironic and ultimately tragic wedding takes place just before the final battle in the film. Ewa and Jerzy take their marriage vows in an idyllic church ceremony; the shots are interspersed with humorous scenes of joking altar boys. The young couple leaving the church and marching under the crossed sabres of the uhlan is deeply symbolic of the Polish horsemanship tradition, thus linking the love for horses and the love for women in one isolated moment.

At the end of the row of crossed sabers, the couple approaches Lotna, who stands waiting for them. Only now does Ewa express a deep dislike for the horse; when Jerzy touches Lotna lovingly, Ewa says, disapprovingly, "You and your horse!" in an obvious fit of jealousy. The postwedding ceremony shows typical scenes from the lives of Poles. An innkeeper, a drummer—played by Roman Polański in a cameo role— vodka for the soldiers, and sexual jokes at the wedding table (referring to the forthcoming consummation of marriage) all illustrate stereotypical Polish customs. Yet the celebration is interrupted by another scene of jealousy on Ewa's part. The new bride, unable to find her husband at the wedding table, goes to the stables, where she finds Jerzy lovingly touching the horse's back. Ewa states that she will not share Jerzy with anyone, and leads him away from the stable. In a surreal dance sequence, the newlyweds go to their bed; Ewa takes off the veil, undresses slowly, and turns to the bed only to find a corpse in it. The two flee from the grisly scene in shock, only to find refuge and love back in the stable.

The morning sees the regiment, along with Ewa, leaving the manor, the men singing a soldiers' song such as "Wojenko, wojenko."[81] The blatant iconography of the uhlan is supplemented with an equally disturbing iconography of waiting and suffering women, so profoundly represented by Artur Grottger[82] in his drawings and paintings. A shot of a lame girl standing against wooden crosses is especially heartrending, as she solemnly watches the passing soldiers. She represents the very real outcome of the war, where death and despair will reign supreme. "Will you remember me?" asks Wodnicki of the girl, illustrating his desire to be remembered after his impending death. Seated on a wooden cart drawn by horses, Ewa asks Wodnicki to take care of her new husband. In a display of motherly love (a common trope in the presentation of women in Polish films—and in Wajda's films in particular), Ewa thinks only about her young husband, an immature lad who combines the characteristics of both son and husband. However, Ewa is once again overcome by her jealousy of Lotna. "Take her," she says, "the horse brings bad luck." At the company's stopover in the woods, Ewa puts out plates and cutlery for herself and her husband, oblivious to the surprised looks on the soldiers' faces and to Jerzy's protests. The young woman desperately wants to be happy, so she talks only about the house, the wedding, and other joyful matters, Jerzy protesting all the while and interjecting with his own discussion of soldiers' duties and responsibilities.

Throughout these scenes, the director plays down images of the impending doom to which the film leads. Of course, the film tells the tale of the first wave of German attacks on Poland, a tragic story known all too well to Polish audiences; from the very beginning of the film, Wajda's spectators ultimately know what to expect. The intrigue lies in the way these events are presented on the screen, for at this juncture Wajda begins the surreal combination of tragic horror and dark, uniquely Polish comedy. One such humorous event takes place in the trenches: A soldier, clearly of peasant origin, plucks a hen he has caught from a nearby peasant hut. His fellow soldiers joke about the dinner he is preparing for them while the bombs fall around them. As if playing with the audience's expectations, Wajda stretches out the time leading up to the final battle, taking great pleasure in leading the spectators slowly through these humorous little scenes, right up to the total obliteration of the Polish forces.

When the German bombers finally approach, Lotna becomes frightened and runs into the fields, away from the hiding place. Jerzy runs after her, but too late. It is only because of the frightened horse that the German bombers discover the hiding place of the uhlan regiment in a nearby wood. After the planes attack, only the dead and wounded, horses and people alike, can be seen among the strewn, smoking debris. In complete silence, the camera pans, revealing the sad remnants, stopping only briefly at the unfinished meal so elaborately set up by Ewa a short time before. The next image is an apple tree in full bloom; Ewa, distraught, cries bitterly as her young husband is buried. In a desperate rage, she goes to the stable planning to kill the horse for which Jerzy and so many others have died. She and the few remaining soldiers all blame Lotna for the carnage. Understanding this reasoning but still ready to protect the horse, Wodnicki appears suddenly in the stable and takes the gun from Ewa's hands, and then embraces the horse lovingly. This emotional treatment of the horse is masterfully captured by Wajda in all its intensity. Wodnicki saddles the horse, finally the possessor of Lotna, a wish he has held since the moment he first saw the horse. The oddly sexual connotations of the soldiers' desire for the mare run as a striking undercurrent throughout the film.

The men leave the village, abandoning the wounded and the women. Outside the village, Wodnicki dissolves the regiment in a ritualistic ceremony of kissing the saber and tearing the regiment's banner, which bears the epigraph "Honor and Motherland." After giving each of the remaining soldiers a piece of the banner, admonishing them to put the fragments back together only when the regiment unites again, Wodnicki rides away on Lotna. He is next seen on a hill with windmills, in a scene symbolic for its connotations related to the futility of fighting (as in Miguel de Cervantes's *Don Quixote*). Fatigued, the lieutenant drinks water from a puddle next to Lotna, who drinks water from the same source. When he falls asleep shortly thereafter, Latoń sneaks into his camp to steal the horse from Wodnicki. Thinking Wodnicki asleep, Latoń is surprised by the lieutenant's cry of "Stand up or I will shoot you!" The sergeant tries to escape with the horse amid the debris left by the retreating Polish army, but Lotna is badly injured in the process. The mare lies heaving on the ground with a broken front leg, grotesquely twisted in a wooden wheel. Torn between his love for Lotna and his wish not to see her in such pain, Wodnicki hesitates to shoot the horse, unable to commit the necessary act of what seems to him simple murder.

In the end, it is Latoń who must kill Lotna; he puts his gun to the horse's head and kills her with a single shot. Lotna's death is seen in symbolic terms: The horse represents not only sensuality and sensitivity, but also the unknowing innocence of Poland in 1939, a country desperately believing in its own invincibility. Wodnicki and Latoń together cut the fir branches to cover the horse's body. Sadness and humiliation after their utter defeat, as well as the despair brought about by the death of the horse, are clearly seen on their faces. Wodnicki breaks his saber and leaves it with Lotna, climbing the hill and walking away among the willow trees so common in Polish villages. The last shot of the film shows Wodnicki turning away from the border stone dividing Poland and Germany.

Anna Rozicka delineates several semiotic fields in which the film's overtly, almost painfully stereotypical depictions appear: the palace or noble's residence, the village and/or the peasant's house, and the Polish landscape. The stereotypical representations of these characteristically Polish spaces are further supplemented by the film's depictions of the uhlan; of country governesses and teachers; and of senseless, romantic cavalry charges. The heavy symbolism in this film is so blatant that most of its audiences reacted with impatience. Rozicka remarks that "Lotna constitutes a specific catalogue of symbols, themes and national emblems."[83] Furthermore, she notes the film's ambivalent presentation of the romantic tradition: "Through the prism of the national moment, Lotna reveals not only the greatness of the Polish Romantic tradition but also its anachronistic aspect."[84]

Most Polish reviews of the film were crushingly negative, especially where they concerned the film's unconvincing plot elements, its bizarre love story, and its excessively romantic treatment of the most tragic day in the history of the Polish army. The rich iconography, especially that of Polish uhlans, was considered excessive and baroque. Alicja Helman, for instance, in her derogatorily titled article "An Uhlan on the Burning Giraffe," summarizes the film as an artistic failure in its cheap and obvious symbolism: "In Lotna we find cheap, flashy and unambiguous symbolism which is neither artistically justified nor thematically needed. The images do not delicately allude to meanings but shout them out. The ideas lightly suggested in the subtext become vulgar and unacceptable."[85]

Other reviewers also noted that the film relies heavily on the "cult of cavalry," officially encouraged by Edward Rydz-Śmigły and Marshall Józef Piłsudski before World War II.[86] Krzysztof Teodor Toeplitz compared Wajda's uhlans to "the merry Hungarian dragoons in operettas,"[87] while Stanisław Grzelecki criticized the film's aesthetics: "Lotna became a film dedicated to the poetry of props and—it grieves me to say it—it is a poetry of form, rhythm and colours rather than of content."[88] Likewise, Stanisław Ozimek opines the beauty of the film, which, despite itself, cannot match the filmmakers' attempt "to employ this intoxicating vision in the service of people and issues."[89]

Other Polish critics referred to this intoxicating vision as "baroque" or even "surrealistic." Zygmunt Kałużyński, for example, describes the film's baroque mise-en-scène and the surrealistic approach in the following way:

> Lotna is the result of a cross between surrealism and Polish uhlan traditions.... Everything which in this film is "surrealistically menacing" rings consistent. This seems a mad paradox, because there is so much "surrealism" in Lotna, and it is so forced, that it takes on the characteristics of parody, and furthermore it is blended into a theme which, on the surface, seems less suited to it than almost any other on earth: the story of the last Polish, traditional, patriotic cavalry charge![90]

This almost parodist aspect of the film has been compared to "vulgar" historical productions such as *Quo Vadis* or *Ordynat Michorowski*.[91] Andrzej Werner offers a very interesting, if rather crushing interpretation of *Lotna* in his book *Polskie, arcypolskie (Polish, Arch-Polish)*[92] as quoted by Chris Caes: "[Werner] argues carefully that consciously or not, the film legitimized the communist government (which by 1959 had more or less successfully reinstated the essentially Stalinist one-party system) by helping to destroy the stereotypical iconography of the nation, which served as a link in popular memory to the deeper vitality of the nation."[93]

While Western reviewers also noted the surrealistic, baroque style of the film (see Marcel Martin[94] and Guy Gauthier[95]), they were not as devastatingly critical as Polish critics. Most importantly, though, the official reception of *Lotna* by Polish authorities was so negative that they took a great deal of time issuing payment for the work. Wajda writes in a letter to the Board of Cinema chair, Minister Tadeusz Zaorski,[96] and asks him for remuneration for the making of the film—a humiliating situation for the director of *Ashes and Diamonds*.[97]

Wajda himself had many reservations concerning *Lotna*. In his own notes, he summarizes the weaknesses of the film in three ways: (1) mistakes of the screenplay, (2) mistakes of film realization, and (3) mistakes in film casting. Of the screenplay, he writes, "there were no clearly delineated characters, with no defined approach to their environment. Consequently, the characters appear fictitious and avoid any conflicts among themselves." Of the second point, regarding the film's realization, he says, "The ideas marked for particular scenes in the screenplay have not been properly developed. The hurried and disorganized film production process did not allow for a careful look at these scenes."[98] Although clearly disappointed and saddened by Polish reviews, Wajda realized that there was something in this film that made it different from the other celebrated films he had made before this one. In time, he decided to look at the whole matter in a different way:

> "Maybe my mistakes denote originality while the 'good' features of the film indicate routine, nothing different from other film directors. Although *Lotna* has not become better thanks to my change of approach, I

have begun to think about myself in a different way: about what I like, what I can do, and what I would like to see on the screen myself. I have been working on this film in my imagination for years, and this is the only film I would like to make again. I love this imperfect child and always call it 'mine.'"[99]

Other common criticisms of the film state that although the cinematography in *Lotna* is expressive and beautiful, motivated by romantic paintings of revolutionary and war efforts, the narrative and especially the actors are poorly chosen. The young uhlan, Jerzy, is handsome but passionless and stiff, without the usual articulation of emotions so characteristic of other actors in Wajda's films. The film's narrative focuses on one main plot while other subplots go unresolved; for instance, the exact nature of the mystifying relationship between Wodnicki and Ewa (the two of whom are old acquaintances, we find out late in the film) is never adequately explained.

Unlike other reviewers, however, I am not so devastatingly critical of the film. For one thing, I agree with Zbigniew Kałużyński[100] that *Lotna* is one of the few extant films to describe the events of World War II from the point of view of Polish army, with their naïve tradition of honor and their absolute inability to anticipate the enormity and power of the German war machine. In this sense, the film is neither critical nor sentimental in its assessment of the officers' reactions. Considering the importance of the cavalry charge in Polish iconography and historiography, Wajda did his best to appropriately present this tragic event on the screen. The suicidal cavalry charge in September 1939 on the German tanks has become legendary in Polish social consciousness, as Caes discusses in his essay on the matter.[101] Its presentation on the screen will always invite virulent criticism, for no portrayal of the event, no matter how beautiful or stunning, would satisfy the expectations of all Poles. The arguably pretentious images depicting this event in Wajda's film are perceived as such partly because the cavalry charge itself was so senseless and hopeless. Nevertheless, the film contains moments of incomparable beauty, which stay in the spectator's memory long after seeing the film. The scenes depicting Chodakiewicz's death and funeral and those surrounding the cavalry charge in particular are striking, unusual, and beautiful without being ironic or parodist.

At the end of the 1950s, Wajda's position as a filmmaker was firmly established: Although a very young man, he was by this time already widely recognized in Poland and abroad. During this decade he mastered his core filmmaking techniques and created a consistent aesthetics for himself. He also established his main thematic interests: a focus on the feelings of people within the context of major historical events, and abundant references to Polish culture with rich visual and aural symbolism. With regard to his filmmaking techniques, he uses primarily medium shots and close-ups. In constructing the narrative, Wajda opts for fast pace manifested in quick editing, various positions of the camera, and, late in 1950s, he conspicuously uses a moving tracking camera. He chooses his music carefully so that it will illustrate or complement the events, not overwhelm them with musical commentary. Already in his four fiction films, he has experimented with ambitious orchestral tunes but also introduced specifically Polish songs or music notes.

Most important to Wajda's developing style is his films' visual fabric: He carefully composes every shot, preceding the filmmaking process with a detailed storyboard, where his painterly eye is especially visible. His tableaux-like shots startle spectators as if each were a miniature art composition. These memorable images stand out in the four films and even in the early études. Examples of such scenes are as follows:

- In *A Generation,* the gallows scene, with silent onlookers standing still; the Italian neo-Realist depiction of interiors; the expressionist lighting in the portrayal of main heroes; the Dickensian factory in which both Jasio and Stach work; and, finally, the spectacular scene of Jasio's death on the spiral staircase in an old tenement
- In *Kanal,* a number of memorable images linked to the iconography of the canals, including the scene showing corpses drifting in the sewers; the scenes of Stokrotka and Korab walking slowly in the canals at the end of the film; and the scene of them both facing death at the grid-covered canal entrance
- In *Ashes and Diamonds,* a collection of exquisite images that serve as an anthology of quintessentially Wajda imagery. Among the most memorable are the bucolic church scene at the beginning of the film; the scene presenting the lovers in bed from above; the scene with the white horse running in the streets; the bar scene with the flaming shot glasses; the scene in the ruined church; the scene in the hotel in which Maciek waits for his victim at the hotel stairs; and the final scene of Maciek's death, commonly called the "laundry scene" by film critics.
- In *Lotna,* the cavalry charge against the German tanks at the film's end; various sequences presenting Lotna, the horse, in full gallop; a grotesque, Bunuelian scene in the stable with coffins full of apples; and finally the repetition of the apple motif at the scene of Ewa's husband's burial

Each of these scenes in Wajda's films functions as a tableau combining numerous graphic elements in an intricate design. The foreground and background elements interact in a meaningful way—they display strong contrasts in color (usually black and white); in configuration (e.g., the intricate design of a love scene in *Ashes and Diamonds*); or in a compilation of surrealist elements in a scene (e.g., Christ hanging upside down in the ruined church in *Ashes and Diamonds*). These exquisite images constitute characteristics of the Polish School in general. *Ashes and Diamonds* is the most prominent representative of this movement. The aesthetic style of the Polish School is characterized by static images; slowly unfolding sequences; and a focus on the explication of political arguments and events and on human emotions. In my opinion, however, it is the quality of the images that adds to the school's greatness. Finally, in terms of general influence, traditions of neorealism, documentary, surrealism, and romanticism all inform Wajda's artistic sensibilities, coming together in his first four films.

FIGHT FOR PERFECTION
Films of the Sixties

This chapter describes the films Wajda produced near the beginning of his career. *Innocent Sorcerers* portrays the emotions and unfulfilled desires of young people in a new, post-World War II Poland. *Samson* is the first film in Wajda's career to describe the fate of Jews in contemporary Poland, a subject Wajda will revisit in three later films *(Promised Land, Korczak,* and *Holy Week). Siberian Lady Macbeth,* based on Nikolai Leskov's story (itself based on Shakespeare's play), relates the events of a brutal murder in distant Siberia. *Siberian Lady Macbeth, Love at Twenty, Ashes,* and *The Gates to Paradise* all illustrate Wajda's search for mastery in accurately depicting historical periods as well as mood and human expression.

In the late 1960s, a time of political turmoil in his country and uncertainty in his private life, Wajda produced films demonstrating a new array of issues and genres. The first of these films, *Roly Poly,* expresses a deep sense of foreboding related to the impersonal nature of scientific discovery. *Hunting Flies* transports the viewer into Wajda's own feelings of helplessness in relation to both his first and second wives, Zofia Wajda and Beata Tyszkiewicz. *Everything for Sale* is a marvel in Polish film. Shot in the mode of the French New Wave, it is a study of grieving and despair following the death of Zbigniew Cybulski, the famous star of *Ashes and Diamonds.*

Innocent Sorcerers (1960)

Wajda's first film of the 1960s presents young people who, as did Wajda himself at the time, taste freedom and love in the extraordinary time of the political "thaw" in the late 1950s and early 1960s. The thaw was triggered by the October 1956 uprising in Hungary (brutally crushed by the Soviets only a month later), by the Polish workers' riots in Poznań against the Communist regime, and by the return of Władysław Gomułka to power in October 1956. During the thaw, Poland woke up from the Stalinist nightmare and started the long, painful process of social and cultural reconstruction. For the first time in his career, Wajda tries to portray young people and their lives and lifestyles in an apolitical fashion. Other films following this interesting path are *Love at Twenty, Hunting Flies,* and *Miss Nobody.* In all these films, Wajda moves away from strictly historical or political themes and concentrates on social themes instead. *Innocent Sorcerers* initiates a new development in Wajda's filmography: the production of films with strong social content, illustrating simple realities of their time, amusingly and at times painfully accurate in their depiction of Polish customs and mores. Although Wajda made only several such films over the years, all of them contain interesting social observations.

Innocent Sorcerers, written by Jerzy Andrzejewski and Jerzy Skolimowski,[1] tells the story of a young doctor, Andrzej, who spends his free time chasing girls, playing jazz, and socializing with his young friends. As Andrzejewski admits in an unpublished document on the film,[2] the screenplay is based on a manuscript he had received in the mail just after World War II; its author, whom he met briefly and who introduced himself as Hektor, asked Andrzejewski to have a look at the work. "Hektor, a platoon officer cadet from the Zośka battalion, and Ewa, the liaison officer, were approximately 18 years old. Ewa was possibly one year younger. In their earliest youth they wandered at the brink of oblivion, revived as if they were disappearing shadows during the time in which the clash of forcible weapons during World War II stamped its dramatic mark."[3] Several years passed, but "Hektor" did not resurface.

Skolimowski, something of a youthful rebel, introduced many "radical" touches to the short story on which the film was based, such as jazz, a playful presentation of sexuality, young men on motorcycles, and girls in tight blouses. All these elements were deemed suspect if not outright forbidden before the thaw. In its light, humorous narrative fashioned after the French New Wave, the film's jazz motif lends a kind of universal significance amid the new, exciting times; the music follows the protagonist Andrzej as he shaves, goes to work, or talks with his friends, or it reappears diegetically in the film when he engages in his favorite pastime—playing drums in a jazz band.

Because *Innocent Sorcerers* was so unusual for its time (in that Wajda barely touches upon questions of Socialist ideology) the director had to explain his motives carefully during a special meeting of the Screenplay Assessment Commission before making the film.[4] The members of this commission, especially Minister Tadeusz Zaorski, had many concerns related to the image of Polish youths, whom they feared would be presented as consumerist and apathetic to the nation's many postwar crises. They wanted the film to be more didactic, with a healthily positive portrayal of young people; however, this idea was strongly opposed by Andrzejewski himself during that meeting. Wajda defended his making of the film in the following way: "I want this film to bring something new into our lives. This is a film about masked feelings or their lack altogether—a theme we have the ability and the right to comment upon. This is a film that shows this idea in a highly ethical manner. I can assure you that this theme will be depicted on the screen in such a manner."[5]

The film's jazz motif also illustrates the process of the post-World War II reconstruction of Warszawa, where the action of the film takes place, that is explored, for instance, when Andrzej rides around the city on a motorcycle near the end of the film. Not only does the film reflect Wajda's world off-camera, but it is also wonderfully self-reflexive, as we see when Andrzej's abandoned girlfriend Mirka passes a poster on the street that advertises the very film in which she is appearing—*Innocent Sorcerers*. The film thus turns into a sort of a general commentary on all such young people at the time, as represented by the character Andrzej in the film, but also a commentary on the life of Wajda, the director, himself a young man making his first optimistic film, one full of vitality and humor.

In the opening sequence of the film, set in Andrzej's spacious apartment, the protagonist completes a crossword puzzle while he listens to a tape recording of himself and his former girlfriend speaking; all the while, she throws stones at the windowpane in an effort to draw him out so she can speak with him, to no avail. She finally leaves the house with Andrzej's friend Edmund. In the following scenes, Andrzej is shown in everyday situations in his life: He enters the sports arena where he works as a doctor, talks to the young boxers whom he supervises, and flirts briefly with a nurse. In a remarkable long shot, the boxing ring is seen from his point of view, as if expressing his desire for fierce, violent action, suggestive of his virility and enthusiasm. This type of exuberant, optimistic young masculinity is recapitulated in several of Wajda's other films, such as *The Wedding* and *A Chronicle of Amorous Incidents*, only to be cynically downplayed in *Hunting Flies* and *Landscape after Battle*.

After leaving the boxing arena, Andrzej goes to a jazz club where he plays drums along with Polo (Roman Polański in another cameo role) and Krzysztof Komeda. From this point forward, the film often reads rather like a documentary regarding the currently budding intellectual and popular cultural life in Poland, casually presenting various Polish stars: Polański and Jerzy Skolimowski, filmmakers; Zbigniew Cybulski and Kalina Jędrusik, actors; Krzysztof Trzciński Komeda, jazz musician; and Sława Przybylska, singer. During the jazz sequence, the director's acumen is seen in the way he mixes the sound of the jazz played on the drums with the sound of the roaring crowds at the boxing ring, as if commenting on the excitement of both kinds of activities so popular among the young men of those times. After playing his piece, Andrzej is approached by Jędrusik, who plays the part of a young journalist interviewing the musicians; he asks her for a date and she accepts.

After a short walk through the dark but lively Warszawa streets, Andrzej enters a café called Mannekin, where he attends the performance of Sława Przybylska, a well-known singer, and talks to his friend Edmund about "girls." In a humorous sequence, the two young men introduce themselves to an attractive young woman named Magda; in a witty ploy concocted by the two men, Edmund soon tricks Magda's date into sharing a taxi with him, leaving Andrzej and Magda behind together. The chemistry between the two is tangible and immediate. A flirtatious exchange takes place as they walk through the streets of Warszawa toward the railway station; because of their leisurely strolling, she misses the last train home. Seeing no better way out of the awkward situation, Andrzej invites Magda back to his apartment, where their innocent flirtation continues and they play games with one another.

In one of their games, Magda pretends that her name is Pelagia and Andrzej calls himself Bazyli. Pelagia writes a series of instructions they have to follow during their encounter and engages in more flirtatious dialogue with the bemused Bazyli. As if anticipating the style of Jean-Luc Godard's *Breathless* (1960), the young people flirt and drink tea while strong undercurrents of youthful vigor and sexual desire emerge and re-emerge from the conversations. The young people also talk about their dreams and their futures. The camera moves ceaselessly between Andrzej and Magda, from close-up to medium shot, from one place in the room to another. Despite the fact that they are confined by the space of the room, they do not go to bed or even kiss, as if delaying the moment of sexual gratification. Shortly, Edmund comes to the window to talk with Andrzej about his crying ex-girlfriend, and the boys exchange some lighthearted remarks about women in general. After Andrzej comes back to the room, he and Magda chat, play some more flirtatious games, eat breakfast, and eventually fall asleep, each on a separate bed.

Suddenly, the sound of a trumpet wakes them. A friend of Andrzej from the jazz band (played by Krzysztof Trzciński Komeda) calls Andrzej outside; he leaves the room and joins his friends, amidst a joyful exchange of jokes and playful remarks. The four young men ride together on a motorcycle, all perched dangerously atop it, fooling around after a sleepless night playing jazz in the café and flirting with the women they meet there. This merry state of the young men reflects the positive and hopeful atmosphere of the late 1950s, when people tried to rebuild their lives after World War II and the years of Stalinism. After the thaw, controversial artists did not have to hide anymore. Consequently, Komeda the jazz musician did not have to hide behind an assumed name (jazz playing was considered a decadent activity by Stalinists); likewise, Skolimowski also plays himself, the boxing champion. Nevertheless, the realities of the 1950s and of the postwar cityscape reappear in one shot after another. The Palace of Culture in

Warszawa, an atrocious architectural creation of the Stalinist regime, looms in the background; the streets are dark and full of rubble, the apartments ugly and seemingly hastily erected.

When Andrzej frolics with his friends, Magda leaves the apartment. In one of the most stylish sequences in the film, Andrzej, riding a motorcycle through the streets of Warszawa, looks for her—the audience also looks for her through Andrzej's eyes. Warszawa, seen from the perspective of the worried Andrzej, is a lonely place in which the jazz motif only helps to add an element of estrangement. Finally, the young doctor goes to the boxing arena, where he approaches Edmund with his frantic questions about Magda. Suddenly, he is attacked by Skolimowski, who, we find, has a grudge against Andrzej for banning him from the upcoming boxing competition. Fully in control of the situation, however, Andrzej returns the boxer's blows and then goes slowly back to his apartment; to accent his loneliness, he is shot from a high angle, a small, solitary figure upon his motorcycle.

Upon his return, anticipating an empty room, Andrzej is surprised to find Magda sitting at his table, which she has covered neatly with a tablecloth, two cups of tea sitting on it. The young people behave as if nothing has happened, both hiding their dread at being separated and their happiness at seeing one another again. Andrzej drinks his tea and listens to the news, then closes his eyes as if falling asleep. Magda starts to say something, but she does not finish; she puts on her scarf instead. Andrzej does not stop her when she leaves. In a moment of painful suspense, the spectator sees Magda leave the apartment without a word. However, pausing outside the door, she hesitantly comes back in, and the film ends in the mode of a classical love story, Magda having returned to Andrzej.

This amusing, light film makes no direct political commentary on the era of the late 1950s. Despite this absence of the political pronouncements, though, Wajda nevertheless makes important statements about the current young generation in Poland and their desire for normal, happy lives. With its references to jazz culture and a focus on the lighter aspects of everyday life, the film celebrates the culture of the West, which, despite bans and political prohibitions, has made a slow inroad into this deeply Socialist society. In a sense, *Innocent Sorcerers* is one of the first films to illustrate the vitality and exuberance of the new Poland. At the time of its screening, however, the film was poorly received not only by government authorities but also by the Catholic Church, which had slowly yet surely re-emerged from obscurity after the thaw. Both authoritative bodies came very close to condemning the film for promoting a "decadent lifestyle." The characteristics of Andrzej and his friends—"chaos, laziness, filth, boredom, day-dreaming and self-pity"—were thought to reflect negatively on real young people's state of mind. In an ironic twist, both the church and the party agreed that "The young people's piecemeal, decadent and illogical reasoning [was] in tandem with their rebellious paralyzed wills and the whims of their imagination."[6]

Equally condemnatory were leading Polish film critics, such as Janusz Wilhelmi, Jerzy Płażewski, and Stefan Morawski,[7] who, in their moralistic diatribes, completely ignore the film's freshness and exuberance— as well as its documentary value as one of the first films produced after the death of Stalin to reflect on the changes in Polish society. Non-Polish critics pointed to the film's general nature in its presentation of young people in Poland: Robert Vas comments, "[Wajda] shows his anti-heroes as amiable, innocent, rebellious victims of a world-wide atmosphere impregnated with the fallout of fear and nihilism."[8] Loguin Seguin also stresses the universal nature of the film, its carefree humor and its undercurrent of sexual awareness, as do both David Robinson and Pierre Lefebour.[9] *Innocent Sorcerers* initiates a new area in Wajda's filmography: films with social content illustrating the truth of the time, amusingly and at times painfully accurate in the depiction of society's mores.

Samson (1961)

After the amusing social commentary that was *Innocent Sorcerers*, Wajda returns to the subject of World War II and produces this serious film about the persecution of Jews in occupied Poland. *Samson* initiates another field in his filmmaking oeuvre: films dealing with the painful issue of anti-Semitism, such as *Korczak* and *Holy Week*. Based on a novel by Kazimierz Brandys,[10] this static, somber film tells the story of a young man, Jakub Gold, "Samson," a Polish Jew persecuted by both Germans and Poles.

The film opens with a point-of-view shot of Jakub walking in the streets of Warszawa. The audience does not see his face, only his back, which signifies the protagonist's anonymity—and that in turn is representative of the fate of Polish Jews in general. The voice-over commentary explains the situation of Jewish people in Poland during World War II. The film's action takes place in the late 1930s, just before the beginning of the war; Jakub is about to begin attending university at the time of growing fascist tendencies in Poland.[11] One of the outcomes of these tendencies was the *numerus clausus*, "which sought to restrict Jewish pupils in selected schools and faculties to numbers proportionate to their position in the population at large. Humiliating 'Jew-benches' made their appearance."[12]

Shortly before his first day at the university, Jakub's mother, full of foreboding, warns her son to be careful of these fascists; she tells him not to talk to anybody and to mind his own business. Jakub passes just such a group on his way to the university hall; when he enters, he sees the enforced segregation of Jews, and later, as fate would have it, he finds himself surrounded by them as he leaves. The students present at the meeting play with Jakub as if he were a puppet. First, they beat him savagely and shove him around, and then one of them throws a stone at his head, only barely missing. When the stone accidentally comes into Jakub's hands, he throws it back at his tormenters, but his aim is true; he hits one of his attackers in the head, killing him. This disturbing opening scene provides the tone for the remainder of the film. Mistreated, cornered, and forced to protect himself, Jakub epitomizes the fate of Jews in Poland before the outbreak of the war.

As a result of the fateful stone-throwing, Jakub goes to jail; he is deeply hurt and humiliated because he feels he was justified in killing his assailant. His despair is relieved by a Polish cashier, Malina, an older prisoner with whom Jakub shares his cell and who also believes that Jakub has been unjustly thrown in prison. Expressionistically lit and carefully framed, the prison shots fully reveal Jakub's despair and loneliness. This aesthetics is especially interesting in those sequences presenting Jakub in his prison cell and the Communist activist Pankrat in the neighboring cell: They talk about Jakub's sentence, with Pankrat clearly indicating the unjust character of his case. The two windows of the prison cells are side by side; their occupants cannot see each other, but the audience can see both so that the panning camera shows the two men engaged in a sorrowful dialogue of two lonely souls.

Samson has many such static scenes, with only some violent interludes. One such violent scene is that which presents the fight between the students and Jakub, while another depicts a violent skirmish between the prisoners and the prison guards during a prison revolt. Another dynamic scene shows the prisoners talking to their relatives during the visitation time; the only person who does not say a word amid the clamor is Jakub's mother, who looks silently at her son, a look of utter devotion and despair on her face. Neither Jakub nor his mother utter a sigh during this painful scene, doing nothing more than exchanging loving, pitiful looks while surrounded by shouting prisoners and their shouting family members.

On 1 September 1939, however, war breaks out and all the prisoners are released. Being a Jew, Jakub is forced to go to the ghetto, where he joins the crowd of people with yellow stars on their backs. As one of his fellow Jews comments, people there are condemned to the ghetto for the simple fact that they exist at all. The ghetto is surrounded by a tall wooden wall symbolic of the victimization and incarceration of Jakub and his fellow Jews. After a difficult time spent in the ghetto, Jakub's mother dies and Jakub decides to leave the ghastly place; he is persuaded by a man called Fiałka to help him jump the wall. At a distance, Germans with dogs are seen pursuing would-be escapees.

Now on the other side of the wall, Jakub tries to find refuge at the house of Fiałka's girlfriend. Quickly chased away for his obviously Jewish appearance, however, he soon finds himself among a party of strangers; Lucyna, an elegant young woman, notices him hiding behind the window and invites him into her home. Everybody there accepts Jakub without a word, clearly aware of his situation. When the guests leave, the young woman asks Jakub to stay, declaring that she is Jewish as well. Jakub wants to leave, however, to return to his own people in the ghetto. He shouts at her in frustration, claiming that nobody understands what it is like in the ghetto, that "everything is black there."

Suddenly, carolers knock at the apartment's door. Lucyna, frightened, clings to Jakub and maintains that they should leave together. In a symbolic gesture redolent of racial purification, she dyes her dark hair to become a fashionable blond. She insists that Jakub leave with her for a quiet life in the country, the only place where they might live without being harassed by the Germans. Jakub refuses her invitation, though, and leaves, seeking refuge with his former friend from prison, Malina. A group of carolers helps him to disappear into the crowd by giving him a white mask, in another ironic symbol of racial cleansing. Once in Malina's house, he is taken care of by Malina and Kazia, the older man's niece. However, Malina's neighbor happens to notice Jakub in their apartment and intends to denounce Malina for sheltering a Jew; as a result, Jakub is relegated to the cellar.

From this point onward, the film turns into a grim tale of incarceration, tedium, and despair. Shot in medium takes, the scenes are static, with rare close-ups of Jakub's face, as if the young man had disappeared from life. He does not fight his imprisonment, and there are rarely any emotions other than despair and loneliness on his face. The cellar's grim and dirty interior is highlighted by dense framing, and an almost documentary precision of detail invokes the atmosphere of misery and dejection surely understood, if not shared by all the Jews at that time. In the cellar, Jakub is reduced to little more than a voyeur, watching life's events from a small cellar window just above ground-level. After several months of this life in hiding, almost a worse state than that of the jail cell he previously inhabited, Jakub has turned into a mute and helpless prisoner. When Malina dies, Kazia, who has since fallen in love with Jakub, wants to keep him to herself; unable to return her feelings, Jakub realizes that he must somehow leave and go back to the ghetto. Lucyna, unable to live as a non-Jew, also decides to go to the ghetto. Soon, however, the tragic and famous Warszawa Uprising takes place and the entire ghetto population is brutally exterminated—destroyed buildings and broken corpses are all Jakub can see from the wall he tries to climb in an attempt to get back to the ghetto.

Desperate and grief-stricken, Jakub climbs down from the wall and hides on the roof of a nearby building. Even here, though, he is surrounded by hostile Poles; one of these, a "Jew-catcher," hopes to get money from Jakub in return for not denouncing him to the Germans. Fiałka, Jakub's prison acquaintance, who by chance happens to be nearby, saves Jakub from this new danger and brings him to the Resistance Center, where Polish freedom-fighters try to hide him. Unfortunately, during a routine inspection, German soldiers come upon some clandestine literature in the yard of the building. On seeing this, Jakub throws a grenade in a final act of despair and revenge; crucified by a falling iron pillar, he dies in the ruins of the Resistance Center, and the film ends.

While many of the scenes in *Samson* are static and monotonous, there are several remarkable moments that make it fascinating to watch. In one deeply symbolic scene, Jakub finds himself in contrasting shades: When he leaves Malina's cellar, it is bright daylight and the sun shines on the streets and upon the white, elegantly dressed people who walk by; on the contrary, Jakub is dirty and dark, relegated to the shadows. In another scene, Jakub looks through his window in the cellar, through which he sees children playing in the dirt and people coming and going, life going on in all its beauty and normalcy. At one point, the suspicious neighbors look into this window hoping to find a hidden Jew; Kazia, who is present when this occurs, then decides to cover the window. Afterward, the small space of the cellar becomes even more claustrophobic and horrible, and from this moment on Jakub undergoes a process of physical and psychological deterioration.

In the end, the film leaves one reflecting sadly on Jewish history and on anti-Semitism—of which envious neighbors, "Jew-catchers," national socialists, and other Poles refusing shelter to Jews are but a few examples—both in twentieth-century Poland and in other times and places. With his constant desire to go back to the ghetto, Jakub represents a fragmented Jewish consciousness, the main objectives of which are to maintain social solidarity and to retain a sense of cultural identity. Wajda presents these poignant vignettes pertaining to the Jewish question for the first time in *Samson*.

Upon its release in November 1961, *Samson* provoked mixed reactions among audiences. Initially a number of enthusiastic reviews appeared in all the major weeklies: *Przekrój, Życie Literackie, Film, Ekran, Sztandar Młodych,* and *Nowa Kultura*. Yet there were also strong objections to the film, one of the greatest of which concerned the lack of historical accuracy in the presentation of the historical-social climate of the German occupation. In the opinion of these disobliging critics, Wajda presented improbable events that could not have happened under German occupation. This negative assessment is countered by such critics as Michał Mirski, however, who declares that all the facts presented in the film are highly probable.[13] Mirski analyzes the film scene-by-scene and corroborates the historical validity of every single event, from the fight at Warszawa University, through the grim and depressing prison scenes, to the scenes of the ghetto. Mirski also devotes significant attention to the state of resignation experienced by the Jews under occupation and to their desire to stay with their own people. As historical sources confirm, the feelings of resignation and apathy in the ghetto were skilfully orchestrated by the Germans, who greatly influenced the Judenrats (Jewish Councils in the ghettos) in this matter. In both style and thematics, the film clearly grapples with themes of suffering and despair that cannot be expressed with spectacular action. Its portrait of a passive, suffering Jew is one of the most interesting aspects of the film, as Mirski notes:

> The Jew who tried to hide himself did not cease to suffer. Even when he was somewhere else, he was linked to the ghetto by thousands of threads, he lived its life. Sometimes, after extended exile, he would return to the ghetto. At one time, he was not able to stand the nervous uncertainty of hiding, so he went back to the ghetto. Later, nervous that his hiding place had been discovered, he returned to the ghetto again. From time to time, he returned hastily to the ghetto not to die but to live, as he hoped that he would survive with his brethren.[14]

Later, Polish critics were surprisingly derogatory in their assessment of the film. Kazimierz Brandys himself suggests that these critics were significantly influenced by the fact that the film did not receive any prizes at the Venice Festival. While reviews occurring before the Venice Festival were almost universally enthusiastic (the film was an official Polish entry to the festival), those after the festival were much less positive—the cynicism and opportunism of many Polish journalists was manifested in the tone of their postfestival reviews. This negative reaction was initiated by Andrzej Kijowski in *Przegląd Kulturalny* and Krzysztof Teodor Toeplitz in *Świat,* soon followed by Janusz Wilhelmi in *Trybuna Ludu.* Most of these articles, Brandys writes in a private letter to Wajda, were written with ill will and completely avoided the discussion of the film's positive aspects; worse, they very much influenced the response of wider Polish audiences. As a result of this, *Samson* was generally not well received by Polish audiences.

Foreign critics were more sympathetic to the film. For instance, the influential French critic Georges Sadoul considered the film Wajda's best to date, and confirmed that it was in fact highly regarded by the Venice Festival critics in 1961, despite the fact that the film won no major prizes there.[15] He writes, "[Wajda] says what he has to say firmly, even brutally, while using a minimum of effects, in shades nearly classical."[16] In presenting its protagonists' feelings of fear and loneliness, *Samson* surpasses even *Kanal*. Miron Czernienko is especially vocal on this issue.[17] The element of fear, as he states, appears in many of Wajda's films, but in *Samson* it reaches its zenith, the invisible border behind which fear turns into cool determination. The director's style in *Samson* was critically noted in almost every review as it was somewhat of an enigma; some critics considered his style "baroque" while others called it "somber" yet "economic." Yet some reviewers considered its baroque style an obstacle to revealing a necessary depth of emotion. For instance, Maria Oleksiewicz states that Wajda has given his *Samson* "the form of an elegiac poem. His rather too obvious Biblical references, however, writer's narrative and commentaries largely deprive the film of the emotional and philosophical climate contained in the theme."[18] Jerzy Płażewski suggests that "when the visual effect wins, the truth loses. Wajda's stylistic colonnades and powerful volutes can be thrilling when viewed close up, without regard to the entire edifice. Once their usefulness and logic is questioned, however, it turns out that the pillars support nothing and the volutes needlessly blot out the structure of the whole."[19] Wajda partly agrees with this harsh assessment of the film's aesthetics. He explains that one of the reasons why the film favored stylization was caused by the film technique: "*Samson* was the first film I made in Cinemascope technique. The panoramic picture favored stylization and measured narrative, with lengthy takes and deep sets. In a word: it drew us away from what Kazimierz Brandys' *Samson* should have been: an action film.... I stylized realistic scenes from the novel to resemble biblical tableaux—static and therefore slightly annoying."[20]

These words would explain my general feeling that *Samson*'s film aesthetics occasionally transcends the mere presentation of events. Even the grimmest episodes of the prewar portion of the film reveal the quiet harmony of the frame, its symmetrical composition, the diffused, static lighting; nevertheless, Wajda breaks this peace with an unexpected and bright metaphor, one of many present in the film. An example of such a metaphor is the moment of the locking of the gates to the ghetto; this shot, taken from the point of view of the German soldiers, shows the Jews looking up silently at the Germans, who are busily hammering spikes into the wooden gates. The Jews simply watch, meek and resigned. Hands in black gloves pound in the nails. The small gap in the gates, through which the Jews are seen, slowly but surely decreases, so that ever fewer and fewer Jews are seen through it. With the final plank, no more Jews can be seen. This moment acquires the accumulated weight of an entire cultural consciousness, and sums up the film itself. As Czernienko notes, "Wajda does not allow for the luxury of symbol for symbol's sake, even if the symbol is the most spectacular. The symbol should be simple and result from the sense of the story.... Only in *Innocent Sorcerers* and later in *Samson* is Wajda able to reach another style, losing nothing from the look of a saturated metaphor."[21]

The debate concerning the film's aesthetics was not the only controversy surrounding the film reception. Another criticism relates to the choice of the actor playing Jakub, Serge Merlin. According to Klaus Eder, Jakub differs greatly from the usual active, romantic heroes present in many of Wajda's films: this Jakub is a passive, inactive protagonist, who does nothing to change his fate.

> Jakub Gold has nothing in common with Polish Romantic heroes: there is not a trace of Maciek Chełmicki in him. A kind of hero new to Wajda, to his experience as well as to his understanding of history, he [Jakub] is certainly closer to Brandys than to Wajda himself. Jakub Gold is deeply rooted in Jewish mythology. Throughout at least two-thirds of the film, his attitude toward history is passive: he experiences history and succumbs to it. Rather than act, he lets himself be carried along by events...[22]

Zdzisław Beryt also openly blames weakness of the film on the casting of Merlin, who is, he argues, able to communicate "loneliness, alienation, and confusion ... [only at] the expense of the psychological credibility, depth, and richness of the character."[23]

However, Wajda himself considers the character of Jakub and Jerzy Wójcik's photography to be the strongest features of the film. Merlin was supposed to play the part of silent witness of the tragic events, not its active and passionate subject. In the choice of the actor and the presentation of the events, Wajda makes the spectator aware of the absolute tragedy of the Jews' fate and the hopelessness of their situation at that time. Jews could do almost nothing to save themselves as they had very few supporters among the Polish society, the theme later voiced more brutally and openly in *Holy Week*. Undoubtedly, this striking film dealing with the issues of World War II differs greatly from his earlier and later films on the subject. While other films devoted to these themes are more dynamic, *Samson* is meditative and mature. With its expressive aesthetics and solemn tone, it presents its subject matter with the seriousness it fully deserves.

The four films discussed in the following section, *Love at Twenty*, *Siberian Lady Macbeth*, *Ashes*, and *The Gates to Paradise*, are not well known either in Poland or beyond. None of them has ever been considered one of Wajda's masterpieces. Only *Ashes* provoked intense commentary on the part of both average filmgoers and historians, at least in Poland. Nevertheless, all four films reiterate Wajda's major thematic preoccupations: World War II (in *Love at Twenty*), history (in *Ashes*), and the presentation of human passions (in *Siberian Lady Macbeth* and *The Gates to Paradise*, both of which are also adaptations of important literary works).

Love at Twenty (1962) Segment *Warszawa*

Love at Twenty is a short film about love that constitutes part of a larger film composed of five film novellas made by French, Italian, Japanese, German, and Polish filmmakers. Each tells the story of a 20-year-old man and a 20-year-old woman who fall in love, with various results. The hero of the first film, made by Francois Truffaut, is a young blue-collar worker in a record album factory, who has fallen hopelessly in love with a classical music lover whom he often accompanies to concerts. Despite the fact that he resides near her apartment, visits her parents, and accompanies her to concerts and other events on a regular basis, however, his love is never reciprocated. When he finally sees her with another man whom she openly adores, he leaves. The second novella, made by Roman filmmaker Renzo Rossellini, tells the story of a young lower-class couple who have fallen madly in love. However, the young man, Leonardo, is the kept man of a wealthy older woman. When he decides to terminate the relationship with the aristocrat, she confronts the younger woman and tells her about Leonardo. The film ends with a shot of the despairing girl.

The third novella was produced by Shintaro Ishihara of Tokyo. This film is a poetic portrayal of poor factory workers, one of whom, Ishtara, falls in love with a girl whom he sees every day on his way to work. Unable to approach her out of an indescribable feeling of dread and love, he simply smiles at her helplessly. One night, he dares to approach her and, in an inexplicable act of love/hate, he strangles her with his own hands. The fourth novella, produced by Marcel Ophuls, tells the story of a young journalist who learns about the birth of his only son by a former lover. Although he had no plans for fatherhood or indeed for any serious relationships, he unexpectedly falls in love with the woman. The film ends on a happy note: the lovers decide to spend their life together.

In the context of these first four novellas, Wajda's film, the last in the series, is arguably the most interesting, as it manages to present many diverse themes in its diegesis. Mixing several elements, Wajda produces a complex little film in which history, memory, and love come together into a simple story of courtship that still elucidates the protagonist's war tragedy. *Love at Twenty* begins with a young couple who kiss and embrace at the zoo. Suddenly, now near the bear's cage, they hear the screams of a little girl who has accidentally fallen into the cage. Władek, the young boyfriend, is afraid to risk his life to save the child. However, a middle-aged electrician called Zbyszek, played by Zbigniew Cybulski, jumps into the cage and saves the little girl. Impressed and mystified, Władek's girlfriend, Basia, invites the man to her apartment. Zbyszek gets onto his bicycle and takes the girl with her while her boyfriend watches, stupefied. Back at her apartment, the girl insists that Zbyszek clean his coat and take off his funny cap; he wants to leave the apartment, but Basia insists that he stay. He leans against the wall, drinks some alcohol he finds in the apartment, and finally approaches the girl somewhat aggressively. They look at each other, and then Zbyszek pushes her against the wall and tries to kiss her. In this dynamic and highly theatrical scene, clearly aimed at enhancing Zbyszek's part, he looks at the girl's neck with obvious desire and presses her aggressively.

Just then, a group of students burst in to visit Basia. Surprised to see the "bear man," they begin to sing and dance, capering around Zbyszek, who quickly feels awkward and out of place. When the music grows louder, he becomes frustrated and afraid. He begins to bluster, describing his war experiences as a Home Army soldier. Yet what is a painful experience for Zbyszek means almost nothing to the young students; they continue their waltz while he leans against the wall, now a lonely figure in the corner of the room. Finally, Władek comes in and Basia greets him warmly. The taunting of Zbyszek gets rougher now— the students begin to play at blindman's buff. Forcefully blindfolded, Zbyszek feels hunted down; he hides in the corner of the room, shivering from the imagined sounds of shots his mind has produced. When the young people laugh, he remembers executions by firing squads during World War II. Finally, the students leave Basia's apartment, singing the song "Biały niedźwiedź mocno śpi" ("The White Bear Sleeps Hard"), an ironic reference to the earlier incident with the bears. Calm now and subdued, Zybyszek also leaves the apartment and rides away on his bicycle. The film ends with a shot of the reunited Basia and Władek running in the fields.

Although only a part of a larger film, Wajda's segment attracted viewers' attention to the social complexity of the love story. In fact, the romantic aspect is not as important as the feelings of claustrophobia and anxiety that the situation in the film evokes. Again, Wajda concentrates on his own obsessions rather than on the theme of the film, which is "love." His next film, *Siberian Lady Macbeth*, on the other hand, concentrates only on romance and its dire consequences.

Siberian Lady Macbeth (1962)

Siberian Lady Macbeth, made in the former Yugoslavia, is a grim story of love and murder. Shot in black and white, it is a stylized film rendition of the famous story of would-be king Macbeth in a Slavic setting. Taken from a short story by Nikolai Leskov based on that tale, the film opens with a panning shot of a village somewhere in Siberia. Solemn orchestral music, based on the motives from Dmitri Shostakovich's opera *Katerina Izmailova*, introduces the mood of the film. These introductory scenes set the mood for the film, in which the bored wife of an old, rich landowner seeks to murder her father-in-law after falling in love with a young suitor.

The film opens with Katarzyna Ismailova, daughter-in-law of the landholder Zinovy Izmailov Nikiticz, looking indolently through the gates of their house. Nikiticz himself catches rats, while Aksinia, the servant, obediently brings food to the abusive landlord. The latter complains that Katarzyna avoids people since her husband left on business five years ago; she walks around the house and does nothing, he grumbles. The following sequences show Katarzyna doing just that—sitting, walking, humming, lonely and bored; always exquisitely photographed against the landowner's beautiful house. The next sequences introduce Sergei, a young man looking for work; he wanders from one house to another, but when he knocks on the doors, nobody answers. However, Nikiticz takes the young man on as a swine-herd for a trial period.

Katarzyna gets to know Sergei when, startled by the joyful laughter of servants in the farm buildings, she goes to investigate the matter. The flirtatious, cheerful Sergei proposes to weigh her on the big scales; when he proceeds to do so, a spark of erotic interest and fascination passes between the two young people. Nikiticz later leaves the house for the evening, and Aksinia knocks at Katarzyna's door to tell her that they can try a fertility charm with a young mare: Katarzyna has no children with her husband, it turns out, and she yearns for them. Dressed in a long white dress, Katarzyna engages in a pagan, quasi-erotic ritual of fertility, in which she rubs her body against the belly of a pregnant mare. A short time later, now back in her bedroom, Katarzyna is started by Sergei, who enters on the pretext that both of them are lonely, bored, and restless. At first against her will, but then with her reluctant consent, he makes love to Katarzyna to the sound of a music box. Only when Nikiticz returns home do the lovers awake.

When he discovers Sergei, Nikiticz beats the young man savagely into unconsciousness; then, worn out by his exertion, he demands food. Katarzyna begs him to let Sergei go and not to hurt either of them any further, but he replies that he does not yet know what he will do. In an intense outburst of hatred, marked in the film by the burning look in Katarzyna's eyes and the dismal musical accords, she warms a pot of mushroom stew for her father-in-law and picks up a knife. From the living room she takes a wooden box and opens it to find the rat poison kept inside, all under the eyes of an Orthodox icon that stares at her and at the audience—reminiscent of Sergei Eisenstein's reproving icons in *Ivan the Terrible* (1945). Hatred still burning in her eyes, Katarzyna brings the poisoned dish to Nikiticz, who looks at her questioningly. After several spoonfuls, he falls to the ground, begging her for water. She refuses. When Aksinia comes in, she sees Katarzyna crouching over the dead body of the old man. Heavy musical accompaniment bears witness to the film's terrible events. The images at this point are static, like tableaux, allowing the spectator to admire the composition of the image and to ponder the ethical dimensions of the event.

The following sequences, static, show the slow funeral procession and also Sergei waking up after his terrible beating. In a single beautifully composed shot of a small stable window, through which Sergei sees the farm's dogs, the funeral, and the neighbors discussing the absence of the deceased man's son, Wajda comments on both the simple reality of village life and the most complex reality of death itself. Just after the funeral, Katarzyna goes to see Sergei in the barn: She wants him to stay with her. When he asks how Nikiticz has died, she replies that it was God's will. She then tends to Sergei's wounds and treats him as if he were now her husband. She also asks him to live with her in the manor. Soon, dressed in white, they look out over their property from the house's porch. However, Sergei, uncertain of his new position and aware of his lower social status, tells Katarzyna that sooner or later she will try to get rid of him. She denies it, saying that they will soon be married in a proper church ceremony, as he himself wishes.

In the meantime, the villagers gossip about the new situation, but they do not disturb the lovers; their peace is troubled only by Katarzyna's horrible dreams. Before long, however, Katarzyna's husband Boris Izmailov returns from his five-week business trip. First, he goes to the cemetery and kisses the cross on his father's grave; next, he travels to the church; and only then does he go to the house, where the lovers are still dallying in bed. Hearing a strange sound, Katarzyna chases away her lover and calmly welcomes her husband; suspicious, acting on a hint from the villagers, he looks for proof of his wife's betrayal: He finds them in a crumpled bed made for two and in Sergei's shirt band, which he left there during their tryst. When Katarzyna comes back from the kitchen with the samovar, he confronts her about her lover. As arranged beforehand between Katarzyna and Sergei, the latter comes up the stairs and helps Katarzyna kill her husband. However, Sergei feels physically and psychologically exhausted after the deed. He wants to drink some tea, but Katarzyna warns him not to drink it and then pours the poisoned tea out. In a scene very reminiscent of that in Shakespeare's *Macbeth*, Sergei carries the corpse out of the house and Katarzyna washes the stairs, which have been covered with blood during the murder. In the dark of the night, Sergei drags Zinovy's corpse out and buries it among the pigs.

Later, at a party that Katarzyna has organized for the members of the service and the villagers, Sergei behaves strangely: He is seen hiding behind a huge wooden column that cuts the frame in two parts. When Aksinia brings in the pig's head for the feast, he cannot eat it and suddenly leaves the room. The distressed guests leave when Sergei shouts that it is Zinovy's head they are going to eat. Hereafter, the villagers' distrust of the couple rises incrementally with each bizarre bit of behavior evinced by the two, such as when they gallop brazenly in a cart pulled by three horses; the magnificent troika gallops around the property while Katarzyna shouts excitedly to Sergei that everything he sees belongs to him.

When they approach the house after their ride, they see a woman with a child waiting at the gate. They prove to be relatives of Katarzyna's late husband, with some claims to Katarzyna's land. The aunt and her son, whom Katarzyna invites to live with them, behave as if they own the place, checking the land books and counting their possessions. Katarzyna and Sergei watch these developments with growing resentment. Finally, they decide to kill the boy, who stands to inherit most of their property. Despite her own pregnancy and growing maternal instincts, Katarzyna actively participates in yet another murder, which happens on Easter. The Easter ritual, exquisitely photographed, reminiscent of many sequences in Sergei Eisenstein's *Ivan the Terrible*, shows a procession of believers around the church. During the procession, one of the villagers accidentally sees the lovers trying to strangle the child. All the villagers rush into the house. When they try to lynch Sergei, Katarzyna intercedes and surrenders, promising to tell the truth to a judge.

In a decisive court verdict, both lovers are sentenced to a labor camp in Siberia for their crimes. They leave the village dressed in exile garb while the disgusted villagers listen to the verdict. In these final shocking sequences, the lovers are seen with their legs chained, marching slowly to their destination in Siberia. On the way, Sergei abandons his lover and tries to charm another young woman in the chain gang, Sonietka; he explains to her that Katarzyna is actually a curse, the real reason for his exile. Despite Katarzyna's pained efforts to lure her lover back, he walks only with his new acquaintance and refuses to have anything more to do with Katarzyna. On the ferry, Sonietka and Sergei keep to themselves while Katarzyna looks on, desolate and heartbroken. Finally, devastated by Sergei's sneering remarks toward her, she suddenly throws herself at Sonietka, whom she pulls into the water and drowns. The last sequence shows Katarzyna drowning herself as the ferry moves on, slowly, inexorably, through the fog.

As Wajda explains in *Wajda Films*,[24] one of the reasons why he decided to make *Siberian Lady Macbeth* was that he wanted to try something new after what were, in his opinion, the disastrous experiences of *Lotna* and *Samson*. He had been working on this story by Leskov for some time leading up to 1962, so he pitched it to Avala Film in Belgrade when they invited him to make a film in Yugoslavia. The film was to be a series of retrospective narratives told by individual deportees trudging to Siberia. The story, according to Wajda, lost the "visionary quality"[25] the trek might have given it due to its classical, linear progression. However, many critics agree that this very progression makes the story remarkably powerful. Richard Roud asserts that "Wajda has renounced his typically baroque style to tell a simple, and yet powerful story of a Lady Macbeth who kills for love rather than for ambition.... Not only has the director succeeded in catching the spirit of the time and the place; he has also managed to create the sense of timelessness inherent to tragedy."[26]

Painted in "broad symbolic strokes,"[27] the film's tale is a universal story of love and betrayal. Wajda, clearly fascinated by Orthodox paintings and icons, textures of wood, and the barrenness of the steppes, has made a film of extreme narrative simplicity and visual clarity. The critic Józef Hen admires the director's ease in moving around the nineteenth-century Russian village and his intimate understanding of the mentality and motivations of the Russians.[28] Surprisingly, though, this same powerful story lacked any "inner fire" for others and was seen by such critics as "an alien and cold film,"[29] an observation acknowledged and partly explained by Wajda himself. The filmmaker has stated that he felt somewhat alienated and uneasy in a new and foreign reality of the Yugoslavian production scene and, in fact, worried constantly about the political and social situation at home throughout the making of the film. Directorial freedom abroad was not enough for him: he needed more freedom at home, in Poland.[30]

Nevertheless, the beauty and magnificent composition of the film's images make the film an exceptional aesthetic experience, a fact noted by all of the film critics who have reviewed it: broad vistas of the Yugoslavian landscape; slanted frames meant to indicate the intense feelings of the main characters; the texture of plain wood or sand; dramatic close-ups of faces distorted by pain; and slow, lethargic figures clad in white or black. Indeed, some reviewers have found this aestheticism so overpowering that it "borders on the academic."[31] The film in many ways resembles a Greek tragedy, its richness surpassed by Wajda only in his theatrical realizations of Fyodor Dostoyevsky's texts. Tragically, this film has never been seen by public audiences in Poland; following its cool reception, Wajda decided to produce a film on Polish history, *Ashes*.

Ashes (1965)

The film *Ashes* was a part of the extensive movement on the part of Polish cinematography as a whole to increase film production in Poland. Other such productions made in the 1960s were *Faraon* (*The Pharaoh*, Jerzy Kawalerowicz, 1965) and *Rękopis Znaleziony w Saragossie* (*The Saragossa Manuscript*, Jerzy Has, 1965). The major Polish studios, Tor, Wektor, and Plan, employed thousands of people at that time and needed to find work for their employees. The production of the film *Ashes* and other huge film productions gave them a possibility to do just this.

Ashes is a black-and-white film shot in two parts; the first part is divided into twelve sections, the second into eight. Based on a well-known novel of the same title by Stefan Żeromski, it deals with the years of the

Napoleonic campaigns, 1797–1813. This era is historically important to Poland, which, under partition at that time, wanted independence from Russian rule. At the time, the nation's idealistic aristocrats hoped that Poland would be liberated by Napoleon in the general movement to set free the whole of Europe. Three such idealists are presented in the film: Prince Gintułt, Rafał Olbromski, and Krzysztof Cedro.

The first sections of the first part of the film introduce the general context of the piece, the Napoleonic war campaign and Polish participation in it. The audience is made aware of Napoleon's promises that he will free the Polish from Russian occupation if they join him in his fight. The first part also introduces one of the protagonists of the film, Prince Gintułt. Through his eyes, we see the battleground in Italy as well as the Polish legion, Gen. Jan Dąbrowski's fusiliers, who participated in Napoleon's campaign in Italy and Africa; Gintułt sees the Polish soldiers, bloodied and tattered, marching downhill in formation. Polish historical and nationalist themes are present in this introductory sequence not only in the presentation of this most famous of Polish legions, which represents the fighting spirit of Poland, but also in the music, *Marsz Dąbrowski (Dąbrowski March)*, that accompanies the march.

In the following scenes, Wajda presents some quintessentially Polish customs, such as the *kulig* (sleigh cavalcade), a ritual common to the Polish village and its manors. During this celebratory custom, nobility and yeomanry go from manor to manor in great horse-drawn sleighs. At each manor along the way, a party is organized for the participants, and then the cavalcade moves on to the next manor. Wajda paints this typical Polish scene exquisitely. The sleighs themselves, the riders on horseback, the peasants accompanying them, the coachmen, and the nobles in their lustrous fur coats are shot with long tracking shots of the cameras, from various angles and positions. They frolic in the snow, revel in the manors, carry their noble ladies across half-frozen streams, all the while watched solemnly by impoverished peasants who are silently critical of the customs of the nobility. Amid the dancing crowds, young Rafał Olbromski, an impoverished nobleman—and the primary protagonist of the film—flirts, dances, and drinks inordinately.

The next scene highlights the fierce independence of the Polish nobles. A Habsburg official criticizes a manor owner, stating that he has not appeared at Habsburg's reception at Wawel (the residence of Polish kings), and upbraids him for not properly respecting Habsburg laws. In response, the landholder retorts that he is the master of his own land and that he will respect only Polish laws. The reference to Polish nationhood reinforces Wajda's didactic predilections concerning the issues of nationality and national identity, as if Wajda downplayed the joyous celebration of Polish customs with the reminder of the historical reality. In the following scenes, however, the romantic component is introduced, linking love and war in a fashion similar to his previous films. Helena de With, a noblewoman, is on the verge of a budding romance with Rafał. At night, he gallops to see Helena; then, after a brief romantic dalliance in the woods, soon interrupted by her jealous former lover, Rafał rides back toward his village only to be attacked by a pack of wolves along the way. Brilliantly photographed, the fight between Rafał and the wolves ends with his victory, although his beloved horse Basia perishes in the struggle.

The next section introduces Rafał's brother Piotr, a patriotic young captain whose health has been irreparably damaged in fighting for Poland's independence. Rafał finds Piotr in the pitiable village of Wygnanka, living among peasants. In his modest hut, Piotr talks to Gintułt, an old friend and confidante, about the situation of the legions, the Polish insurrection, and the Poles' desire for freedom. Gintułt responds with a tale of disgrace and betrayal: In a brilliant flashback, the story of Polish soldiers betrayed by Napoleon in Mantua unfolds in painful detail. After the city's capitulation, Napoleon had promised freedom to Poles who supported his campaign. However, in a secret exchange with the Austrians, one of the three Poland's occupying nations, the French officer in charge leaves the Polish forces under Austrian arrest. Betrayed and humiliated, the Poles return to their country cordoned by Austrians.

In a heated exchange concerning the freeing of peasants, Piotr and Gintułt begin to quarrel about their respective political views. Their argument progresses to the point where they choose to settle their differences in a duel. Before they can commence, however, Piotr's injuries get the better of him and he crumples to the ground. The duel does not take place, for Piotr soon dies and the former friends part unreconciled. Only the poor local peasants, whom the feeble captain has always helped and treated with respect, are shown mourning his death. Gintułt leaves the village with Rafał, whom he has invited to stay in his house in a gesture of goodwill and out of guilt for the deceased brother and friend.

At Gintułt's house, Rafał matures and studies under the prince's tutelage. He learns table manners, philosophy, history, and art, eventually becoming able to assist the prince with his writings. During one of their outings in the city of Warszawa, Rafał meets his former schoolfriend, Krzysztof Cedro. When Rafał is offered a place in the Masonic Lodge, he eagerly accepts, considering the offer to be a great honor. Shortly, in a spectacular ritual among the Masons, Rafał notices Helena, apparently one of the few women also participating in the Masonic ritual; he realizes that she is the wife of the Masons' leader. In all, Wajda shows members of the Polish aristocracy engaging in an array of enjoyable activities; however, this trend ends abruptly in a scene, in which an orderly in Wygnanka is beaten by its new ruler, who is disrespectful of the liberating wishes of the village's late master, Piotr. This brutal sequence, especially when juxtaposed with those occurring immediately previous, is a memorable commentary on Poland and its people around the turn of the eighteenth century.

The final sections of the first half of the film, provide a conclusion to the first romantic story arc in *Ashes*. Helena writes a letter to her husband telling him that she loves Rafał and wants to spend the rest of her life with him. They leave together but they are later ambushed by highland robbers. Helena is raped and beaten, eventually jumping off a cliff to escape the ordeal while Rafał is forced to watch helplessly. Krzysztof brings him to the palace of his wealthy father, feeds him, and slowly brings him back to life, but Rafał is now matured beyond his years and saddened by the state of his country and his compatriots.

The second half of *Ashes* begins with Rafał and Krzysztof, both young and naïve, listening to a Polish Napoleonic legionnaire tell war stories about the legion's recent mission in the Antilles. There, the Polish soldiers fighting under Napoleon's banner had to suppress the mutiny of the "Black Regiment" by force. A striking flashback in bright white shows the murder of black soldiers being executed by shocked Poles. To the accompaniment of distorted Polish nationalistic tunes, the soldiers leave the scene of the slaughter disoriented and disbelieving, many making the sign of the cross as they go. Despite these horrific details concerning the Napoleonic campaign, Rafał and Krzysztof decide to join Napoleon to win freedom for Poland; early in the morning, they saddle their horses and try to sneak away. However, Krzysztof's father hears the commotion and tries to stop his son.

A lengthy sequence ensues, showing the legionnaire with whom the two young men had been speaking: he is being hanged for fomenting sedition. With the shout, "Let the Emperor Live!" he calls to the watching peasants that Napoleon offers freedom to everybody and that serfdom is the thing of the past. Positioned against a white, cold sky, the gallows soon halts the shouts of the insurgent. In the tradition of expressionist cinema, the hanged and the gallows seem remote, abandoned by God and society, presented as a long shot with the camera slowly zooming out. The section closes with Rafał and Krzysztof arriving at the castle of the chamberlain Orłowski, where Princess Elżbieta Gintułtówna dwells.

In the second section, Rafał and Krzysztof participate in a court ball; during the dance, they manage both to flirt and to plot an escape from Austrian jurisdiction. Rafał declares his love for Elżbieta and arranges a furtive meeting with her; she agrees to help the young men pass safely across the river. Despite the danger of a possible discovery by her husband and the imminent danger of the river-crossing, Rafał spends the night in her room, wrapped in white muslins with the princess at his side. Again, love, death, bravado, and patriotism are mixed in dialogue and action; aware of the danger, but also welcoming it, Rafał exclaims during the dance that he may get himself intentionally killed during the crossing of the river. Intentional or not, Rafał is nearly killed when the boat chartered by Elżbieta is shot at by Austrian soldiers. When the ferryman is killed, the two young soldiers continue across the river on the ice floe. In a stunning sequence, reminiscent of Vsevolod Pudovkin's famous scene on the ice in *Mother* (1926), Rafał and Krzysztof escape the Austrians, Rafał mocking the enemy soldiers all the while for their poor marksmanship. He treats the crossing as a boy would treat an exciting game, even to the point of berating Krzysztof for his clumsiness—as a result of which the friends part in bitterness and later end up in different regiments.

The next section is an account of the battle between Polish legionnaires fighting for Napoleon against the Austrian regiments. When combat starts, Prince Józef Poniatowski leads the charge, Rafał next to him. Shot from various positions of the camera in medium shots, the battle scenes show the physical act of killing in explicit detail. However, the battle is shot without a comfortable distance usually accomplished in long shots when a battle scene is depicted, so it appears to be a slaughter executed by legionnaires and Austrians alike. As if to cynically reinforce the realistic look of the battle, Wajda has it accompanied by a Polish national anthem in a slightly ironic arrangement. In doing so, the director almost sneers at the idealistic but misguided efforts of Polish warriors who fled the Austrian occupier at home to join the ranks of the supposed "freedom-fighter," Napoleon, somewhere outside Poland.

This momentous battle scene is followed by another one, the famous Battle of Saragossa, a famous siege that occurred during Napolean's Peninsular War. Krzysztof, a light cavalryman, announces his arrival with Captain Wyganowski. In conversing with the captain, Krzysztof learns that the town must be conquered the following day, and a discussion regarding Poland's liberation once again ensues. The battle starts with the storming of the town's gates, which, suddenly opened, reveal a group of strange figures, as if taken straight from medieval times: dressed in masks and strange attire, the townspeople try to stop the superstitious soldiers by frightening them out of their wits. Horribly laughing women, figures of devils and of Death, hideous beggars, all bring to mind images from Luis Bunuel's *Viridiana* (1961) and from Jeronim Bosch's paintings. The Polish soldiers manage to pass by and march on, but are indeed afraid to come too near the eerie figures.

The subsequent dynamic, powerful sequences show the soldiers attacking barricade after barricade along the narrow streets, conquering the town with relentless energy. Once Saragossa is taken, the spoils of war fall into the soldiers' hands: Women are raped, interspersed with scenes of feasting and gorging, slaughter, and the torture of civilians. These brief scenes are punctuated with dialogues between Krzysztof and Wyganowski, who, dazed and horrified, both renounce the soldiers' brutal actions. One of the most striking bits of conversation between the two takes place by the corpse of a young nun who has taken her own life rather than be raped by Napoleon's soldiers. In this sequence, Krzysztof learns the realities of war, and he also hears Wyganowski's decision to take a dismissal from the army. The final sequence of the section, however, shows Wyganowski's naked corpse outside the Saragossa cloister. Stripped of his uniform and insignia, he lies helpless in the drifting sand. Krzysztof asks some passing soldiers to bury the captain, but they refuse; they act as if he were a traitor and want nothing to do with him. In the end, Krzysztof tries ineffectually to bury the body. The officer's saber, perched at his head, is a symbol of yet another pointless death.

The next section shows the aftermath of the Saragossa battle: carts full of corpses drawn by mules, destroyed huts, starving and abused women and children, and dying horses. Krzysztof stumbles slowly over the rough terrain. His sick horse having fallen from a cliff, Krzysztof wanders about through the carnage and destruction resulting from the retreating armies. Meanwhile, his memories of the Samosierra charge come back to him; this flashback scene of the charge, added to the script by Wajda himself,[32] is one of the most spectacular cavalry charges in the history of Polish cinema. Shot from various angles, it shows riders charging barricades, jumping over cannons, and galloping madly in the Samosierra Ravine. The cleverly matched soundtrack contains a constant sound of hoofbeats. The sequence, while beautiful, is also rather grotesque in portraying young cavalrymen shouting "Hurrah!" only to fall from horses when hit by cannons. Horses without riders, hundreds of them, gallop aimlessly to the loud shouts of "Let the emperor live!"

The shouts blend into the battlefield after the Samosierra charge. In a field full of wounded, dead, and dying soldiers, Napoleon casually inspects the aftermath of the battle and allows the soldiers to applaud him for the victory. The splendor of the victory is belied by the images of crawling and moaning soldiers, one of whom is Krzysztof, who begs for an answer from Napoleon on the future of his campaign. The liberation of Poland is, of course, Krzysztof's main concern. Moaning softly, he proclaims his loyalty to Napoleon and to his own country. The section ends with solemn, inaccessible Napoleon walking among the soldiers, who are once again shouting "Let the emperor Live!" and "Vive La Pologne!"

The following parts of the film concentrate on Rafał, who, having been wounded, rests in a manor near Sandomierz. He shares the room with Gen. Sokolnicki. Rafał asks to serve as an aide-de-camp to the general, while the latter responds that the fate of the impending battle is doomed. Only a handful of soldiers have returned from Spain. Nevertheless, the optimistic and naïve Rafał wants to fight on. In the morning as they ready for battle at Sandomierz, the reality of their plight becomes clear, for they are now outnumbered by the Austrians roughly four-to-one. Rafał meets Gintułt near St. Jakub's Church, the prince wandering around and quietly observing the damage. At the beginning of the battle, Gintułt suddenly finds himself in the middle of the battle trying to protect the church. Sokolnicki refuses his request, however, and pushes the prince brutally aside. Hit by the legionary's bayonet, Gintułt utters the Masons' summons: *Do mnie dzieci, wdowy* ("Come to me, children and widows"). Hearing this, Rafał immediately comes to the assistance of his friend and Mason comrade.

This particular scene and the following one are instrumental in demonstrating Rafał's transformation from a naïve, enthusiastic young officer into a mature, prudent man. When he is ordered by the general to be executed for his insubordination, Rafał resignedly complies, having accepted the consequences of his measured actions. Suddenly, however, and rather ironically, an Austrian grenade saves him at the last minute. Rafał rescues Gintułt, and brings the prince and his orderly, Michcik, to the Olbromski family home, Tarniny (as seen at the beginning of the film in the *kulig* scene near the beginning of the film). The film's complicated time frame has now come full circle, and this scene marks the choice that Rafał makes between past and present: In saving Gintułt, he has declared his bond with the aristocratic past and the importance of tradition.

The link with tradition and the past is further reinforced in the following scenes in which Rafał rebuilds his family's burned house after an invasion by Austrian soldiers. When he raises a huge log, a fresh inscription of the year 1812 is clearly seen on it. The date is important because it marks the beginning of Napoleon's campaign in Russia. Shortly, a lone rider approaches, proving to be Krzysztof, Rafał's former friend and confidante. Krzysztof tells Rafał of Napoleon's war with Russia and tries to convince him to join. Rafał refuses to take part in another war, however, stating contemptuously that only three years have passed since the last one. Krzysztof, mature and solemn, leaves Rafał to his work. However, before much time has elapsed, Rafał changes his mind and joins his erstwhile friend as he crosses a river, suggestive of the earlier scene in which the same two young men fled the Austrians across the ice floes, and also representing the Napoleonic army's crossing of the Niemen River into Russia. Before crossing the river, Rafał looks back at his house—as he did in the beginning of the film, at the onset of Napoleon's campaign in Spain—as if trying to etch the image of the newly built manor in his mind.

The film ends with a scene that takes place on the Russian plains in winter, during Napoleon's doomed campaign (of the nearly 650,000 men who followed him to Moscow, less than 100,000 would ever return to their homes). Driven by horses on the white, barren, windswept plains, Napoleon looks solemnly ahead. A bizarre flashback recalls the time of Napoleon's glory at Samosierra; horrifying music accompanies Napoleon on the inspection of his troops as, in slow motion, he passes slowly on his horse along the proud soldiers. The return to reality in Russia is brutal and jarring: scattered troops, dying soldiers and horses, and, all around, death and decay. Suddenly, a ragged figure rises from the snow—it is Rafał, blind and clad in tatters. He tries to ask the direction from the passing riders, but no sound passes his lips. Once the pathos of this scene is established, the director again leads the viewer into another bizarre flashback of Napoleon's glory. Then, amid shouts of "Let the emperor live!" the screen fades to white.

This aesthetically beautiful and convincing adaptation of the great novel is a romantic tale of the fight for freedom of Poland, and for love, honor, and devotion to great ideals. The film also includes some iconographic national elements, lovingly portrayed by Wajda. Among them are the *kulig;* the courtly ball; the construction of a house, a symbol of national unity; the stork, a symbol of rejuvenation and new beginnings; romantic love; and an almost suicidal sacrifice of one's life for the future of Poland. All of these elements of the narrative and the visual symbols reiterate Wajda's strong national feelings, but unlike in the films *A Generation* and *Ashes and Diamonds,* they constitute a delicate fabric of the film's narrative, their cohesion disrupted by battles and conflicts in which the film protagonists willingly participate. However, despite this strong diegetic support for heroic action, the film is also full of criticism of Poles' naïveté and the gullible belief in the goodwill of others, such as Napoleon.

Consequently, *Ashes* was received with interest as a film adaptation of the famous novel, but also with criticism from politicians due to its uncompromising portrayal of Poles as naïve and idealistic victims of historical events. The most astonishing attack on the director concerns the film's ideology. In the 1960s, government authorities controlled all aspects of Polish cultural and social life, including the production of films. In the case of national classics, they were especially vigilant— they did not want controversial filmmakers to use classical texts for their own dissident causes. *Ashes* was no exception. Unfortunately, one of the most ardent critics was the influential former Chief of Police and Interior Affairs, Minister Mieczysław Moczar. Wajda comments: "[Party Secretary Mieczysław] Moczar and his men were only too happy to divide the nation—or at least the national artistic elite—into revisionists and true patriots. Thus, I became a 'revisionist,' which was not very helpful in my later work as [a] film-maker."[33]

In the extensive discussion on this subject in popular press, the subject of "revisionism" came up quite often. According to the party line, a true patriot would not question the validity of Polish participation in the Napoleonic wars: Poland's involvement has always been interpreted as a worthy romantic endeavor, consistent with Poles' approach to the liberation of their country at any cost. Wajda's "revisionist" interpretation, by pointing out the senselessness of this romantic effort, effectively sought to deconstruct the faithful integrity of Poles in fighting under Napoleon. Consequently, Wajda was forced to respond to many virulent remarks made by Moczar in the government press.

I would suggest that this attack on Wajda was politically motivated because of his Aesopian tactics in this film, the only tactics he could apply in the politically repressive 1960s. Themes of liberation and social protest could only be conveyed between the lines, so to speak, using historical films as a (relatively) safe medium. As Wajda recalls, "The censorship fiercely traced and eradicated all analogies to the current political situation."[34] Consequently, an historical drama proved a useful device for expressing thoughts—through analogy, metaphor, or any number of similar methods—about the state of politics in contemporary Poland. Thus, hiding behind Stefan Żeromski's acute criticism of Poles in the eighteenth century, with their aristocratic preoccupations and political naïveté, Wajda presented his own dissatisfaction with the state of his contemporary Poland at the time. However, his inherent criticism was immediately noted by Polish authorities.

Other less politically minded critics addressed the film's great length and seeming incoherency. Wajda himself sympathized with this line of criticism, for he found the novel extremely difficult to adapt. Revered in Poland not only for its criticism of the Polish approach to history but also for its romanticism, the book has always been widely discussed by literary and historical theoreticians and is well known to the Polish public at large. As Andrzej Żuławski recalls,

> Wajda complained about the tedious need to relate the events, 'the things that must be shown for the spectator to comprehend the story,' which took up miles of tape and left too little time for registering the current moment.... If a film is to occupy the viewers for three hours, should the camera be left free to wander, or should it stick to the hero?... Wajda is one of those strict rationalists who sculpt one solid scene after another in the solitude of their studios and impose them on nature, people and objects.[35]

In effect, the film constitutes an intricate mosaic of historical facts, romantic plots, and character developments (especially that of Rafał), shot against a panorama of artistically portrayed landscapes. Adding to the director's difficulties was the fact that *Ashes* was a black-and-white film shot on 35 mm with anamorphic lens: This format, as Wajda recalls, was very difficult to edit properly; in fact, despite some critics' comments that the film demonstrates a baroque aesthetics,[36] Wajda himself, ever his own worst critic, has always felt that *Ashes* does not form a unified visual whole.

Amid the finite criticism concerning, among other things, particular scenes (especially the final scene of the film), inadequate film techniques, the "shallow" psychological motivations of the protagonists, and the film's excessive aestheticism, critics were generally satisfied with the film. Stefan Morawski writes of "the tragedy of a generation swept into the heat of battle on the most noble intentions, only to die a senseless death";[37] for Stefan Żółkiewski, the film is a masterpiece of "both poetry and social and intellectual passion."[38] The film's adaptation from the novel is praised by Żółkiewski, Tadeusz Nowakowski, Wiktor Woroszylski, Kazimierz Wyka, Konrad Eberhardt, and Maria Kornatowska, the most prominent critics of the time.[39] On the other hand, Wajda's exaggerated style and the film's aestheticization of cruelty are matters of concern to Rafał Marszałek and Andrzej Lam, respectively.[40] Western critics generally had difficulty understanding the complexity of national symbolism, starting from the national anthem sung at the beginning of the film through to its rustic scenes; likewise, they tended to miss the cultural significance of the scenes depicting Polish manors and cities and ending with hopeless military charges. As a result, their reviews focused on the aesthetic qualities of the film, praising both its "realistic manner"[41] and its "Russian-style epic broadness," as well as its parallels to the Brazilian Cinema Novo in the passionate treatment of political issues.[42]

Ashes comments astutely upon Poland's historical improbabilities, and Wajda is not altogether wrongheaded in casting Poles as politically naïve, passionate romantics. Due to the novel's temporal and spatial scope, any sort of accurate cause-effect narrative proved to be impossible. Likewise, Rafał's character development as it occurs in the novel could not be appropriately presented. The film therefore takes the form of a series of historical tableaux that illustrate the major plot developments of the novel but are too historically complex to constitute obvious points in the plot. Nevertheless, in an heroic effort to produce an understandable plot, Wajda re-created Rafał as a protagonist with whom his audience could easily identify. This decision brought about two primary effects: (1) It made the film easier to understand, and (2) it launched the career of Daniel Olbrychski, one of the most gifted Polish actors of the decade.

The Gates to Paradise (1968)

Pleased with the cooperation of Jerzy Andrzejewski in making *Ashes and Diamonds* into a film, Wajda had long thought about adapting another of his books. As Andrzejewski comments in 1958,

> We are thinking about the next screenplay with Wajda. At present, I am writing a book entitled *The Gates to Paradise*. It is an historical novel tak-

ing place at the beginning of the 13th Century, at the end of the Crusades. The protagonists of the film are French children who have decided to initiate a similar crusade themselves. What fascinated me in this theme? The immutability of human feelings and longings—in this case, those of teenage children. These longings and dreams collapse when confronted with reality.[43]

Wajda wanted to make this film in Poland, in the snow-covered region of the country. It seemed to him that both the themes and the atmosphere presented in the book would look best in the context of a wintry Polish landscape. When the project was rejected by Polish film industry authorities, however, he decided on an international coproduction with Jointex Film in London and Avala Film in Belgrade, and this fact dictated the production conditions. In the former Yugoslavia, neither the climate nor the crew proved helpful. This strange, mystical film, unlike any other film produced by Wajda, nevertheless repeats some general themes present throughout his other films: those of loneliness and despair, betrayal and forgiveness. *The Gates to Paradise* is quite static and monotonous, with the camera following the youths from the left side only; yet, even with this static concept, it has many changes of shots. The film's score is composed entirely of medieval music.

The Gates to Paradise opens upon a beautiful landscape, with voice-over narration explaining the course of events up to the present. Several young people, the protagonists of the film, frolic in the fields and then slowly walk up the mountains. These sequences introduce the Children's Crusade from afar, seemingly basking in the beautiful composition of the frames. Jacob, the main protagonist and leader of the crusade, slowly approaches the others on horseback and looks at the walking youths with a solemn face. In the following scenes, a group of soldiers escorting wounded aristocrats from the Crusades ask the approaching youths where they are going. When they respond that they are going to Jerusalem, the soldiers and aristocrats laugh cruelly, relentlessly mocking the youths' endeavor.

However, the aging monk who accompanies the soldiers takes pity on the youngsters and decides to join their crusade. Later, as the only adult in this march, he becomes the youths' confidante and the narrator of their stories. In fact, the remainder of the film's diegesis is told via the conversations between the elderly, well-wishing, and sympathetic monk and the five youthful protagonists: Maud, Alexis, Robert, Blanche, and Jacob. Initially approaching him to discuss matters of faith, the youths soon open up, revealing their respective psychological problems. The first to approach the monk is Maud, who tells him about her early life in the village and of the sudden appearance of Jacob, the young "prophet" who appealed to the other four youths to join him in his crusade. She talks about Jacob's rejection of both her and Blanche's romantic advances, and about her indescribable passion and love for the young spiritualist. Finally, crying helplessly from emotional exhaustion after her confession, she leaves the monk.

Robert soon takes Maud's place: He tells the monk about his own love for Maud and his wish to marry her. In a flashback from Robert's point of view, the audience sees the developments in the village before the start of the crusade. Robert is a helpless voyeur to the joy and exhilaration Maud shows in the presence of the newly arrived Jacob. After Robert's tale is finished, the priest wants to speak with Jacob, but Alexis, who is nearer, intercepts the priest himself. Alexis describes the homosexual love affair he had with Count Ludovic; despite the fact that Ludovic used his position of power to win Alexis, the orphaned youth accepted the count's advances with gratitude and love. In a flashback, the spectator sees the unfolding love affair between the two, a romance diluted with elements of both guilt and sadomasochism. Suddenly, though, Jacob appeared on the scene; Ludovic accidentally met the beautiful young Jacob in a shepherd's hut and a love encounter between the two soon ensued. Later, Alexis, realizing that the count had been unfaithful to him, did not save the count's life when Ludovic accidentally slipped on his horse when crossing a raging river. The perplexed and dismayed monk listens to Alexis's admission of guilt and realizes that the youth has committed a grave crime. He now wants to hear Jacob's version of the story, so he calls the young "prophet" to his side.

Jacob talks of his meeting with the count and confirms Alexis's version of the tale. He talks about his conflict with himself, his problems with the admiring young women, but also reveals the fact that Ludovic convinced him to lead the children's crusade. Thus, it is not the boy's religious convictions that have made him a prophet, but manipulation by the powerful count that led him to his current role. At this point, overwhelmed with disgust and sadness, the monk does not wish to hear any more confessions from any of the youths, for he realizes that innocence and religious faith are not their virtues, and that they go to Jerusalem for reasons other than spiritual—their all-too-human feelings of betrayal, love, hatred, jealousy, and loneliness. The monk leaves them to their own fate, shouting loudly that Jacob is no prophet. The children's crusade leaves him sitting in a deep ditch and its participants slowly climb the hills, while the monk sits alone and unheard.

Wajda considers *The Gates to Paradise* one of his worst films. Shot in the former Yugoslavia with a non-Polish production crew, the film seems pretentious and unconvincing in its presentation of both the story and the feelings of the protagonists. As Wajda recalls in *Wajda Films,* he experienced innumerable problems during the film's production. Photographs of Wajda during the production of this film generally depict a person obviously upset, presumably by the slow pace of production and by the numerous problems he had during that time. Wajda was sure of neither the precision of the dialogues translated into English, nor of the expressive power of his young actors. As he remarks, "I felt trapped and confined. I worked hard, trying each day to spark more effort from myself and from the cast alike, but the loose mob of people who had never worked [in film] before resisted my demands. Each new day made our project smaller, weaker and more trivial ..."[44]

In a revealing letter to Jerzy Andrzejewski, dated 23 February 1967, Wajda expresses his dissatisfaction with the film (which was nevertheless not corroborated by film critics later on):

> You ask about the film. It is not good. All in all, neither religious nor anti. Nor a work of art—but one can not say that it isn't at all, either. Nothing shocking—yet full of filthy discussion. Boring—yet watchable. To sum up: "Mediocrity which was to be greatness." Why so? For a number of reasons. I think I should start with a screenplay. In order to convey the message of your book, the story would have to have been completely dismantled, re-thought and re-written.... So much for the screenplay, now it's my turn to take the blame: I was unable to invent or add anything, continuously busy holding together all the existing elements while they shot out this way and that, like live fish from my hands.[45]

Not every critic was as hard on the film as the director himself, however. Robert Benayoun, for example, had this to say about the film: "Direct and bold, condemnatory and yet wonderfully lyrical, the film has become a bit lost in the customary cinema distribution channels, but is bound to be fished out by lovers of film art interested in this unusual chapter in the great director's career."[46] However, others, both in Poland and elsewhere, noted the discrepancy between the text of Andrzejewski's novel and the film. Claude Michel Cluny talks about Wajda's betrayal of the original "by remaining faithful to it—an eternal problem—the fiasco of translating from the language of one art into that of another";[47] Bolesław Michałek calls the film "a limp piece of filmmaking, but worst of all a completely damp squib as far as striking any contemporary sparks was concerned."[48] Still, while Wajda tackled and did not entirely overcome certain difficulties in this film, his efforts are nonetheless masterful. The film's beautiful images and composition only reinforce its crucial questions of love and betrayal, which are handled with maturity and understanding.

After making *The Gates to Paradise* and the controversial and highly criticized *Ashes*, Wajda concentrated on projects of a more personal nature. This period in his life is characterized by films in various genres. First off, he produces *Roly Poly*, a humorous film made for TV based on Stanisław Lem's short story; next, he produces the important self-reflexive film, *Everything for Sale*. During this period, Wajda also tries his hand at comedy in *Hunting Flies*, which also incorporates elements arising from his personal relationships with women.

Roly Poly (1968)

A playful and amusing science-fiction film, *Roly Poly* is noteworthy in particular because Wajda used the comedic talent of Bogumił Kobiela, one of the greatest Polish comedic actors of the latter part of the twentieth century, who played the lead roles—those of race-car driver Tomasz Fox and, later in the film, of his brother Richard. The film is the story of various people who die in car accidents and whose bodies serve as sources for transplantation experiments. Tomasz is one such victim. Unwittingly anticipating many of the ethical questions related to the problems of organ transplantation, Stanisław Lem touches upon crucial moral issues in a humorous way.

The film starts with Tomasz and his codriver/navigator Richard exchanging good-byes with their family. The brothers get into their race car amid the exuberant laughter and shouts of the excited family members and race off into the darkness. Swift swish pans follow the car and the smiling faces of the drivers. The race goes on until there is a loud crash signaling an accident; to reinforce the film's amusing atmosphere, Wajda uses a comic-book drawing of the word *Bum* (Crash) in the middle of the screen rather than showing the car crash. This unusual and uncharacteristic insertion, completely foreign to Wajda's otherwise realistic style, introduces a moment of playfulness and irony.

The next sequence opens in a bright, clean hospital where attendants carry the victims of the crash along on gurneys. Only then do the credits begin to roll, accompanied by jazzy, lighthearted music and shots of Warszawa taken from within the racing car. Thereafter, a lawyer enters the Stalowy (Steel) Hospital and is approached by strange figures with four eyes. He is led to a hospital room where Richard exercises while suspended in a cagelike structure; however, Richard is now played by Kobiela. (Tomasz's face/head has been transplanted to Richard, so Kobiela actually ends up playing both parts.) Although he had already showed his comedic talent in *Ashes and Diamonds* (in which he played the part of the opportunist Drewnowski) and in Edward Munk's *Zezowate szczęście* (*Bad Luck*, 1960), in this film Kobiela truly shines.

Richard proceeds to explain his problem to the lawyer: The insurance company does not want to pay his brother's life insurance because Tomasz is not completely dead—his body parts in fact live on in Richard's body (as well as in others') thanks to a series of transplant operations performed by Dr. Burton and the staff of this unusual hospital. In the surreal atmosphere of the bright hospital, beautiful young nurses and handsome doctors running in all directions, Burton's explanations sound unlikely as well. He explains that he is not concerned with the identity of the accident victims, nor does he care whose body parts he must borrow to create a "complete" human being. In an attempt to explain his transplantation policy to the bewildered lawyer,

Burton explains that humans should get used to the discrepancy between the body and the mind. Of course, this mildly amusing philosophical and political comment was made in the 1960s, when Socialism prevailed in Poland and when poor living conditions were compensated by relative freedom of expression; this simple fact advanced the film to a more important political statement comparable to those made by the Polish masters of the grotesque and the political parable, such as Sławomir Mrożek, Jerzy Grotowski, and Tadeusz Różewicz.

When the lawyer leaves the hospital, he is approached by several young people offering their organs for money. The lawyer looks for an explanation from the insurance agent, who launches into a rather convoluted monologue about the "percentile existence"[49] of the deceased Tomasz. In a series of amusing exchanges the lawyer shares (with the insurance agent, with Richard himself, and with Tomasz's wife) the legal and social improbabilities of Richard's existence and his rights to his brother's insurance gradually become clear.

After undergoing several transplant procedures at the hospital, Richard decides to try his luck at racing again. Again, he has an accident. This time, he comes back to his lawyer as a man with a woman's soul: he cries often, takes out his powder-box during the meeting, and even flirts with the lawyer. In an ongoing series of transplantation mishaps, he becomes a different person yet again, and several other people sue him for their transplanted body parts. Richard eventually turns entirely into a woman—even his psychoanalyst no longer recognizes him because his behavior changes so drastically. The film ends with Richard visiting the lawyer as his former replacement codriver/navigator, Ali Stevens. Although the face still belongs to Richard, his mind is wholly Ali's: The transplantation of the soul is complete this time. The lawyer and Ali/Richard exchange final looks. Ali, unaware of his body's former personas, has come to the lawyer because he knows him personally. However, this third transplantation is too much for the lawyer to endure, and the film ends with a shot of his disbelieving face. Wajda does not go any more deeply into the moral and social consequences of transplantation than to produce a lighthearted, amusing, and very short (thirty-nine-minute) film. He concentrates on the improbability of the events and only hints at the deeper philosophical connotations of Lem's story. Such connotations did not evade him altogether, though.

This small film attests to the director's skill at constructing a convincing yet highly amusing story. *Roly Poly* is also a rare example of a literary adaptation that managed to please both the critics and the author of the source text, Lem. The following correspondence between the director and the story's author attests to this fact:

Dear Sir:
Two days ago I watched *Roly Poly* on television. Both your work and the actors' as well as the set decorations seemed very good to me.... The

imminent, indefinite 'future' has been very cleverly constructed, especially considering the scant means you had at your disposal. The best scenes are, in my opinion, those in the hospital and the insurance agency, while the one at the psychoanalyst's seemed to me to be slightly too exaggerated, i.e., more grotesque than the other two.[50]

Everything for Sale (1969)

In January of 1967, Wajda's favorite actor, Zbigniew Cybulski, died suddenly. Wajda had long considered Cybulski to be one of the greatest Polish actors and employed him in two of his films and also in many theatrical plays he directed. In this film, Cybulski "appears" as a nonexistent but beloved figure. *Everything for Sale* is a fascinating account of the director's effort to produce a film about the deceased actor; the entire film shows or tries to reveal the mystery of the legendary actor, who was both loved and hated by everybody. In the process, *Everything for Sale* became a film about the production of films, an astonishing account of the director's work with his actors and the medium itself—a self-reflexive film about the making of films.

Unlike the screenplays for Wajda's other films, the script for this film was written by Wajda himself. He has often said that he considers *Everything for Sale* to be his most personal film. The film starts from a sequence restaging the fatal accident in which Cybulski lost his life; while jumping onto a train in Wrocław, he slid under it and was crushed under its wheels. In that scene, Andrzej, the Film Director *within* the film (played by Andrzej Łapicki, a well-known Polish actor), and Elżbieta Czyżewska, the deceased actor's wife in the film, suddenly realize that her husband is dead. The Film Director is plainly Wajda's alter ego, a fact Łapicki conveys through his distant, cool, but engaged acting. This realistic scene, referring to the real past event, is suddenly interrupted by the Film Director scrambling out of a hole on the platform and shouting "How was the scene?"

Everything for Sale seems to take place on two planes: that of the past, when the actor was alive, and that of the present, in which the director and his crew are making a film about the legendary Cybulski. When Andrzej and Ela talk about the scene and Andrzej's reaction to it, they mention the real feelings of the deceased actor; at a certain moment, for instance, Ela says of him that "he also was nervous when the scene was shot," as he was nervous when a similar scene was shot in *A Generation*. Of course, by this she refers to the scene in which Cybulski played a small role—that of a young man jumping onto a moving train. Similarly, Daniel Olbrychski, playing himself in the film (a young actor waiting for his chance to replace the famous Zbigniew) clearly refers to the real Zbigniew when he talks about the deceased actor in the film: about his metal cup, his behavior, his tardiness, and so on.

Beata, the Film Director's former wife in the film, is played by Beata Tyszkiewicz, Wajda's former wife in reality; her character is disgusted by the fact that the actress Elżbieta Czyżewska—again, the actor's wife *in the movie*—is also to play the part of his *real* wife, Ela, in the film. Beata questions the ethics of this casting decision, saying, "This is your film, but our lives. I do not know whether you have the right to mix everything like this." Thus, the Film Director's ex-wife (and, ironically, the real director's ex-wife) explains the complexity of the Film Director's life, in which reality and fantasy mix seamlessly together. Of course, the fact that all the main characters use their real names in the film stretches the irony of the situation that much further (not to mention the fact that Łapicki, as the Film Director in the film, while not portraying his real-life self, still shares the name of the actual director of the film).

In one of the most striking sequences of the film, the characters' reality and the actors' reality are almost entirely juxtaposed. Ela comes to Beata's house looking for Zbigniew. Beata, with her young child, is not surprised by Ela's intrusion; she knows Zbigniew can never be trusted and often disappears for days at a time, for she was also his former lover and now wants nothing to do with him. The two women exchange several accusations and bitter remarks toward both Zbigniew and one another. Ela sits on Beata's bed, drinks vodka, and tells Beata that she had tried to make herself similar to Beata in a desperate attempt to win Zbigniew's love. The following scene, in which Ela takes off her false eyelashes and loosens her hair, is as powerful as the doubled image in Ingmar Bergman's *Persona* (1966) or that in Margarethe Von Trotta's *Marianne and Juliane/The German Sisters* (1981), where the sisters look at one another in jail. Shortly, Ela disappears into the bathroom and proceeds to slit her wrists.

Immediately, though, the constructedness of the moment and the presence of the real director become palpable: As the camera zooms back from the bathroom, the audience sees the crew that has just filmed the whole scene. In this particular scene, Wajda's awareness of the French New Wave is clear. Jean Luc Godard and his colleagues were known to Polish artists and cinephiles, their intellectual films were admired though reluctantly copied. In this attempt at applying the French New Wave philosophy, Wajda produces a self-reflexive scene in which he comments on the role of the director in exploring various facets of reality and on the process of filmmaking itself.

The crew, the director, and the actors wait for Zbigniew to arrive on the set—but of course he will never come because he is already dead. Beata, Ela, Andrzej, and Daniel constantly wonder where he is, just as they all had so many times in real life. In its self-referentiality, *Everything for Sale* crosses many lines. At one point, a conversation between Ela and Daniel about Zbigniew's whereabouts takes place against huge photos of Zbigniew himself. Despite the fact that the name of the missing actor is never mentioned in the film, Cybulski's images appear on billboards, signs, photographs, and the like throughout the film, which make his presence/absence conspicuous. In another scene, for example, when Beata and Ela reach the latter's apartment, Ela refers casually to the film *Everything for Sale*. Next, we see her entering the apartment, relieved that the light in the bathroom indicates her husband's presence; after a while, having delivered a vicious diatribe full of threats and accusations, she realizes that Zbigniew is not in the bathroom at all.

In the following sequences, Wajda changes genres from fiction film to documentary. The scenes shift constantly between documenting this particular film being made and documenting the process of filmmaking in general. In one scene, the famous Polish actor Bogumił Kobiela comments on the cynicism of filmmakers and on the impossibility of capturing the comedic essence of a human being. This sequence leads us directly to a party where many young filmmakers and actors scrutinize Ela with amusement and incredulity: They know all about Zbigniew and his philandering, and none are surprised by his long disappearances. In this scene, Ela dances energetically, nervous and alone, not looking at anyone around her. The dance is shot dynamically, with rapid zooms of the camera in and out, focusing on her tense face, a nervous smile pasted on. When Ela leaves the party, she has a long conversation with the Film Director Andrzej, revealing the personal drama of an unloved and unwanted wife who wants and needs to be loved—by anyone, even by the Film Director himself. After the party, several drunken people, along with Ela and the Film Director, come upon a merry-go-round; in a moment of revenge for their earlier callousness, Ela turns the motor on and watches the party-goers spinning helplessly. (As well, this scene links the topos of the merry-go-round to that occurring in two of Wajda's other films, *A Generation* and *Holy Week*.)

Next, Daniel appears, playing the fiddle, while Beata and Ela engage in a conversation about the man they both loved so desperately. Beata tells of a man who always seemed lost and unhappy, wearing a rucksack and sneakers, always immature, running from life's many responsibilities. Still trying to find Zbigniew, the women drive to the cultural hall in a small town, where he supposedly went to a lecture. There they learn that he left the hall with a young woman—an obvious hint that he may be cheating again. From their car windows, the women see the winter landscape, galloping horses, and birches, all of which constitute an intertextual mosaic accompanying the dialogue and the many exchanges of glances between the two women, both of whom know Zbigniew intimately, and the young girl, apparently Zbigniew's most recent love interest.

Suddenly, a radio communiqué is heard over the car's speakers: Cybulski is reported to have died that day at Wrocław Railway Station.

The faces of the two startled women are frozen behind the car window as they absorb the tragic news in complete silence. This emotionally charged scene, eerily silent, is followed by a shot of galloping horses, which lead us directly to the scene of the actor's death just being shot by the crew nearby. Ela and Beata run along the railway tracks to see police officers taking measurements at the death scene. When the huge locomotive passes by, their faces are seen through the passing wheels, helpless and solemn. In the next scene, reality and imagination mix even further. In the Ateneum Theater, where Cybulski worked as an actor, the Film Director complains that he now has nobody to work with anymore. In this way, Wajda refers to his own successful career as a prolific theater director. In the subsequent sequence, the scene of the actor's funeral—which is staged realistically, shot in grainy black and white—all the wives, lovers, friends, and colleagues of the deceased actor are present, yet despite the realism, they all somehow appear as strange, life-like apparitions.

From this point forward in the film, the actors talk about the legendary Cybulski, who is of course no longer with them. Bobek, Andrzej, and Daniel concur that Zbigniew deserves a film about himself—"about Zbigniew without him," as Bobek puts it. However, in the manner of Fellini's $8\frac{1}{2}$ (1963), the film they are in becomes a film less about Cybulski than was projected and more about the director and about the making of films in general. Zbigniew's tin cup and leather jacket become mere film props, albeit props that drive the story: Both objects are passed on to Daniel, who will become Wajda's next favorite actor, cast in many well-known films throughout the 1970s.

The final sequences in *Everything for Sale* show moments from Wajda's own life, presented in an autobiographical format: scenes of work on the set; of his cooperation with his technical staff; of conversations about Zbigniew's imagined, unwritten screenplays; and of the pleasures and torments of filmmaking. Wajda's favorite paintings by famed Polish artist Andrzej Wróblewski appear suddenly, and then the director's famous statement is heard, mouthed by the Film Director: "Don't you think that I can fall in love with another actor again?" The Film Director then chooses Daniel as a replacement for the film he had planned to make with Zbigniew. The final scene shows Daniel running after the herd of galloping horses seen earlier; he is young, energetic, and full of life. Yet his image becomes blurred at the very end, almost indistinguishable, unfocused. His face is reduced to a fuzzy blob on the screen, a blurred image that reflects both of the identity of "the chosen actor" and on the essence and the texture of the film itself.

In this intriguing film, Wajda tackles several issues including the personality of an actor; filmmaking as both creative and human processes; and the ambiguous border between the fictional and the real. This nostalgic film is unconventional in its treatment of both content and form.

First, it is the only film made by Wajda without a clearly unfolding narrative. Second, it seems to privilege contemporary, documentary images over the static, well-composed scenes of his earlier fiction films. Wajda creates Godardian metaphors by using such tactics as blurred images, slanted lines, and faces seen through window panes, which add a moment of freshness to his efforts to present the impossible: a love for an actor who is no longer alive.

These tactics have been noted by critics; for instance, Krzysztof Teodor Toeplitz describes the film as an inventive way of saying good-bye to the deceased colleague:[51]

> The situation gives Wajda the occasion for confronting legend with reality, but he is aware of the danger of facile, shallow "debunking"; the film is far more complex than that. Instead, Wajda is interested in collecting the gestures, impressions and various incidental fragments of personality or image which the dead actor scattered among the living and showing how these "crumbs" constitute an awkward "gift," like some heirloom one is dearly attached to and yet can do nothing with.[52]

Other critics noted the self-centered cynicism of the director, who freely employs images of the deceased actor in order to present only himself. While Louis Marcorelles notes the film's self-reflexive "coquetry,"[53] Philip Strick refers ironically to the film's title when he says that "the film is a definition of the film director in general and of Andrzej Wajda in particular.... Everything they had (or imagined they had) was for sale and they sold it; now Wajda even sells Cybulski's death, and his own loss of direction, for the sake of the cinema."[54]

Yet Strick's criticism, which might be harsh, only highlights the shift in this film from the presentation of the deceased actor to the self-reflexive focus on the director himself. The subject of the film—the deceased actor—is no longer under scrutiny once the director realizes that he is interested more in the way the film is made, in the ethics and the realities of filmmaking, the cynicism of the profession itself, than in a truthful presentation of the actor. Similar arguments have been raised by Krzysztof Mętrak, Zygmunt Kałużynski, and Joanna Guze,[55] among others.

The similarity of *Everything for Sale* to Fellini's *8½* is evident in the many self-reflexive moments in the film, such as the scene mentioned by Penelope Houston, in which the director cuts his forehead on his windshield when forced to brake suddenly: "He immediately gets out to photograph his own blood-stained face—a masochistic comment on life as art, based on an awareness that all that 'real' blood has been put on by the make-up artist."[56] The film's self-reflexivity is also unprecedented particularly by comparison to Wajda's other films. As Toeplitz mentions, Wajda "for the first time ... examines formal problems which have preoccupied the world avant-garde for some years," especially

"the question of authenticity of film as a document of reality, as well as
the question of moral and intellectual justification for telling invented
and often conventionalized stories about non-existent characters."[57]
While Wajda deals with his own fascinations and exasperations in his
work with Cybulski over the years, he also embarks on an examination
of difficult moral questions related to the relation between the real and
the imagined.

Upon its release, this film hit a nerve especially with relatively sophisticated audiences, who immediately recognized the influences of
the French New Wave movement, and of Godard in particular: its in-
consistent, choppy narrative; the mixture of fiction and documentary
genres; the self-reflexive presence of crew and director, camera and
lights, and so on. There is also a certain blandness and uncommunica-
tiveness in the actors' facial expressions, as if, in a truly Godardian
fashion, the actors have distanced themselves from the roles they play
(despite the roles being *themselves*). Yet Ela's theatrics and Beata's cold
response to her behavior, for instance, make the film ambiguous and
strange; in his effort to recall the memory of the deceased actor, Wajda
tries to portray Zbigniew candidly but also to distance himself from the
painful and unbearable fact of his death. Finally, one has the distinct
feeling that the emotions presented in the film are too personal and too
revealing about the director himself.

Hunting Flies (1969)

Hunting Flies is one of the rare films in Wajda's filmography in which
the director shows his comedic talents. The script of this amusing film
is based on Janusz Głowacki's short story "Hunting Flies." Głowacki,
known as a great comic satirist, presented his readers with the Poland
of the 1960s, along with the ambitions of this society and all the dilemmas and uncertainties that accompanied the nation's newly emerging
economies. In the 1960s, Poland reached a level of modest economic
prosperity, called by some *gomułkowszczyzna* ("Gomułka time," referring to Władysław Gomułka, the First Secretary of the Communist Party
at that time), wherein Poles had access to basic life necessities but could
not reach a living standard comparable to the one enjoyed in Western
democracies. As Norman Davies comments, although Gomułka "was
empowered to make a series of strategic concessions to popular demands and to permit the three specific features of the Polish order—an
independent Catholic Church, a free peasantry, and a curious blend of
bogus political pluralism," he did not abandon the idea of "the more
orthodox model of socialist society."[58] The film illustrates the dilemmas
of the representatives of the intelligentsia who would like to live a normal, successful life but are limited by the ideological and economic

restrictions of Socialism. The time of the 1960s is portrayed as the time of the grotesque and the bizarre. At the same time, the film seems to reflect at least indirectly on Wajda's personal problems in his marriage with actress Beata Tyszkiewicz, whom he divorced in 1969.

The design of the credits and the film's musical score are very contemporary, a trend Wajda began with *Innocent Sorcerers* and continued in *Everything for Sale*. The protagonist, Włodek, and his wife and his ten-year-old son live with his parents-in-law in Warszawa, dwelling in a typical small, crowded apartment—a common enough scenario in the 1960s. The director immediately introduces the reality of the cramped apartment by using close takes, medium shots, and close-ups. Furthermore, a journalistic account of the fishing industry plays on the TV in the background, and in this way Wajda metaphorically introduces the elements of claustrophobia and dread: Like fish out of water, Poles have no way out of their current horrible way of life; similarly, the black-and-white television screen introduces another enclosed space—that of the television itself, as if confining the space of the protagonists even further. Yet, at the same time, the television leads the spectator and the apartment's inhabitants out of the cramped space, to some "otherwhere." It therefore also provides a possibility for maneuver and escape.

The protagonist, Włodek, is a library clerk in his thirties with some ambitions as a writer and translator. Włodek is first seen working on his typewriter and reading aloud the Russian texts he is translating into Polish. Amid the clutter, the conversations of his parents-in-law, and the constant complaints of his wife, Hanka, he is trying desperately to concentrate and do some work. Both his wife and her mother are vituperative, overbearing women, complaining loudly and constantly about Włodek's ineptitude. The mother-in-law suspects him of breaking her precious teacups, his wife berates him for his inability to get them a larger apartment, and both his son and his father-in-law ignore him completely. To add to this situation of overwhelming oppression, Hanka, a nurse, periodically gives Włodek painful shots of vitamins.

The delicate love story soon to follow is shot against the backdrop of the social context of Warszawa life in the 1960s. Indeed, following Włodek out into the street, the camera takes in several draft dodgers talking in front of a students' club, exchanging remarks about women, cars, and money, cracking jokes and enjoying themselves. Włodek smokes a cigarette and waits for his friend, a "new rich" colleague who will take him to the club. The wandering camera, changing lights, and various positions in which the shots are taken create an atmosphere of nervous excitement and fun.

Before long, Irena, a student at Warszawa University's Polish Philology Department, enters the club and is immediately approached aggressively by two young men. Włodek sees their attempted assault of the young woman and hits one of them, allowing her to pass safely. Irena's face is shown only in passing; she is almost an ethereal apparition of femininity when compared to the two overwhelming women with whom Włodek is forced to live. To express her gratitude, Irena starts a conversation with Włodek, who looks upon her with admiration. They dance closely, clearly fascinated. Włodek eventually takes Irena back to her apartment, which she shares with her aunt. In contrast to the claustrophobic space of his own apartment, the space in which Irena appears is open, brightly lit, and inviting. After some time spent in this intellectually and sexually attractive space, Włodek returns to his family afraid that they have noticed his lengthy absence. However, no one seems to have paid any attention to his disappearance. His father-in-law watches a TV program about bears, his mother-in-law and his wife are interested in their own affairs. When his wife addresses him, she talks only about a bigger apartment for the family.[59]

To add to Włodek's feelings of inadequacy and helplessness, he is also belittled by his pregnant female superior where he works, at the Palace of Culture;[60] when he asks for a raise, she explains that he cannot get it because he has not yet got his graduate studies diploma. Overpowered by his place of work, with its high ceilings and gaudy interiors, and always in need of explaining his motives to himself and to everyone around him, Włodek feels helpless. When he later goes to meet Irena at the university gates, he suddenly feels apprehensive and shy and does not approach her; Irena looks for Włodek, but then passes by him, not noticing his small figure. Włodek again returns home only to be met by the same oppressive scenario of wife and mother-in-law accusing the men in the house of breaking teacups or of other such inanities. As if in response to the constant nagging, Włodek's father-in-law catches flies on long strips of adhesive celluloid, a common contraption at the time. The act of catching flies (which gives the film its title) is the response of emasculated males to domination by overpowering women.[61]

The next time Włodek tries to find Irena, he approaches her openly and they go to her apartment together. She immediately takes control of the conversation—and of Włodek. She tells him that, with his intelligence, he should seek another career. His private life, his relationship with his wife and parents-in-law, and his monumental unhappiness all fall under Irena's scrutiny. Wanting to see Włodek as "manly," she persuades him to take part in a physical altercation during their walk in the street. Włodek feebly protects the victim, doing so primarily for Irena, who wants to mold him into a "real man." Later, they talk about new possibilities for him, such as the translation of Russian poems into Polish.

On returning to his home, the anxious Włodek again fears the reaction of his family to his absence. Nothing happens, though, as usual. In a routine manner, Hanka tries to make love with him while talking about some household errands. When she falls asleep, Włodek begins to translate poems, as he has promised Irena he would do. The next day, in one of the most amusing sequences of the film, Włodek is summoned to collect a prize at the Warszawa police department for his actions in the altercation the previous day. In an elaborately arranged police department hall, Włodek receives a crystal vase—a common official present handed out for good deeds—together with a typically unimaginative official proclamation for his help in "reigning in the hooligan elements" *(za poskramianie elementów chuligańskich)*. This lengthy sequence clearly aims at making fun of the detested militia, parodying their low intelligence, their cynicism, and their willingness to obey party officials blindly.

Irena waits for Włodek and takes him to her apartment. Alone with him, she undresses suddenly and tells him that it is time to end with the bourgeois prejudices. While they make love, she talks about philosophy, linguistics, and their future plans. She then assesses his translated poems critically, dresses him up as an "intellectually awakening artist," and tells him that it would be good for his career to make appearances in certain social circles. When Włodek returns home, life goes on as usual. His mother-in-law looks for broken dinnerware, his father-in-law watches television and catches flies, Hanka complains about the apartment, and Włodek's son talks to himself. This time, however, Włodek does not care whether they have noticed his absence and quietly falls asleep on the balcony.

In another scene highlighting the damaging role of women in men's lives, Daniel is Irena's former lover, a competent—but not gifted—sculptor who tries to produce masterpieces amid the squalor of a studio that Irena rented for him. Drowning his discontent and frustration in alcohol, he waits endlessly for Irena, whom he credits with saving his sanity and his creativity. To his admonitions at her sudden appearance, Irena responds that Daniel has ceased to interest her and promptly throws him out of the apartment to make way for her new man. When Daniel leaves the studio crying, Włodek passes him on the stairs; resignedly, compassionately, he shakes the broken sculptor's hand. In the studio, while Włodek thinks only about making love, Irena pesters him about writing and then, when he does so, controls his every word.

Events take a somewhat different turn when Irena and Włodek go for a walk—or rather, when Irena takes Włodek for a walk. Suddenly, the unhappy Włodek tries to climb a fence in a desperate attempt to escape her; he fails. In the following sequences, he attends a fashionable party in Nieporęt, to which Irena takes him in an attempt to arrange some lucrative deals for him. Pushing him to make contacts for himself, Irena has an eye only on potential clients or influential people, and not on Włodek himself. In an amusing sequence conveying the cynicism and opportunism of the new Polish intelligentsia, Włodek feels lost and uncertain. Disgusted with and uncertain of himself, Włodek wants only to leave the party. While Irena is involved in her wheeling and dealing, constantly on the lookout for contacts and people who could be of use to her, and finally surrounded by men with whom she will dance in a surrealistic dance, Włodek looks for a way out. Finally, unceremoniously pushed away by an influential and fashionable writer, he is promptly thrown out of the hotel room by a female publisher.

Later, back in the apartment, the atmosphere of distress and anguish escalates when Irena walks around Włodek with her hands covered in blood: The chicken she is cutting in half, when seen through his terrified eyes, seems to transform into Włodek himself. Włodek tries to write poetry, but cannot do it in this atmosphere. Finally, humiliated by the female editor of another journal who says, "if a cucumber does not sing, it means that it is not able to" (*"jeżeli ogórek nie śpiewa to widocznie nie może"*), Włodek hears from Irena that she has another idea for him—instead of poetry, he should study sculpture. In a dream, Włodek tries to strangle her; in the following dream sequence, he hides her body in a sewer pipe.

The final sequence of the film shows Włodek back at his home, safe and happy once more. However, to his bewilderment, Hanka has changed: Her clothes, eyeglasses, and behavior now all remind him of Irena. While Włodek is happy to be home, Hanka has apparently turned into an ambitious woman with high hopes for Włodek. In a final scene of terror and distress, Włodek dreams about the three suffocating women in his life surrounding him amid a mass of dead flies. Hanka, her mother, and Irena, all wearing the same huge eyeglasses, dance a strange dance; finally, they push him down into the celluloid strips with dead flies stuck to them. Only Irena's white teeth can be seen, glistening in the bright lamplight.

Hunting Flies is a satire on Polish society and its reality in the 1960s. It is also a deeply touching film indirectly commenting on the director's frustrations related to women in his life at that time. Włodek becomes Wajda's helpless "alter ego," the representative of emasculated man who felt helpless when confronted by emancipated, liberated, and educated women. Whether based on personal worries or not, the film clearly portrays women in a negative light, thus also presenting Wajda as a subconsciously misogynist filmmaker. The film portrays men as victims of women who are visibly superior, physically bigger and stronger than the men on the screen and who are also more "masculine" than men in their level of education, their resourcefulness, and their stamina. Although presented as a satire, the men's victimization is biased in the film, portrayed from a position of patriarchy that assumes the superiority of men from the start. Reinforcing this position is the heavy-handed treatment of this satire, which portrays all women as grotesque and unreal, cruel and inhuman in their treatment of men in the film.

In reviews of the film, most critics at the time suggested that the satirical approach has never been Wajda's forte.[62] Others point out to the fact that, in the tradition of the satiric pamphlet or feuilleton (which is also the specialty of two most highly respected weeklies of that era, *Kultura* and *Polityka*), Wajda tried to produce a "sarcastic pamphlet" on the sixties.[63] Years later, Mateusz Werner suggests that, in *Hunting Flies*, Wajda shows a different face, that of "the chronicler of the trivial and the commonplace who hunts human 'flies' in order to encase them in his celluloid ambers."[64] Certainly, when seen from the perspective of his other films, *Hunting Flies* is clearly a testimony to the emptiness, selfishness, and meanness of his contemporaries engaged in their busy career pursuits.

Piotr Borowiec admires this film, considering it a surrealist work reminiscent of the theater of the absurd: "Almost every response in the film is ambiguous or devoid of logical sense, but the plot is excellent. The film shows a powerful criticism of the snobbery of some pseudo-intellectual circles and an apt parody of a specifically Polish form of matriarchy (according to which the wife holds her husband strongly underfoot)."[65] Granted, *Hunting Flies* is patently different from Wajda's overpowering war films, with their rich images and heartrending plots. In his attempt to produce a satiric film, Wajda had to create a different aesthetics. Toeplitz states that "[Wajda] no longer attempts beautiful images intended to suggest through their intensity some profound meaning. Film language now serves modestly to create a reality which is conventionalized enough to escape the demands of mimetic verisimilitude, while remaining sufficiently realistic and convincing to prevent an immersion in illusion."[66]

In his attempt to create symbolic images in *Hunting Flies*, Wajda is apparently too literal, too obvious, and too sarcastic. This begs the question of whether he was not excessively influenced by his own personal problems. Engulfed by divorce proceedings from his wife Beata while making this film, he seems to have been unable to distance himself personally from the script. The result is a pointedly and poignantly misogynist portrayal of women. As Toeplitz notes, "Wajda is interested in the paradoxical, often psychologically novel situations which result from the headlong emancipation of women, accompanied as it is by widespread emasculation and weakening of man's position."[67] Wajda, whose portrayal of women is generally rather outdated—in fact unfriendly and predominantly misogynistic in many of his films (with notable exceptions in *The Young Ladies of Wilko* and *Man of Marble*)—reveals an openly hostile misogyny in *Hunting Flies*. He opens the quintessential feminist can of worms with this film, which is invariably referred to when his other depictions of women are discussed or questioned.[68]

The films produced in the 1960s reveal Wajda's versatility as a film director: He is capable of presenting grave issues *(Samson* and *Siberian Lady Macbeth)* and, to a lesser degree, light and humorous ones *(Roly Poly* and *Hunting Flies)*. His portrayal of young people is open-minded and fresh *(Innocent Sorcerers* and *Love at Twenty)*; he presents young Poles as innocent and happy, hungry for new life experiences and eager to forget the war events. Undoubtedly, the most important films of this decade are *Samson* (for its unabashed presentation of Jewish issues), *Ashes* (for its controversial portrayal of historical events of the Napoleonic campaign), and *Everything for Sale* (for its detour into the French New Wave aesthetics and an exceptionally personal treatment of the subject).

Samson is an especially important film in that it addresses issues vital to Poles only fifteen years after the end of World War II. Many participants of these fateful events were still alive at the time of the film's screening and could respond openly and directly to the events presented on the screen. However, partly due to the unconvincing acting of the main protagonist, the film does not have the desired intensity of effect. Also, the film may be subliminally anti-Semitic, as well. After all, it portrays the fate of a "stereotypical Jew" who neither stirs the spectators' sympathy nor interest.

In *Ashes,* the director reveals his openly nationalistic stance once again, his concern for the fate of Poland, and his interpretation of its past and its future. Yet this beautiful film, although black and white, gives the spectator an opportunity to look into Polish manors and huts and to admire the sublime Polish landscape. The film fascinates with its attention to detail in the portrayal of both Polish palaces and spectacular battles. Again, Wajda continues his presentation of romantic protagonists who believe that they will be able to liberate Poland on their own. The moments of disillusion are even more poignant here than in *Ashes and Diamonds* because they are repeated over and over again in several scenes of defeat. This repetition of trauma signifies a site of mourning and despair over the lost ideals, a site that will later be revisited even more bitterly in *Landscape after Battle.*

However, what stands out after watching all of these films is, again, the intensity of emotions portrayed on the screen and the beauty of the images. Starting from *Innocent Sorcerers* with the image of Andrzej on a motorbike, which he rides through empty Warszawa streets, and even in *Hunting Flies* with its vicious presentation of women, the director creates aesthetically striking images. Despite heavy criticism garnered by both *The Gates to Paradise* and *Siberian Lady Macbeth,* the films contain sophisticated, austere images aptly illustrating the meaning of the stories on which they are based. Simple lines and color strategies characterize both films. Against this bland background, the films' powerful emotions stand out all that much more remarkably.

My favorite film of this decade is *Everything for Sale,* for its emotional intensity; its attempt to document the ungraspable moment of the death of an actor; its intellectual complexity; and its striking aesthetics, alluding to the aesthetics and intellectual accomplishments of the French New Wave. In its self-referentiality, the fragmented structure of the images, several planes of narration (the wife and lover of the actor, the director, and the friends and colleagues who knew the deceased actor), and the structure of the images, all of which metatheatrically denote the film apparatus itself, *Everything for Sale* breaks ground in Polish film by moving away from its classical and traditional visions. Two images especially stand out in my memory: that of the frozen faces behind the car window when the women in Cybulski's life learn about the actor's death; and the last image of the actor Daniel, who will replace Cybulski, his face fading to an ambiguous, blurred blob that blends into the background, as if signifying a young life that might end as abruptly as did that of Cybulski himself.

4

BETWEEN POLITICS AND THE THEMES OF LIFE AND DEATH
Films of the Seventies

The 1970s mark Wajda's consummate creative period, during which his most highly celebrated films were made. *The Birchwood* garnered the highest praise both in Poland and abroad for its mature treatment of the subject of death and for the film's tasteful aesthetics. *Landscape after Battle* is the subtle portrayal of a young man's internal struggles after the end of World War II; in it, the cynicism of the internment camps is juxtaposed with the death of a young woman ready to start a new life after the war. The third film, *Pilate and Others*, treats themes of Christianity in a contemporary context, while *The Shadow Line*, on the other hand, deals with the issues of personal responsibility during a voyage at sea. *The Wedding* portrays the wedding celebration in both historical and political contexts.

In *The Young Ladies of Wilko*, as in *The Birchwood*, Wajda excels in his depiction of the Polish landscape with all its tranquility and grandeur; this film deals with the passage of time and with the loves of the four female protagonists. Wajda continues to use well-known literary texts as the basis for his films and to concentrate on themes of people's inner dilemmas in the face of adversity. These films were honored highly both in Poland and abroad, and *Promised Land* won an Oscar nomination. In *Promised Land*, however, the uncompromising portrayal of Poles as morally corrupt opportunists opened a hornet's nest of attacks and accusations. The director was criticized for his representation of minorities in Poland, his cynicism regarding Poland's strengths and weaknesses, and a generally hypercritical treatment of his compatriots.

From his criticism of Polish society in *Promised Land*, Wajda moved in his subsequent films to scathing condemnations of Socialism, of politics in general and politicians in particular. In *Man of Marble*, he presents major political events that occurred in Poland throughout the 1950s and 1960s, ending with the momentous wave of strikes that signaled the end of Socialism in 1970. *Without Anesthetic* dissects the inner workings of the totalitarian system and tells the tale of previously untold discriminations and repressions. *The Orchestra Conductor* is a study of human nature in another sense; it is the story of a leader who understands and respects the people with whom he works.

The Birchwood (1970)

Following *Roly Poly, Hunting Flies,* and *Everything for Sale,* Wajda made his most mature and accomplished films to date; the 1970s mark the pinnacle of his artistic output. In this era, Wajda has learned to maintain a balance between content and representation. The first of these "mature" films is *The Birchwood,* based on Jarosław Iwaszkiewicz's short story by the same title. Wajda had thought about making this film for years, but had considered himself too young to start the project in his thirties. However, as he notes in *Wajda Films,* Polish television eventually commissioned the film from him, thus "cutting short his growing pains."[1] Immediately after its premiere in 1970, the film garnered critical attention as a visual masterpiece strikingly different from his political films of the past. Both in its pace and its emotional understatement, the film was a departure from the highly passionate former screen creations. The simple story of two brothers, Stanisław and Bolesław, struck a chord with audiences wanting answers to the eternal questions of life and death.

    The Birchwood takes place in a small village, in the house of Bolesław; Stanisław returns from the grand salons of Europe because he knows he is about to die of tuberculosis. At first, Bolesław greets Stanisław reluctantly, but gradually accepts him and the inevitable decline of his health. Within this basic premise, the tragic events unfold slowly and stunningly, revealing a remarkable complexity and psychological density. The film starts with a sequence showing the countryside landscape in a sweeping panorama of panning shots: Willows, birches, lowlands, and streams provide the backdrop to Stanisław's pale and tired face as he takes in the surroundings on his way to Bolesław's house. A simple home, almost a peasant's hut, emerges. This house will provide a refuge for Stanisław in the last months of his life.

    Unaware initially of Stanisław's terminal illness, Bolesław, whose beloved wife has died a year earlier, treats his brother's arrival as an intrusion into his secluded and quiet life. He does his best to ignore Stanisław's apparent exhilaration and lust for life, his love of music, and the friendship he offers to Bolesław's daughter, Ola. For his part, the dynamic Stanisław seems alternately euphoric and depressed, spending much of his time looking out through the windows in his blue room, taking his medication regularly and otherwise doing little more than attending to his own routine needs. Despite his exuberance, he is all too aware of his impending death and the inexorable passage of time. Bolesław, aloof and taciturn, tends to the daily matters of the farm; every evening after supper, he visits his wife's grave in the birch grove. Gradually, though, as he sees the dying Stanisław express his unquenchable zest for life, Bolesław begins to wake up to his own.

Bolesław accepts with disdain his ailing brother's wish to rent a piano, and he observes Stanisław's loud, animated behavior with disgust. Wajda ingeniously uses the opportunity of Stanisław going to rent the piano (from another tuberculosis victim in the nearby town) to provide snapshots of the various social classes living in a small town in Poland at the beginning of the century; in this striking sequence he presents the lifestyles of a broad range of peoples. In this aesthetically dense and thematically complex sequence, Gypsies, Jews, and Poles, peasants, townsfolk, and shopkeepers alike all vie for Stanisław's attention.

When Stanisław brings the piano to the house, Bolesław welcomes him coldly. In response, Stanisław finally reveals the purpose of his visit to his brother. He explains that, usually a short time before death occurs, the tuberculosis patient often experiences a brief improvement attended by a period of euphoria. During this time, doctors generally want the patient to go back to his or her family—or at least somewhere outside the hospital. Fir woods are thought to provide the best environment for such patients, so Stanisław has decided to come stay with his brother, who lives in the countryside. Sardonic, he says that this improvement phase soon passes and that he will die in next to no time. Stanisław then discusses the emptiness of his former life in Europe, having known during his time there that he could never touch life's essence because of his impending death.

In a very short time, Stanisław gets to know Malina, the hired help in Bolesław's house; he is immediately attracted to her openly manifested sexuality, and they soon begin to have an affair. After a playful bicycle ride with Malina that leaves Stanisław totally exhausted, he goes for a walk and reaches the birch grove where Bolesław's wife is buried. There he hears Ola walking nearby, and she quietly explains the circumstances of her mother's death. When Stanisław and Ola go back to his room, he shows her photographs from his recent past. In a remarkably beautiful sequence, making an explicit connection between the worlds of cinema and of painting, both so dear to Wajda, Bolesław looks upon Jacek Malczewski's painting *Kobieta z kosą (Woman with a Scythe)*[2] hanging behind him. The painting, which combines the concepts of love, beauty, and death, is a famous icon of the Polish Symbolism movement in art. [+]

When Bolesław finally opens up to Stanisław about his wife, describing her as a modest, good woman whom he began to understand and love only after her death, his face, partly hidden from view, is contorted by pain. Almost immediately, though, the distraught man suddenly bursts out with condemnations concerning Stanisław's affair with

Malina; unusually excited and indignant, he condemns carnal love, comparing it to animal passion. When Malina unexpectedly bursts in, asking the brothers for help in treating her wounded brother Janek, Bolesław and Stanisław reconcile for a moment only to quarrel again hours later. In a subsequent series of exquisitely composed sequences, Stanisław wakes up to a beautiful morning, plays the piano, and impulsively throws the whole battery of medications out of the window. He then makes love passionately with Malina, walks aimlessly through the birch bower, listens to the sound of an accordion in Malina's hut, plays the piano (parodically recalling the tunes of vaudeville), dances on the small footbridge over the stream, and despairs over the inevitable course of events. Alternately anxious and blithe, he awaits his own death.

Meanwhile, Bolesław is strangely roused to life by the romance unfolding between Malina and his brother; he suddenly seems eager to embrace his wife's death, understand it, and move on. In one of the most distressing sequences in all of Wajda's films, he approaches his daughter with a series of questions concerning her mother. The mournful widower, desperate to come to some profound understanding of his wife and of her life, tries to extract it brutally from his young daughter. He bombards her with questions about her relationship with the young farmhand Michał, Malina's brother; when Ola does not respond, he verbally abuses her and impulsively hugs her in turn.

In another scene that follows shortly, it is Bolesław, not Stanisław, who follows Malina to the meadow where she cuts her yellow marsh flowers. She is radiant, young and desirable. However, in a clear allusion to Malczewski's *Woman with a Scythe*, she is also shown as a death-figure, clad in white and holding a scythe in her hands. Bolesław tries to seduce her; startled by his advances, she tries to run away from him. He chases her, though, and begins to kiss her passionately. The wakening process has begun for Bolesław. Agonizingly, he starts to turn away from his deceased wife and, through coming to terms with Stanisław's impending death, is slowly invigorated thanks to Malina, young Michał (whose strength and agility he admires), and the sublime natural world that surrounds him.

Yet that same nature, in all its beauty, finally leads Stanisław to his death when he is soaked with rain after a visit to the hut. He wakes up the next morning only to realize that his mouth is full of blood; as the owner of the piano comes to claim his property, Stanisław realizes that his time has come. In a metaphoric shortcut, Wajda shows the rented piano being driven away to its new owner. The piano, resembling a black coffin, is a metonymic signifier of Stanisław's imminent death. In the death scene, Wajda combines a love for life, nature, music, and cinema in one brilliant metaphor: The dying Stanisław wakes up suddenly in the morning as the piano-coffin wends away, looks upon the birch grove, half rises from his bed, and then collapses. The scene is shot with a revolving camera, giving an impression of dizziness reminiscent of the scene of a kiss in Alfred Hitchcock's *Vertigo* (1958).

In a conversation with Jerzy Niesiobędzki, Wajda comments on Stanisław's death scene:

> "In the finale to the film, *The Birchwood,* we see a piano being taken away through the wood. I could introduce this scene because I have not pro-
> duced the scene of Stanisław's funeral. I only showed him dying. The pi-
> ano is black, it is being taken in a carriage, as if it were a coffin. This
> image is a metaphor because a film has to aim at being a metaphorical
> and a condensed statement."[3]

This scene, forecast by both the protagonists and the audience since the film's very beginning, is followed by scenes showing Bolesław as he chases Malina away from Stanisław's body; orders Stanisław's room to be thoroughly cleaned; and then rides away with Ola, both of them dressed in liberating, radiant whites. The dark colors of death—in ocher, blues, and browns—give way to sunny whites, which have symbolically been present in the whites of the birch grove throughout the film.

The Birchwood is one of my favorite films, thematically sophisticated and mature. The themes of life, death, sexuality, and nature are not over-whelming or visually outrageous, not given to emotional excess, but are gently alluded to through paintings well known to Poles (e.g., iconic images of birch groves and dark peasant huts), and through pi-ano music and the iconography of the piano instrument itself, which are linked to death and mourning. The superb performances of Daniel Olbrychski and Olgierd Łukaszewicz reinforce the contrast between the hysterical and despairing Stanisław and the subdued, deeply suf-fering Bolesław. Both Malina and Michał are symbols and catalysts, as well as fully realized characters, supplementing our interpretation of the lust for life expressed by Stanisław and the submergence in death symbolized by Bolesław; the raw sexuality of each of the young sib-lings triggers, simultaneously, the dying and the waking processes that both experience.

The film's impact has been universally noted. It was heralded a mas-terpiece, both in Poland and abroad. As Etienne Lalou summarizes it, the film is "beautiful because each scene is emotional and meaningful and each is absolutely indispensable and necessary."[4] It is worth noting here that death and sensuality are common motives in European and Polish art: Wajda was aware of this, of course. In his attempt to present the affinity between death and sensuality, Wajda actually delved into Ryszard Przybylski's essay on Iwaszkiewicz's "Eros and Thanatos," an effort that clearly produced a stunning result noted by many Polish and foreign reviewers.[5] For instance, André Cornand states, "The con-currence of the messages in the literary text, its critical analysis, and the

paintings by Malczewski, has changed Wajda's film into a poetic med-
itation on the battle of the forces of life against the forces of death."[6]
Cornand's views on this subject are reflected by both Robert Chazal[7]
and Angelo Signorelli.[8]

Aside from the philosophical and compositional balance struck by
the film, perhaps its most remarkable feature is Wajda's consistent allusion to various well-known Polish artworks. The scenes with Malina
are immobile tableaux at times, making associations with Jacek Malczewski paintings (*A Woman with a Scythe* and *Zatruta Studnia [A Woman
at the Well]*). Wajda comments on this allusiveness in the following way:

> **Jerzy Niesiobędzki:** Do the scenes in *The Birchwood* recalling Mal-
> czewski's paintings reinforce the metaphorical aspect of the film while
> they function as autonomous scenes in the film?
>
> **Andrzej Wajda:** A film director can reinforce the film message with a
> work of art which has a completely different meaning. But this work of
> art should not produce an impression of something added on artificially,
> next to something else, or, outside of film events and film action. On the
> contrary, it should be perceived as an integral part of the action.[9]

The Birchwood garnered many awards both in Poland and abroad, signaling the emergence of a mature, gifted filmmaker who presented complex human emotions with profound accuracy. No social or political
criticism obfuscates the clarity of the film, in which love, life, and death
take center stage. Here, Wajda has moved in the direction of the highly
philosophical films of Ingmar Bergman rather than in that of his earlier
films, which dealt with general social or political issues in specific historical contexts.

Landscape after Battle (1970)

After *The Birchwood*, Wajda returns to the same subject matter that constituted much of his early career: World War II. *Landscape after Battle*
deals with the consequences of the war for Poles: particularly, the disillusionment and bitterness felt by young and old alike. Based on a
novel by Tadeusz Borowski, *Landscape after Battle* depicts the days after
the opening of the concentration camps, a setting that provides the
landscape for an ill-fated romance between two former prisoners: a
Polish student, Tadeusz, and a young Polish Jew, Nina.

The film opens with the loud sound of artillery, the concentration
camp visible from afar. It is winter, and snow covers the fields around
the camp. Antonio Vivaldi's *Four Seasons* accompanies the ecstatic freeing of the prisoners by the American forces. Dressed in their striped
uniforms, the prisoners move joyously out of the barracks, touching

the electrified barbwire fence that is no longer active; they run on the snow, break glass in the windows, burn their hated stripes, change into civil clothes, and eat voraciously, all the while proclaiming their freedom loudly and exuberantly. The narrator informs us that the year is 1945 but that the prisoners are still kept behind bars—the liberators, seeking to maintain some order among those they have freed, keep them in the old SS camps.

When the American officer tells the prisoners that they should respect his commands to remain lawful and orderly, they look at him in disbelief. He explains that any criminal behavior will be punished accordingly, but they respond shortly afterward by murdering the former kapo, whom they drown in sewage. Tadeusz, who is always seen reading books, as if in an attempt to block out his memories of war, witnesses these events. The memories that haunt Tadeusz and the other prisoners are overlaid with the diegetic music of a violinist within the context of the film who, performs Henryk Wieniawski's concerto in accompaniment to the surrealistic scene of their freedom.

Shortly thereafter, Tadeusz and another prisoner, Karol, carry on a bitter conversation, commenting sarcastically on the activities of their compatriots. The former prisoners' main occupation is tending to their daily needs and necessities—food, hygiene, and occasional sexual encounters—highlighted with constant petty squabbles over these basic privileges. This degrading state of affairs is presented by Wajda as a pathetic effort by the prisoners to retain sanity in the conditions of imprisonment. Their cynicism, bickering, and quarreling are overpowering, presented by the director against a backdrop of the claustrophobic interiors and dirty exteriors of the camp's buildings. The atmosphere of misery and helplessness is conveyed by several means: someone reads a bleak poem penned by Tadeusz Baczyński; a Gypsy sings sadly amid the squalor; and Karol and Tadeusz continue their pusillanimous bickering about food, the kitchen, and the sanitary conditions.

In the next sequence, Tadeusz cooks a meal on a makeshift stove, something the prisoners have been forbidden to do. When the American officer approaches him and orders him to stop, Tadeusz bursts out in anger, saying that he never gets enough food in the camp. For breaking the rules, he is led into an improvised cell in an old cellar, all the while demonstrating illogical and disoriented behavior: He tries to run away, whistling and raising his hands, even though no one really tries to force him into confinement. Once he is in the cell, however, he is perfectly happy to be left alone to read. The claustrophobic space of the cellar *cum* cell reminds the spectator of the scenes from *Samson*, with its long sequences of Jakub's incarceration. However, whereas in *Samson* the cellar served as the protagonist's final refuge in a real situation of oppression, here it symbolizes the psychological prison in which

Tadeusz finds himself trapped. When the priest tries to release him, Tadeusz refuses to leave the cell despite the fact that he is free to go.

Later, during the camp's mass, a solemn and important occasion for all the inhabitants of the camp, a bus arrives with female ex-prisoners. Looking through the metal fence, the women approach male prisoners with interest; Nina, a young Jewish Pole, is among them. She joins the men during communion, where Tadeusz and Nina exchange glances for the first time. Tadeusz, distributing the communion, is alerted to Nina's awkwardness and hesitation when she accepts the communion wafer: He does not yet know that Nina is a Jew, and that this ritual is unwelcome to her. When, after the mass, they talk with the old professor about Poland after the war, the three of them are cynical and bitter. In the meantime, polite visits from the Westerners disrupt the strange logic of the camp.

After a time, Tadeusz pulls Nina away from the other prisoners; he tells her of his will to live, his desire for women, and his overwhelming fear of death. They are interrupted suddenly by a brutal scene unfolding in the camp: a German kitchen maid is brought to justice by the former prisoners. Suspected of having stolen food, she is dragged half-naked to the commanding officers. Disgusted and mortified, Nina begs Tadeusz to flee the camp with her. His lack of will makes this flight impossible for Tadeusz, however; he suggests a walk in the woods instead. Nina and Tadeusz run joyously on the waste heap beyond the prison fence. When they cross the road, though, they hear gunshots. Terrified, they hide in the nearby woods and lie down in the carpet of autumn leaves. Nina kisses the reluctant Tadeusz, but he rises and runs away to a pile of leaves.

In the flirtatious conversation that ensues, the young people talk about poetry, love, and life, but their dialogue is constantly disrupted by the reminders of war: the concentration camp numbers on Tadeusz's hand, which Nina kisses; the appearance of a German woman who had interrogated Tadeusz in Warszawa; and the arrival of a German soldier, in uniform, who asks for a cigarette. The beauty of the autumn afternoon with its red leaves, warm sun, and idyllic patter about love, is also marred by Tadeusz's angry outbursts and desperate cynicism. It is not only outside reality that interferes, but also Tadeusz's constant filtering of this reality through his painful memories. These intrusions, both external and internal, lend the scenes a meticulous poignancy.

Nina tries to calm Tadeusz; she thinks about the future, a possible escape to the West, study in Paris, and a quiet, peaceful life. To this, Tadeusz responds with uncertainty and questions concerning his "Polishness" and his (lost) sense of belonging. Nina admits that she too is unsure of her own identity: she is a Polish Jew who feels that she is neither fully Pole nor fully Jew. (This topic of identity crisis among young people brought up in Poland during the World War II era is forcibly thrust upon the audience, but never fully explained.) The final love scene between the two is interspersed with painful exchanges concerning their fear of/for the future, and their notions of nationality and patriotism. When Nina finally asks Tadeusz whether he wants to return to Poland or stay in the West, he responds that he is not sure; she decides to go back to the camp, with a hesitant Tadeusz in tow.

However, when they approach the camp, Nina is accidentally shot and killed by an American soldier who automatically responds to the warning of the military guard concerning the ex-prisoners appearing at the gate. The death sequence begins with the tolling of a bell from a nearby church. Tadeusz, hiding in the nearby trenches, is unsure of what has happened; the setting sun blinds him and the other prisoners, helpless spectators who become the unwilling witnesses to the tragic death. Repeated takes of Nina's fall portray her death as especially cruel and unjust; the last smile she sends to Tadeusz is brutally cut short by her sudden fall to the ground. When he is questioned about the event, Tadeusz tells the camp's commanding officer that his soldiers have just killed an innocent girl. "We are used to it," he adds, "First the Germans, now you—what's the difference?" Tadeusz returns to the camp without looking at the body of Nina lying outside the camp. Amid the debauchery of his fellow (ex-)prisoners, the sadly singing Gypsy, and the squalor of the camp quarters, he voraciously consumes another meal and tries to read another book.

Ironically, Nina has been killed on the camp's last day; later, the exhilarated former prisoners burn effigies of German soldiers and watch a kitschy reenactment of the Battle of Grunwald, a legendary battle fought and won by Poles against Teutonic knights in 1410. The battle was the biggest one fought in Europe in the Middle Ages and attested to the ferociousness and patriotism of Polish and Lithuanian forces. The outcome of this battle seriously weakened the importance of the Teutonic knights. This well-known historical event has a grotesque portrayal in *Everything for Sale*, however. Shot against a huge white sheet hanging in the background, the mock battle is grotesque in its stylized movement: As if in slow motion, the antagonists engage in a symbolic exchange of gestures. Played to Frederic Chopin's *Polonaise in A-major,* the Battle of Grunwald also serves as a backdrop to later conversations between Tadeusz and the camp's priest, who wants Tadeusz to go to the morgue to identify Nina's body. The seemingly dispassionate Tadeusz at first refuses to listen to the priest's pleadings and turns back to his food; finally, though, they go, leaving behind the infuriated prisoners who, now engaged in yet another argument, have forgotten all about the play going on in front of them. The Jewish violinist finally brings them all to attention by playing the Polish national anthem.

The naked body of Nina is displayed on a catafalque. The priest calls Nina's death a symbol of all the atrocities of the recently ended war. Tadeusz, a self-proclaimed atheist, refuses to listen and begs the priest to leave. Once he is alone, the young man crawls under the catafalque with an animal cry, and remains there, silent. The next scene is the last of the film, with Tadeusz leaving the camp, a small cart full of books in tow. In evident contrast with Vivaldi's exuberant music, his face in this last sequence is pale, a study in horror and resignation. The closing shot is of Polish soldiers marching out of the camp singing a well-known song about the end of the war ("Zakwitały pęki jasnych róż").

Landscape after Battle treats the war theme in a way that is rather unconventional, particularly for Wajda. While his earlier films dealing with the Second World War were crafted in the mode of heroic historiography, this film stresses the war's pointlessness, and the despair that governs even after the war ends. War, the film avers, destroys people's dignity and sanity, making them helpless victims unable to function on their own. Tadeusz, played brilliantly by Daniel Olbrychski, recedes from view at the end of the film a broken man, unable to put the past behind him. In his cynical, bitter treatment of the theme, Wajda remains faithful to the artistic and literary tradition of many Polish artists. "Żeromski, who scratched wounds, Matejko, who was condemned as a slanderer for the bitter meaning of Rejtan, Chopin and his melancholy, the Kraków Historical School with its revisionism."[10]

As in *Kanal*, *Ashes and Diamonds*, and *Samson*, the bitterness and cynicism resulting from participation in horrific war events come fully to the forefront; here, though, they are not obfuscated or invalidated by the romantic tradition of heroism encountered in the former films. *Landscape after Battle* is a mature film, painful to watch because Wajda does not coddle the audience, but rather forces them to see the prisoners as perpetrators of degrading crimes and not as powerless victims. Of course, the prisoners' situation is a matter of the historical context, but Wajda keeps this context remote, visible only through memories and apparitions, and no longer an imminent threat—thus making the behavior of the prisoners all the more appalling. Krzysztof Teodor Toeplitz rightly notes that "Wajda presents a terrifying picture of the camps, and does it in a situation where there were no more guards, police dogs, and when the furnaces of the crematoria had already cooled."[11]

Notions of homeland, country, and nation feature prominently in *Landscape after Battle*. As Waldemar Chołodowski comments, however, here Wajda questions these notions in a way that does not occur in his earlier films. "Is the homeland synonymous with a trolley loaded with books, a commonwealth of language, landscapes remembered from childhood and transfused into the blood stream as Tadeusz would have it, or—to define this notion negatively—does the homeland cease to have any significance, when one cannot find one's place in it—as is Nina's experience through her very existence?"[12] As John Pym suggests, this film is "less romantic and more honest in its reassessment, twenty five years on, of the period covered by the director's more widely known trilogy (1954–58) celebrating the Polish resistance."[13] In a private letter to Wajda, Agnieszka Osiecka compliments the director on the way he manages to "convey our greatness and our baseness, and in such a way that each is reflected in the other, as in a mirror."[14] Other reviewers expressed their admiration for Wajda's ability to express the love of homeland[15] and his "deep Christian feeling for suffering and the determined will of a layman to discover the reason and the sense of everything that surrounds us."[16]

Landscape after Battle contributes to Wajda's long time commitment to the portrayal of Jewish characters in his films. Nina represents those Jews who survived World War II but who are confused and uncertain about their identity. She is unsure what to do and where to go. She is "here and there": in Poland and willing to go somewhere else at the same time. Paradoxically, her dream of Europe and of the world, where her Jewishness would be fully embraced, is cut short by death, the only viable solution, the film suggests, to her dilemma. Again, Jewish passivity and/or an internal need to escape and wander (the myth of "the wandering Jew") is addressed but not answered. Helpless in view of the complexity of the Jewish fate, Wajda lets Nina fall silently to the ground, as if overpowered by the impossibilities, paradoxes, and absurdities of her fate. As in his other films portraying Jews, Wajda here raises controversial historical issues concerning the place of Jews in the liberated country or, rather, their lack of a future there. As in *Samson*, he does it in an honest and mature way, not expecting any answers to these difficult questions.

Opinions regarding the film's style are varied. While Osiecka sensed a sort of imperturbability or stylistic calmness on the part of Wajda the director others understood that Wajda had to locate the film firmly in Borowski's world and to portray it "in the same cool, staccato style."[17] Alicja Helman provides a most interesting description of the film: "Wajda balances constantly on the verge of kitsch, bad taste, and effects that can give a nasty shock to the viewer. At times, the film makes us hold our breath as we observe the artist's ventures like a flight over the precipice, but each risky tension ends in fortunate relief."[18] For many, the film leaves a bitter aftertaste because of both the nonsympathetic presentation of the protagonist, Tadeusz, and the negative portrayal of the ex-prisoners. Regardless, *Landscape after Battle* also affirms the transition of Wajda, first witnessed in *The Birchwood*, from a young and enthusiastic director into a mature, successful filmmaker who is not afraid to deal with controversial subjects in his films.

Pilate and Others (1972)

The film *Pilate and Others* is a contemporary rendition of Christ's story. The film was made during the height of the Socialist system in Poland

and in other countries of the Soviet bloc. The beginning of the 1970s was a time of significant economic prosperity thanks to the sympathetic approach of Edward Gierek, the Communist Party Secretary. As Norman Davies explains, "unlike Gomułka, [Gierek] was fully aware of the gulf which separated the living standards of working people in Poland from that of their counterparts in the West, and was willing to listen to their aspirations."[19] He admitted to the party's failures and paid attention to ordinary folk. He increased wages for workers, eased censorship, and lowered restrictions on travel and foreign contacts. In all areas of life, there was a considerable moderation of party control that raised everybody's hope for a better life.

Soon, however, even under Gierek's leadership, the political situation reached an impasse, the government and party control tightened, and a series of confrontations with workers ensued. The 1970s was a decade of organized opposition movements in Poland, both clandestine and open rebellions, and, finally, the growth of the Solidarity movement at the end of the decade.[20] In *Pilate and Others*, political criticism comes to the fore, in that it openly reveals power relations in a Socialist society. The film was shot in Nuremberg, the site of many Nazi rallies, on the ruins of Third Reich. This place was turned into the palace of Herod, the ruler of Judea, while Frankfurt's Zeil Avenue, Via Dolorosa, and the garbage dump near Wiesbaden, high over a motorway, played the part of Golgotha. The film consists of three parts, "Pilatus," "Mathias," and "Judas," in a classical drama about love, betrayal, and death.

Pilate and Others opens with a shot of a flock of sheep being herded to the slaughter house. In a voice-over, Wajda himself carries out an interview with the shepherd who, resigned, says he knows that he too is being led to slaughter. "Others will take my place," he pronounces calmly. The sequence, full of biblical references, yet referring clearly to the situation of citizens under the totalitarian regime (e.g., those in Poland), leads to the interrogation of Jeshua by the emperor's representative, Pilat. Jeshua is questioned about his subversive activities and his wish to demolish the churches of the old faith and to build the church of a new Christian one. This long conversation is shot with various static and mobile positions of the camera and with frequent pans and tracking shots, and it presents a startling commentary on the real power of the emperor. Despite the fact that Pilat, paralyzed, is lying on a stretcher and Jeshua (called Jeszua Ha-Nocri in Bulhakov's novel) stands above him, it is Pilat who holds the power and not Jeszua, so they are shot accordingly: Pilat is seen from a low camera angle and Jeshua from high up.

This solemn dialogue, taking place in the past, is witnessed by contemporary spectators, positioned high above the protagonists on the platform from which Hitler greeted his followers during the Nuremberg rallies. The past is reinterpreted, reworked so to speak, by the present time; contemporary sequences in the film are later interspersed with those of the biblical tale in a startlingly logical crosscutting between the two. For instance, the contemporary timeline in the film leads us to a conversation between Judas and Jeszua, a young, naïve hippie, at a café somewhere downtown. When Judas reports this conversation over the phone, a handful of silver coins suddenly falls out: This clear reference to *srebrniki* (thirty pieces of silver) seamlessly links the past with the present, as when two young men dressed in contemporary garb, sitting in the middle of a busy street, converse about the time of Christ. Likewise, when Jeszua is led to the commander of security, Afranius, it is not a Roman official who appears in front of him, but an agent in contemporary security officer's clothes. Here, as elsewhere, the biblical discourse mixes not only with that of the Germany of the 1970s, with its youth rebels and the impending doom of the Red Brigades, but also with the discourse of Nazi Germany (the emblems of which appear in the images of the Nazi eagle); thus, the gallows we see allude both to the Romans and to the executions during the Second World War, as well as to the greetings of Pilat delivered to the crowds from the Nuremberg platform.

The main protagonists are not the only people dressed in contemporary clothes. For instance, Afranius in a black coat and black glasses, checks the stadium for bombs, fliers, and other accruements of subversive activities. While the tried criminals, among whom Jeszua finds himself, are dressed as gang members and hippies, ancient Roman soldiers on horseback stand guard and later mix with the crowds. Wajda explains his Mathias/Matthew and Jeszua/Jesus with reference to the so-called "Jesus revolution" movement born in the United States during the late 1960s. "My film has nothing in common with this movement," Wajda says. "The screenplay is based on a novel written in 1938. *Pilat* is a completely secular film. However, I am interested in the reaction to my film during the development of this particular movement."[21] In another interview, Wajda states that he was also fascinated with another movement: the *prowosi*, represented by young people using signs of the Crucifixion as one of their symbols and wearing shirts with the image of Christ on them. "I even cut out from the newspaper a photograph which presented three young boys in American battledress. I thought these were Christ, St. Peter, and St. John, and this is how I signed this photograph."[22]

The admixture of the apocryphal and the contemporary continues throughout the film. When Jeszua is led to the execution, he is taken in a cart led by horses and surrounded by Roman soldiers who wear peplum, sandals, and swords along with contemporary police helmets and gas masks. The whole scene takes place in a modern setting, with cars passing by. Mathias, the reliable friend and confidante, is a beatnik who wants to accompany his master on his way to his death; among the contemporary passersby, he looks lonely and bedraggled. In a dream, Mathias embraces Jeszua and promises to help him end his life. To do this, he needs a weapon; Mathias enters a German bakery and steals a knife, and then follows Jeszua to the garbage heap/Golgotha, to the accompaniment of music by Bach. When Jeszua is crucified, young children in contemporary clothes look on, while the Roman guards speak German. Jeszua refuses a cigarette before being nailed to the cross. The scene, reminiscent of death row scenarios, precedes the arrival of Afranius, who is to supervise the final moments.

After the Crucifixion, Mathias hides inside the wreck of a burned car behind the garbage dumps and watches the scene in agitated silence. When he tries to approach the dying Jeszua, he is brutally pushed away by the guards. Returning to the car, he begins a monologue accusing God of allowing the death of Christ. During this passionate outburst (completely improvised by Daniel Olbrychski on the set), he begs for Jeszua's death. Meanwhile, dying slowly on the cross, his face covered with innumerable flies, Jeszua reminisces about his happy past life, thinking of his travels and of discussions held with his disciples.

While tourists in buses photograph the whole scene from their windows, Afranius sits patiently in the full sun and waits for the end to Jeszua's ordeal. Mathias, on the other hand, dreams about Jeszua's quick death. In a dreamy sequence in slow motion Mathias climbs to Jeszua and tries to end his life, only to be interrupted by Afranius. A short time later, when a vicious storm front moves in, Afranius and the guards quickly run away. With the storm raging around him, Mathias cuts Jeszua from the cross and drags his limp body into the dump. In the meantime, Afranius calls Pilat to tell him that his orders have been carried out, and is asked to return to join a meeting. Their conversation centers on Judas, who is supposed to collect money for his betrayal of Jeszua—but as the phone call concludes, Afranius is commanded to assassinate Jeszua's betrayer. This sequence initiates the last part of the film, "Judas."

The assassination scene takes place in an amusement park, among joyous crowds. Afranius first visits a prostitute, then arranges a meeting with a paid killer and, helped by a transvestite he has paid for this purpose, lures Judas to the botanical garden. Loud contemporary music and shots depicting people at play accompany these scenes. The assassination itself takes place amid the lush greenery of the botanical garden; he is killed during a kiss with the transvestite, who seems to hold something in his/her hands. Later, when Afranius turns Judas's body over, he pulls a pouch full of money from his hands. After washing his own hands in a beautiful tropical pool, the officer meets Pilat and explains what has happened.

The film ends with a meeting between Mathias and Pilat, in which the latter explains to a surprised and mistrusting Mathias that he has ordered the assassination of Judas. Soaked in sweat, blood, and tears, with an image of the head of Jeszua on his T-shirt, the disciple is ready to run. When he begins to sense Pilat's sympathy, he starts to trust him and shows him Jeszua's words written on the parchment. Finally, he asks Pilat for a clean sheet of paper. Huddled over the typewriter, he begins to type but his head turns upward and, in a mysterious dream sequence, he sees himself dragging a wooden cross along the highway.

In Poland, this film was neither well known nor well received; it appeared in repertory cinemas only three years after its release on West German TV. Abroad, it was also criticized, particularly for its lack of empathy in the presentation of Christ's plight. Some critics even suggested that the film re-creates (or even imitates) the Passion performances in *Oberammergau* and the fashionable *Jeszua-Superstar* shows.[23] Wajda responded to this criticism in the following way:

> I wanted to show the indifference of the world saturated with technology and material prosperity to the death of a human being, the indifference that was shown during the actual moment of the shooting of the scene. The crucifixion scene was shot in a visible place near the highway. After the events taking place in the West, one could think that a man's crucifixion was really taking place. Nobody stopped at the scene. There was a sign forbidding people to stop; this sign released people from the moral obligation to stop. One must not stop, one must go on. Some people took photos ...[24]

The film was highly controversial among religious Poles, who were offended by the images, the language, and the message of the film. Particularly troubling for such audiences were Christ's death on the dumpsite and the fact that both Mathias and Jeszua were presented as young beatniks, representatives of controversial underground youth movements. The Catholic group who claimed authorship of an unsigned letter sent to Prime Minister Piotr Jaroszewicz calls *Pilate and Others* a tiring film that mocks their faith. The tone of this letter, however, is itself highly offensive: the director and the film producers are called "scoundrels" by the authors, who demand unquestioning respect for Catholicism.[25]

Official critics are more positive in their assessment of the film. Rafał Marszałek, for instance, calls it "a marvelous manifestation of the talent of the director and actors, a work of great imagination."[26] Similarly, Jacek Fuksiewicz calls the film "a brilliant game of imagination and intelligence"; he sees Wajda applying "the language of paradox, mental short-cuts, absurd jokes with such gusto as in *Roly Poly* and *Hunting Flies*."[27] Most critics were interested in Wajda's decision to place the story's action in a contemporary setting. Klaus Eder, for instance, describes the credo by claming that "Wajda was interested not only in Jeszua, but also in the question of why today's youth trust Him so much and make Him their idol …"[28] For Ugo Buzzolan, Wajda presents this theme with a passion characteristic of that apparent in his other political films:

> This film leaves no one indifferent. Wajda conveys his ideas in a light, imaginative way, and even though they cause anxiety, they are certainly unique. One must also discuss the film since the deep meaning of the parable—the appearance of Christ and the living presence of his two thousand year old message in a consumer, technocratic society—forces one to ask questions and gives rise to many painful doubts.[29]

Although rarely watched in Poland, the film must be treated as a continuation of Wajda's ongoing political work. The story of Christ serves as a general message for both Polish politicians and Western society as a whole; Christ's story has a universal meaning, especially for the young and the disadvantaged—his ideals of honesty and of moral and ethical behavior were very much alive and important to young people in the 1970s. The film is a fascinating attempt to present Christ's plight convincingly, but as a story with direct reference to the present times. In my opinion, Wajda wanted to make a statement that the ideas of Christ live on for young people in the 1970s with equal force as they did in the past. One aspect of the film in particular I find to be questionable, however: The film addresses those in power in too obvious a manner. This direct political address is too blunt, especially in the scene with the sheep led to slaughter and in the portrayal of Afranius, the security agent. In this film, as Zygmunt Kałużynski notes, Wajda does not whisper about political addressees, but instead roars.[30]

The Wedding (1970)

One of the most interesting and enigmatic films produced by Wajda in the 1970s is *The Wedding*, an allegorical tale that illustrates dramatically the historical dilemmas of Poland embroiled in historical conflicts in the nineteenth century, cynically exposing Poles' inability to take their fate in their own hands.[31] Wajda had been interested in the textual and filmic possibilities of *The Wedding* for a while. The making of the film followed a 1963 staging of the play in the Old Theater in Kraków.[32] However, due to the extremely heavy allusiveness of the original text, the film is virtually inexplicable to Western viewers who know little of the intricacies of Polish history.

The film's events occur over the course of the day and night of a wedding that takes place in a peasant's hut. The film is based on the actual wedding, in which the playwright Stanisław Wyspiański himself participated, of the poet Lucjan Rydel to a country girl (called simply "Bride" in the play and in the film). The event takes place at the house of another historical figure, the poet Kazimierz Przerwa Tetmajer, around the year 1900, when Poland was partitioned into three occupational zones by Austria, Prussia, and Russia, respectively. At the end of the nineteenth century, the most favorable conditions for Polish national life were in the Austrian zone, especially in Kraków; there, politically engaged persons, intellectuals, and artists arrived from other parts of the country that were subject to severe Russian and Prussian oppression. Kraków's Bohemia had a strong feeling of guilt toward peasants, who expected signals and programs from them for their revolutionary movements. The epidemic of misalliances, one of which is depicted in *The Wedding*, arose from the resulting sense of guilt: The aristocracy expected to purify itself, to reinforce itself through unions with the "folk," and at the same time to instill the indifferent country population with national spirit.[33]

The wedding is seen from the perspective of "the poet," a sophisticated Bohemian, who is both fascinated and slightly disgusted with the peasants swirling and sweating around him. In order to correctly capture the passionate shaking and swirling of the peasant dancers, Wajda presents much of the film as a dance, with music always in the background. He punctuates the dances with the brief appearances of guests, who present the dialogue, the story, and thus the essence of the play. These appearances function as visual metonymy, signaling the presence of such historical figures as Wernyhora, Stańczyk, and Zawisza.[34] Three primary areas of interest converge in *The Wedding*: (1) Wajda's interest in great Polish works of literature; (2) the thematic linking of past and present; and (3) the incorporation of allusions and topoi from other works of art, such as paintings[35] and music (here, both classical and folk music). The result of this merging of interests is a visually stunning film that fairly shimmers with energy and passion.

In the film's opening sequence, the wedding procession leaves the Mariacki Church in Kraków[36] accompanied by loud peasant music. The bridegroom and the bride, parents and guests, and various representatives of the peasantry and the intelligentsia are shown in close-ups, with handheld cameras, their faces and figures passing swiftly in carts driven by colorfully dressed horses. On their way to the Bronowice village hut where the wedding will take place, the wedding participants pass soldiers on maneuvers, who watch the passing guests solemnly. By thus contrasting moods in this sequence, Wajda introduces a moment of tension and uncertainty as to the historical and social circumstances of the wedding.

When dusk falls, a journalist, one of the invited guests, arrives late and approaches the hut, which radiates light and music. He looks sadly at this place of joy after having passed the sad willow trees in the dark; when he enters the hut, he is embraced by the energetically dancing crowd. The wedding participants wear traditional wedding clothes characteristic of the Kraków region. Immersed in their dance, the crowd is oblivious to critical looks of the members of the intelligentsia who, invited by the bridegroom (who is also "the poet"), look upon the wedding spectacle in awe. They start polite conversations with the peasantry, only halfheartedly expecting any response, talking of politics—a popular theme in Poles' social life at any time. When the journalist is asked about politics by Czepiec, he responds reluctantly, as if afraid the peasant will not understand him. Then, suddenly alert, he seems to notice something outside the window. The host also seems unusually alert as he looks outside at the sheaves of corn, resembling men, in the nearby field; the straw men look ethereally beautiful, glowing in the warm light coming from the hut.[37]

The film is not only about the debate regarding the liberation of Poland, but also about the impossibility of a mix between the two strata of society who are present, the dilemma articulated by the poet in his condescending words about their hosts.[38] He expresses the beliefs of Wyspiański himself, who referred to peasants as "the populace" but at the same time embraced and revered their straightforward openness. In a series of vignettes during the long dancing sequence, several dialogues confirm the poet's stand: The peasant bride and the upper-class bridegroom have nothing to talk about: their social and cultural incompatibilities are conspicuous. The older peasants comment on this unusual wedding, saying that the lords *(pany)* are bored with each other so they turn to the peasants to amuse them. Radczyni, the Councillor's wife; Maryna, a young woman of the Kraków intelligentsia; and the poet scornfully acknowledge the passing dancers, not taking part in the festivities. In a telling dialogue between Radczyni and the bride, we realize that the young girl has not even talked to her new husband about their future life together. Amid the dancing crowds, the journalist wanders and has a premonition that something unusual is about to happen.

In the meantime, a Jewish man enters the hut and tells the bridegroom that the members of the Kraków intelligentsia are merely playing at ideas of nation and nationhood. The Jew then asks the one question that frames the entire wedding: "Why does the poet marry a peasant girl?" He gets no response. Suddenly Rachela, the Jew's daughter, appears, seeming a beautiful ghost, all in reds and blacks. She also has a poet's sensibilities, so she sees the hut, the light, and the warmth it exudes as an event full of poesy and wonder. In a self-reflexive moment, the bridegroom exclaims, "I feel it, I hear it, I will describe everything in the future" *("Ja to czuję, ja to słyszę, kiedyś wszystko to opiszę").*[39] Meanwhile, the Jew and the priest converse about the peasants and their indebtedness to the Jew; later, the priest scolds Czepiec for not returning what he owes to the Jewish tapster. This ordinary discussion is

interrupted by dreamlike sequences depicting occupant soldiers passing the hut, and later the bridegroom dancing among the straw men
with his naked feet stomping the mud. Czepiec laughs when he sees
this folly, clearly amused by the poet's exultation. When the bridegroom enters the hut, Czepiec tells him about a possible insurrection
against the occupiers.

The next sequence with Rachela reveals all the prejudices of Poles
against Jews; the latter, often the owners of inns and taverns, were generally envied and despised for the income they generated at the expense of Polish peasants. Rachela clearly invites this reaction. Initially,
she stands against the wall, looking at the peasants dancing around
her. Nobody is interested in her except the poet, who, fascinated by her
beauty and sophistication, dances with her. All the peasants move back
and look with silent awe and distrust at the dancing couple. Rachela
talks loudly about the poetic aspect of the wedding and the hut, enam-
ored with its beauty and colors. With the exception of the poet, no one
compliments her on her soliloquy, however. In another part of the hut,
Czepiec talks about the pogrom of the Jews, presenting a clear commentary on their fate in Poland. To this, the Catholic priest reacts with
laughter, while the intelligentsia sit in the back of the room and listen.

Suddenly, Rachela looks through the window at the straw men; she
then tells the poet to invite all the ghosts outside to attend the wedding,
as the old tradition requires, and disappears among the weeping wil-
lows. The straw man sequence begins a series of appearances triggered
by the ghosts' invitation: Stańczyk, jester to Polish King Zygmunt August II, appears to the journalist; the black knight Zawisza, legendary
hero of Grunwald, appears to the poet; Rejtan and Hetman, famous
Polish commanders-in-chief, appear to the bridegroom, who experiences a vision of the Polish partition; Wernyhora, legendary prophet of
the Ukraine, materializes for the host; and the old man at the party sees
Szela, the famous leader of the peasant uprising in nineteenth-century
Galicja.[40]

These "ghosts" and their living counterparts all engage in dialogues
full of historical and national idiosyncrasies. From now on, historical
references appear continually in the form of paintings in the barn and,
as ghosts, in the rooms of the hut. Furthermore, the apparitions trigger
actual events in which the participants of the wedding engage. For example, the host gives Jasiek the golden horn of Wernyhora, which symbolizes a call to arms, and prompts him to go out and call the peasants
to action. When Jasiek leaves on a white horse with the horn in his
hands; the host returns to the hut and, exhausted, falls asleep in his
chair; Jasiek rides around the countryside calling peasants to join the
insurrection.

These ghost scenes are interspersed with a series of vignettes in
which peasant women talk about the future life of the unusual wed-

ding couple, while children sleep contentedly in poses carefully emulating those found in portraits by Stanisław Wyspiański. For instance, a little girl sleeping at a table, her head bent over her forearm, is an allusion to Wyspiański's iconic portraits of peasant children. Thusly, Wajda directs the audience's attention to an array of Polish masterpieces, among them the paintings by Jan Stanisławski, Józef Chełmoński, Stanisław Wyspiański, Aleksander Gierymski, Teodor Axentowicz, and the poetry of Kazimierz Przerwa Tetmajer. One of the most explicit references in the film is to Wyspiański's painting *Studium Dziecka—Helenka z Wazonikiem i Kwiatami* (1902).

Despite the sleeping children, though, the festivities are now in full swing. Continuing the earlier ghost theme, the sleeping girl dreams that the straw man outside the window sings to her and wants to enter the hut; meanwhile, the woman called Emilia dreams about her lover, a painter, long deceased. Similarly allusive, this brief flashback scene, set in a birch grove, reminds us of Wajda's earlier film, *The Birchwood*—both in its locale and, more interestingly, in the fact that Emilia and her dead lover Stanisław are portrayed by the same actors who played the parts of the lovers Malina and Stanisław in the previous film.

In another series of vignettes, the bridegroom seems to appreciate his bride, but only on the surface, as if looking for the source of health and robust life in his wife. In this, Wyspiański criticizes both the idealization of Polish peasants' robustness by the aristocracy and the desire of the upper classes to draw from this supposed health. In the nineteenth century, this idealization was realized in many ways, one of them a persistent belief among the intelligentsia that they might find solace and medical cure in villages, especially those located in the mountainous regions around Kraków. This idea is cynically exposed by the bridegroom, played brilliantly by Daniel Olbrychski.

Finally, morning comes. Jasiek, with the golden horn, is lost in the fog and stops at the point where three borders—those of the Austrian, Russian, and Prussian zones—intersect, revealing the impossible situation of a Poland that, politically and geographically at least, did not really exist at that time. The soldiers from the three occupied zones surround Jasiek and he gallops away. In the meantime, the tired wedding participants lie drunk on the floor, some still wanting to dance, while Czepiec talks about one of the most pervasive addictions in Poland, alcoholism. When the quarrelsome Czepiec calls upon the peasants to take scythes from the barn, the atmosphere in the hut changes from a joyous to an aggressive one. When Jasiek returns without his cap or the horn, he finds the terrified members of the intelligentsia pinned down by the scythe-wielding peasants.

They are let go only when the host explains the strange vision in which Wernyhora calls for an insurrection. All the wedding guests listen to the hoofbeats in apprehension. No feelings or desires are important now; everyone kneels down and waits for Jasiek with the golden horn. The white light embraces men with scythes, other participants of the wedding, and the straw men. Finally, Jasiek emerges out of the morning fog, without the horn, and tries to wake the participants of the wedding out of their stupor. The first to wake up is the groom. He leaves the hut and approaches the white horse lying exhausted in the mud. Others gather around the straw men amid the wailing voice of Chochoł, who sings *"miałeś chamie złoty róg"* ("you had a golden horn, peasant"), clearly referring to the lost opportunity to liberate Poland from its occupiers.

The Wedding is a film unique in Polish cinema, based on a play widely considered one of the best theatrical works in Poland; it is a text well known to almost every Pole, studied by both literary critics and school children alike. Choosing this text for a film was an act of courage on the part of the director, for bringing such a well-known piece to the screen is almost always a doomed enterprise. Wajda was prompted, though, he claims, not only by the text's vitality and social importance for Poles, but also by the visual possibilities it created for the cinema. The text's appeal to Poles, its presentation of the conflict between intelligentsia and peasantry, and its highly critical portrayal of all the social spheres in nineteenth-century Poland, was crucial to the director, who has always been critical of Poles' naïveté and political inertia. He presents these ideological conflicts against a backdrop of fantasy and reality, intersecting in a relentless dance, surrounded by constant drinking, bickering, and hysterical joyfulness. This blend of high spirit and excessive emotion translates into a visually stunning film.

Most of the film's action takes place while the participants are drunk and unruly, with the general atmosphere thickening, the guests drawn slowly into drunken stupor. This is when the ghosts appear in what Zygmunt Kałużynski calls a "montage of the stream of consciousness," which, according to him, Wajda borrowed from the French New Wave representatives Alain Resnais and Jean-Luc Godard. This "stream of unsuspected depictions, suddenly cut[,] reflecting on the interior states without any introduction,"[41] gives the film its ferocity and emotional intensity. The film is quite satisfying in this respect, but other reviewers do not agree. For instance, Paul Coates feels that

> [the] quest to bring together all the threads can even issue in the lack of an organizing idea of which Krzysztof Mętrak complains. The Aesopian possibility of reference to seventies Poland borders on academicism, and ironically exemplifies the very inability to criticize the system pilloried by Wyspiański himself. It may well be as compensation for this that Wajda fetishizes technique, setting the camera zooming compulsively to engender the sense of instability that heralds, and then accompanies, the manifestations of the otherworldly.[42]

Of course, the film tells its story in pictures. Himself a painter, Wajda understood deeply the visual potential of the film. As Krzysztof Teodor Toeplitz notes, the filmmaker applies the same artistic criteria to the structure of both his paintings and his films: Such basic principles of painting as harmony, balance, and proportion are also important to the structure of film shots and sequences.[43]

Most critics praised Wajda's artistic vision, including his addition of some scenes not present in the literary work—for instance, the scene portraying the aristocrats attacked by peasants raised serious objections. While Toeplitz considered this scene justified within the spirit of the film, Kałużynski contended that the scene is unnecessary and excessive, filling a highly expressive film with unwarranted emotional intensity.[44] Many critical voices were concerned regarding the film's contemporaneity in the sense that *The Wedding* could be interpreted as referring to both the nineteenth-century past and to the 1970s. Jarosław Iwaszkiewicz, however, one of the greatest Polish writers, declared that "*The Wedding* is still current after 72 years!"[45]

Especially in the Polish press, the film triggered extensive discussions concerning its adherence to the play on which it was based, its interpretation of historical events, and its aesthetic impact. Other critical comments concerned "the film's links with Polish Romanticism, the nature of the main protagonist in the film which is the 'group subconscious,' historical realism, the presentation of events in the oneiric space, the manifestation of helplessness in view of historical events and even 'shrieking realism.'"[46] *The Wedding* has been evaluated quite highly by French critics, on the other hand. Gilles Jacob and Louis Chauvet call the film "interesting," "beautiful," and "highly emotional," with a clear structure and a style "full of emotional tension."[47] The French critics perceive the symbolic importance of Wajda's national and social obsessions and compare the film to Fellini's *La Dolce Vita*;[48] they understand its importance in explicating the historical fate of Poland,[49] and many also stress the film's beauty, to the point of calling it "formal perfection."[50]

I find the negative Polish criticism concerning the film's adherence to the text of the play baffling, given the director's mastery in his attempt to combine the difficult text of the play with the film medium's visual aspects, pace, and energy. While the referential density in this film requires good knowledge of Polish history and art, Wajda seduces the spectator with his aesthetics, arising from his love for spectacle. By structuring the film around the image of the dance, with its movement, its frenzy, and the ensuing exhaustion of the dancers, Wajda presents important social and historical issues as if in passing, not thrusting them demagogically in one's face; rather, he smuggles them in between swirls of intoxicated peasants. Again, what really remains in the spectator's memory is the stunning power of the images presented to the monotonous, though intoxicating beat of the music. However, while the visual potential of the film is realized first in the dance, it appears also, and equally, in the verisimilitude and complexity of the characters, spinning as they utter their monologues breathlessly, and in the intricacy of the ideological and political issues they espouse or represent. The film fulfills all the postulations of the play.

Promised Land (1974)

After *The Wedding*, Wajda's next film seems to be made by a different director, although the same passion is evident in its approaches to historical data and to the emotions of the protagonists. *Promised Land* tells the story of three young entrepreneurs, Karol Borowiecki, Moryc Welt, and Maks Baum, who build a factory in Łódź at the turn of the century. Based on a well-known Władysław Reymont novel by the same title, the film tells the story of the first attempts at Poland's industrialization. Unlike *The Wedding*, in which the emotional intensity is obtained largely by sweeping camera movements, the "emotional excess" in this film is achieved with the use of close-ups and broad sweeps of the wide-scope lenses of the camera.

The first part (of four) in the film starts with a sweeping panorama of the gloomy suburbs of Łódź, where the rag-clothed workers live in shacks, malnourished and sad. At dawn, they go to their jobs in the factories. Meanwhile, the film's protagonists open a champagne bottle in the woods as they discuss the construction of their factory. Karol is a young member of the landed aristocracy who tries to make a fortune with the backing of his Polish family; Maks is a German, heir to an industrial fortune; and Moryc is a Jewish businessman who decides to support his friends in the investment endeavor. Wide-angle shots reveal them admiring the rapidly growing city. Shortly thereafter, though, they show Karol ruthlessly conducting business in Bucholz's factory, where he is employed as a supervisor; Maks shouts at his aging father, who refuses to give him money for his new venture; and Moryc engages in feverish dealings at the stock exchange.

These sequences introduce the fervent but also merciless atmosphere of the new industry, where workers' demands for better working conditions are ignored. When an intern at the factory, Van Horn, demands compensation for the wife of a deceased worker, he is brutally dismissed by the insensitive Karol. The world of industry is presented as a place in which there is no compassion, where feelings of helplessness predominate. Ambitious Karol, who functions well in this harsh setting, is later approached by Muller, a German factory owner, with an offer to come and work for him. Karol refuses, saying that he plans to build his own factory.

From this scene forward, the story focuses on Karol and his transformation from a relentless and enthusiastic, if slightly naïve entrepreneur into a ruthless industrialist. Karol has two love interests: Lucy Zucker, the wife of a rich Jewish factory owner and financier; and Anka, Karol's fiancée, who lives on the estate of Karol's father, in an old country manor at Kurów. These love interests also epitomize two Polish cultural traditions, that of the old gentry (represented by Anka), slowly disappearing with the approach of the twentieth century, with its hunger for monetary gain at any cost, and that of the Zuckers, the representatives of the new era.

The three friends go to the opera house, where they amuse themselves at a performance of *Swan Lake*. Shot with a wide-scope camera, the sequence reveals all the unpleasant aspects of the nouveau-riche society to which the protagonists belong. With the exception of a few young men and women, nobody treats the theater as a place of high-quality entertainment; rather, it is a place of "wheeling-and-dealing," where businesspeople start new partnerships and renew old acquaintances. When talking about women such as Lucy, the friends exchange remarks about the value of her diamonds and not about the beauty of her person. Moryc confirms the cynicism of this segment of society when he proclaims that the theater is as important for doing business as for anything else.

Mada Muller—a naive, narrow-minded, and poorly educated young woman, daughter of the German factory owner—is also at the theater. She is attracted to Karol and asks him, in a thinly veiled invitation to further encounters, for books to read; Karol reluctantly agrees, sensing the urgency in her voice but also, and more importantly, recognizing the usefulness of such contacts in the future. He agrees to come to her house later. Suddenly, there is commotion in the theater. During a burlesque piece performed on the stage during the break, the businesspeople sitting in the theater loggias are approached by messengers. The three friends notice these developments and Moryc runs to learn what has happened. When Zucker leaves his place to attend to business, his wife, Lucy, nods at Karol, invites him into her loggia, and then persuades him to leave the theater with her. On his way to her, Karol notices several men who have committed suicide because of some unfortunate business dealings.

A short time later, when Lucy and Karol indulge in a sexual encounter in her carriage on the way to the Zuckers' house, she tells him about the rising prices of cotton, which is the reason for the commotion in the opera house. The most explicit sexual moment takes place when Karol learns from her that he will profit enormously from this inside trading; she passes on the information she has obtained from her husband just as Karol is on the verge of an orgasm. Later, Karol comes to the restaurant seeking Moryc so that he can communicate this new and exciting business opportunity. With his information, the three friends stand to make a great deal of money before the new cotton regulation is in place. The drunken Moryc sobers up immediately.

When the three friends discuss this opportunity the following morning, Maks is surprised and touched by Karol's generosity. Moryc is all business, and considers the friendly revelations to be sentimental folly; he dreams only of the factory the three of them will build and is not interested in any other business opportunities. Polish generosity and fairness, when compared to Jewish shrewdness and greed, smacks of a stereotypical depiction of Jews, a volatile matter for which the film was severely criticized.[51] In all, Moryc is portrayed as a clown, the "resourceful Jew" common in literature at the beginning of the twentieth century. Wajda himself, aware of these stereotypes, frequently defends his portrayals as based on those of the original novel from which the film is composed.

The second part of the film shows Wilczek, a pawnbroker and usurer who lends money to the impoverished local women in return for their possessions. In intense sequences shot with wide-screen lenses, the workers are shown on their way to the factory. The voice-over commentary states that Łódź suffers from an economic collapse because of market fluctuations. This commentary attends feverish depictions of pulsating factory machines and marching workers. Next, a much quieter sequence depicts the aristocrat Trawiński, who engages in a quiet conversation with his wife in his upscale house. Trawiński is bankrupt, like so many other aristocrats at the time. The old-fashioned aristocracy cannot adapt to the new times and do not know how to function in this environment of greed and duplicity. Trawińsky's wife, unaware of the situation, has ordered a beautiful mosaic tabletop from Italy; her husband is too proud to explain to her the gravity of their situation and leaves their house to seek financial help.

Trawiński approaches Karol at Bucholz's factory and asks him for a loan. Karol refuses, explaining that Trawińsky has no luck and thus he cannot risk any business with him. When he returns to his wife, Trawińsky realizes that her aristocratic upbringing, where honesty in business dealings was of paramount importance, would not allow her to accept her husband if he involved himself in any sort of swindles, which the ruthless commerce of the time generally required if one wished to be successful. Devastated by the impossibility of his situation, he leaves the house and commits suicide with a gun. The scene is punctuated by the ever-present clatter of the factory where Moryc and the German Kessler discuss still another business venture; afterward, demonstrating the moral decrepitude of the era, Kessler approaches young female workers and asks his assistant to choose young, pretty ones to attend an orgy at his estate.

This orgy soon takes place in Kessler's palace, and the nouveau-riche guests are shown to be completely debauched and immoral. Naked young women dance among rich men, young and old alike. The scene is observed by the workers through the windows of the palace, by the disgusted Moryc inside the palace, and by an amused Karol outside. Kessler, accompanied by a frightened village girl, Zosia, approaches Karol and bombards him with arrogant comments regarding "modern civilization" and German superiority. In a telling sequence, the Pole proudly responds that pigs (a popular term for Germans in Poland at this time) would never understand eagles (a reference to the Polish national emblem and, indirectly, an allusion to Polish independence and romanticism).

Here, Wajda deals openly with a volatile theme of Polish nationalism, always linked to Polish Romanticism, which considers freedom to be superior to any capitalist practicalities. This ill-concealed nationalism also triggers action against Kessler, who must be punished for his abuse of young girls—but worse, for the fact that he is an arrogant German industrialist abusing young *Polish* girls. Abuse and power are linked with the early developments of industry and counteracted by nationalism, naïveté, and romanticism. Zosia's attendance at Kessler's castle ends with her being banned from her parents' house upon her return from the orgy the following morning. Her mother does not want to see her, and only her brother follows the poor girl to the door. Again, this tragic scene is punctuated by crowds of workers going to work, silent factory chimneys witnessing the scene and relentlessly rattling machines. Kessler dies miserably in his own factory, thrown by Zosia's enraged and desperate father, Malinowski, under the wheel of his machinery.

Elsewhere, Karol cynically woos the young Mada Muller, whom he met at the opera, approaching her with a superficial exchange of pleasantries. Ominously, a flowerpot falls from the window upstairs, as if commenting on their future. The girl's rich German father invites Karol to see his palace; in its poorly conceived opulence, the palace surpasses everything that has been built in Łódź so far. Karol asks Muller why he does not live there, and the German responds that he keeps the palace only to show it off to others—after all, he quips, everybody is building something. The panning movement of the camera sweeps over the huge ceilings and walls full of ornaments, while the men discuss future bridegrooms for a rich young woman like Mada.

In further developments concerning Karol's plans to build a factory by himself, since Moryc and Maks have backed out of the plan, Moryc learns from the old Jew that all the Jewish and German industrialists have set up a front against the young Pole, for they perceive him as a threat: He might introduce the rules of fair play and create an honestly run factory. This goes against the business interests of all of Łódź, so

Glinczman, a prominent and wealthy Jew, withdraws credit from the three friends. Shocked and disgusted, Moryc leaves his older compatriot when the latter refuses to lend him money. The next scene shows another development: Mrs. Trawińska, the impoverished wife of the deceased aristocrat, stands in line at a soup kitchen operated by the Catholic Church, and then eats her modest meal among the many unfortunate townsfolk. In a parallel sequence, Maks, Moryc, and Karol count the money for the factory at the building site. Unlike the Trawińskas, each of them was able to acquire some funds. The serenity of the scene is marred, however, by Maks's admission that he extracted the money from his own father by cunning and force.

The third part of the film opens with the young and energetic Moryc and Karol discussing the cotton price hikes in the factory. The dynamic scene is soon contrasted with the peace of the manor, Kurów, outside Łódź, where Anka and Karol's father live; the three friends approach the beautiful manor on bicycles, laughing and joking, admiring the idyllic landscape full of birch trees, sand, and chirping birds. Anka, Karol's young fiancée, emerges from the house in a white dress. The sentimental appearance of the scene is reinforced later by the young couple's romantic walk among the birch trees, their ride on black and white horses, and their conversations full of love and tenderness. All of this is illustrated with the music reminiscent of that from the film *Noce i dnie (Nights and Days)*, a romantic account of the rural life in the nineteenth century.

During dinner, the young men talk only of the factory they plan to build. In their enthusiasm for "the new," they do not consider tradition, which is represented by Anka, Karol's father, and the manor in which they reside. Moryc in particular seems to see everything in terms of its dollar value; Karol persuades his father to consider investing in his new factory. The next day, images and scenes full of references to Polish tradition—the design of the manor's rooms, for example, and Anka's sentimentality—shift into a harsh reality. Dawn arrives unusually bright and sharp, showing Karol awakening with a tense look on his face.

At the breakfast table, the young entrepreneurs discuss their ambitious plans while the new buyer of Kurów, the parvenu Kaczmarek, the future owner of Kurów, throws a bunch of banknotes in the middle of the breakfast table. Arrogant, he demands coffee and talks loudly and rudely about his new possession; Anka's silent bewilderment is punctuated by his loud, haughty behavior. The next scene shows a carriage bringing Anka and Karol's father to Łódź. The industrial landscape in Łódź provides a shocking contrast to the beauty of Kurów. The city, seen from Anka's point of view, is an ugly place full of contrasts. Rich palaces of industrialists are surrounded by the poor dwellings of the workers. Hungry, dirty children play near the sewers while merchants and moneylenders go about their business. Karol welcomes the newcomers and graciously accepts money given to him by Anka, who does not hide her love for Karol.

The following sequences deal with Bucholz, the affluent owner of the factory in which Karol works. In a stereotypical presentation of a rich and arrogant German, the legendary Bucholz is an abrasive bully who treats his Polish doctor, his personal servant, and his clerks in an equally ruthless manner. He boasts about his riches and physically abuses his servants and employees; he throws out Horn, the honest clerk who tries to protect the workers; he holds cynical conversations with Karol about business dealings. Finally, as he takes a lonely walk around his factory, Bucholz dies, alone and unnoticed. The factory continues to function without him; nobody is troubled by his death, and life goes on. During the funeral, Jews and Poles converse about the deceased financier and industrialist, who owned almost half of Łódź at the time of his death. Suddenly, some of the carriages leave the funeral procession and the workers go back to their offices: someone has declared that the cotton prices rose and, soon, almost everyone abandons the funeral.

Finally, the three protagonists stand at the construction site of their factory. Karol complains that his line of credit is depleted and nobody wants to have anything to do with him. His luck seems to have left him. Lucy informs him that she is pregnant, and Anka willingly engages in charity work in his own factory. Surprised and shocked by Karol's brutality and ruthlessness (for the young businessman does not want any charity workers in his factory), Anka cries desperately and rebels against him. Karol's father reacts to this turn of events with disgust; he shouts at Karol that he has hurt Anka by not marrying her and by keeping her at bay. Finally, he condemns his son for having forgotten his past and his ancestry, for having "sold his soul to the golden calf," and throws Karol out of his house.

The fourth part of the film starts with Moryc counting out the money he owes Glinczman. During their subsequent conversation, Moryc wins the money back from the lender by blackmail and deceit. He takes the sum he needs for the newly built factory, where Maks and Karol see to the last-minute details; excited by the good news about the money, the friends decide to open the factory at once. They join hands with each other in a close-up reminiscent of those in Wajda's other films about the glory of work and entrepreneurship, such as *Man of Marble*. The factory is consecrated with holy water—and then by another sort of water, as the three friends lightheartedly urinate against the factory's wall.

However, their jubilation is interrupted by Zucker, who brings Karol a letter, obviously from Lucy even though it is unsigned, stating that the young man is the father of her child. Karol lies about his affair with Lucy, and thus reveals himself to be an unconscionable, cynical young man who has compromised his integrity, his beliefs, and his honesty. Eventually, he turns into an unfeeling businessperson whose only desire is to make money at any cost, even if it means distancing himself from everyone and imperiling the quality of his goods. Like his integrity, Karol's love for Anka also disappears. In a telling good-bye sequence, he leaves the honest young woman only to meet with his clandestine lover, Lucy.

During their secret meeting, Lucy tells Karol that her husband plans to send her to his relatives in Berlin. Convinced by Karol's oath, Zucker now believes the child to be his own, and he wants to protect his wife during her pregnancy. She begs Karol to go with her; he dissuades her from this idea but then, with another glance at her deeply décolletage dress, decides otherwise. The lovers plan to leave Łódź together on the same train. However, when he enters Lucy's compartment, Karol is noticed by Bum-bum, a criminal paid by Zucker to watch his wife covertly. When Bum-bum reports this fact back to Zucker, the jealous husband decides to burn Karol's factory. Two sequences are intercut throughout the following scenes: Anka sadly playing the piano and the lovers on the train engaging in sexual play. Suddenly, someone throws a stone at the window in Anka's room and shouts that the factory is on fire. When Anka enters the burning factory, she sees Moryc and Maks terrified by the burning flames, mad looks in their eyes. Karol is soon informed about the fire by telegram and returns to Łódź immediately.

In the next scene, Karol speaks a monologue addressed to his deceased father. In impassioned words, he tries to explain the motives of his actions, his ruthlessness, and his lack of principles. He says that what his predecessors won with the saber and the cross, he has been forced to obtain through cruelty and ruthlessness: He must conquer the Jewish and German industries in Poland with the same weapons they use against him. Finally, after Anka has returned his engagement ring, Karol leaves the house. In the morning, the three friends deliberate over their future when they learn that the factory was burned on Zucker's order. Realizing suddenly that their misfortunes have been caused by Karol's indiscretions, Maks and Moryc are infuriated and attack Karol viciously.

The final sequence of the film shows Karol several years later with his wife, the daughter of the German industrialist Muller, at a lavish party he holds for his guests. Portraying him with his children, wife, and guests, surrounded by insurmountable riches, the scenes are cut with black-and-white shots of empty factories. Suddenly, a stone smashes through the window into their living room, signifying the beginning of the workers' strike. Supported by members of his board of executives, Karol gives the order to shoot at the workers. The film ends with a shot of a worker holding a red flag in his hand.

Promised Land was universally heralded a masterpiece and received an Oscar nomination as the best foreign film of 1976. At the same time, it caused a stir among critics both in Poland and abroad. Most commentators of the film noted the following areas that required explanation and interpretation, especially for foreign audiences:

1. The inaccurate portrayal of Karol as a ruthless Polish industrialist, unlike his positive and rather benign portrayal in the book;
2. The demonization in the film of industrial progress, which, according to Reymont and many historians, actually had a beneficial influence on Łódź;
3. Stereotypical, at times parodic representations of Germans and Jews;
4. The "Americanization" of the film, in both content and form, particularly in its presentation of complex situations in superficial black-and-white, well-composed, quick-paced tableaux and sequences.

The major consequence of these "inadequacies" was that the complex historical reality and the ideological intricacies of the book were only superficially presented in the film. First, Reymont's *Promised Land* illustrated the progress in Łódź in an almost documentary fashion, while Wajda concentrated on the fate of one of the book's protagonists, Karol. This change was widely commented upon not only by film critics, but also by historians and literary critics. To all these and to other criticisms, Wajda unvaryingly responded that the film was governed by other rules than a novel and that he was interested in producing a good, well-paced, "Americanesque" film. In fact, in one of the many interviews he gave after the film's screening, he stressed the fact that it was "the realization of the film, the energy of actors, the explicit and interesting stage design and the explosive nature of action" that particularly appealed to the spectators.[52]

One of the most interesting commentaries regarding Wajda's "inaccurate" portrayal of Karol was proposed by Bożena Krzywobłocka in *Ekran:* "Promised Land in the book is the land of happiness and hope for the capitalists of mainly foreign origin, not for Polish capitalists who have not been accepted as partners in 'real business'.... Borowiecki, as presented by Wajda, epitomizes the capitalist evil, the presentation so anachronistic and unrealistic that it brings only laughter."[53] In the later part of her essay, Krzywobłocka reveals all the transformations or reinterpretations by Wajda of major events in the book, and even some inconsistencies concerning historical facts as presented by Reymont. These changes have been meticulously documented by Anna Pyszny in the academic interpretation of the film as a "reinterpretation" of the book that is filtered through the filmmaker's "personal sensitivity, his mentality, individual obsessions and his own philosophy of life."[54] In a similar approach to the film, Michał Komar reveals differences and similarities between the original text and the film in a detailed analysis of both, supported with historical material from the epoch.[55]

Regarding the film's demonization of industrial progress, Wajda's approach is again dictated by an almost American attention to narrative structure in terms of morally unambiguous characters. In presenting industrialists in homogeneously negative colors, his purpose was to contrast them with the traditional idealistic and "good" representatives of the nobility and aristocracy, represented by Trawiński, Anka, and Karol's father. In the novel, Karol is a charismatic, successful industrialist who mourns the departure of the idealistic past, and decidedly not the ruthless capitalist depicted by Wajda.

One of the most controversial topics in critical discourse surrounding the film is its presentation of Jews, one considered offensive by most reviewers. Anna Pyszny comments on the anti-Semitic presentation of the Jewish character Moryc, which according to her is an excellent illustration of the political obsessions of the Stronnictwo Narodowo-Demokratyczne (National Democratic Party), "the political party at play,"[56] at the time of the novel. In the novel, Moryc is cunning and ruthless, constantly taking advantage of the collaborators who are portrayed as his friends in the film. While he takes care only of his own business, he causes the collapse of their enterprise by starting the fire in the new factory and withdrawing his money. In the film, however, Moryc is "toned down," changed so drastically that it implies a far-reaching interpretation not only of this protagonist, but of the whole meaning of the novel as well. In the film, Moryc is a cunning person who minds his own interests. However, he is no more rapacious than his companions, a Pole and a German. In some cases, he is even unselfish and loyal. He participates in the construction of the factory, gets the money by cunning, and, after the fire in the factory, defends Karol against Maks's justified complaints.[57]

Once again, Pyszny calls Wajda's modification a "reinterpretation." Wajda eliminates *endecja* attitudes and shows a world in which "people act according to specific rules of the game, notwithstanding their nationality. Their actions in the film are motivated not by specific predispositions of particular nations but by historical and social determinants."[58] In this context, the anti-Semitism of which the film was accused was especially upsetting to Wajda, who tried hard to eliminate the most incendiary elements of the novel as he wrote the screenplay for the film.

Wajda was especially embittered by the fact that, despite its Oscar nomination, *Promised Land* was rarely shown in the United States because of its negative Jewish stereotypes. Like Reymont's novel, the film offers a brutally honest portrayal of nineteenth-century Polish society; its matter is controversial, and at times explosively so. After its release, the film provoked strong reactions not only in its presentation of Jews, but also of both Poles and Germans. While Wajda hoped for accolades in the United States, he most certainly underestimated the impact some scenes would have on the American public. Distribution agencies in Los Angeles and New York would not show the film at all. The Manggha Center in Kraków has amassed a wealth of correspondence between Wajda and American film distributors who voice their ambivalence regarding the film. For example, Daniel Talbot writes,

> "Finally, I screened *Land of Promise*, this time with a few spectators who are prominent in the New York Jewish community. For me, it is a masterpiece of filmmaking, so rich and wonderfully made, a feast for the eyes. Unhappily, however, the feeling among several people in the audience is that the film is open to anti-Semitic interpretation.... This said, it will be impossible for me to open the film in New York."[59]

Another screening of the film in New York in 1988 met with similar reaction. In reviewing this film, critic Caryn James talks about the stereotypical presentation of Jews in *Promised Land*, which most viewers watched with disgust. "Not all of Mr. Wajda's 19th-century excesses sit comfortably in the 20th century. Too many secondary characters are stereotypes of Jews, especially a repulsive, piggish woman with whom Karol has an affair and her merciless, vengeful husband. There is so little historical perspective on these characters that Mr. Wajda's own judgement seems to have failed him."[60]

The reception of *Promised Land* demonstrates that understanding a film's wider cultural context is an absolute interpretive necessity. Wajda's intention to produce an honest film about the industrial growth of Łódź in the nineteenth century never materialized; the film was universally acclaimed as a masterpiece, but criticized in Eastern Europe for its presentation of the greed, ruthlessness, and moral decrepitude characterizing early capitalism in Poland. Yet in the reviews of English-speaking spectators, all attention was focused on the inappropriate presentation of minorities, especially Jews—although Wajda was equally damning in his portrayal of (greedy) Poles and Germans, it was his portrayal of Jews that raised Western spectators' eyebrows.

It is important to understand that the issues of representation, stereotyping, and political correctness were highly debated in research and political circles in the West during the 1970s (as they remain today), while in Poland these debates started only in the late 1980s and early 1990s. Wajda's—or perhaps more accurately Reymont's—naturalistic, though perhaps exaggerated portraits of ethnic minorities were conducive to these discussions. Poland has long been thought a country with latent anti-Semitism simmering deep in its collective subconscious, so *Promised Land*, although brilliantly made, perhaps unnecessarily threw some fuel onto the fire of these discussions. Probably, as Wajda stated in 2000, he never thought at the time of making the film that the complexities of historical Polish-Jewish relations in Poland could still ignite such heated debates elsewhere in the world.[61] Nonetheless, he came to realize that he could not appease his critics in this matter, however noble his intentions might have been in making the film.

As far as the fourth common area of criticism—that of the Americanization of the film's form and content—is concerned, all of the critics at the time of its release contended that the film is essentially brilliant. In all of the interviews and critical treatises, one prevailing commentary reigns: The film is an aesthetic masterpiece in which Wajda's painterly talent shines. Zygmunt Kałużynski calls the film "a spectacle" that "suggestively combines ugliness and beauty, lyricism and shock, caricature and poetry. This combination of aesthetic values makes *Promised Land* a quintessentially Wajda film, and not just an adaptation of a well-known novel."[62] This view is also supported by Krzysztof Teodor Toeplitz, who calls the film "an excellent artwork, manieristic in its outlook."[63]

The spectacle in the film attacks the viewer with a direct appeal to both emotional and aesthetic sensibilities. A viewer must side either with Anka and Karol's father, representatives of the conservative aristocratic past (shot in a like manner, using medium shots, diffused light, and romanticized portrayals), or with Karol and his friends, and thus with the industrial world they represent, with all its dirt, clutter, noise, ruthlessness, and greed (mostly portrayed in wide scope). Such a "black-and-white" portrayal of the protagonists is conducive to superficial generalizations, though, and flattens the overall meaning of the novel. However, such a simplification allowed Wajda to present the protagonists as elements of a well-composed tableau of the film spectacle. In such a tableau, the protagonists, their movements, and the elements of the background against which they are filmed constitute equiponderant elements of the whole. The complexity of the characters and of their motivations would only obliterate the clarity of the spectacle itself.

The simplification of character motivation thus allows Wajda to dazzle the spectator with wide sweeps of the camera, with the quick pace of the film, with the aesthetic brilliance of the shots, and with the consistent spectrum of color. Sequences in dark colors signify the hopelessness and brutality of the industrial world, while light, romantic sequences refer to the past, to the romantic approach to life, to the rural Polish landscape, and to the nationalistic bliss. This consistent aesthetics creates a clear ideological division between the nostalgic past and the ruthless future, and, paradoxically, between nations as well. On one side are the idealistic Poles (Karol being an exception), and on the other, ruthless Germans and Jews. This unequivocal portrayal allowed Wajda to make a fully Americanized film, with events unfolding in a clear cause-effect pattern. The film dazzles with color, hypnotizes the spectator with the monotonous clatter of machines, and thus provides a clear interpretation of the film's events.

The Shadow Line (1976)

After the storm raised by *Promised Land,* Wajda's next film brought peace, calm, and introspection. *The Shadow Line* is another example of adaptation of a famous literary text to film, this time of a short story by Joseph Conrad. The film portrays the sea adventures and moral dilemmas of a young sea captain. The screenplay by Bolesław Sulik and Wajda and the cinematography of Witold Sobociński combine to evoke a lyrical film that captures the beauty of the sea, the ship, and the man in command of it. Although basically an adaptation of a story that takes place in the nineteenth century, the film turns into a universal statement on truth, human self-determination, and basic questions of morality. When explaining his intention to make this film, Wajda says, "I think that there exists a great need for true purity, something very positive, something with basic principles. This was the first reason for making this film—the reason of moral nature."[64]

The film starts with a series of stills from the nineteenth century, depicting scenes of nautical life. The narrator tells about the mysterious abandonment of the ship *Vidar,* which for eighteen months was left drifting in the southern seas without explanation. The narrator leads us to the Officer-Sailor Home in Singapore, where Capt. Joseph Conrad, played by a young Marek Kondrat, sits at a table with other captains, among them Giles and Hamilton. In a nostalgic autobiographical statement, the young captain tells about his sad experiences at sea and about the fact that he does not plan to take on a new command. However, when an attractive offer arises, supported by the recommendation of an experienced Giles, he changes his mind. He learns from Giles that it has been difficult to find a captain for the *Regina Maris* because the former captain seems to have died under mysterious circumstances; the ship is thought doomed.

When Joseph sees the ship for the first time, he is struck by its beauty and splendor. The *Regina Maris* is an English three-master manned by an English crew and formerly commanded by an English captain.[65] In a loving shot of the ship, accompanied by the nostalgic music of Wojciech Kilar, Wajda tries to convey the mysterious qualities of seamanship, the sea, and nature. When Burns, the first mate, introduces the crew, the magic of the moment disappears: The crew all look sickly, aptly rendered by shots in brownish colors. Soon after they set sail, problems begin to occur: There are difficulties with the cargo when the ship enters Hong Kong harbor, and Burns is found to suffer from cholera. Despite the doctor's warnings about the cholera outbreak and his conviction that Burns should be left in the hospital, Conrad decides to take Burns with him. The proud ship leaves the port in the descending sun.

The ship experiences more serious problems at sea. First, a dead calm descends, and the ship is trapped for many weeks. Burns blames the ghost of the deceased captain for this predicament; the calm and inscrutable young captain merely drinks tea and listens to the barely audible waves. Then, the remaining crew members get sick, so he distributes quinine among them and silently wanders up and down the ship. The tropical fever, heat, and humidity create an atmosphere of fear and apprehension. Burns continues to complain about the dead captain, while the sickened, shivering crew members wait passively; they all behave as if the ship were bewitched. All of these events and phenomena are depicted by cinematographer Allan Starski in mysterious and beautiful images, illustrated by Kilar's music.

Conrad begins to have bad dreams in which he overhears strange exchanges between Burns and the deceased captain. When he wakes up, he realizes that the curse of the sea is not yet gone. Not only is the dead calm still there, but the quinine jars, he discovers, are full of sand. The young captain gets increasingly angry and exasperated. In the captain's diary he writes about his own insecurities and worries; he wonders whether he is any good as a captain and whether he should be onboard at all. Suddenly, the wind rises, clouds appear on the horizon, and the crew members' hopes are aroused. After an initial spell of good wind, however, everything dies down again. Burns, laughing, curses the sea. As if in response to his curses, the wind rises with tremendous force and the ship charges forward madly. The sails screech in the wind and water sprays up onto the deck. Burns leaves his cabin and sees the young captain steering the ship by himself. With the crew too weak to help him, the captain heroically leads the ship with the help of his faithful steward, Ransom. Land appears on the horizon; the fight against nature is finally over. All of the crew members live, and are taken by health officials to the hospital. In a final conversation with captain Giles, Conrad says that he feels old; Giles responds that he *looks* older, as well. Despite his horrific predicaments, however, he now wants to go to the Indian Ocean.

The Shadow Line did not raise a great deal of interest in Poland or abroad. Considered an interesting, meditative tale on humanity's responsibility in the face of adversity, it did not communicate the passion and openness found in most of Wajda's other films. Both the landscape and the social problems were alien to Wajda, and he could not properly translate the power and intensity of Conrad's prose into the language of film. The intense silence of the sea in Conrad's prose translates into a painful stillness in the middle of the film, an impasse; while inactivity can be described in words as well as activity can, such a thing is monumentally difficult to translate into the language of cinema, the foremost principle of which is "movement."

This impasse translated into unconvincing performances and what Piotr Kajewski describes as "a sort of a lack of coherence between the abundant text and the image, accompanied by actors who seem to stand next to everything that happens on the screen."[66] Andrzej Markowski also comments on this dilemma, especially in view of the incompatibility between the text and the lack of action:

> Wajda set out to accomplish what seemed like an impossible task: that is to transfer every scene and nearly every line of dialogue of Conrad's novel to the film, even though *The Shadow Line* seems to have no film action. Cast in half-tones, it can, however, be given only one interpretation. This unambiguous meaning is lightly indicated, often lost in the shadow, its action introverted. Its dramatic power does not lie in external and fairly uncommon events but in the interplay of internal forces.[67]

It seems that even in the presentation of general themes, such as a man's strength in the face of adversity, death, and sickness, Wajda feels at his best when these themes are set against the landscape and social conditions of Poland, which he understands implicitly. In both *The Birchwood* and *The Young Ladies of Wilko*, general themes of life and death are set in a Polish environment, and the two films are powerful and passionate because of it. *The Shadow Line*, on the other hand, while dealing with similar general themes, is suspended in a social emptiness that, unfortunately, cannot be filled by the subdued performances of the actors, however strong their characterizations. Nevertheless, the film charmed many spectators with its exquisite images of the sea, both in its calm majesty and rage.

It seems that the philosophical reflections of Conrad found their expression in the quietly passionate images of Witold Sobociński, the film's cinematographer. For this beauty, the film earned many awards, including one from the Third Festival of Polish Feature Films (Gdańsk, 1976) and from the International Week of Maritime Films (Cartagena, Spain, 1979). Many critics, among them Juliet McLauchlan, admired Wajda's humility in adapting Conrad's prose to the screen: "[He] left aside his personal approach to Conrad's story and restrained from imposing anything foreign to the text."[68] Her words aptly summarize those positive impressions the film made on many spectators: "in this film the characterization of protagonists is subtle, the psychological tensions are pertinently alluded to, and the sea and the ship itself are vividly presented thanks to the dazzling but delicate and subtle applications of color and sound."[69] For Aleksander Jackiewicz, the film toys with light and color in a subdued tone, "as if diffused in the light of William Turner's paintings."[70]

Man of Marble (1977)

Man of Marble belongs to a group of films that openly revealed the past and present social and political structures in Poland.[71] Considered part of a trilogy along with the films *Man of Iron* and *Danton,* it is crucial to the formation and development of the Polish cinema's School of Moral Concern (or Cinema of Distrust), terms referring to "realistic films that examine contemporary issues and were made primarily between 1976 and 1981."[72] Generally, the most important films of this school, apart from Wajda's three, are considered to be Krzysztof Zanussi's *Barwy Ochronne* (1977), *Constans* (1980), *Kontrakt* (1980), and *Spirala* (1978); Feliks Falk's *Wodzirej* (1978); Agnieszka Holland's *Aktorzy Prowincjonalni* (1979); and Krzysztof Kieślowski's *Amator* (1979).[73] In all these films, the situation of Poles in the late 1970s is discussed candidly with attention paid to detail in an almost documentary fashion. Likewise, in *Man of Marble*'s convincing images, Wajda relates the fate of contemporary Poles in their struggle for liberation from an oppressive system.

Man of Marble is about a young film student, Agnieszka, who in the 1970s wants to produce a student graduation film about her father in his youth, which occurred during the 1950s. The producer, Bogusław Sobczuk, opposes Agnieszka's project because such a dangerous theme has never been presented on the screen; he wants her to make a film about steelworkers and the results of the Socialist economy, which would be more in line with party policy. Agnieszka insists on her project, claiming that it would be of interest to a wider range of viewers. Sobczuk refuses to give her forbidden film material, however, and reminds her that she has only twenty-one days to finish the film.

Eager to complete her project despite obstacles, Agnieszka and her crew sneak into the National Museum in Warszawa, where they film the marble figure of Birkut (Jerzy Radziwiłowicz), a Stalinist hero, along with other sculptures from the 1950s, despite a formal prohibition by the director of the museum. Agnieszka's older cameraman expresses his doubts, feeling that the theme Agnieszka is dealing with is potentially dangerous. Agnieszka does not offer comfort, but merely asks him to shoot the whole film with a handheld camera, not from a tripod.

Later, Agnieszka watches films from the 1950s in a studio projection room. The projection starts with discarded footage from the film *The Beginning of the Town;* we see the film director Burski taking shots of living conditions at a big construction site: the muddy boots of the workers, food lines, the destruction of the cherry orchard, construction equipment sinking in the mud, and the throwing of food at a party official. The next film from the 1950s, *Architects of Our Happiness,* shows Birkut as a distinguished worker who has contributed to the development of the country. The film footage is a brilliant collage of actual old footage and contemporary re-stagings of scenes from the 1950s. It shows Birkut's life full of successes, from his origins in a small village near Kraków to his career as an exemplary worker and union activist. Astute audiences note that he is also the worker whose huge portrait was being taken down in the documentary footage at the beginning of *Man of Marble.*

Agnieszka decides to meet Burski. From her cameraman, she learns that *Architects of Our Happiness* won a prestigious prize in the 1950s. Agnieszka is next seen at the Okęcie airport in Warszawa, where Burski is returning from a film festival. She accompanies him to his house and, on the way, tells him about her plans for her own film. Burski agrees to meet her again. From this point forward, *Man of Marble* is told in two intersecting narratives, the past and the present, the former realized in a series of flashbacks.[74] Through this process of uncovering the past, the spectator slowly uncovers the story of Birkut and his many successes, finding that his life was also filled with disappointment and deceptions by the government.

In the first flashback, triggered by a conversation with Agnieszka, Burski describes the making of his film at the construction site in Nowa Huta. He starts with a conversation he had with Party Secretary Jodła, who helped him in the creation of Birkut, the new "Stakhanovite."[75] In this sequence Wajda shows a calculated and careful construction of a Stalinist myth by a cynical film director and a condescending party official, despite initial opposition to the plan by more rational representatives of the party committee. The next flashback recalls a meeting between Burski and Michalak, the security officer who had taken care of Birkut in the 1950s. Michalak accompanied Birkut on all his propaganda shows. Michalak describes the infamous show in Żabinka Mała, during which the Stakhanovite and two co-workers had to lay 30,000 bricks during a one-day shift: During an otherwise typical propaganda show, someone had passed a scalding hot brick to Birkut, who dropped the brick and screamed with pain; the whole event was stopped while Michalak looked for the guilty party. Michalak accused Wincenty Witek, Birkut's friend, of the sabotage.

The next scene shows Birkut involved in social work in Nowa Huta. As Michalak explains, Birkut could no longer work as a bricklayer since his hands did not heal properly. Following a cut to the next scene, we see Witek called to the security office in Nowa Huta for questioning, concerning his presumed contacts with the West. Birkut, who is waiting for his friend, eventually realizes that Witek has been detained in the office. In an effort to learn what has happened to him, Birkut goes to the central security office in Warszawa. This scene marks the ideological turning point for Birkut. From an idealistic party member, he becomes a disillusioned former worker seeking the truth about his friend Witek. At the meeting in Nowa Huta, to which Birkut comes directly after his trip to Warszawa, he addresses fellow workers with a desperate plea to save Witek. The workers dismiss his plea and start singing a Party song. Birkut leaves the meeting hall alone. The following scenes show Birkut moving out of his new apartment in Nowa Huta, going on a drinking binge with a Gypsy troupe, and then throwing a brick at the Kraków Party Headquarters.

During a conversation between Agnieszka and her producer, the latter is plainly displeased with the results of her work, and insists that she does not touch forbidden subjects. Instead, he demands that she go to Huta Katowice and conduct an interview with Witek himself, so she goes to meet Birkut's former friend. In the 1970s, Witek is now one of the managers of a construction site. He takes Agnieszka for a ride in a helicopter and describes Birkut's life after his return from the prison, where the former Stakhanovite had been thrown after Witek's trial. In the following flashback, Birkut is seen returning from prison, greeted enthusiastically at the railway station, and then later looking desperately for his former wife, Hanka, who left their old apartment without leaving word where she was going. Agnieszka arranges an interview with Hanka, who describes how her former husband came to Zakopane to find her, only to learn that she had betrayed him both as a husband and a comrade.

Next, Agnieszka is back in Warszawa. The introductory materials for her film are being viewed by the producer and the television commission. She sits in the corridor, smokes a cigarette, and waits for the verdict. The producer leaves the projection room and complains that Agnieszka found neither Birkut nor his son during her research. He tells her that he cannot give her any more tape or equipment. When Agnieszka insists that she must finish the film, she is given only two more weeks for final editing and sound. In disappointment, Agnieszka goes to see her father. This scene embraces a kind of stillness, a pause in the action, a recharging of batteries. Agnieszka tells her father about the decision of the authorities to take her film away from her. The father insists, however, that she finish the film without the equipment; he would like to find out what happened to Birkut. Cheered, Agnieszka leaves for Gdańsk where she hopes to meet Maciek, Birkut's son (Maciek is played by the same actor, Jerzy Radziwiłowicz).

Agnieszka and Maciek meet at the Gdańsk shipyard. She explains the reason for her arrival and asks Maciek to come with her to Warszawa. The last sequence in the film presents the two of them at the TV studio, going to meet the producer. This final scene complies with the Hollywood principles of a movie with a happy ending, thus introducing a point of departure for the reflections concerning the relation of Wajda to the American film industry, his fascination with Hollywood films (especially *Citizen Kane*, 1941), and with American film technique. At the same time, though, the American trait is mocked to some extent, appropriated by Wajda with a decidedly Polish, sarcastic sense of humor. The last scene reveals the Hollywood paradigm of a patriarchal plot with man and woman united by love, as *he* delicately takes control of the situation (Maciek puts his hand over Agnieszka's shoulder in a paternal gesture). This discourse of such traditional values reemerges in this film's sequel, *Man of Iron*.[76]

Man of Marble is a precisely constructed and rhythmic work combining two temporal planes, the contemporary and the past. The first ten sequences deal with Agnieszka's work on her diploma film. In this part, flashbacks from the past play an important role in reiterating or reinforcing the diegetic equivalence of the two plots in the film. Agnieszka's plot would not be able to exist without Birkut's. This mutual dependence functions on many levels in the film: diegetically, since Agnieszka's misfortunes with her diploma film are similar to Birkut's own in the 1950s (both protagonists are driven by a desire to be honest and sincere in their lives); structurally, since both of them constitute the axis along which other protagonists of the film meet; and in terms of characterization, since both protagonists reveal similar behavioral traits (being naïve and outspoken at the same time). All the protagonists in the first ten sequences appear both in the time of the 1950s and in the time of the 1970s, united by the person of Birkut and exhumed by the persona of Agnieszka.

This is a complex film in which many diverse interests of Wajda coalesce. The film is an important contribution to both the Cinema of Moral Concern and to those social content films that combine various cultural and historical traits in multisemantic layers. For this reason, the film has been carefully analyzed elsewhere, some elements of that analysis being contained in this text.[77] The intricate structure of the film, its brisk pace, and its many references to cultural discourses such as Socialist Realism, Romanticism, Hollywood cinema, and others, are the main characteristic features of the film.

However, these are not the main reasons for the enthusiastic reception of the film in Poland: That honor goes to the fact that the film recalls the horrific Stalinist times, with their politics of terrorism, and deceptions and manipulations by the government against decent, well-meaning, and hard-working citizens.

> It was the only film which claimed the blood, sweat and tears of the working people. Although the film was seen by 2.5 million viewers, Wajda got only a bag of insults for his efforts.... It is not a film about a Stakhanovite, as the official critics were trying to convince the general public, it is a film about the notion of the proletariat dictatorship. In those years, the proletariat was given the conditions indispensable for their taking part in governing the country, but, on the other hand, a gigantic propaganda manipulation machine and terrorist security apparatus were initiated to control them."[78]

Man of Marble deals openly with these deceptions and investigates their mechanisms. It presents the consequences of governmental manipulation for ordinary people, who suffered economically, emotionally, and ideologically. This unprecedented act of bravery earned Wajda the highest accolades from every segment of Polish society and caused long lines to form in front of the few cinemas where the film was shown.

All of these social and political discourses are brilliantly presented in an ideal match with the film's aesthetic discourses. For instance, the exuberant tone of the propaganda in the 1950s segments describing the life of Birkut matches the enthusiasm of the young generation in the 1970s. Both young people are described by means of two diverse styles: Birkut by Socialist Realism and Agnieszka by the Hollywood style, expressed in the film's brisk and energetic pace. This enthusiastic double voice of the young people, shored up by the music of both the 1950s and 1970s, respectively, is restrained by the grim interiors in which the dirty secrets of the system are revealed. The light, open spaces in which Agnieszka and Mateusz are found contrast with the dark spaces of the Security Headquarters, the shadowy space in which Agnieszka conducts her conversation with Michalak, the darkness of the screening room, and the dim office of the TV producer.

Newsreels and documentary footage add an element of historical authenticity to the film. The re-creations of films from the 1950s are brilliant accomplishments by Wajda, who produced a masterly collage of old reels and contemporary film touched with age-inducing color effects, so that both look as if they came from the same period. An example of such a film within a film is *Architects of Our Happiness*, supposedly a prize-winning documentary made twenty-four years earlier by the fictional director, Burski. *Architects* would be a parody if it were not such a precise re-creation of the era's Socialist propaganda, albeit one that incorporates Birkut. We see him on a reviewing stand as effigies of Harry S. Truman, Francisco Franco, and other enemies of Socialism file past. To the upbeat Poland-on-the-march narration ("They sallied forth to join the struggle for a better future"), *Architects* dramatizes Birkut's official life, which, if one can judge from the optimistic workers' chorus, went on happily ever after. Wajda does not parody blatantly, but the mild satire is unmistakable, trenchant.

Man of Marble takes place here and now. The whole film can be read as a documentary. It deeply affected spectators thanks to its many allusions to the very recent past and to contemporary references to which spectators could relate immediately. One of the first examples of this precision is the sequence in the TV studio,[79] where Agnieszka views the films from the 1950s. Most of the people taking part in the screenings of the films in the studio are older than Agnieszka; the times depicted are presumably well known to them or to their families, so they doubt Agnieszka's ability to make a film based on the forbidden past. However, a series of significant glances are exchanged between the woman who assists with the reels and Agnieszka; this woman seems to understand fully the risk Agnieszka is taking. Hers is a motherly look, full of pity for the aspiring young director, but at the same time admiring. This simple exchange of glances signifies a rich historical discourse on the totalitarian system, which itself allows for such an unspoken exchange but forbids an open verbal exchange.

Another sequence refers to the class differences in Poland in 1970s. Agnieszka's conversation with Burski depicts him as the director of a film about Birkut. By the 1970s, Burski is a well-established artistic personality living in a villa with his family and a servant. The villa bears all the signs of luxury and comfort; Agnieszka does not fit in here. The class and status differences are demonstrated by Agnieszka's dress, her lack of material belongings, and her inelegant behavior. The meeting between the older director and the younger one is read by the spectator as a contrast between old and young, powerful and weak, upper and middle class, and perhaps most importantly the opportunistic and the rebellious. After all, class differences, although officially absent in Socialist Poland, were nevertheless present in a society where the distribution of power and influence was no longer dependent on family background or on material assets, but on one's position in the party ranks or relation to party officials. As a consequence of this power structure, the representatives of artistic circles often compromised artistic autonomy in exchange for positive discrimination that guaranteed a comfortable life equivalent to that of the upper classes in the West.

The scene with Burski opens up a retrospective scene from the 1950s, surrounding his film about Birkut. In this sequence, Burski decides to produce staged screening of the workers' competition. Secretary Jodła, the security members, and the director all take part in this conspiracy. However, the final word concerning the arrangement of the mise-en-scène, the action, and the choice of actors belongs to the director. Party corruption goes hand in hand with cynical manipulation by the media. The event Burski orchestrated was the construction of a wall from 30,000 bricks within one day. Such an event had to be carefully prepared, and a worker had to be chosen who would not jeopardize the propagandist value of the whole event—he had to be extremely young, strong, and naïve. Birkut served this ideal in the best way imaginable. As a young man from a village, he knew nothing about manipulation by the media; he wanted only to be a good worker and comrade.

This depiction of Birkut as a representative of his society at that time contrasts strikingly with the scenes in the beginning of *Man of Marble*. Certain ominous signals of social awareness had already appeared in Burski's early films from the 1950s: the cutting of the cherry trees, mud at the construction site, lack of food, forced labor, and a party official running away from furious workers all constitute a kind of overture to forthcoming events.[80] Birkut believes naïvely in the good intentions of Burski and in his positive presentation of the workers' effort as a joint effort of his team.[81] At the end of the dramatic bricklaying competition, the spectator is exposed to the twisted face of Birkut, whose eyes are filled with bestial exhaustion. The scene is striking because of another emotionally loaded concatenation of images: that is, the faces of the viewers of the humiliating spectacle, the older workers, tired and disinterested, looking with disbelief at the circus.[82]

On the other hand, some Polish spectators considered Wajda's Birkut to be a mere caricature of a worker in the 1950s—an unsophisticated individual who enthusiastically accepts the exposition of his image in the Social Realist monuments.[83] These viewers detected a dialogic coexistence of several discourses in the film's presentation: for instance, bitterness in Wajda, fighting for the upper hand against the discourse of historical presentation in the depiction of Birkut's heroism and naïveté; and the discourse of irony that made Birkut a comic-strip figure of the Social Realist drama.[84] In the production of Burski's film, the historical discourse is discernible in other parts of the film as well. The spectator, prepared by the film's exposé of the truth of the historical discourse in the 1950s, is not surprised by the monstrosities of the authorities in the 1970s. The chilling picture of the discourse of "great manipulation" serves as an ideological and moral explanation for all the atrocities committed by the officials, and of the moral degeneration of the people surrounding Birkut. Thus, the moral degeneration of Polish decision-makers in the 1970s—the producer who makes decisions about Agnieszka's film, and Burski, now a famous director—is an irrefutable consequence of the moral depravity in those early times of Socialist Poland.

One of the most important aspects of the historical reality in the film is the frightening and oppressive presence of the security forces, which inevitably introduce the discourse of Stalinism. The totalitarian threat of Stalinism is revealed especially in these forces. Both in the contemporary discourse and in the discourse from the past, the *bezpieka* (a derogatory term for the security forces) is presented as a threatening force and a tool of total oppression, mere acquaintance with which can be harmful. The discourse of bezpieka dominates in Burski's film about Birkut, where security officials "take care" of the safety of the participants and keep a close eye on any potential subversives. An example of this type of action occurs in the sequence that constitutes a flashback describing the activities of the bezpieka from the security agent's point of view. Michalak, assigned to Birkut and Witek during and between their propaganda shows, describes the building event and the fate of Birkut as a social worker (which he later became).

Birkut emerges from Michalak's retrospective as an idealistic and naïve social worker, not frightened by the apparent sabotage during the fateful event. This made Birkut a dangerous type, impervious to any kind of political and ideological influence from the authorities. As Michalak tells it, Birkut's naïveté was challenged only when his friend Witek was arrested for "probable contacts with the West" (a lie fabricated by the authorities). Despite many warnings from his wife and friends, who begged him not to jeopardize his future, Birkut goes to the Central Security Office in Warszawa to ask about Witek. He is received by the security official with patronizing nonchalance, but gets no promises. In its ambiguity, the scene is similar to that in which Witek "disappeared"; Birkut had accompanied him to the secretary's room and had waited patiently for his reappearance. When after several hours he demanded to see his friend, the secretary pushed him into a cell-like room with a cool and frightening interior—and then he was told cynically that nobody had entered the room before.

Witek's abduction by security forces symbolizes a common practice performed in the 1950s by the Stalinist regime, which considered individual human lives largely irrelevant. Czesław Miłosz relates the atmosphere of fear that such actions of the security apparatus provoked: "[A] long period of terror demands an established apparatus and becomes a permanent institution.... Fear is well known as a cement of societies. [Under Stalinist rule] if all one hundred thousand people live in daily fear, they give off a collective aura that hangs over the city like a heavy cloud."[85] This collective aura of overpowering and ever-present fear is vivid throughout the film: in the linguistic texture (ambiguous statements and remarks based on common knowledge); in the image texture (the exchange of looks between Agnieszka and the woman in the screening room, the exchange of looks between the security official and his secretary, and many other instances); and in the musical score.

One of the most striking sequences in *Man of Marble* is that of Agnieszka's interview with Witek. A former political prisoner, he is now director of one of the numerous Polish "industrial miracles," the gigantic construction site of Huta Katowice. He seems to enjoy the role of a successful manager and boasts of his own achievements. Not much is said about Birkut, however. His statement, "Oh, Birkut was a truthful man. There are not many like him nowadays, he would be useful at our construction site" (*"O, Birkut to był prawdomówny człowiek. Dzisiaj już mało takich, a przydałby się na budowie"*), is shockingly banal and jars the ears of the Polish listener with its ideological "newspeak."[86] This sequence constitutes an historical recapitulation of the 1970s, with its fascination for industrialization, its technocratic propaganda system, and its subordination of human needs to the requirements of "historical necessity," as propagated by the power system.

The sequence presenting the Huta Katowice site has been widely criticized by film analysts and public audiences alike in Poland. Alicja Helman of Kraków University, for instance, considers this sequence (especially the part in which Wajda presents an idealistic picture of the industrial landscape from a bird's-eye view) as an act of capitulation to the system on the part of Wajda, and final proof that Wajda did not in fact reject Socialism, that he in fact still found some of its premises and properties (e.g., industrialization) to be fascinating and worthy. The

Poland of the 1970s in this particular sequence seems to be a country of "success" (in line with an official line of state propaganda) marked by the modern, contemporary buildings of Warszawa, the Łazienki route, and the enthusiasm of the builders of Huta Katowice. Poles are seen as active and industrious. This optimistic presentation of Polish reality in the 1970s is ironically contrasted with the discourse of the Poles' own experience. When audiences saw this sequence, many looked on in disbelief and wondered how Wajda dared include a typical official "success" story in his film. In the context of the 1970s in Poland—a country of gray and neglected cities, their impatient and unhappy citizens working without any enthusiasm or belief in "the good of the cause"—a colorful scene from Huta Katowice introduced a dissonance into the film.[87]

Wajda is more faithful to his public in terms of historical discourse during one of the last sequences in the film, the Gdańsk shipyard. A kind of grimness is apparent in the shipyard early in the morning when the laborers go to work. The atmosphere of apathy gives way to growing dread and to the imminence of final solutions to the political crisis. (Although Wajda claims that there is no causal relationship between the film and the strikes in Gdańsk, he thinks that "it's not unreasonable to see a connection between them, if only of mutual concern."[88]) As Godzic notes, the presentation of the Gdańsk shipyard reminds one of the famous fog sequence in the port after the murder of Vakulinchuk in Eisenstein's *Battleship Potemkin* (1925), when the imminence of the final, dreadful solutions to the crisis is equally threatening.[89]

The historical discourse in *Man of Marble* evokes certain reactions in the spectators who, in their attempt to match their personal historical truth with the history on the screen, try to appropriate the latter in their act of spectatorship. Yet all of these historical truths that spectators recognized are told in an aesthetically consistent way, which integrates Socialist Realism, Romanticism, and Hollywood cinema. The discourse of Socialist Realism, an artistic version of Stalinism, produced a whole artistic school in the former Soviet Union and in Poland that propagated the ideals of Stalin in paintings, sculpture, and film. All of the artistic creations from this time in Polish history (the Socialist Realist period is said to have been at its peak from 1950 to 1954) propagate the cult of Stalin; these works were uniformly based on a black-and-white dichotomy in terms of character presentation.

In *Man of Marble*, for instance, Birkut is serious and self-righteous throughout most of the film. However, there is a moment when the director allows him some ironic doubt, when he looks in disbelief at the marble figure of himself carved by a Socialist Realist sculptor; Birkut almost winks at the spectator.

A strict division of roles was characteristic for Socialist Realism plots, regardless of whether in a "production" novel, a drama or a film. These parts were predetermined and pre-formulated, as in folklore. An enemy was always an enemy, easily recognized, even if he or she were in disguise; a hesitant intellectual was always a hesitant intellectual, even if he or she meant well and did not want to help the enemy in the realization of his nefarious plans; and, a positive hero was always a positive hero, even if, in the moments of weakness, he or she was over-eager or acted in a thoughtless way.[90]

Socialist Realism is an important cultural discourse, within which Wajda functioned as a film director (after all, Burski is Wajda's alter ego[91]); the discursive legacy is vivid in most of the film's sequences. In this sense, the film moved but also irritated Polish spectators, who discerned the presence of this discourse in every layer of the film.

Polish Romanticism arose sometime time after 1820, but continued to influence literature and art during the two world wars and up to the time of Solidarity. In the nineteenth century, Romanticism was the artistic outlet for the ideological foment that was stirring the whole nation. Feelings of insecurity and injustice caused by the partition of Poland by Russia, Prussia, and Austria in 1795 found an outlet in this movement, which embodied the nationalistic notion of rebellion against the state. Since Poland did not officially exist between 1795 and 1918, the caretakers of Polish lore and letters before 1914—figures such as Adam Mickiewicz and Frederic Chopin, and later Stanisław Wyspiański and Stanisław Reymont—constituted a Polish "government of the soul" in lieu of an autonomous political entity. In Poland, it is still considered the mission of the artist to do no less than to mould history. Romantic themes such as the fate of the common people, the nourishing of national consciousness, and the desire for freedom appear repeatedly in many of Wajda's films, for instance in *The Wedding*, *Ashes and Diamonds*, and *Mr. Thadeus*.

In *Man of Marble*, similarly, the common man is romanticized and glorified: Birkut is always presented in a favorable way. His image on the screen is surrounded by a halo of diffused, orange light, and the contours are soft, as if enveloping him in the mist of the spectator's sympathy and understanding. Birkut's depiction as the romantic hero who fights for the fate of a fellow man (and who suffers in the process) also reiterate this tone. One of the most striking scenes that illustrate this romantic discourse is the one showing Hanka and Birkut as they move from the apartment in Nowa Huta; in fact, this scene is annoyingly romanticized. After his return from prison, Birkut is told that he no longer has a state-sponsored apartment and must move to the slums on the outskirts of the city. On the cart there are modest pieces of furniture, the table, the chair, and the bookcase, but the most important of Birkut's belongings seems to be a traditional red geranium, which Birkut and his wife handle with great care. This symbol of love for Polish peasant tradition seems to epitomize Birkut's love for truth and honesty. As a romantic hero, Birkut suffers at the hands of authorities but endures this hardship with dignity and calm. The visionary aspect of Romanticism—the messiah as redeemer—is seen in Agnieszka, who tries to undo (or at least to unwrite) history, and also in Birkut, who tries to open the eyes of the spectator to the historical truth. He believes in social utopianism, becoming a social worker after his fateful accident.

The discourse of Hollywood cinema is seen in the film's references to *Citizen Kane*, in terms of its theme and method of production. Like so many Hollywood films, it leaves open the possibility of a sequel. Jan Dawson refers to *Man of Marble* as "an East European *Citizen Kane.*"[92] Both films are concerned with the mechanics of mythology: *Man of Marble* explores the creation of a public image while simultaneously pursuing its own investigation into the reality behind official myth. It is also concerned with the power of the media in manipulating truth. Furthermore, like *Citizen Kane*, Wajda's film is multilayered and multidimensional; the reminiscences that structure the narrative of *Man of Marble* all reveal something, usually ironic, about the characters themselves and the kinds of choices they make. The plot of *Man of Marble* almost literally reproduces Herman Mankiewicz's plot of "the film about the life of a famous American, as seen from several different points of view."[93] *Man of Marble* is a mixture of flashbacks, crosscutting, and contained discontinuity. Both films show refinement in their plot construction, where, "chaotic as it seems at first, every loose end turns into an elegant bow."[94] David Thomson notes, "*Kane* confirms the way Hollywood films progress, not like life but like a clever toy or a perfect construct . . . . *Kane's* development grows out of cuts, slow dissolves, flashbacks—all of which were common, if not normally put together with such mannered ingenuity. They are also devices of dislocation making for an artificial coherence."[95] Copied, transformed, or ironically alluded to, the discourse of *Citizen Kane* is a source of frequent references and additional subtexts in the film.

These analyses cannot, of course, exhaust all of the complex themes in the film. One might analyze the multilayered relation of Wajda to the position of Burski in the film, for example, or his identification with Agnieszka and his complex relation to the discourse of Socialist Realism, Romanticism, and classical Hollywood films. Wajda treats all of these themes with seriousness, but also with irony, maintaining arm's length even as he embraces them. For the purpose of this book, however, the analysis of *Man of Marble* must end with attention devoted to the film's enthusiastic reception by the audiences in Poland and elsewhere.

Wajda expected only negative comments from government officials. However, Minister Tejchma considered the film an outstanding achievement and, despite warnings from the Censorship Office, the political leader Piotr Jaroszewicz, and members of the Ministry of Culture, he did not ban the film. *Man of Marble* was screened for the first time at the "Wars" Cinema in the Nowe Miasto (New Town) section of Warszawa on 25 February 1977, and was received enthusiastically by audiences. Long lines formed in front of the cinemas and Wajda received many letters from all over Poland commending him for the film.[96] Lino Micciche notes that "one fifth of the Polish population has seen the film,"[97] despite what Jerzy Płażewski called "prophylactic censorship": "Not only [were] the prepared texts ... censored, but a list of colleagues who had the right to voice their opinions about the film was compiled."[98] Although the film was sent to the Gdańsk Film Festival in September, "authorities arranged that neither *Man of Marble*, nor any other film made by Wajda's 'X' unit, would win any award.... However, Andrzej Ochalski, the leader of the ad hoc awards committee, presented Wajda with another award: a brick tied with a red ribbon."[99]

In a short time, the film became one of the best known from among Wajda's corpus in Poland, and was lauded as one of the most interesting Polish films ever made. It cemented Wajda's position as a political filmmaker. As with Maciek Chełmicki in *Ashes and Diamonds*, the spectators easily identified with Agnieszka and considered her an apt representation of the 1970s in Poland. The reception of *Man of Marble* was nearly as enthusiastic abroad. Wajda was applauded for his bravery, for the journalistic accuracy in his presentation of events, for his originality of vision, for his excellent casting, and for the complexity of the attitude he presented toward Birkut.[100]

Without Anesthetic a.k.a. Rough Treatment (1978)

While *Man of Marble* depicted the enthusiasm of youth, which could conquer any obstacles on its way to truth, *Without Anesthetic* addresses the bitterness and disillusionment of a mature man, prominent journalist Jerzy Michałowski, in the face of the convoluted ideological meanderings of Polish politics. Considered one of the later films of the School of Moral Concern, it shows the conflict between Polish authorities and citizens in a much less optimistic way than *Man of Marble*. This film belongs to that group of political films that, together with *Man of Marble*, criticized social and political relations in Poland in the 1970s, paralleling and to some extent instigating the rise of Polish democratic movements.

The end of the 1970s was characterized by uncertain social and political conditions in Poland: growing disenchantment with government policies—not only among the working class, but among the intelligentsia as well—and stagnation in the standard of living, a worsening party reputation, and general discontent across the country.[101] The first important strikes in 1976 started the period of gradual disintegration of the Socialist system and led to the emergence of the Solidarity movement in the 1980s. Finally, the appointment of Karol Wojtyła as Pope John Paul II in October 1978 accelerated the social processes leading to the transformation of the political system in Poland and throughout East-Central Europe.

Without Anesthetic is a realistic portrayal of the Polish intelligentsia at that time. Jerzy's life literally disintegrates when those at the top of the party structure take note of his politically controversial statements. The film, from a screenplay by Agnieszka Holland and Wajda, takes place in Warszawa, the locus of political power in Poland. It starts when Jerzy returns from a business trip only to experience a series of events that bury him like an unexpected avalanche. His wife Ewa decides to leave him; his television interview on the TV program *Three against One* is negatively received by party officials; his position at work deteriorates; and his classes at the university where he teaches are canceled. Shot in a documentary tradition, the film cuts between the televised scenes from the interview and those depicting the film's protagonists in "real-life" situations.

In the interview, Jerzy appears as a self-assured, wise man. We see the interview being watched closely by several observers: Ewa and their daughter Gapcia, along with Ewa's young lover Jacek Rościszewski; party officials; and Jerzy's colleagues. Awed and jealous, all watch Jerzy deliver an eloquent speech on democracy and freedom. He ends the speech with a statement about history (especially referring to "silences" in history, as if foretelling the course of events soon to come), and about Solidarity developments at the end of the 1970s, leading to the momentous strike in 1980. The speech does not appeal to party officials, of course, who, through a whole mechanism of persecutions and denials, trigger a series of disastrous events for the journalist. Jerzy's assessment of an ambitious and critical book is downplayed by a younger, more orthodox colleague; his position on the newspaper's editorial board is undermined, his place at his desk literally filled by someone else; even his access to international press is denied. This professional disembowelment is accompanied and paralleled by the psychological crisis caused by Ewa's demand for a divorce. Especially poignant are the scenes in Jerzy's apartment, shot with wide-angle lenses, in which Jerzy leans against the walls, lost in the loneliness of empty rooms deserted by wife and daughter.

In the scene that yields the film's title, Jerzy goes to the dentist and wants to have his tooth pulled out without anesthetic. The dental iconography of a painful extraction functions here as a symbol for the extraction of truth from often ambiguous, undefined reality. Wanda, the dentist, reveals to Jerzy that Ewa has a lover and wants to end their marriage. Unlike the befuddled exchanges with his colleagues, when nobody tells him the truth but treats Jerzy's downfall evasively, the open exchange with the dentist is straightforward, painful but appreciated. There is no way back to his marriage, just as, it seems, there is no way back to his old life of privileges.

One of the most politically revealing scenes takes place during a meeting of the editorial board. Jerzy is denigrated by Jacek Rościszew-ski, a young orthodox Socialist who "plays by the rules" and who wants a different, politically correct book to receive a major award. With no support from his editorial chief or from his colleagues, Jerzy loses his fight for the publication of the controversial collection of essays he supports written by an ambitious young author, and realizes that he has lost his own battle for freedom of expression as well. The demagogic speech of his younger colleague is explicit and painful: The winds of change have reverted the dominant ideology to that of the xenophobic 1950s.

Concurrently, Jerzy's personal life also unfolds dramatically and pathetically. While Jerzy is professionally uncompromising, in his private life he tries desperately to win his wife back. He has no pride as he pursues her wherever she goes, rejects her request for divorce, and clings desperately to his young daughter. He feels even more powerless and degraded when he finds out that the young demagogue whom he had fought (and by whom he was soundly defeated) at the editorial board meeting is his wife's new lover. The cancellation of his ambitious student seminar at Warszawa University only adds to his humiliation. The students understand the cancellation as a political disservice, a theme they undertake during a long discussion one evening in Jerzy's apartment. The young student Agata, played by Krystyna Janda, who appears in many of Wajda's political films, does not really participate in the discussions; she does not leave the apartment, but remains silent throughout most of his political and personal ordeal, even later on.

Jerzy breaks down, disillusioned and sad. He cannot live any longer in such an intemperate political climate. Abandoned by everybody, save for the silent Agata, he slowly turns to alcohol for comfort. Accused of becoming an alcoholic, he loses the last privileges at his editorial office. When he asks Broński, a high party official, about the disastrous developments, his old friend reveals that he is no longer in a position of power and that he will soon leave the country as an ambassador to France. The friends talk about the political forces manipulating their fates. In an Aesopian moment, Broński, sitting in a suit plainly too tight for him, deliberates about the principle of rotation: Those who are too good at their work have to be relocated.

In the final scenes, as part of a final attempt to gain his wife back, Jerzy invites her to dinner at his home. Meticulously dressed, he tries to re-create the atmosphere of their life together. In the middle of his elaborate and carefully staged dinner, however, Ewa leaves; they meet later only at the divorce proceedings. Like the political developments involving Jerzy, the court proceedings progress according to a specific scenario created by the inhuman requirements of the law. For the divorce to take place, reasons have to be found, witnesses have to be called, and the course of reasoning has to be presented in a logical way. As a result, Jerzy is confronted with unbelievable accusations concocted by his wife and her divorce lawyer; feeling that he has nothing else to say, he leaves the court in disgust. When Ewa goes to talk to him after the hearing, she runs to his house only to see that an explosion has occurred; ambulance attendants take Jerzy to the hospital. The film ends on this ambiguous note, leaving the audience uncertain as to whether the gas explosion was accidental or whether he was attempting suicide—and, in either case, whether he lives or dies.

Without Anesthetic is a painfully accurate account of the Polish political climate at the end of the 1970s. It illustrates aptly the feelings of frustration and uncertainty prevalent among Polish citizens; a pertinent example of this political malaise is Wajda himself and his beloved filmmaking group called Unit X; in this film, Wajda may have uncannily forecast his own fate, for Unit X was taken from him several years later and the group of young filmmakers was dissolved. *Without Anesthetic* presents such frustrations in a straightforward way, without any symbolic or metaphoric shortcuts, but with a frank comment on the political reality. In both the Polish and the foreign press, the film was widely embraced. Polish critics praised Agnieszka Holland as the author of the screenplay; she raised important issues concerning the paranoid, Kafkaesque situation of those members of Socialist intelligentsia who had risen to the top of their career ladders—yet who could be demoted at any time, losing their jobs, their means of sustenance, their families, and even their lives. All of the actors' performances were universally praised as well, for presenting so clearly and captivatingly the universal problems of political interference, human weakness, and moral strength in the face of adversity, jealousy, love, and the end of love, all of which together contribute to the protagonist's demise.

Nevertheless, there was some negative criticism as well. Zygmunt Kałużynski, one of the most probing critics of the Polish film community, casts doubt on the historicity of the events presented in the film. The ambiguity of the chronology in *Without Anesthetic* (nowhere in the film is it made clear when the film action takes place) is also noted by critics such as Vincent Canby.[102] Others complain that the motivations of the protagonist are not always clear and, generally speaking, that his professional ordeal seems improbable in the context of his otherwise highly successful career. After all, they argue, under Socialism it was impossible to establish a solid professional career based only on the merit of one's work: as Zygmunt Kałużynski, Janusz Zatorski, and Zbigniew Kłaczyński all observe, one had to have at least *some* connections and be adept at maneuvering through the corridors of workplace politics.[103] While the thesis of the film is highly political, its treatment was called "naïve and melodramatic (in the derogatory sense of the word)"[104] or "demagogic and simplified."[105]

In *Kultura*, Andrzej Kuśniewicz, Rafał Marszałek, Anna Tatarkiewicz, Janusz Tazbir, and Krzysztof Teodor Toeplitz all stressed the fact that *Without Anesthetic* has to be seen in the context of other important "political" films of those times: Feliks Falk's *Top Dog* (1978) and Andrzej Zanussi's *Camouflage* (1977). As occurs in these two films, the filmmaker raises important social questions. These critics similarly support the view of other reviewers, stating that the character of Jerzy is not particularly well defined. Toeplitz supports Wajda's own view when he says that *Without Anesthetic* is "a psychological film, the essence of which is based on the historical issues of contemporary times and our reality; it is a drama with the elements of satire and bitter humour."[106] Although not considered a great accomplishment stylistically, the film was thought important for other reasons. In it, Wajda touches upon the sophistication and multilayered complexity of the abuse of power by Polish apparatchiks in the 1970s. While *Man of Marble* was demagogically "in your face" with its explicit presentation of the abuses of power, Wajda attempts, not entirely successfully, to portray other aspects of such abuse in *Without Anesthetic*.

The Young Ladies of Wilko (1979)

Wajda's next film, *The Young Ladies of Wilko*, transports the viewer into the world of emotions and nostalgia. In this film, the discourse of nostalgia[107] emerges strongly for the first time in Wajda's oeuvre. Like *The Birchwood* and a handful of other films by Wajda, *The Young Ladies of Wilko* is about daily life, which constitutes an introspective trait in Wajda's film production. Again, in seeking a screenplay for this film, Wajda turns to one of the most accomplished writers of Polish literature, Jarosław Iwaszkiewicz. As in *The Birchwood*, the pace of the film is slower than in many of his other films, matching the pace of the story. The film is a meditative tale, unfolding among the meadows and birch groves of the Polish landscape and the niches of an old manor, about four sisters, their young cousin Tunia, and their cousin Wiktor Ruben.

The film opens with a sequence presenting Iwaszkiewicz, the author of the short story on which the screenplay is based; a violin concerto by Karol Szymanowski is heard in the background. Iwaszkiewicz looks solemnly at the graves at the cemetery during *Zaduszki* (a holiday commemorating the dead) and quietly deliberates on the lives of those who are long gone. Only then does Wajda make his transition to the diegetic cemetery. Wiktor, the protagonist, stands at the edge of the still open grave of his brother Jurek. Distraught and pale, he does not leave the grave even though the priest waits for him to go. Later, Wiktor tells his doctor that he cannot stop thinking about his dead brother, who worked himself to death in a rapidly developing Warszawa. The doctor recommends country rest, and convinces Wiktor that he should go away for a while. The young man decides to visit Wilko, where he spent his childhood. Aboard the ferry, Wiktor observes the quiet landscape on either side of the river, admiring its rural simplicity; when he finally disembarks, he looks around carefully, as if seeking his own perspective and making sure that the reality he perceives is from his own point of view. On entering the old family manor in Wilko, Wiktor hears women's voices, happy and content. His eyes fall on the sumptuously set dinner table at which the female protagonists sit; this table will function as a centerpiece to most of the film's events.

In response to their questions, Wiktor tells the women about himself while Julcia, Jola, Zosia, Kazia, and Tunia listen to him attentively. All dressed in light colors, they explain that they have been coming with their children to the old manor every summer for the past fifteen years. Only Fela does not come because she died, as they explain to the surprised Wiktor. After exchanging greetings with the ladies, Wiktor goes to his uncle's house, where he intends to spend the three weeks recommended by the doctor. He falls into a deep sleep and does not awake until the following afternoon. In the meantime, the youngest of the five women, Tunia, comes to Wiktor's uncle with some preserves. After a moment of hesitation, clearly interested in the quiet and pleasant man, she asks about Wiktor.

The following morning, after a quiet breakfast with his uncle and aunt, Wiktor again visits the manor in Wilko. The idyllic landscape fills him with peace. On his way, he passes Iwaszkiewicz slowly walking among the trees (Iwaszkiewicz agreed to Wajda's request to play himself in the film). Tunia looks on from the porch, and then suddenly disappears; Wiktor enters the seemingly empty house. Wiktor discovers a half-dressed Julcia and her husband in one of the rooms; Jola with her guests from Warszawa in another; and Kazia teaching her children French in the next one. Casually dressed and quite at ease with her semi-naked femininity, Julcia looks at Wiktor longingly. Wiktor feels strange, uncertain as to what is happening. He enters Zosia's room and asks her if she would go for a walk with him. Zosia refuses ambiguously, but recommends Tunia, who, in her words, has enough health and energy to go with him. Tunia takes Wiktor to Fela's grave, where Wiktor suddenly grows quiet and asks Tunia to leave him alone.

During a conversation in the evening, in the subdued atmosphere of the old manor, Wiktor talks with his uncle about the essence of happiness. At breakfast, his aunt informs him about various family matters, including recent marriages or divorces of his cousins at Wilko. Wiktor shows no interest, while the concerned aunt muses about a possible marriage to Tunia, when Jola enters and invites them to dinner. Wiktor seems tense and unhappy during the visit. Clearly feeling uneasy, he asks Jola about her frequent male visitors. Jola, surprised, asks Wiktor if he is in love with her. When he does not respond, she tells him that she only saw a moral authority in him. After a tense static scene in which the now mature people look at each other for a long moment, Jola suggests that Wiktor take her around the farm, saying that soon a carriage will come to pick her up. In swift, panning movements, the camera follows the two people, laughing and smiling, until Zosia comes and picks Wiktor up.

When Wiktor enters the dining room at the manor, the children recite a poem at the lavish table, which is surrounded by guests. Jola's husband asks Wiktor how he spends his time in Wilko. He responds that he goes for walks, reads, and often naps. Jola's husband replies that Wilko indeed makes one meditate on life more than any other place; in response, Jola begins to laugh hysterically, and her husband comments that she is a fastidious wife. The sexual undertone is explicit and Wiktor feels embarrassed. He looks around as if he wants to understand the people around him, but then goes out to the hall. There, he hears Julcia's husband scolding Kazia for inviting so many people to the party. When Julcia's husband leaves, Wiktor approaches Kazia and they start talking. In a quiet conversation, Kazia tells Wiktor that all five sisters were at one time ecstatically in love with him, especially the deceased Fela. Wiktor responds that he did not know. Kazia is surprised that Wiktor has become more subdued. In a sad conclusion to this conversation, Wiktor declares that he ran from love, like a coward. This brilliant scene is marked by such delightful "mini-events" as children bursting in trying to grab desserts and Kazia petting Wiktor on his head.

The film proceeds in slow strokes, revealing the complexity and uniqueness of women's lives. Marital conflicts (between Jola and her husband), the naiveté and passion of Tunia, the quiet despair of Kazia, the detachment of Zosia, and the sensuality of Julcia, all appear in small vignette scenes. Ordinary events like family meals, walks in the countryside, evening dances, and conversations in the storeroom are lovingly painted by Wajda in rich detail and amid an earthy, "homey" atmosphere. Still, a delicate current of sexual tension and desire runs through the whole film. All the women seem to desire Wiktor more or less passionately. All the amorous scenes, however, are presented through the amused and slightly distanced eye of Wiktor, who tries desperately to reclaim his youth in these encounters. He makes love to Julcia, tries to kiss Tunia, and then talks lovingly to both Kazia and Zosia. At the end of this series of encounters, Wiktor says *"lato się w nim przełamało"* ("the summer broke in me"), and he goes to Fela's grave. Jola meets him there and invites him on a romantic horseback ride.

At his uncle's house in the morning, Wiktor announces that he wants to leave. On hearing this, his uncle faints and later talks with Wiktor about the imminence of death. The same morning, Wiktor goes to Wilko to say good-bye. During a lyrical breakfast scene, Jola and Julcia eat voraciously while Kazia tends to the household chores. This delicious breakfast, shot in light, luminous colors, is one of the most enchanting scenes in the film. Wiktor is an observer only, an outsider. When he announces that he will leave, the women remain silent. Julcia then faints suddenly and Jola's laughter dies down. Wiktor wants to say good-bye to Tunia, but she does not respond. He then leaves the manor.

Suddenly, a lonely shot from a rifle is heard from Tunia's room. The sisters run to see whether Tunia is all right. When they realize that all is well, Kazia states, "now everything will be fine," as if relieved that the women will again stay alone without the unnecessary turmoil and passion that Wiktor's presence arose in them. Bidding farewell to his aunt, Wiktor says that he does not want any more change in his life, and that he can no longer love. On the ferry, he takes a sip of water from the river, a clear symbol of absolution. On the train, he sees Iwaszkiewicz looking at him with a faint smile. The film ends with a dedication to Iwaszkiewicz.

The Young Ladies of Wilko, like *The Birchwood,* brings to mind a different set of themes than Wajda's political films. The passage of time, the meaning of life and death, femininity, love, and emotionality are Wajda's major preoccupations in this film. He tries to depict the quiet mystery of Iwaszkiewicz's prose. Wajda introduces a completely different rhythm in *The Young Ladies of Wilko:*

> They play slowly because they are in no hurry, because their lives, their existences, and their longings are different. It is *time* I am talking about. I have no time because I am painting this time. I have no time because usually I am painting something that requires a different, quicker pace. So, how can I move into this other time and do what. Look at when they are lying in the grass, yet there is nothing coming out of this lying. This is the real subject of this film.[108]

Most critics agree that the themes of death and the passage of time are the dominant ones in this film. However, as Piotr Lis states, these themes are not necessarily presented merely through the act of dying: Wajda is able to depict things that are untranslatable and illusory. He shows them in the way he portrays nature, both summer and autumn at once, through the masterful cinematography of Edward Kłosiński.[109] The color of the visuals makes the film sadly optimistic, although it tells a story of death and melancholy.

The film is unique in Wajda's filmography in that it contains superb portraits of women. Here, women are "the mainstay of order and grace," exemplary members of society, "responsible for themselves and for others. That is why everything that these women do—cook and fry, some red currants, raspberries with cream, they lay out flowers, sometimes play the piano, they read something to children in French—all of this is important. It is something that we desperately miss and need, while all this selflessness disappeared under the brutal stamp of contemporary life."[110] *The Young Ladies of Wilko* is generally considered one of the most beautiful and mature films produced by Wajda. In it, Wajda's feeling for the beauty of the Polish landscape, his maturity in the treatment of life and death, and his feel for the passage of time contribute to the formation of a richly subdued portrayal of life, with all of its complexities. Music, color, and mise-en-scène, all essential but none excessive, create an atmosphere of peace and contemplation. Thanks to the film's slow pace, Wajda allows the women to play themselves and to improvise during the prolonged, serene scenes. In this film, the director does not present any thesis or didactically try to teach his audience what to do or how to behave. Rather, he lets the cameras roll and leisurely account for the events in front of and around them.

By contrast, when this film was made, the country was in turmoil. Formal opposition movements began to emerge, one of the most powerful being the Komitet Obrony Robotników (Workers' Defense Committee), created in 1976. The strikes in June 1976, caused by soaring prices, signaled the decline of the Gierek regime. Two years later, in October 1978, Karol Wojtyła, Archbishop of Kraków, became Pope John Paul II. The following year he made his first official pilgrimage to Poland.[111] Wajda's next film, the last one produced in the 1970s, presents this atmosphere of turmoil in the country and contrasts it with the persona of a quiet charismatic leader, the ideal political "conductor."

The Orchestra Conductor (1979)

The Orchestra Conductor belongs among Wajda's other political films. It contains hidden messages in the Aesopian manner, in which the director expresses his opinion on the nature of the nation's political leadership. The film tells the story of an orchestra conductor, but in fact it is about a charismatic leader who loves people and who cares only about the music he creates, not about his own status. The Orchestra Conductor, played by Sir John Gielgud, is widely construed as a representation of Pope John Paul II, who was turning into a major social and political figure at the time. Andrzej Kijowski wrote the script based on the experience of the real conductor, Andrzej Markowski.

The film starts with a long pan of New York City, accompanied by Beethoven's Fifth Symphony. Marta, a young Polish musician on a musical scholarship in New York, enthusiastically admires the sky-scape. The sequence ends with Marta and the female Kościuszko Foundation clerk talking about her stay in New York in front of the foundation's office. At the same time, in a crosscut to Poland, Marta's husband Adam reads a postcard from his wife, in which she says that she misses her husband and feels completely dependent on him. Back in New York,

Marta notices a poster for a concert featuring the famous Polish conductor John Lasocky, and she decides to go.

After the concert, Lasocky stands on the stairs panting heavily.
Marta observes him quietly; surrounded by the crowds in the foyer, Lasocky sees camera operators attempting to make a film about him, but
he dismisses them impatiently. The only person who apparently does
not want to get an autograph from him is Marta, quietly standing in the
corner. Slightly bewildered, Lasocky approaches her, and she explains
that she is on a musical scholarship and is to return to Poland the following day. Lasocky asks her about her mother and, when he hears the
name Anna, has a moment of strange recognition, as if the past has
come back to haunt him. He wants Marta to stay another day or two,
but she responds that she must return to Poland.

Back home, a strangely distant husband welcomes Marta; while she
seems excited and happy, he looks on her with calm, emotionless eyes.
Despite his kisses and presents, there is no real excitement in him. Tension and uneasiness mark their relationship; even in bed, Adam asks
desperately whether Marta loves him. After her reluctant *yes,* silence
embraces them.[112] In New York, Lasocky tries to dissuade the persistent
filmmakers from bothering him. He is angry that his peace has been destroyed, and promises to go to a place where they will not find him. In
the meantime, in Poland, Adam conducts his provincial orchestra; preoccupied with his own interpretation of the music, he pays no attention
to the players. When they do not respond to his directions, he is bitter
and sarcastic, unable to communicate well with them. In fact, he alien-
ates everyone with his sniping remarks. He warns his players that they
must do better because the great conductor Lasocky is coming soon to
conduct their orchestra. Not all are happy about this. Some gripe that
Lasocky is too old for this task, that he left the country a long time ago
and is thus out of touch with them, and so forth.

Suddenly, Marta, who plays the violin in her husband's orchestra, notices Lasocky sitting in the back row quietly observing the rehearsal. She
approaches him and then Adam, visibly touched, introduces Lasocky
to the orchestra. The maestro greets every musician in the orchestra
individually, and then calmly asks them to play. Happy, warm, and
powerfully charismatic, he listens, enrapt, to the tones of Beethoven's
symphony (the camera leans on his hands while he conducts), and he
then compliments the musicians on their fine performance. During a
short break, he explains to them the nature of Beethoven's Fifth. The
players are mesmerized and thereafter play slowly and accurately.
Adam also listens to them play and realizes that the musicians have
picked up the tones they could not earlier.

After the rehearsal, Lasocky, Adam, and Marta walk around the
town accompanied by Beethoven's melodies. When Lasocky leaves the
couple to perform an errand, Marta asks Adam why he wanted to be a

conductor. She asserts that one has to love the orchestra, as he does not. Upset by her critical remarks, Adam reminds her rudely that she should take greater care of their child. Later, the spouses explicate the differences between their two musical styles. Marta reports that Lasocky told her, privately, that they are a very good orchestra, while Adam complains that they need more discipline. He then criticizes the older conductor, telling her about Lasocky's professional problem in the past and his desire to leave the country as a result. In fact, Lasocky had apparently lost his place in the middle of a concert because he was thinking about his former lover, who indeed turns out to be Marta's mother: She had decided to marry someone else, not him.

Quick crosscutting brings us to a sequence with Lasocky, who is on the phone with his doctor in New York talking about his heart problems. He is irritable and uncertain, and tells his doctor that he would like to feel as healthy as he felt long ago. Despite his doctor's demands that he take his pills, Lasocky throws his medication into the bathroom sink. In the following scenes, Lasocky's upcoming concert is transferred to a bigger hall with all the accoutrements suitable for such an occasion— only because it is the great conductor who will direct the orchestra and not Marta's husband. Adam's jealousy and narrow-mindedness emerge from this talk, as he complains quietly but bitterly. On the contrary, Lasocky's portrayal is warm and compassionate. He talks concernedly with the orchestra players about their personal problems, their living conditions, and the like. Shot with a hidden camera, the sequence shows their ecstatic faces as they communicate their worries to Lasocky, who proves to be a good listener. He assures them that they should let go of their personal worries and uncertainties concerning their performing abilities; they must realize, he explains, that the music is most important, and that, if they let it, it will speak for them.

By demonstrating Lasocky's good-heartedness, Wajda comments on the superiority of the public good, which supersedes petty misunderstandings and weaknesses. Even the color palette of the next sequence reinforces this moment of "truth." The orchestra plays while the camera portrays it lovingly in warm colors; also in warm light, depicted with a sort of halo, Lasocky directs the orchestra blissfully. Sometimes, he exchanges glances with Marta, who regards him with contentment and fascination. Adam notices these glances and, when they come home, expresses his feelings of betrayal and alienation. The sequence at their home after the rehearsal shows them engaged in a strange exchange of gestures. First they make love, then Adam takes the covers and goes to sleep in their child's bedroom; Marta follows him, but Adam wants to sleep alone.

During dinner at candlelight, Lasocky addresses Marta as if she were his erstwhile lover, Marta's mother Anna. He says he came back especially for Marta and kisses her on the lips. Next, we see Marta during a dinner with her grandfather, Adam, and the couple's daughter. This occasion stands in great contrast to the charming dinner with Lasocky: The former is awkward, everybody behaving demurely. Later, Adam is engaged in an equally awkward exchange with party officials, who suggest that the whole concert be moved to Warszawa or that the Warszawa Philharmonic players should come to reinforce the ranks of the provincial orchestra. Adam opposes this offer vehemently. He says that doing either would be a slap in his orchestra's face—and that, moreover, Lasocky would not agree in any case, for, having become closely acquainted with the musicians now, knowing them all on a first-name basis, he would not wish to replace them. In a fit of pique, though, the party official suggests that Lasocky would not notice the change anyway. This particular scene comments sharply on the arrogance of those in power and their complete disregard for the preferences of ordinary people.

The next sequence shows Adam conducting the orchestra at Lasocky's request. He conducts impatiently, interrupting them constantly and verbally abusing them. This tense sequence, in which the young conductor is shown as a despotic monster, ends with the open revolt of the orchestra; Adam breaks his baton and leaves the podium in disgrace. Marta approaches him in their apartment later and asks what is wrong with him. She does not understand his state of mind, especially when he ruminates on the role of The Orchestra Conductor in general. Marta declares that he has hurt her badly, and that she has decided not to perform in his orchestra for this particular concert. Marta leaves the apartment and goes to Lasocky, in tears. Confused and upset, he decides to order breakfast for both of them. In response, Marta asks him why he has come back to Poland and leaves his room.

Lasocky takes a walk while the Warszawa musicians arrive to support the concert. The suspicious local orchestra players watch them wearily as they approach the building; when Adam tries to convince them that they should play with the new musicians, they are angry and resentful. Adam uses typical arguments about social and political duty, but the provincial musicians are not convinced. Lasocky comes to the hall and sees strange faces among the orchestra players. He is annoyed and unhappy; declaring, "This is not my orchestra," he leaves the hall. In spite of Adam's protests, all the original orchestra members leave the hall as well.

Lasocky goes for a walk and sees a line of people sitting in front of the theater where the tickets for his concert are about to be sold, most of them young people waiting quietly. They talk about Lasocky and the enthusiasm and hard work he is rumored to have inspired in the musicians. The old man listens amazed to the great praise for his person. He sits down with them, clearly not recognized by the potential members of the audience. In the meantime, Marta and Adam look for Lasocky. They finally find him at the end of the ticket line, sitting quietly with his hat over his eyes. When they try to wake him, they think that he must have fainted, but when she tries to lift him she realizes something is terribly wrong. An ambulance is called, but when it arrives Lasocky has no pulse. Marta, astonished at his death, asks herself what his role was to her; both as an artist and as her mother's former lover, he plays an important part in her personal and her private lives.

In a later sequence, Marta's father says that he is surprised that Lasocky died before him. He advises Marta to leave her weak and cowardly husband, whom he feels does not deserve his daughter; he claims that Adam reminds him of himself when *he* was a young man. Marta responds calmly that she will not abandon her husband, but in the last sequence she tells Adam that he should pick himself up and play the concert. This painful sequence finally reveals Adam's true colors, for he is egoistically apprehensive only about his conducting, while Marta thinks only about the deceased director. She asks Adam to play because that is all they can do for their deceased friend. In the last monologue, Marta tells her husband that he is jealous not of Lasocky himself, but of the way he understood music. For Lasocky, music was the essence of life, while for Adam music is merely a means to an end (i.e., to privileges, prestige, and money). Marta tells him to abandon his profession because he loves neither music nor the people who play it. Against this barrage of bitter words Adam offers only silence. His face slowly fades to black while Beethoven's music plays in the background.

The film is an allegory regarding bureaucrats in Communist Poland. For such people, political work is associated with perks and privileges and means nothing in itself. Adam represents this segment of Polish society. Lasocky, on the other hand, represents the "enlightened" people who care about others, disregarding their own narrow interests and needs. Wajda clearly compares Lasocky to the charismatic Pope John Paul II, who visited Poland when this film was being made. The film met with varied success. On the one hand, it was received enthusiastically abroad: for instance, during the 1980 Berlin Film Festival.[113] On the other hand, it was severely criticized for its superficial treatment of what should have been complex characters, whom Wajda didactically portrayed using "clear oppositions between bad and good, small and great."[114] Maria Malatyńska also openly criticized Wajda for a superficial and negative depiction of a woman who adores Lasocki but who viciously criticizes her husband.[115] Even more damning were the opinions of Krzysztof Teodor Toeplitz and Andrzej Lipiński, who stated that the film has very little to do with reality; Toeplitz suggests that "the film fails convincingly to convey the message by means of the film story as it evolves on the screen,"[116] while Lipiński states that, in the film, "everybody is pretending to be everybody else, supposedly alluding to what is commonly described as "reality".... Everything you touch in this film simply crumbles."[117]

As usual, foreign critics were not so devastating in their criticism, and expressed an understanding for Wajda's didacticism, his need to show precisely what kind of leader the Poles should have: someone like Pope John Paul II and not some petty bureaucrat. They also accurately interpret the political message conveyed by the film. For instance, Nicolas Wappshot states that, "In *The Orchestra Conductor*, Sir John Gielgud plays an orchestral conductor returning to Poland who is embarrassed to find musicians apologizing for the poor standard of their music under the restraints of communism";[118] similarly, Pedro Crespo says that "Wajda, with splendid asceticism, depicts the contemporary social organism in the guise of [a] symphony orchestra."[119] Jeanne-Pierre Le Pavec compares this film to Fellini's *Orchestra Rehearsal* (1979), which also viewed an orchestra as a social organism in microcosm.[120]

Like many other Polish critics, I also find myself baffled by Wajda's superficial treatment of the protagonists. The problems in the marriage of Marta and Adam seem unclear and unexplained, the couple's motivations and acerbic treatment of each other uncorroborated by the events unfolding in the film. As in Wajda's earlier film, *Without Anesthetic*, the elevated thesis seems to have eliminated the need for the presentation of character complexities. Eager to portray a positive leader in the best light, Wajda presents him in a beautiful color spectrum and romantic light, while almost all of the other characters and situations are murky, grim, and strange. Nevertheless, the film appropriately reflects on Poles' longing for a charismatic leader, someone who would understand their needs and himself play "the music of their lives." Despite its numerous shortcomings, some of which have been discussed in the preceding paragraphs, the film confirms Wajda's consistent ideological line in his concern for Poland and for the fate of his compatriots.

Beyond doubt, those films produced by Wajda in the 1970s constitute the pinnacle of his filmography. The mature filmmaker demonstrates great insight and complexity, being in full command of his filmmaking abilities. In general, in the films dealing with Polish history, he is perceptive and careful, handling the literary material on which the films are based with great attention. Nevertheless, he is more certain of his position as a filmmaker during this period than he was in the 1960s, willing to get into risky situations with film adaptations of literary material to reach his goals. For example, *Promised Land* dazzles the spectator with its fast-paced, American-style aesthetics, implemented to suit the film's didactic thesis; as an adaptation, the film is little concerned with complete accuracy in portraying the events and moods as they occur in Reymont's famous novel. The thesis (i.e., "the romantic past is good and the industrial present is bad and corrupting") forecasts the nostalgia that will speak with full voice in the next two decades, in films such as *A Chronicle of Amorous Incidents, Mr. Thadeus,* and *Revenge.*

The 1970s also mark the height of Wajda's artistic involvement in the productions of young filmmakers and their socially engaged films, crafted under Wajda's tutelage in Unit X. In his own work, Wajda remains politically engaged, both in his films about the past *(The Wedding* and *Landscape after Battle)* and in those about the present *(Man of Marble, Without Anesthetic,* and *The Orchestra Conductor).* Undoubtedly, the initiation of the School of Moral Concern with *Man of Marble* led indirectly to a political avalanche that culminated in the Solidarity movement. I would suggest that both *Without Anesthetic* and *The Orchestra Conductor* belong to the School of Moral Concern: Both of them are realistic portrayals of the 1970s, and both reveal unsettling characteristics of social and political lives in Poland. Their didacticism, their overtly propagandist overtones, and the histrionics of their protagonists are symptoms of the discontent of Polish society at the time.

Yet the most exquisite films from this period, and my favorite ones, are those belonging to the general films about life and death: *The Birchwood* and *The Young Ladies of Wilko.* Dealing with the universal questions and concerns surrounding life, death, love, sexuality, and the passage of time, they combine all of the elements of Wajda's filmmaking and artistic skills to work in tandem for him. Well-composed images, meticulously structured pacing, and carefully chosen music create a nostalgic atmosphere, a mysterious "something" that still makes an unmistakable statement about the films' universal meaning. These films are not overtly didactic, but instead subdued in tone and modest in message; they present events as they unfold, making the films poignant in their documentary accuracy. The films simply depict life "as is."

Especially in *The Young Ladies of Wilko,* the nostalgic account of fleeting youth is palpable, making the spectator deliberate the position of the filmmaker, no longer a young man himself. In the subdued acting of Daniel Olbrychski (in the role of Wiktor), Wajda may be expressing his own thoughts on the passage of time. The film is nostalgic in another sense, as well. In this film, Wajda portrays the world of the nobility's past, the world of huge houses in which people lead a comfortable and elaborate life rich in dances, sumptuous meals, and slow conversations. In the country on the brink of a social revolution, the film provided a moment of relief and a break from the turbulent times. Laboriously recreated visions of slowly unfolding events functioned as an entry into the world of suppressed emotions and into the discourse of death.

❀ 5

NOSTALGIA AND REMORSE

Films of the Eighties

The four films Wajda created between the end of the 1970s and the beginning of the 80s—*Man of Marble, Without Anesthetic, Man of Iron,* and *Danton*—comment on actual political events in Poland and uncompromisingly criticize the Socialist system for its totalitarianism, opportunism, and moral inadequacy. *Man of Iron,* which illustrates the struggle of the working class for dignity and decent working conditions, shows the historical events leading to the abolition of the Socialist government in Poland and the creation of the Solidarity movement. *Danton,* the last film in this outwardly political series, refers to the implementation of martial law in Poland in the context of the French Revolution. The two first films both won awards, being lauded for their denouncements of governmental corruption, their open-mindedness in the treatment of their political subjects, and their audacity in challenging the political status quo.

Melancholia, mourning, and memory are the mainstays of Polish cinema, dealing largely with events from the past, the detritus of World War II that can never be eradicated, the trauma that can never be appeased, all of which pass into melancholic mourning. *A Love in Germany* transports viewers back to World War II via a love story, in which a German woman and a Polish boy fall in love and are brutally punished by the Nazis for their transgression. Wajda here revisits the most painful of subjects in Polish history: war's inhumanity and the bitterness of Polish-German relations.

The 1980s also mark the beginning of a nostalgic trend in Wajda's films. In *A Chronicle of Amorous Incidents,* Wajda revisits an even earlier time, hearkening back to the events preceding the Second World War. Finally, in *The Possessed,* he returns to his beloved Russian author, Fyodor Dostoevsky. He produces a film version of *The Possessed,* transferring its unsettling mood in camera movements and acting performances.

Man of Iron (1981)

Man of Iron carries on the explicitly political trend in Wajda's filmography. A sequel to *Man of Marble,* it also continues the story of that film's protagonists, Maciek Tomczyk and Agnieszka. Although belonging to the School of Moral Concern in its ideology and outlook, *Man of Iron* employs plainly propagandistic methods, through which Wajda seeks to inform Poles and the world about the spectacular rise of the Solidarity movement and about the strike. The portrayal of the present reaches its apogee in *Man of Iron,* a film produced in great haste during a short, exhilarating period of time when Solidarity was still in power.

This rush, along with a feeling of messianic need, prompted Wajda to put together fictional and documentary footage in order to astound Poles and to inform them and the world at large about the significance of events in the past twelve months, when Solidarity and other democratic movements were in full power in Poland. Uneven in form, as if not completely edited and finished, *Man of Iron* was an important metapolitical event through which Wajda communicated the political event itself. It not only revealed the mechanism of the Polish revolution, but also boldly showed the arrogance and self-centeredness of those in power. For this, but not for its cinematic merits, *Man of Iron* received the Golden Palm in Cannes.

The first scene opens in Warszawa at the Polish Radio Studio, where the recording of a radio broadcast is in progress. One of the most respected actresses in Poland, Maja Komorowska, recites Czesław Miłosz's poem "Nadzieja ("Hope"). Winkiel, a journalist at the Polish Radio Studio, is producing a broadcast with three women about the inconveniences of everyday life caused by the strike. He receives a telephone call from his supervisor, in which he is informed that he must meet with the chief of Radiokomitet (the Polish Media Organization) immediately. At the chief's office, Winkiel is ordered to go to Gdańsk, the heart of the workers' revolution, where he is to produce a broadcast about the events.

On leaving the train in Gdańsk, Winkiel is approached by an older man, the driver appointed to pick him up from the station and take him to meet with the party official, Badecki. At Badecki's office, we see the first evidence of the strike. Badecki watches a French television interview with Maciek Tomczyk, the strike leader. Interviewers ask Tomczyk about the circumstances of the strike, wanting to know its cause; they are sympathetic to the strike. In a brutally honest monologue, Badecki states that the television interview they have just seen serves to introduce a smear campaign to be continued and expanded by means of radio news: Winkiel is to concoct a broadcast that will destroy Maciek, but quickly expresses his surprise and revulsion at that prospect. Badecki immediately reminds the journalist of the time, years earlier, when he had helped to conceal the evidence after Winkiel was involved in a fatal car accident. When Winkiel returns to his hotel room, he finds someone already there waiting for him: Captain Wirski, a security agent, who has brought the file on Maciek. Wirski presents Tomczyk as a reactionary with a suspicious curriculum vitae.

Before Wirski leaves, Winkiel turns on the TV and listens to a speech by Wojciech Fiszbach, the First Secretary of the Communist Party in Gdańsk, who warns the public against participating in the strike. With disgust on his face, Winkiel listens to the unbearable "newspeak," the language of slogans and hidden threats. In response, he unscrews a bottle of vodka, but the bottle slips from his hands and crashes to the floor. Winkiel sops up the spill with a hotel towel and tries to save the remains of the alcohol by squeezing the towel into a hotel cup. He then goes to the hotel bar to get another bottle of vodka, but there he learns that not only can he not get alcohol but, because the telephone lines have been cut, he cannot contact Warszawa either. He also learns that the striking shipyard workers are in total control of Gdańsk and the shipyard. Back in his hotel room, Winkiel witnesses a Catholic mass in front of the Gdańsk shipyard from his window.

To learn more about the revolutionary turmoil, Winkiel decides to go to the shipyard. He listens to the complaints of workers behind the shipyard gate, and he sees women in front of the gate at the shipyard commemorating the workers' deaths in the demonstrations of 1970. At the shipyard gate, Winkiel happens to encounter Dzidek, an aspiring engineer he had met many years previous. Dzidek will function as Winkiel's guide in the world of the striking workers, and will also become one of the journalist's main sources of information about Tomczyk. As the two men decide to go for a cup of coffee, the camera shows workers sitting on the wall of the shipyard, loudspeakers blaring with the speeches of the strike activists, and the general atmosphere of a state of siege, but one also full of joy and excitement.

As in *Man of Marble,* the film diegesis from this point forward is depicted in two parallel temporal paths, present and past. The present path relates the discourse of the society in August 1980, during the time of the strike. The past discourse appears through numerous flashbacks, explaining the development of Maciek as a political activist and referring to historical events that shaped him. The first flashback takes the spectator into the historical demonstrations in Gdańsk in 1970: Dzidek, an ardent supporter of the strike, turns on a projector to show Winkiel an illegal documentary film. At the same time, Winkiel turns on the tape recorder hidden in his jacket, intending to record their conversation, hoping to hear derogatory information regarding Maciek.

In the second flashback, a conversation takes place between Mateusz Birkut (the protagonist of *Man of Marble*) and Maciek, his son. Dzidek witnesses the quarrel between father and son. Their discussion concerns Maciek's participation in the student demonstrations of 1968. Winkiel asks about Maciek, and Dzidek tells him about the events of 1968, when Maciek asked his father to influence workers to join the students in their demonstration against the authorities. Birkut does not allow his son to join the students who have decided to support the liberal outbreak in Warszawa. He justifies his decision with the supposition that their actions will likely mean a provocation.

The film's third flashback leads the spectator to the demonstrations of 1970, showing the room in the students' hostel where Maciek, Dzidek, and other students watch the demonstrating workers below in the street. Suddenly, a woman enters and tells Maciek that his father has been killed at the overpass. Next comes one of the most powerful scenes in *Man of Iron*, partly fictional and part documentary. The restaging of a procession of the workers bearing the body of a dead man upon a door is accompanied by a documentary sound track recorded by the police. In the next scene, Maciek and his student friends arrive at the overpass to get the body of Maciek's father, only to find that it is gone. In the meantime, the boys observe the police beating a worker, a scene taken from a documentary of the police and their methods of abuse.

In the fourth flashback, after the strikes of 1970 in Gdańsk, the students listen to the inaugural speech of the newly appointed First Secretary, Gierek. The balanced, quiet voice of Gierek, providing an explanation for the bloody events, serves as a pacifier, a bitter candy after the demonstrations and killings. In this actual TV footage, Gierek repeats the well-known phrases of all his predecessors, suggesting that specific conclusions should be drawn from these painful experiences of the last weeks. The students in the hall listen in silence, except for Maciek, who shows a completely different reaction. With a frown of disgust on his face, the young man rises from his chair, throws his jacket at the TV, and shouts, *"Nie chcę! Nie chcę!"* ("I don't want to! I don't want to!"). Two students take him away while others look on in silence. When the police arrive, the students politely report that their friend has had a nervous attack and was taken away by ambulance. At the psychiatric hospital where Maciek has been detained, Dzidek carries on a conversation with Maciek's doctor, who tells him that Maciek is normal and healthy and needs no treatment. As they leave the hospital, Maciek tells Dzidek that he has decided to abandon his studies.

When the film diegesis returns to the present, we are still in the radio studio; Winkiel wants to know what happened to Maciek after his conversation with Dzidek, who replies that Maciek disappeared. Another brief flashback, however, shows Maciek and Dzidek after some years in Gdańsk: Dzidek is a young engineer with a diploma who has just sent Gierek a congratulatory telegram; Maciek has finished compulsory service in the army and now works in the Gdańsk shipyard. The conversation in the studio resumes, and when Winkiel learns that Maciek was soon fired from the shipyard, his voice reveals excitement. "Because of the father?" he asks. "I don't think so," Dzidek replies. "Another surname, another shipyard." Winkiel's response to this observation—"It doesn't fit. I am trying to put it all together"—is telling, and it makes Dzidek suspicious. Trying to smooth the matter over, Winkiel hastily shows his cards: "In 1970 I wrote something about his father. Maybe I will write about him now." To this, Dzidek shows no reaction. Later, Winkiel goes to the shipyard fence hoping that he will be able to get into the shipyard. As one of the workers in the shipyard explains, however, access to the shipyard is forbidden even to the workers' mothers. Soon thereafter, he is suddenly surrounded by representatives of the Gdańsk Writers' Union who want him to sign a statement indicating solidarity with the striking workers and opposition to the regime. He reluctantly signs the letter.

The next scene, drawn from documentary footage, takes place in a TV studio where an interview is carried out with the real historical person of First Secretary Tadeusz Fiszbach, of the Communist Party in Gdańsk. Winkiel listens while standing in the open door of the studio. The interview continues when Dzidek approaches Winkiel and comments on Fiszbach's words about the threat of a civil war in Poland. Dzidek also promises a film about Solidarity developments that will consist partly of fictional footage and partly of documentary footage. The fictional footage shows a scene in which Maciek reads the demands of the workers from the Międzyzakładowy Komitet Strajkowy (Inter-Factory Strike Committee). The second part constitutes authentic documentary footage showing Wałęsa and representatives of the government, among them Deputy Premier Mieczysław Jagielski, marching in the direction of the negotiating hall. This part of the footage is followed by documentary scenes of the strike itself.

The following scenes lead Winkiel to a meeting with Mrs. Hulewicz, Maciek's former landlady. In the car on the way to the meeting, Winkiel further discloses his real character to Dzidek, stating that he is not a genuine journalist but a mongrel, completely dependent upon the will of his superiors. Winkiel almost decides not to carry out the interview, carrying on with it only when Dzidek promises that the journalist will get a coveted pass to the shipyard from Hulewicz's daughter, Anna. Hulewicz relates to Winkiel—again presented through a series of flashbacks—the scene of Birkut's death in 1970, followed by Maciek's search for his father's body in the hospital mortuary and its secret burial.

A third flashback relates the process of looking for Birkut's grave on 1 November the following year: This is the Day of the Departed in Poland, devoted to the memory of the deceased, when families traditionally gather at graves, light candles, and lay flowers. However, Birkut's grave is nowhere to be found. In response to the brutal desecration of the grave, in the fourth flashback Maciek puts an iron cross at the place where his father died. In a fifth flashback, Hulewicz refers to Maciek's efforts at the shipyard, where he tries to convince his fellow workers that they should officially support the 1976 strikes in Radom. It is worth noting at this point that the strikes in Radom, Nowa Huta, Warszawa, and other places in Poland erupted in response to Gierek's decision to raise food prices by almost 60 percent.[1]

After leaving the Hulewicz home, Winkiel goes to the shipyard. The next sequence takes place inside the shipyard where Winkiel is let in by Anna. In another flashback, this one introduced by Anna, Maciek is seen in Gdańsk underpasses and streets putting up posters about the events in Radom and Ursus. Suddenly, two security agents in civilian clothes force him into a car. This scene of abduction is observed by a group of opposition members who happened to be nearby. Winkiel's leaving the shipyard is immediately followed by religious hymns before a Catholic mass; the next shot is of Wałęsa reciting a prayer for the striking workers.

Winkiel, now back at the hotel, listens to the prayers on the radio. Suddenly there is a telephone call summoning him to the hotel restaurant, where a man resembling the real-life chief of Radiokomitet at the time, Maciej Szczepański, but called in the film simply "First Representative," awaits him. Winkiel, despite himself, had been drawn in, touched, disarmed by the honesty of the workers and by the truth of their plight, yet he is now brutally reminded that he serves another master. He finishes the telephone conversation with "wrong number" and tries to escape through the hotel's back door. On his way, though, he is stopped by one of the hotel personnel and asked to enter the restaurant.

First Representative demands to know whether Winkiel has had any contact with the striking workers in the shipyard. When Winkiel tries to dodge the question, First Representative answers with a threat that Winkiel will be beaten if he does not answer correctly, and insists that the information Winkiel has gathered will be on the air the following day. When Winkiel tries to object that the material is not finished yet and that he needs time for editing, his superior interrupts rudely and says that Winkiel will not be editing the material. Winkiel reacts violently, shouting that he does not want to do it. In response to this, First Representative blackmails him with evidence of Winkiel's complicity and guilt.

Winkiel wants to do an interview with Maciek's wife Agnieszka, the filmmaker from *Man of Marble,* who is currently in prison; he is an old acquaintance of hers (he worked at the TV studio when Agnieszka was making her diploma film in Warszawa). Agnieszka describes her life with Maciek from the beginning, from her first meeting with him in Gdańsk through to their unfortunate visit to the TV studio where Agnieszka brought Maciek as a proof that Birkut existed, right up to the "silent revolution" in Gdańsk. This portion of the film is an interplay of flashbacks and commentaries, conducted by Wajda in a way similar to that of the interview with Mrs. Hulewicz. Agnieszka's story about

Maciek is of course more personal than those of the others; she talks about their life together, their exhibition of photographs, and their constant struggle for survival. The flashback giving the story about their exhibition is particularly telling.

Maciek and Agnieszka prepare their exhibition of photographs (of past events and atrocities) in Maciek's house, but are interrupted by the human relations officer from Maciek's workplace. The man threatens Maciek, saying that his exhibition will have dire consequences. The following parts of Agnieszka's story describe in detail the growth of love between her and Maciek, her return to Warszawa, their return to Gdańsk, and their wedding at the church there. The continuous interplay of flashbacks and Agnieszka's monologue is interrupted by a parallel insertion of documentary footage from the shipyard negotiations. During this scene, Agnieszka calls the shipyard, but instead of Maciek's voice she hears Deputy Premier Mieczysław Jagielski and the representative of the Inter-Factory Strike Committee, Światło, who are to carry out official talks at the shipyard. In another flashback, the pregnant Agnieszka is seen working in a shop and accepting money from Maciek's colleagues. Maciek returns from prison and persuades her to leave Gdańsk with their newborn son.

After the interview, on his way out of the police station, Winkiel passes the gym at the police headquarters where Captain Wirski, whom he had encountered earlier in his hotel room, notices him and demands material on Maciek. Winkiel refuses and leaves the gym, relieved that he has cut ties with the regime. He then goes to the shipyard and calls the Warszawa Radiokomitet offices from the strike headquarters. He tells the secretary that he wants to resign. The camera leads the spectator to the large negotiating room where the final agreement is being signed by Wałęsa and a government representative. In a series of shots, the spectator sees a triumphant Wałęsa with Maciek in a fictitious tableau; an enthusiastic Winkiel with Anna Hulewicz; and Agnieszka's and Maciek's final meeting after Agnieszka's stay in prison.

The historical sound track relates a speech by Mieczysław Jagielski, who tells about the painful negotiations and signals the act of signing the final agreement documents. The documentary footage continues its presentation of Wałęsa before the shipyard, facing a huge crowd of enthusiastic people, and Wałęsa again, later, on the arms of the workers, the crowds chanting *"dziękujemy"* ("thank you"). Winkiel leaves the empty negotiation hall. He realizes that he has been denounced by the driver who works for Badecki; the driver tells him that he is to meet Badecki in front of the shipyard. Winkiel leaves the shipyard and approaches the car, where Badecki, with a smile, tells him that the agreement is not important because it was signed under duress. The film ends with a monologue by Maciek on the overpass, addressed to his father.

Man of Iron, in addition to winning the Golden Palm at Cannes, was an enormous success in Poland and abroad. It generated feelings of enthusiasm and nationalistic fervor in the spectators; as Wajda notes in some publications, many spectators rose from their seats and sang the Polish national anthem after the film's screening. There are several reasons for which the film was perceived as an important work. First, due to its quasi-documentary character, it made its vision of the strike believable and powerful; it is the most well-known film to date about the famous strike. Second, it openly depicted, in a brutally honest way, the arrogance of the authorities, and their vices, their inhumanity toward common people, their luxurious lifestyle, and their disregard for the well-being of the Polish people. Third, it returned to the idea of a romantic, messianic hero, who, like Maciek Chełmicki in *Ashes and Diamonds*, risks his life and the life of his family for a political cause.

In his presentation of Maciek and Agnieszka, Wajda uses Catholic ideology and iconography. The Christian notions of the Messiah are not only delicately alluded to, but are explicitly framed by the religious symbolism and the documentary footage. In this way, Wajda reveals the importance of Catholicism in Socialist Poland and the political role it has always played there in the past. Due to the film's consistency of vision and passionate presentation of historical events, *Man of Iron* had a tremendous impact on public opinion in the West, and it greatly influenced the course of political events in Poland. Wajda created his own artistic version of the historical event before anyone else; as the first artist to present this vision to the public, he became the coauthor of a specific version of history that would later be proliferated in other parts of the country.

Other discourses, such as newsreels, BBC programs, radio broadcasts, and television programs, prepared by other foreign TV crews, existed as historical documents, but they never reached the general public, especially in Poland.[2] In fact, censorship was still so strong in August 1980 that, although the TV-viewing public knew that stoppages were occurring in the Gdańsk shipyard, they had no idea what was really going on. Filmed six months after the strike, Wajda's work became a prototext, a singular artistic source for the discourse depicting these events, one that the Polish public could trust. Although Polish audiences were aware of the fact that Wajda's film was a fictionalized account and not necessarily an analysis or a document of actual events, they accepted the film as an artistic presentation that communicated not only the historical truth but the spirit of the strike as well.

The film is powerful as a political statement. It draws its power from several film approaches seeking to address the audience directly, in a manner almost like propaganda. Wajda used all the methods of his Socialist Realist background, his knowledge of documentary and propaganda film, to express feelings of outrage and enthusiasm and to influence the audience's perception of events. Moreover, he openly uses Christian iconography, in this way addressing not only the sophisticated intelligentsia but also the predominantly Catholic people of Poland. In the first of these approaches, Wajda mixes documentary and fictitious footage. This creates an effect of authenticity, greatly appealing to audiences tired of the lies served to them through official government media.

Before Solidarity came to power, facts were distorted in the government press, changed beyond recognition or not revealed at all. The truth about the mistreatment of Polish citizens by police and security forces existed in folk discourse, through gossip and conversations among friends. Some of the facts of abuse were eventually documented by underground organizations like the KOR (Komitet Obrony Robotników— The Workers' Defense Committee), at great personal expense and with agents in constant fear of imprisonment and persecution. The sorts of truths they uncovered were revealed openly by Wajda in the form of documentary footage of beatings and police abuse. Additionally, Wajda uses an interwoven mesh of real people (the participants of the strike or its leaders), real songs, and reconstructions of real events.

The authenticity of these images took spectators by surprise. For instance, Lech Wałęsa, the strike leader, and Anna Walentynowicz, the actual instigator/cause of the strike, both appear in *Man of Iron* several times. The combination of real people with the fictional protagonists and their artificial incorporation into the film fiction (as in the scene of the wedding of Agnieszka and Maciek) strike a false chord—even if their appearance in the historical footage or in the staged scenes related to the strike itself strengthens the enunciative power of the film's message. As Mariusz Muszkat notes, "The proportions of ordinariness and sublimity have been obliterated, especially in the scene of the wedding in which Wałęsa and Walentynowicz take part as witnesses. They were not the same people as they had been before August. Confidence, caused by an unprecedented victory, was all too clear on their faces. In this theatrical scene, two times were mixed. This was a serious dissonance."[3]

So, while Wałęsa and Walentynowicz exist in popular memory as the famous participants of the strike, their later political success had nothing to do with the stressful time of the strike itself. The sloppiness in matching these two diverse diegetic times—that of the strike (1980) and that in which the film was made (1981)—was immediately noticed by observant spectators who were hypersensitive to any misinterpretations of the crucial historical time of the strike, the only time in the very recent history of Poland that literally "stood still."

The public demands for documentary truth in the presentation of events put undue stress on Wajda, who, in presenting the "here and now," wanted to make the reality on the screen credible and believable. He also introduced a specific narrative technique, the quintessentially believable and trustworthy "old woman," the representative of simple people, the teller of historical tales, gossip, and jokes, but also the upholder of the national tradition and of the unification myths: Thus, Mrs. Hulewicz serves as a link between past and present.

The historical facts voiced by simple people from the street reinforce the expository power of the presentation. According to Czesław Dondziłło, situating the film's discourse in the minds of "the people" was intentional, since Wajda wanted to reveal the mass character of the reform movement.[4] In particular, history seen from the point of view of the most vulnerable observers of history—old women—is an extremely powerful device. Mrs. Hulewicz, at whose house Maciek once rented an apartment, serves as a point of insertion into Maciek's past life. For instance, the flashback introduced by her that describes the search for Birkut's grave is an example of the return to national traditions, to the most sacred of Polish days, the Day of the Departed. Maciek's grave has never been at the cemetery, he has never been buried there, which is anathema to Catholic Poles, for whom a proper burial is a must. In response to the obliteration of this tradition, Maciek puts an iron cross at the place where his father died. The coarse symbolism of this act is direct; a cross made of iron and polished by Maciek in the shipyard serves as a symbol of Maciek himself, but also as a premonition of times to come: It is a solemn reminder of the dead, but also of the power of the opposition unified under the banner of Catholicism in Poland.

While Mrs. Hulewicz's memories relate mostly to past traumas, the presentation of authorities relates to the traumas experienced by Poles at present. Winkiel, a journalist of small posture, is messy and inept, cynically betraying his former friends and present heroes of revolution. In clothes that always seem too small and somewhat dirty, he represents a small and unimportant member of the society, one who has remained under the thumb of the powerful for too long. Drowning his uncertainties in alcohol, he prefers not to remember that the same authorities who raised him into his place also took away his right to speak freely, and have oppressed his fellow citizens in this way for years. Winkiel's transformation into a convert at the end of the film is, quite simply, unconvincing.

In the presentation of Winkiel, Polish audiences recognized themselves as compromised people who were forced by circumstances to cooperate with the regime. As Jerzy Surdykowski indicates, Winkiel became *chłopiec do bicia* (the whipping boy) through what many felt to be Wajda's caricature of the journalist. Real journalists in Poland reacted violently to such a demeaning portrait of their profession, arguing that Winkiel's cynicism and alcoholism hid acute moral dilemmas much more convoluted and interdependent than a simple fear of incrimination by security agents.[5] In Surdykowski's words, "Although one dreams of seeing the real face of the journalist, Winkiel, and his psychological roots, one is aware of the fact that the cheap caricature of the journalist presented in 'Man of Iron' functions and will continue to function, copied in the thousands by standard literature and screenplay writing. Society needs its whipping boys."[6]

Wajda is equally hard on the representatives of governmental authority. His demagogic portrayal situates the government exclusively within the framework of the "bad guy," unlike in *Man of Marble*, where the position of "them" could still be debated, questioned, and in some cases reluctantly accepted.[7] Here, the representative of authority, Badecki, is presented as a drunkard who shouts that the party will not share power, and that the only way to be rid of the workers is to dispose of Maciek. This aspect of Wajda's presentation irritated many spectators in Poland, who doubted especially its excessively literal quality. As Małgorzata Szpakowska states, "In general, 'Man of Iron' is over-explicit.... [T]he bad guys ooze anger, sweat and vodka. If one is bad, one is also ugly and badly brought up; if one is on the right side, then one is also subtle."[8]

Every spectator in the cinema related personally, to some degree, with the images on the screen, which produced a violent feedback based on individual memories, hidden facts revealed by the underground publications of the opposition movements in Poland, and by the underground discourse of social knowledge circulated in the form of gossip, conjecture, and personal experiences. As Paweł Jędrzejewski states, "In 'Man of Iron,' reality is cold and autumnal. Security agents are dressed in leather jackets or have their hats pulled down over their eyes. The so-called decision makers and VIPs are repulsive and recognizable from one hundred metres away. The world is unequivocal. The appearances of normalcy, so characteristic of Wajda's earlier films, are missing."[9]

In this presentation of the "villains," Wajda shifts into the discourse of Socialist Realism, absorbed at the Łódź Film School and first exposed in his early études. He introduces this discourse deliberately, openly seeking to influence the reactions of spectators, to draw out, so to speak, their feelings of revulsion when they think of the authorities, to warm them up for a fight. As Krzysztof Kłopotowski writes, "The spectators went along with Wajda because the film gives vent to feelings of hatred and hope pent up over the years. 'Man of Iron' destroys the myth that the authorities only wanted the good of the people. For the first time it shows the authorities' ill will and egoism, traits of whose existence the society had suspected the party and government agencies for decades."[10]

The Socialist Realism paradigm of the strict division of roles into good or evil clearly influences character formation in *Man of Iron*. In the film, there are no truly three-dimensional people, only one-dimensional abstractions that represent historical forces. According to this Socialist Realist interpretation, on the one side there is Maciek, a virtuous and courageous working-class protagonist. His enemies admire him; his friends and loved ones include salt-of-the-earth grandmothers and intellectuals who are drawn, moth-like, to the light of his integrity. Even Wałęsa stands in as best man at his marriage, which takes place in a church and signifies the ostensible communion of church, working class, and intelligentsia.

Against the idealistic hero, on the other hand, are arrayed a motley and assiduous crew consisting of scheming bureaucrats, spineless reporters, alcoholic police informers, and unscrupulous security police, all representatives of an oppressive and Machiavellian dictatorship. An example of such an image is found in the sequence in which Agnieszka is presented as a symbol of Mother-Poland. The construction of the mise-en-scène places Agnieszka—the Madonna with unborn child, viewed with pious adoration by Birkut's fellow workers—in the center of the picture. Agnieszka looks monumental, statuesque, presented without any ironic commentary. "In *Man of Iron* Agnieszka and Birkut's son were apotheosised—statufied, so to speak—as pious, forward-straining heroes out of a tradition that can be described only as Stalinist; and the fruit of their hard-working Stakhanovite loins was blessed in a pathetic little cameo appearance, by none other than Lech Wałęsa himself."[11] In this shot, Wajda creates what almost seems a painting, one in a style very typical of the Stalinist period, in which Stalin and his revolutionary heroes are presented as statuesque and monolithic figures. In this manner, Wajda refers directly to Poland's cultural past, but also introduces an insidious mise-en-scène that imposes its sentimentality.

In *Man of Iron*, there is no place for irony. The title is informed by the images of the iron cross Maciek builds for his father after his death; by the place he works in, the shipyard, where most elements of the ship are still welded in an old-fashioned way that imposes the association of iron and its treatment; and by the "iron" characterization of Maciek, who demonstrates inhuman, unbending determination in times of ideological crisis. Socialist Realism is an important cultural discourse within which Wajda worked extensively (after all, Burski from *Man of Marble* constitutes Wajda's alter ego); its legacy is vivid in most of this film's sequences. In this sense, the film moved but also irritated Polish spectators, who discerned the presence of his discourse in every layer of the film.

Perhaps the most surprising overt historical discourse in *Man of Iron*, following years of silence in the films and mass media in Poland, is the role of Catholicism. For the first time, Wajda publicly acknowledged the social and political presence of the Catholic Church, particularly the role the Catholic religion played in supporting the opposition movements and the Gdańsk strike. By including documentary footage of the crowds in their masses, and the images of religious icons on the shipyard fence, Wajda emphasizes the importance of Catholicism in Poland

and also its ritualistic value. As the opposition grew, the significance of the Catholic religion meant not only an impressive spectacle but also a notable addition to the opposition's power, which undermined the authority of the government and constituted a parallel, powerful current of resistance. At the same time, the discourse of Catholicism is reinforced by that of Polish Romanticism; in *Man of Iron*, Maciek is Messiah, one who devotes his life and the well-being of his family to organizing the opposition movement against an oppressive Communist system.

The film's messianism, as Walicki points out, is highly representative of the Polish variety: "A full-fledged Messianism, national and religious at the same time, striving for an imminent and total regeneration of earth life, was born in Poland after the defeat of the November uprising. The real new element in it—an element from which the entire structure of messianic thought could be derived—was the conviction that traditional faith was not enough, that Christianity should be rejuvenated or reborn, and that the fate of Poland depended on the universal religious regeneration of mankind."[12] This Polish messianism is overpowering in *Man of Iron*, present in the images of Catholic masses, crosses, and cemeteries; in the scenes with obvious religious references (e.g., the scene of sharing bread between Anna and Winkiel); and in the scene of help being offered to the pregnant Agnieszka.

Messianism is also present in the sound track when the spectator is exposed to the religious hymns during the lifting of the cross, during the mass, and upon Winkiel's and Dzidek's departure from the Hulewicz home. Religious rituals, such as the wedding in the church, the mass, and the burial of the dead, are openly and, with typical Polish passion, related to the political and the ideological: the political and the religious merge in the presentation of the Romantic Messiah. Passion and feeling, the hallmarks of Romanticism, characterize the presentation of all of the Romantic voices in the films: the religious, the messianic, and the populist.

Sometimes, however, the film's Romantic emotionalism borders on the sentimental. For instance, the presentation of Agnieszka as a symbol of Solidarity and "Mother-Poland" is almost campy in its sentimentality. The scene combines all the necessary ingredients of the Romantic sauce: the messianic function, the populist tradition, and the religious elements, all merged in an elaborate shot of Agnieszka, the saint, humbly accepting money from the workers.[13] The overwhelming role of religion in the film was noted by such critics as Vincent Canby of the *New York Times*, who wrote that "the most interesting thing about *Man of Iron* is the way it dramatizes the immense political importance of Polish Roman Catholicism at this time."[14] Polish critics such as Tadeusz Szyma also notes the presence of religion in Wajda's film; in his opinion, due to the director's moderation in presenting the theme, the symbol of the cross become extremely powerful.[15]

Wajda reveals many social ills in this film, problems not readily admitted to by the public. One such unpleasant truth is the widespread alcoholism that existed in Poland during those times. The spilled alcohol in the bathroom serves as a symbol denoting that the pathetic Winkiel is subjugated to *two* supplementary discourses: those of authority and of alcohol. The widespread consent to use alcohol in every walk of life produced a social phenomenon of camaraderie that subjugated (or at least ameliorated) all opposing discourses and made drinkers "feel at home" with the authorities. Alcohol blurred the differences between the good and the bad, the honest and the dishonest. Not surprisingly, those few who were self-declared abstainers were treated with suspicion and distrust by their colleagues.

In its aesthetics, the film also addresses the spectators in a direct, demagogic way. It is likely that the basic concept of montage was employed by Wajda to produce striking effects in film and to reveal social contradictions; this strategy functions not only through concatenations of images, but also through the juxtaposition of image and sound, image and language, and image and music, creating the effect of a dialectical clash of ideas characteristic of Eisenstein's theoretical reflections and practical approach to making films: *Man of Iron*'s combination of sound and image produces a striking, almost frightening effect. For instance, in the scene of the procession with the dead worker carried prone on the door, the sound track superimposed on the visuals is a chilling counterpoint to the visual images. The dry, crackling observations of the militia groups' short-wave radio communications—all in short, informative sentences such as "a group of people moves in the direction of [x street]," or "several hundred people gather in [y place] and should be dispersed"—brings a cold and unsettling realism to the otherwise passive solemnity of the procession.

In general, audiences reacted emotionally to the film, identifying strongly with its protagonists. They admired Wajda for his bold and unprecedented depiction of the truth, but expressed disapproval of his simplifications and documentary inaccuracies. *Man of Iron* is similar to *Everything for Sale* in its unparalleled display of social anger, grief, and excitement, depicted by Wajda with all the means at his disposal. This emotional excess, however, translates at times into demagogy and propaganda—which, admittedly, were perhaps methods fit for the spirit of the times, "both majestic and kitschy ... full of passion, tragedy and anxiety."[16] On 12 December 1981, martial law was declared in Poland. This state lasted sixteen months, causing irreparable harm to Polish culture as many artists were incarcerated or interned. Because of his international fame, Wajda was not thrown into prison like so many others, but he suffered from other, more subtle persecutions: In April of 1983, while making *Danton* in France, he was removed as the head of the film production studio, Unit X. Notwithstanding these drawbacks,

Wajda focused on the production of the film that many consider the best of his entire career.

Danton (1983)

Danton is set in 1784, during the French Revolution. The film has to be read in the context of its reception in Poland and France, the two countries within which audiences might be expected to have a sufficiently deep knowledge of both Polish and French histories to grasp the film's message. Wajda gives his history a "contemporary feel" even while maintaining a grasp of historical sources and populist legends, yet these two issues—the film's reception in Poland and its reception in France—must orient any meaningful discussion of its issues, merits, and flaws.

In the film, Wajda refers to a well-known conflict between two revolutionary leaders, Robespierre and Danton, which resulted in the death of the latter. Both Stanisława Przybyszewska, the playwright, and Wajda see the conflict as an antagonistic discourse that arose not only from personal differences, but also from two opposing ideologies and points of view. Historians, on the other hand, credit Danton's death to the turmoil of revolution and to the forces remaining beyond the personal control of the protagonists. The "personal conflict" position is the one that Wajda adapts for his film. He presents Danton as a person who loves people and life, a man both warm and caring; by contrast, Robespierre is cold and forbidding.

Wajda dismisses Danton's more questionable character traits, such as his greed and corruption, in favor of his most positive ones. Meanwhile, in the depiction of Robespierre, he avoids whole areas of interpretation of the historical part he played in the revolution and instead concentrates on his dogmatism and earnestness in approaching the principles of insurgency. This simple dichotomy directs the viewer's attention to the questions of politics and human responsibility in general. Not surprisingly, it also provides a discursive "entry" into the areas of political and social references in present-day Poland. Particular scenes in the film attest to this multi-layered complexity of the whole film.

Most scenes in *Danton* occur in the form of tableaux; each takes place in a closed theatrical space and involves the protagonists within an emotional exchange of ideas. Important moments in the film are always connected with speeches by the protagonists or with others' responses to them. The film starts with a scene at a guard post, where guards are checking the carts for aristocratic fugitives. Danton is in one of the carriages returning to Paris. He is greeted warmly and enthusiastically both by the guards and the crowds. At the same time, Robespierre lies in bed sick and feverish; elsewhere in the same scene, his companion washes her little brother in the tub. She forces the boy to recite the Declaration of the Rights of Man and the Citizen, and he trembles with fear when he tries to recite the long and difficult phrases.[17]

In town, angry people line up in the rain waiting for bread, while spies walk around them and listen to their complaints. A young prisoner is led to prison. A girl waiting in line comments on his beauty, which later leads to her arrest. All the while, this scene is watched by Robespierre from a window above the street. In the next scene, Camille Desmoulins's newspaper, *Vieux Cordelier,* which Danton supports, is ordered closed down and the printing shop demolished. Desmoulins opposes this act of vandalism; however, Heron, chief of the secret police, tells him that he is no longer allowed to say anything. The remains of the printed material are picked up by young boys in front of the shop. Later, in a conversation with Robespierre, Saint-Just suggests that, because of Danton, an overthrow of the government may occur in the near future. Robespierre goes to the Tuileries, to the meeting of the Committee of Public Safety, and discusses Danton's situation with his colleagues. Shortly, Amar, the chief of police, arrives with the documents denouncing him.

Danton soon learns about the conspiracy against him. He remains convinced that nothing untoward can happen to him because the working class of Paris is behind him. Desmoulins and others approach Danton and tell him that Desmoulins's newspaper has been closed. Philippeau, a representative of the centrist Jacobins, suggests to Danton that perhaps they should overthrow the government, but Danton opposes this move for fear of a bloodbath. During the meeting at the National Convention, Bourdon attacks the methods of the secret police and Heron. One of the members of the Committee of Public Safety relates this speech to his peers, who blame Danton for Bourdon's accusations. Robespierre decides to meet Danton and warns him of the committee's accusation of treason. During the meeting at Danton's house, the two leaders reveal differences in their outlook on revolution: Danton considers Robespierre's policy inhuman and destructive; Robespierre, on the other hand, considers Danton's arguments childish. Robespierre wants Danton to join his committee, but the latter refuses. They cannot reach an agreement.

Meanwhile, Desmoulins and Lucille, his wife, talk about events at the convention. Lucille is frightened, sensing that something terrible is about to happen. Robespierre comes to visit Desmoulins, whom he considers a close friend, and tries to convince him to make a speech at the convention, arguing that Danton was using Desmoulins. However, Desmoulins refuses and throws Robespierre out. A short time later, the Committee of Public Safety members meet to discuss Danton; Robespierre sets the time of Danton's arrest for 3:30 A.M. that day. Each of the members of the committee presents his opinion, and then Saint-Just writes an indictment. From this moment on, the film picks up speed; everything now happens within twenty-four hours, so the pace of events becomes hectic—people start running, for example, and the tension is vivid in the nervous camera work, on the tense and uncertain faces of the protagonists, and in the sound effects and music. The latter are frightening and jarring, clearly reflecting the intensity of the experience.

Danton comes home in the evening. Desmoulins, who had been waiting for his return, accuses Danton of treason. Danton realizes that Robespierre has visited Desmoulins and concludes that their arrest is imminent. The ensuing film action happens in the crescendo of events. The Convention Hall is full. People talk angrily. Suddenly, a young man announces that Danton has been arrested. The Committee of Public Safety members enter the Convention Hall. Legendre, Danton's supporter, takes the stand and demands that Danton be heard; other speakers want to defend Danton, as well. However, Saint-Just pushes the would-be speakers away from the rostrum and tears up the pieces of paper with the names of other speakers. People shout "Down with the dictator!" as Robespierre gives an ardent speech against Danton. Suddenly, Bourdon betrays Danton, decrying him in a speech that ends with his intonation of La Marseillaise. When he leaves the Convention Hall, Lucille, who heard his declaration, slaps him across the face.

Desmoulins, Philippeau, and Danton are incarcerated. Danton explains to Desmoulins that the trial has nothing to do with justice; he believes that the trial is simply a political duel. Someone announces that the convention has accepted the charges against the three men. On 2 April, the prisoners are tried, along with all of the city's incarcerated thieves—a fact Danton protests to no avail—by the Revolutionary Tribunal. The press is not allowed to take notes when the judge reads the indictment. At the hearing, Danton produces his famous speech and demands a public trial. In court, Danton is continually interrupted by the judge, who uses the decree that the accused is not supposed to address the observers in the hall. The observers react violently to this; consequently, the guards are called and order is restored. Danton then speaks amid complete silence until he loses his voice.

Danton goes to Conciergierie, the famous prison, along with the other convicts. On 4 April, the members of the committee make Legendre sign a false deposition about the plot planned by Desmoulins's wife and Danton's friends. Robespierre and the members of the committee plan to introduce a new law that forbids the accused to speak at all during a trial. During the trial at the convention, Danton states that the trial is "rigged" and that the committee wants to get rid of him while silencing his protests with their new decree. On 5 April, the verdict is read by the members of the court in the now empty hall of the convention. All of the accused are condemned to death and all of their properties and belongings are confiscated.

Next, in a quick scene, we see the guillotine being prepared for the execution. Danton and the others have their hair cut in prison and are led out with their hands tied behind their backs. Outside the prison, Danton looks up to the window of Robespierre's apartment. Soon, the guillotine is at work; the blade moves and blood pours. Robespierre, bedridden due to illness, wakes up suddenly as if he has been having a bad dream. Danton climbs the scaffold and asks the executioner to show his head to the crowd after his death. Simultaneously, Robespierre, pale and trembling, takes the sheets from his face and states that democracy is an illusion. The guillotine is washed after the killing, with Lucille in the foreground, tying a red ribbon round her neck. The young brother of Robespierre's companion now recites the decrees to Robespierre perfectly, while he listens in horror. Fade to black and silence.

Danton is a tense, emotional film, a highly subjective portrayal of a creatively interpreted historical moment, with only a modicum of attention paid to historicity. In *Danton*, Wajda is concerned more with the internal state of the nation than with an objective depiction of the events as portrayed in Przybyszewska's play. As with the later film *The Possessed*, this film mesmerizes spectators with its emotional intensity, the somewhat dirty look of its interiors and exteriors, and its feeling of terror, lack of reason, and rising emotional tension. Wajda's revolution is pulsating with an inner rhythm that forces its participants to act quickly and brutally. The revolutionaries do not sleep much or eat leisurely; on the contrary, they are immersed in hectic, irrational actions, and they run from place to place and deal briskly with whatever issues are at hand. The depictions of common people are as frantic and hectic as the dealings of the Strike Committee at the Solidarity Strike in the Gdańsk Shipyard in 1980.

Understandably, the film reflects the fast-paced revolutionary dealings, the urgency, of Wajda's contemporaries, but also the undercurrent of terror in these dealings. *Danton* is as unmistakably personal as both *Everything for Sale* and *Man of Iron.* In each of these films, there is no place for calculated irony or humor; the films address the viewers directly with an intensity unparalleled in Wajda's other films. In *Danton*, Wajda addresses his own contemporary nation's emotions, clearly and realistically presenting betrayal and terror, both of which Poles had experienced after martial law was declared. Consequently, despite Wajda's continued denial that *Danton* does not have a Polish context,[18] such an interpretation was repeatedly presented in both the Polish and the French press after the first screening. For instance, in *Trybuna Robotnicza*, the popular Communist daily, Ireneusz Łęczek states, "Those who start the huge machinery of a social movement become its victims, thrust out by others. Private intentions mix with social ones. Naive activists operate alongside experienced political players yearning for power and money. All this is very close to recent Polish affairs. Consequently, my opinion is that *Danton* is much more Polish than it may seem."[19] Accordingly, Polish spectators persistently see numerous Polish references in the film. The general interpretation of Robespierre's and Danton's motives was closely related to the Polish historical context of the conflict between, respectively, those of Polish leaders Wojciech Jaruzelski and Lech Wałęsa.

Robespierre himself in the film is an iconographic image from Polish culture. Pompous and stiff-necked, overly concerned with his outward appearance, he is a man who puts on his costume as armor against the outside world. Admittedly, this presentation of Robespierre does not give credit to the great historical person, who, according to Prof. Jan Baszkiewicz, historical consultant for the film, was an advocate of "a utopian, *sans-culotte* program of an egalitarian society who wanted to stabilize the revolution by introducing and strengthening its basic reforms in the years 1789–93."[20] In general, Wajda's Robespierre is a martinet advocate of the revolution obsessed with the ideas of egalitarianism and populism.

Interestingly, this presentation of Robespierre correlates with the popular presentation of Gen. Wojciech Jaruzelski in the Polish mass media. Inflexible, exceedingly private, stone-faced, Jaruzelski was obsessively concerned with matters of raison d'état and the implementation of the repressive regulations of martial law. Like Robespierre, Jaruzelski also wore "a stiff corset" under his military uniform. His image, similar to that of Wajda's Robespierre, is that of a solemn, formal politician, consistently and unflinchingly following the dictates of his own policy. Robespierre shows some positive attributes when he disagrees with his confederates about the accusations against Danton; similarly, Jaruzelski admitted in many interviews after the termination of martial law that he considered it his own private tragedy. Both Robespierre and Jaruzelski seem to have considered the imposition of terror as a necessary, painful condition to be undertaken in the service of the state.

Another instance of correlation between the film's events and recent Polish history occurs in the sequence depicting the meeting of the National Convention, which conjures up the idea of the Polish Sejm and its notorious *sejmikowanie* (deliberations), during which every *voivode* (principal of the province) could frustrate the directives of the government. The Sejm's debates continued endlessly in the sixteenth and seventeenth centuries, leading to chaos in the country and to a lack of solutions for many of its problems. This political culture of constant deliberation, conspiracy, and political fighting was so inscribed in the Polish mentality that even the new union Solidarity could not withstand this tradition. Within the union itself, just after its commencement, various factions and oppositions appeared.

The unavoidable temptation to see *Danton* in terms of Solidarity was corroborated by many critics. Some critics[21] read whole areas of subversive (if not overt) discourse into Wajda's film when they questioned whether the director intended *Danton* to be a metaphor for Polish events, with Danton as a surrogate Wałęsa and with Robespierre as a stand-in for the military government or even for the Soviet regime. Interviewed by filmmaker Marcel Ophuls in *American Film,* Wajda says, "Poland was indeed in a revolutionary situation last year," and that *Danton* attempts to "describe the atmosphere of revolution." David Sterritt goes as far as stating,

> It's possible that *Danton* has more biting political meanings and intentions than Wajda cares to let on, fearing for his status in the Polish artistic community (his next project is a stage production in Kraków) or his personal well-being. "There are moments in the history of our country when we can afford to make a political film that one is not ashamed to put one's signature to," he told Ophuls, adding that "right now, this is not the case in Poland."[22]

However, Philip Strick notes that the reference to the Polish context also signifies the film's universality: "[S]uch parallels as it may contain with events of the 1980s simply confirm the validity of the piece as a philosophical debate relating to the fortuitous (if cyclical) repetitions of history, applicable as much to current French politics (and duly applied, with some uproar, to the 1982 Socialist Party conference at Valence) as to the problems of Poland or anywhere else."[23]

The sequences analyzed here are just a few examples of numerous sites of allusiveness that Polish spectators have recognized in the film. The time of *Danton*'s release—in 1983, only a year after the implementation of martial law—encouraged such a reading. The film was highly appreciated in Poland for its unconventional presentation and discussion of a political message that related to contemporary life. Moreover, it was praised as another example of Wajda's Aesopian tale in which important political messages are communicated between the lines. Aside from the protagonists themselves, certain scenes in the film attest to the film's allusiveness. That is, some scenes in the film closely resemble well-known events or occurrences in recent Polish political culture.

When angry citizens of the republic wait in the rain to buy bread and when spies walk around them listening to what they say, one thinks of the persistent shortages in food distribution in Poland in the 1960s and 1970s. The abduction of a young girl by police after she has commented on the beauty of a passing prisoner acknowledges the horrors experienced during the first months after the introduction of martial law, so well known to the Polish spectator: Ordinary citizens could be interrogated on any charge and kept at the police station without any legitimate grounds for up to two days. Similarly, the scene in which Robespierre reads Desmoulins' newspaper, followed immediately by that in which the paper's office is demolished, transports the Polish spectator into the early months of martial law: Police and representatives of the army could enter the apartment of a citizen under suspicion, carry out a brutal search, and, on finding printing materials or machines, demolish them and turn the whole apartment upside down.

Robespierre's tense demeanor and brutal decisions place him on a par with Jaruzelski, who, at the time of martial law, pressured writers to conform to the standard symbols of loyalty to the regime and reinstated party control over the intelligentsia. The brutal demolition of the print shop, with the smashing of machines and windowpanes, is immediately followed by a scene presenting Heron, who has just executed Robespierre's order, leaving the plant with stacks of the paper falling from his full hands, obediently picked up by young boys who follow him. Thus, the brutality of the police is placed within an ironic framework of impressionable young citizens of the republic,[24] who see how the law is implemented and who are conditioned to believe that it is to be respected and obeyed.

In France, conversely, *Danton* was received icily. Most of the controversy surrounding *Danton* just before and after its release in Paris was of a clearly political nature. President François Mitterand, after a special screening at the Cinémathèque Française, is said to have walked out as soon as the lights came up, hurrying out through a crowd of journalists so that he did not have to answer questions. Critics pointed to Wajda's questionable handling of historical facts and, particularly, his identification with Danton rather than with Robespierre. In the eyes of the French public, *Danton* was extremely pro-Danton and very anti-Robespierre. Wajda seemed very lenient toward Danton's obvious corruption, his venality, and his rabble-rousing, yet very contemptuous of Robespierre's thirst for virtue. As Marcel Ophuls puts it in his interview with Wajda, "Admittedly, both [heroes of the French Revolution] had a great deal of blood on their hands. But should the virtuous, the incorruptible side of Robespierre be considered as nothing more than an infirmity, a psychoanalytic quirk, to be held up to ridicule?"[25]

In Ophuls's opinion, the fact that Wajda's homeland has lived through countless revolutions should make him more inclined to undertake a thoughtful and penetrating analysis of all the aspects of each leader. Alas, there is no predisposition in Wajda to do that. Ophuls, whose opinions match those of the representatives of French Socialism, desired a more thoughtful and sensitive portrayal of the Revolution and its leaders. Their disappointment mirrored the disillusionment of French spectators of various political and cultural orientations, who expected a more enthusiastic depiction of the Revolution from a director also considered a former Resistance fighter.[26] The French spectator inscribed into his or her polemic a similarity between the Polish and French histories and a similar passion for the political and the emotional within the historical. Distressed by the incompatibility of these discourses, the French spectator asks, "Why should any French Socialist today still expect a Polish filmmaker to show any sympathy or even any understanding for the mentality of those leaders of the French Revolution whom he holds, rightly or wrongly, to have been responsible for the ravages of the guillotine?"[27]

Ophuls's opinion reflects the polemical opposition between the intentions of the film director and the response of the local spectator. The spectator may understand the artistic message, but not every spectator could approve of its ideological content. Thus, in the French reception of the film, the clash between various aspects of reception produced a spectatorial tension impossible to pacify, both within the viewer trying to unite the points of view of the two protagonists, and among those spectators representing disparate points of view. As Ophuls sees it, Wajda infuses his Robespierre with all the negative aspects of the Revolution: he charges him with "all the crimes of Stalinism."[28] In attacking the puritanism and ideological hypocrisy of the historical figure, Wajda, in the eyes of the French spectator, attacks the very idea of the Revolution itself that, in the French social consciousness, has come to be embodied by Robespierre.

In fact, a number of Polish reviewers agreed with the opinions of the French critics in this matter. For instance, Jan Sajdak argues,

> The French public opinion rightly states that Danton was a prominent figure with none too clean hands and that he liked to make money in every possible way. Sartre said openly—"We loved Danton as a tribune but we could not respect him as a man." Robespierre was a completely different man. He was an idealist with clean hands, commonly called "incorruptible." The Revolution and the Republic were his beloved only children, to whom he devoted his whole life. He it is who supports the plan of national education—the common obligation to provide a free education. As he considers war the best defense, he knows that war will enable him to crush counterrevolution. Robespierre considered terror as a necessary evil, and he stated that terror can only be a tool in the hands of truly honourable people. It was no accident that his desire to clear the Committee for Public Salvation and Safety from corruption immediately caused his death. A real patriot, democrat, and revolutionary died. He became immortal, and the newest research of Jaurès and Mathiez puts him on a pedestal.[29]

This specific representation of the two leaders of the Revolution results, consequently, in a faulty presentation of history. Two critical remarks in particular are worth presenting in the discussion of the historical discourse in the film. In one of them, quoted by M. Ostrowski in his review of *Danton,* Louis Mermaz contends, "The film is misleading: in the last analysis, there is nothing wrong in this for those who have a modicum of knowledge. However, there is a risk that it will be completely incomprehensible to those spectators who did not learn history."[30] Laurent Dispot from *Le Matin* is even more critical in his remarks:

> The historical period the film deals with is very well known to students. They would fail their history lesson miserably if they reproduced Wajda's

version, without any reference to Herbertists or de-Christianization; without mentioning the fact that France had been attacked and that the war had been the cause and the driving force behind everything—behind the protagonists' every statement, every decision, and every activity.³¹

The arguments of various (but especially French) critics constitute parallel voices in the clarification of the film's political message. They contribute to the reading of *Danton* as a dense, polyphonic text, in which Polish and French voices interact on many levels of interpretation. The literal images of the French Revolution actively engage with those allusive images depicting political activities and historical events within the Polish context; as with any utterance, various discourses are juxtaposed within this filmic utterance. They include the voice of the Polish director, who presents a specific, Slavic interpretation of the Revolution; the voices of French spectators, who each introduce their own unique interpretations of the historical events in France; and the voices of Polish spectators, who, similarly, inscribe their own Polish interpretations into the film.

Danton reveals many aesthetic traits of theater tradition in Poland; Wajda's theatrical activities constitute an important contributing factor to the film's creation. Of course, the film is based on a play, Przybyszewska's *The Danton Affair*,³² which is primarily an intellectual drama addressing the philosophy of history, in which human issues are of secondary importance. Maciej Karpiński, a longtime friend of Wajda who has collaborated with the director on a number of theatrical productions, believes Przybyszewska stresses the ethics of a Revolution that is inspired by reason and not passion,³³ while Wajda's *Danton* overwhelms the spectators with barely hidden emotions. The French Revolution is used by Przybyszewska as an example of an historical confrontation of opposed ideals. While Robespierre adheres to principle, Danton embodies revolutionary compromise. Przybyszewska's text clearly shows her fascination with Robespierre. Although she realizes that his devotion to revolutionary standards could turn at any point into a dogmatic absolutism "that would betray its initial idealism and bring destruction in its wake,"³⁴ her play leads us through political discussions and masterful exegeses of ideological points, sanctioning Robespierre's clarity of argumentation, and, in general, the purity of the intellectual debate.

On the basis of this play, Wajda directed his own production of *The Danton Affair* in Teatr Powszechny (The Popular Theater) in Warszawa in 1975. The part of Robespierre was played by Wojciech Pszoniak (later cast in the same role in the film), and the part of Danton by Mieczysław Pawlik. The stage production's minimalist style (bare stage floor, a heavy wooden table as the basic prop) reinforced the strongly defined behavioral differences in characterization. All of the characters in the play are strongly individualized, with the main dramatic responsibility falling upon the two protagonists, Robespierre and Danton. The acting styles of Pszoniak and Pawlik had one thing in common: "a dominance, an undefinable sense of dangerousness that made their impersonation of the great historical figures truly convincing."[35]

Danton thus reveals a change in the interpretation of Robespierre and Danton, in which Robespierre turns into a dogmatic, cold advocate of the revolutionary idea, while Danton becomes a charismatic champion of the populist cause. But the main principles of the dramaturgic reconstruction of the plot remain the same on stage and on film. The aesthetic of the film is conditioned by the demands of the spoken word. Consequently, *Danton* is largely played out in a series of brief, intimate, beautifully defined dialogues and confrontations that vacillate between the robust, commonsensical Danton and the steely Robespierre.

One of the consequences of this strict structuring of the scenes around conversation is the film's relative dearth of large, populous scenes. Shots involving great numbers of people or horses are few and confined, so that the convention sequences, with their packed assemblies, make a vivid display of a government in turmoil. The court where Danton and his fellows rail against injustice is packed. The film's power comes mostly from its performances and its close-ups, shown in a quick, rhythmic succession of shot-reverse-shots that match the rhythm of the spoken word.

In this, Wajda seems to repeat his technique of a direct dialogue with the audience that he had already used in his first presentation of *The Danton Affair*; minimalist staging inevitably distances the audience from the action and the set, forcing viewers to focus on word, gesture, and context. In his stage production, Wajda carried the action into the midst of the spectators; seated on chairs among the actors, the audience was given the illusion of actively participating in the play, of being part of the scene. Although Wajda was not able to place the spectators within the world of the film in precisely the same way, he uses close-ups with such refinement that the spectator feels he or she to be a part of the conflict. Close-ups, shot-reverse-shots, and facial expressions in the shots cause the spectator to be as emotionally and intellectually engaged in the process of viewing the film as audiences were in viewing the play. In fact, the facial expressions of the protagonists become the most important "words" in the film. *Danton* is as carefully orchestrated a theatrical accomplishment as was its earlier staged forebear.

The film medium allows Wajda to reinforce the dramaturgic structure of the opposing forces of the French Revolution with the color and the construction of mise-en-scène. While the world of Robespierre and his preference for reason is presented in cool whites and blues, the world of the rustic Danton is rich in reds, yellows, and greens. In this application of color, Wajda clearly draws from his experience as a painter. For example, Robespierre's room, unlike Danton's lively, colorful quarters, is cool and ugly, the epitome of revolutionary dogma; it is empty, rigid, and stark in its barrenness. Its bluish walls enclose modest furniture and sparse objects in the same way its austere walls open and close the film, constituting a rigid framework that contains the deeply passionate conflict of the film. In the final scene of the film, the room is an epilogue to the historical lesson of the Revolution. It is no accident that Danton looks up to the room before going to the guillotine. He hopes to see Robespierre at the window, but it is empty; Danton shouts toward the window that Robespierre will soon follow him. The room, again, with its sparseness and coldness, functions as a comment on the imminent terror that will annihilate both oppressed and oppressor.

By contrast, Danton's Revolution is of the masses, heavy with the desire to live, to eat well and drink much, and to make love: In Danton's quarters, passion and vitality reign. The predominant colors are red, brown, and orange, while the rooms are cluttered with an abundance of objects. This vitality, evident in the life Danton lives and in the ideas he promulgates, is rendered irrelevant at the end of the film by the image of Robespierre's spartan, lifeless room. Wajda displays once again the sensitivity of a painter, an art connoisseur, and an intellectual who understands that a true depiction of those times requires a presentation of historical facts in a spectacular manner.

Music also constitutes a clearly distinguishable voice in *Danton*. In Philip Strick's words, "an apparently anachronistic modern music composed by Jean Prodromides succeeds in capturing the essence of the picture: the sense of things tearing apart."[36] The compositions convey magnificently the immediacy of the oppressed characters' terror through their grim, metallic orchestrations, which seem continually on the point of explosion. The executions, seemingly unattended, are "almost Bressonian matters of blades and blood in brief proximity";[37] the jagged, nervy score, with its opposition of jarring sounds, yet lively and rough in the scenes with Danton, adds a discordant note regarding the dialogic clash of attitudes, emotions, and judgments.[38]

Danton's theatrical and cinematic elements create an absorbing mosaic of glossia; the spectator is indulged with the beautiful presentation of the ideological conflict and also with the artistry of the film's images. Here, Wajda reveals his plurivocalism, combining his experience as painter, filmmaker, and theater director, creating a passionate film that presents its political argument in an artistically refined manner. Due to this brilliant combination, *Danton* is revered by some critics as "one of the best films of [Wajda's] career."[39]

A Love in Germany (1983)

In this film, Wajda again returns to the theme of World War II, but this time from the perspective of ordinary Germans living in a small town.

As Jerzy Płażewski writes, "Hochuth's book allowed Wajda another look at the Germans. He could show in a film what kind of people they were, how they lived in their own world and what shape their world had, for the first time,"[40] showing fascism as an everyday social phenomenon. The film follows the story of a young Pole, Stanisław, addressed by Germans as "Stani," and a young German woman, Paulina, who fall in love under the Nazi regime. Of course, Nazi policy did not allow Germans to associate, let alone intermarry with those Hitler defined as "subhuman," including Poles, Czechs, Hungarians, Jews, and Gypsies.

The film was made in a village called Tumringen, many of the locals of which actually participated in the film production. An article in the *Stuttgarter Zeitung* describes the circumstances of making of the film in this way:

> The production of this movie creates agitation, [for] the confrontation with the past still ignites peoples' emotions. The film production has split the population of Tumringen into two camps. "We get strange looks, even get looked at as the enemy," says an extra from the village, "and only because we are participating in the movie." Younger people also, she describes, do not understand why "these old stories keep having to be dragged up again." Angry exchanges take place in Tumringen: There is talk of "communistic backstabbers" and "Jew lovers" who produce the movie. The atmosphere is tense: The population of the village is now divided: Into those in the movie and the others.[41]

As is demonstrated by this excerpt, Wajda's production raised emotions to an unprecedented level, especially in Germany. Consistent once again with his overall historical and political interests, he raises controversy and uncertainty with his choice of subject matter for the film.

A Love in Germany starts with a sequence in a train, upon which we find a middle-aged man, Herbert, and his young son Klaus. They are on their way to Brombach, a small town in southern Germany where Herbert grew up, the only child of a German soldier posted in Bavaria during the war and his wife, store owner Pauline. During World War II, Herbert was a little boy who witnessed a budding love affair between his mother and a Polish laborer named Stani. We are informed of the time frame through the troubling flashback of Herbert as a little boy licking a lollipop with a swastika on it—a startling reminder of the times, in which innocence mixed closely with horror.

From sentimental contemporary sequences showing Herbert and Klaus in Brombach, a beautiful little town among rolling hills, the film shifts to the past so that the doomed love affair takes center stage. We see Stani helping his employer to deliver fruit to Pauline's store: He brings in a large basket of apples when Pauline notices him, and the two young people exchange meaningful looks for the first time. The apples spill on the ground and Stani helps Pauline pick them up, but

he also casts a simmering glance at her naked knees. In a scene recalling the famous apple scene in the film *Lotna,* associations of fertility, desire, and romantic love come to the fore.

The next sequence shows Wehrmacht officers coming from the war
for a short respite, the husband of Pauline's neighbor Maria Wyler being one of them. The film unfolds from this point onward in a succession of intercut sequences showing the budding romance on the one
hand and the reaction of the town's inhabitants (but most especially
Maria) on the other. Usually, non-German workers such as Stani were
treated as subhuman, but he is treated differently by his employer, as
shown in scenes where the young man eats dinner at the same table as
his employer. This display of resistance to Hitler's interracial politics is
accompanied by a radio commentary stating that communication with
such people is strictly forbidden by Hitler. Stani's employer expresses
his anger at the proclamation loudly, saying that the young man is also
a human, like everybody else around them.

The romance between Pauline and Stani grows rapidly in intensity.
Pauline is open and honest about her feelings and prepares herself
fully for the illicit tryst; she buys condoms at the pharmacy, shocking
the pharmacist. Later, on the way to the town, she encounters Stani,
who has stopped with his horses for a moment; she approaches him
and the young people quickly embrace and undress hastily. Suddenly,
they hear an approaching car. Two German officers exit the vehicle for
a moment to admire the view. However, they do not notice the lovers
and quickly resume their travel. Pauline and Stani look to each other
with alarm but continue their lovemaking.

Herbert notices the growing attraction between Stani and Pauline,
who in turn notes her son's disapproval; however, consumed by desire,
she can do nothing about it. When she happens to see her neighbor
Maria making love with her husband, she looks at the photo of her own
husband, but she thinks instead about Stani. In her sexual frustration,
she asks Stani's employer to allow her to "rent" Stani as a help for her
shop for a while. When asked about her husband in Bavaria, Pauline
indicates that she is not eager to visit him. Soon, the affair becomes obvious to the inhabitants of the small town; Maria and Stani are unable
to hide their feelings. Their display evokes feelings of antipathy and
jealousy among the townspeople, especially in Maria. The latter is envious not only of Pauline's young lover, but also of her success in business. Maria's husband is more forgiving, stating that some orders issued
by Hitler are senseless.

Back in the contemporary time line of the film, the sight of the store
brings another memory to Herbert. The scene begins with Pauline serving a customer while Stani helps her behind the counter. Making her
sexual attraction for the young man conspicuous to the customer, Pauline serves the older woman offhandedly, then closes the store and goes

to the cellar where Stani first helped her with the delivery of apples. Oblivious to the outside world, they start to make love while young Herbert looks on from the cellar stairs. When Pauline notices her son watching, she closes the cellar door, excluding him from their presence.

In later developments, Pauline's friend Elizabeth Schinnitgens enters with the letter informing her that Elizabeth's husband, Hans, has died in the war. Pauline visits Stani and tells him that she wants him to leave. However, when asked about her young lover, Pauline admits that she loves Stani and does not want him to go anywhere. Under pressure from Elizabeth and from the townspeople, though, she plans to visit her husband, now stationed in another part of Germany. During a storm that night, Pauline goes to Stani and tells him that their affair must end. Angry and frustrated, he leaves her and returns to the horses, which have become extremely agitated both by the storm and by the lovers' quarrel. He tries to calm the animals down, but is ultimately trampled by them.

The following morning, Pauline goes with her suitcase to the station. On the way, a wagoner offers her a ride and informs her that Stani is in the hospital. She immediately runs to the hospital in distress and expresses her love for Stani openly. Shocked by her behavior, the German patients and nurses force her to leave the hospital. Under great social pressure, Pauline goes to see her husband. In the meantime, Elizabeth takes care of Pauline's store and her business; however, Pauline has also asked her to give Stani any love letters she sends while she is away.

The action of the film now shifts again to the present time. Herbert enters his family's old store and asks about his mother's love letters. Maria now owns Pauline's store, personally and financially benefiting from her erstwhile neighbor's downfall. We find that the lovers were found out and punished by the Nazis. Herbert finally learns the truth of the love letters when he visits the elderly Elizabeth at the hospital; she explains to him that one of the letters accidentally got in the hands of the Gestapo. Elizabeth's lawyer explains the whole event to Herbert in detail.

Now the film returns again to the past, to the scene of the interrogation taking place at the Gestapo station. Both Pauline and Stani are questioned about their affair; to protect Pauline, Stani denies everything. However, when he sees that she is also in custody, his face changes. Pauline and Stani embrace, not paying attention to anyone around them. Stani is taken away from the interrogation room while Gestapo officers question Pauline about the affair. She admits that she loves Stani, to which the Gestapo officers respond with revulsion tinged with pity. Nevertheless, they try to find a way out of this dilemma. Following Hitler's dictates about the purity of the German race, they try to match the characteristics of Stani's body with the required "ideal." After a long, absurd discussion, the officer in command, Meyer, declares that a match is possible after all, and that Stani can become a German citizen. However, Stani rejects this "generous" offer: He does not want to renounce his Polish citizenship and thus leaves no way out of the Nazi dilemma for the German officers. The Gestapo leader decides to hang Stani publicly as a warning to other prisoners. Pauline is also punished, sent away to a concentration camp.

Although reviewed warmly by some critics, *A Love in Germany* provoked many negative comments. It touched upon sensitive and rarely discussed issues—the silent collaboration of ordinary German citizens within the system of terror and extermination employed by the Nazis, and the consequent moral dilemmas this collaboration created for ordinary Germans. The fact that it is Wajda, representative of the victim nation, who raises these issues irked many Germans. Add to this the negative representation of all Germans in the film (the openly seductive, almost shameless Pauline included), and the film seemed to many people—but particularly to German audiences—an outright slap in the face of Germany.

In *Tygodnik Powszechny*, critic Tadeusz Szyma suggests that Wajda's treatment of German responsibility for the World War II atrocities may have touched too many sensitive nerves. According to historical documents, German citizens not only acted officially as per the dictates of Hitler's racial policy, but also functioned as the silent collaborators of Hitler, in this way contributing to the eradication of prisoners.[42] After all, as Szyma argues, it is thanks to an army of nameless clerks, neighbors, and citizens of small towns such as Brombach that the process of extermination could take place. Wajda points to the administrative and human sides of the totalitarian system, aspects often omitted in the official accounts of World War II.

There was another kind of criticism, as well; many German critics expressed an opinion that the strong political beliefs of Rolf Hochhut were watered down by Wajda's focus on the story's love affair itself. *Der Spiegel* criticized the film for its depiction of an ordinary and rather base love story, more similar to "a farce which in no way resembles the accusatory novel of Rolf Hochhut. The latter described the banality of evil and the almost paranoid climate of fear and hatred":[43]

> *A Love in Germany* is an uncharacteristic Wajda film. Love as a destructive passion has seldom if ever interested Wajda as a filmmaker, *The Siberian Lady Macbeth* and perhaps *Everything for Sale* being the only other noteworthy examples of films with such themes. Yet this film may nonetheless be one of his most effective, effortlessly evoking sweeping, haunting associations from a small set of extremely specific circumstances.[44]

Kevin Farrington is also quite critical in his assessment of the film, drawing attention to the discrepancy between the gravity of the sexual transgression in view of strict Nazi rules and the reaction of the Nazi officials in the film, a discrepancy that shows them as just "nothing more than bureaucrats in the uniform of the Third Reich. They are back-slapping, beer-guzzling oafs, nothing at all like the rigid, boot-clicking sadists with whom we are accustomed."[45] Such a depiction of the antagonists does not lend credence to this love story, which ends so tragically due to documented historical circumstances. Rodo Fruendt also distrusts the depiction of the German soldiers, noting that the film does not explain all the reservations the Nazi officials had concerning the infamous race rules:

> In its original framework, [*A Love in Germany*], in which Otto Sander as narrator revisits the past, shows even more of the bitterness and self-righteousness of the losers. After his experience in Venice, Wajda short-ened the film by approximately 12 minutes. Unfortunately, one scene was left out which was especially effective in showing what the film re-ally is about, but maybe the German viewers really would not be inter-ested in this: In the second half of the movie, when the lovers are exposed to the "Gestapo machinery," Wajda shows not a "Gestapo machinery" but humans. As well, Armin Mueller-Stahl, assisted by Ralf Wolter, ac-complishes a grotesque balancing act in the role of the chief of the secret state police from the neighboring city.... With even-tempered exactness, he tries to follow insane decisions about "questions of race," the most in-human regulations. And when others refuse his rational-seeming insan-ity, he is insulted, deeply disappointed. The hangman who cannot understand that his hard work is not laudable, who does nothing evil but only does his job—that is Mueller-Stahl in sum.[46]

It seems that in his attempt to present the humanity of the Germans, their hesitations and their doubts concerning the nature of Hitler's in-famous race rules, Wajda trivialized sensitive matters and did not give credence to the complexity of criticisms presented by Hohchuth. Be-hind his relatively benign presentation of German officers, however, there may have been a more complex explanation of the filmmaker's motives.

In the 1980s, a new political trend, one that moved toward the nor-malization of German-Polish relations, was initiated by the Polish au-thorities. Some reviewers suggest that Wajda wanted to participate in Polish politics by unflinchingly addressing such a controversial issue. In fact, Angelika Kaps asserts that, by making this film, Wajda wants to help reestablish relations between Germany and Poland: "Wajda's in-terest in this project is explained not only in his esteem of Hochhuth as one of the most important political narrators and dramatists, but also in a close need for the argumentation of the subject of the relationship between Germany and Poland with the possibility or impossibility of a love in a—past or present—supremacy state."[47]

Whether this political justification led Wajda in his filmmaking or not can never be proved. However, as in his other films, again we see

Wajda's preoccupation with history and its impact on the fate of an ordinary man. As Kevin Farrington notes, Wajda's concern in the film is
"the mechanism of history and the drama of the common man swept
up by events beyond his control. Sex is therefore only a corollary to the
larger picture."[48] Wajda makes the film not to justify or explain Nazi
atrocities but, as Rex Reed states, because he believes that "we must
never forget, lest we be condemned to relive it now."[49]

Although the film expresses Wajda's continuous interest in the themes
of World War II, it failed to raise as powerful emotions as his earlier
and now famous war trilogy. As a representative of the victim nation,
he may have not grasped adequately the enormity and complexity of
German guilt—and even if he had, he might not have expressed it fully.
As Tadeusz Szyma suggests, Wajda may have "distanced the German
spectators of the film because he did not really understand the historical phenomenon of Nazism for Germans."[50] His German characters are
not particularly convincing, lacking complexity and insight. Likewise,
the film cannot be read as a universal human drama due to the lack of
balance in the presentation of human feelings. While the love of Pauline is fully portrayed, especially in the first part of the film, Stani's feelings are depicted in broad, unfocused strokes; at times he seems merely
a passive respondent to Pauline's advances, an issue noted by many reviewers.[51] Wajda blamed himself for the unfortunate casting of Piotr
Łysak; a competent actor, he nonetheless had little chance to show his
acting ability when in company of one of the greatest German actresses,
Hanna Schygulla. Her expressive and powerful performance completely sidelined her counterpart's and other actors' efforts and made
the surrealist orders of Hitler particularly poignant.

A Chronicle of Amorous Incidents (1986)

A Chronicle of Amorous Incidents, a nostalgic film and one widely appreciated by Poles, returns to the year 1939, set during the period leading
to the very beginning of World War II. The action takes place in Wilno,
at the eastern border of Poland. It starts from a highly original sequence
in which past and present merge. Two men, one young one and one
middle-aged, are on a train. From the window they watch uhlans on
horses ride along the train tracks. They seem to be performing a mounted
military charge, attacking the enemy at a full gallop. As in *Lotna,* Wajda
once again presents the whole iconography of uhlans and their culture.

At a certain point in this sequence, there appears a superimposition
of two faces, the young and the old, and a dialogue ensues between the
two passengers. The young man, Witek, wonders aloud where he has
left his old cap. The other man, played by the renowned writer Tadeusz
Konwicki himself, responds that he knows which cap the younger man

has in mind, and adds that he will not have to change it for another one. Following these mysterious words, the unknown older man disappears. The appearance of this Stranger, "Konwicki-actor, Konwicki-ghost," as Maria Malatyńska calls him, is "the most exquisite narrative invention in this film."[52] It produces a moment of uncanny combination of past and present, as if it were the very epitomization of nostalgia through which the past seems to live in the present.

At Witek's home, his mother greets him enthusiastically and asks about his student cap. They talk about his imminent graduation and his future university life. Witek's terminally ill grandfather, lying in bed in the same room, is also interested in the young man's plans. Death and life mix in this beautiful scene, the room lit with a diffused summer light. Suddenly, a neighbor drops in and asks Witek to deliver a telegram to the manor-house, and Witek agrees. At the destination, a young woman approaches him and picks up the telegram. Her mother soon follows and the two women speak French, not paying attention to the young man standing in the hall. When the young woman wants to tip Witek, he responds in French as well. He explains that he is no postman, but simply delivers the telegram as a favor. From the moment he first sees her, Witek falls desperately in love with the young woman, whose name is Alina.

Witek follows Alina wherever she goes and engages in flirtatious conversations with her whenever he meets her. The whole film turns into a story about the delicate romance between the two youths. Wajda intersperses these romantic moments with important scenes presenting conversations between Engel and Lowa (friends of Witek from Germany and Bielarus, respectively) and between the Puciatowny sisters (young girls from the neighborhood whom Witek, Engel, and Lowa have befriended). These light, yet socially significant encounters display the sarcasm of young people in talking about sex and romance; the scenes function as a sobering contrast to the idealistic and romantic love affair unfolding between Witek and Alina.

As in his other films, Wajda presents in *A Chronicle of Amorous Incidents* important social situations that highlight a complex Polish social landscape. Before World War II, Poland was a multinational country with Jews, Ukrainians, Germans, and Belarusians richly represented in the Polish population. In one scene portraying other nationalities, Engel scolds his father, a German protestant priest, when he complains of the German language being used by the latter in his sermons. Engel wants desperately to be assimilated into the Polish community. This scene and others like it introduce tension and uncertainty into a seemingly romantic film. Seemingly a lighthearted film about the young protagonists' erotic awakening, the marching soldiers, war preparations, and scenes of nationalistic tension create an emotional discord that Wajda accentuates with music.

Wajda maintains the film's narrative division into present and past in the sequences with the Stranger, who appears again when Witek runs through the wood in search of Alina. The contemporary merges with the past when the Stranger shows Witek his radio headphones; the startled Witek recovers from the shock on seeing such a marvel, and just has the time to ask where the Stranger knows him from. However, the Stranger disappears suddenly. Next, the Stranger appears at the Jewish market, and he and the pair pass each other without a word. These strange scenes involving the Stranger are interspersed with those that introduce the atmosphere of erotic tension in the film.

Next, Witek leads Alina and her cousin, Sylwek, to the river's edge, where the boys fight over the girl. Shortly thereafter, Witek appears at the manor where the Puciatowny girls freely converse about love, sex, and pleasure. In the meantime, Engel's sister Greta tells Witek, whom she secretly loves, about the impending war; she mentions the fact that she will have to leave Poland for Germany very soon. However, Witek is very much in love with Alina, whom he follows, takes for walks in the country, and dreams about day and night. During these nervous nights, he also dreams about the Stranger. The former comes to Witek's bedroom as if it were his own, and looks for old German documents or talks about future events.

Witek becomes more insistent in trying to see Alina, until her father threatens him with his gun to warn the youth that this behavior is intolerable. Finally, Alina agrees to come to meet at the river bend, where the young people declare their love for one another. They promise to meet in the near future for a secret "wedding" ceremony. In the meantime, the state of war becomes more visible: Polish and German soldiers can be seen everywhere. Greta's and Engel's family leave for Germany while Lowa goes to join the Polish army.

The wedding ceremony takes place in the final part of the film. It starts from a brightly lit, dreamlike sequence of their communion in the water, a romantic sequence portraying the young people kissing and making love and, finally, lying down on the riverbank in a futile attempt to commit suicide together. At that moment, the war starts: Artillery shots erupt around them and it appears that they are both shot. The film ends with two significant sequences: In one, Alina and Witek submerge themselves in the water, as if disappearing slowly into nothingness. At the same time, endless army squadrons approach and walk along the river. According to Tadeusz Szyma, this last scene of the suicide attempt was in fact "conditioned by external circumstances: the negative reaction of Alina's parents against Witek to avoid misalliance and the fact that Witek failed his graduation exam and thus ruined his aspirations and plans. However, Wajda sees this futile attempt in a more symbolic sense—as a gesture of saving their own romantic world from final destruction."[53] At the same time, the disappearance into the water is ambiguous: the young people wake up after their suicide attempt. Still, they disappear in the water later on. As Szyma proposes, Wajda "merged the contradictions between the realistic and the symbolic aspects of the whole film and created its ideal and organic unity which resulted in the effect of the mutual overlapping of various levels of the film and in the subtle opalization of its meanings."[54]

A Chronicle of Amorous Incidents is a nervous and intense account of the atmosphere dominating Poland just before the start of World War II. This atmosphere is shown along with the experience of young people oblivious to the coming events. The two young people in love, in particular, are only vaguely aware of the impending doom. Despite marching soldiers and numerous emigrations from the town, Witek and Alina remain suspended in their own constructed "unreality," in the world of love. According to some reviewers, the film is one of the most touching love stories not only in Wajda's filmography but in Polish cinema as a whole. This Polish "Romeo and Juliet story" is told by Wajda "in pastel images portraying the life of a small town near Wilno with its hidden dramas and with its feverish and delicate love between Alina and Witek in the foreground. This love had no chance at that time, it was brutally destroyed by the contradictions of that world which finally culminated in the sick cry of anti-aircraft sirens."[55] Despite its ending, the film's aesthetics are sweet and beautiful, as if we watched a series of "sugary post-cards."[56]

Most Polish critics received the film enthusiastically, underlining its mastery in the presentation of the Mickiewiczian landscapes and of the social realities of Poland before World War II. One such enthusiastic critic is Szyma, who emphasizes Wajda's almost documentary presentation of the "as of today exotic cultural tradition of the multi-national Polish Republic which he places in the mythical space of this specific place on Earth which also produced Adam Mickiewicz."[57] Like Kazimierz Młynarz, Szyma also stresses the fact that the film recalls the Romantic tradition not only in the presentation of the landscape and the love story, but also in the inclusion of the figure of the Stranger, like the ghost in Romanticism. This figure is "Witek's double-ganger, who knows his past and can tell his future and expresses the increased/strengthened awareness of Witek's being."[58]

Romanticism, an overarching trait in Wajda's filmography, again comes to the fore in this film. As in *Lotna*, Wajda portrays Polish uhlans as beautiful, imaginary figures with all the accruements of their military might: lances, ensigns, and badges. Yet these imaginary figures also function as a link between past and present. "[T]hey epitomize past military glory, and symbolize the longings of Poles concerning their importance in the past. The uhlans, directly transported from the sanctuary of the national imagination, signify a transition point between two worlds: the past and the future, the passing world and the coming one."[59] Similarly, the town is unrealistically beautiful and stereotypically idealistic, with all of its inhabitants living together in harmony.

The film is a feverish depiction of a beautiful love story, one that could not have been consummated in any way at the historical time it represents. The summer of 1939 produced a particular tense, volatile atmosphere that Wajda aptly depicts through the film's rapidly changing scenes. In the scenes of rural life, Wajda shows the versatility of Polish people, their heterogeneity and passion, in a similar way as in *The Wedding* and in *Ashes and Diamonds*. The uncertainty and anxiety of the times is vivid in these scenes, as well as in the scenes in the marketplace, those at the Puciatowny house, and the final scenes at the riverbank. Both images and music contribute to the creation of the anxious atmosphere in the film.

As in *The Young Ladies of Wilko*, Wajda shows an interest in the search for lost youth and in a return to the past. In these two nostalgic films, Wajda experiments with the ways of presenting the fond (yet difficult) past. In *The Young Ladies of Wilko*, color and light represent the passage of time, as summer turns into a premature fall; in *A Chronicle of Amorous Incidents*, it is the Stranger persona of Konwicki and the pastel colors of the images that render the film a visual fugue on the passage of time.

The Possessed (1988)

After the nostalgic *Chronicle of Amorous Incidents*, Wajda returns to his great literary passion, the texts of Fyodor Dostoevsky. *The Possessed* has to be seen in the general context of Wajda's interest in the works of Dostoevsky, who was famous for his shrewd portrayal of human feelings and obsessions. Fascinated with Dostoevsky's deep understanding of emotions and psychological states, Wajda often approached his texts for theatrical realizations: *The Possessed* in 1971, *Nastasja Filippovna* (based on *The Idiot*) in 1977, and finally *Crime and Punishment* in 1984. One of the reasons why Wajda wanted to make a film based on *The Possessed* was the fact that he wanted, thanks to the cinematic means he could employ, to portray the revolutionary spirit in a convincing and perceptive way. A veteran of the "silent revolution" (as Solidarity's rise to power was known in Poland) and witness to the strike in Gdańsk, he deeply understood the feelings of uncertainty, constant fear, and sheer determination that the revolutionary effort created. He was fascinated by the events of nineteenth-century Russia and by Dostoevsky's presentation of doomed characters who are blinded and terrified by forces they simply cannot understand.

As the film opens, we find Szatow running through a darkened wood; he stops, digs a hole, and buries a large copy machine. The atmosphere is dark and gloomy, the winter landscape illustrated with jarring music.

The uncertainty and the agitation are underscored by the nervous moves of the camera, which will accompany all the characters in their actions in a similar way from now on. In the subsequent scenes, a group of insurgents returns to Russia from Switzerland. The year is 1870. Several young activists in a spacious house converse about the abolition of the present regime in Russia. They are awaiting the return of Mikolaj Stawrogin, the group's ideological leader and their new messiah. In Russia there is discontent, as the voice of the narrator explains, and the country is on the brink of a revolution. The film proceeds in a series of nervous, passionate scenes in which the protagonists establish their viewpoints on the subversive revolutionary activities in Russia.

In a conversation with Stiepan Wierchowienski, Szatow explains that he wants to leave the revolutionary assembly because he has lost contact with "simple people" in living outside Russia. He believes that, without a link to the common folk, one cannot foment revolution. The intensity of these discussions arises largely from the dialogue between Szatow and Piotr, Wierchowienski's young and impetuous son, but it is reinforced by the aggressive behavior of all the young participants. Piotr wants quick solutions to the social and political situations in Russia; he wants *action*, stating that books are unnecessary, that what they really need are deeds to change the world. The forceful and feverish atmosphere of *The Possessed* is expressed by the dynamic Szatow, who walks edgily in the rooms and on the stairs, and by the atmosphere of tension and uncertainty presented in various shots, in a fast pace of sequences, and in the flickering play of light and shade. Additionally, the atmosphere is reinforced by excellent music full of disturbing tones, composed by Zygmunt Konieczny, which adds to the uncertainty and thus ominously forecasts the sinister events about to happen. This musical discourse is reminiscent of Wajda's earlier solutions in a similar context, especially in *Danton*. In this film, Jean Prodromides's music also accentuates the elements of horror and fear in the plot.

Szatow visits Kirylow, another member of their revolutionary group, on the way home. Kirylow is restless and morose; he looks at the maps in front of him, spills ink accidentally, and talks to Szatow about suffering and death. Szatow calmly leaves and goes to the railway station; there, Maurycy and the governor's daughter Lisa await the arrival of the revolutionary leader Stawrogin, with whom Lisa is infatuated. Captain Lebiadkin is also waiting at the station with his physically disabled sister Maria; he raises a disparaging drink to Russia, which he cynically describes as a "pigsty" and a "freak of nature." When Stawrogin finally arrives, both Lisa and Maria approach him; the latter suddenly kneels in front of him, but Stawrogin calmly picks her up and explains that although he saved her from the attack of strangers some time ago, he is neither her husband nor her lover. Lebiadkin leads his sister away, and then Szatow attacks Strawrogin, striking him in the face, causing Lisa to faint. This strange, intense scene full of unexplained emotions and actions introduces several concurrent narrative developments that constitute some of the film's plots and originate from Dostoevsky's complex and overwhelming novel: relationships between Lisa and Stawrogin, between Maria Lebiadkin and Stawrogin, and between Szatow and Stawrogin. The latter remains tense, cynical, and unresponding to the emotional demands of all three people.

The previous scene is followed by another in a church, in which Szatow strolls around and looks upon the faces of members of various Russian social classes represented, rich and poor alike. As well as introducing the spectator to another plot in the film, the relationship between Lisa and her father, this scene also presents social differences in Russian society amid the opulence of the Russian Orthodox Church. The apparent poverty of the masses, the plainness of their dress, mixes with the riches on the walls and the beauty of the church interior. Lisa is also in the church; she approaches her father, who tells her that precious pearls have been stolen from the church. He also explains why he prefers, in the face of the common unrest, the safety of the church to the hostilities in his office. The governor's comment is an apt observation on the situation in Russia at the time.

In the meantime, Stawrogin visits the depressive Kiryłow. Their bizarre conversation revolves around the issues of death and religion; Stawrogin asks Kiryłow if he still wants to commit suicide. Kiryłow assures him that that is indeed his intention. On the way out, Stawrogin encounters Szatow, who holds a gun in his hand; Stawrogin asks why Szatow wants to shoot him. Szatow explains that he wants to shoot Stawrogin because the latter has changed Szatow's life dramatically. The cynical Stawrogin replies that it was his purpose to change Szatow's life, and, demonstrating his arrogance, announces that once he thought about changing Russia in the same way. Szatow begs him to do this, to raise the flag for all the young people he had influenced in the past. However, Stawrogin answers that right now he questions his beliefs in God and in revolution, and he wonders whether he wants to live or to kill himself. Finally, he warns Szatow that the latter will be killed by ruling of his own revolutionary association. In shock, Szatow learns that Stawrogin actually considers Maria his wife, despite his earlier protestations at the train station.

In the pouring rain, Stawrogin visits Lebiadkin and Maria. From the disturbing conversation between Lebiadkin and Stawrogin, we learn that the latter was married to Lebiadkin's sister for four years, a fact they held secret from everybody. Lebiadkin is trying to use this fact against the man by blackmailing him, trying to extort money for keeping the secret. However, Stawrogin refuses to put up with this state of affairs any longer and declares that he will reveal their secret. After Lebiadkin leaves the house to give Stawrogin and Maria some privacy, Stawrogin enters the room in which she lies on the couch. He approaches her quietly, sits next to her, and looks at her. Maria responds strangely, asking him to enter the room again, as if she wants him to repeat some script known only to her. When Stawrogin does as she asks, she pretends that it is not him who has entered, but a demon in his form. The enraged Stawrogin storms out of the house. The unusual dialogue reveals the bizarre nature of their relationship. Wajda underlines these aspects of the conversation by portraying Maria as unstable and paranoid. Her face is covered in heavy white makeup, her eyes are burning and sad, and her theatricalism adds to the emotional intensity of the encounter.

On the way out, Stawrogin encounters the beggar who, as we learn later, has robbed the church of its pearls and has overheard the quarrel between the spouses. The beggar offers to kill Lebiadkin and his wife for 1,500 rubles (an enormous sum of money at the time). Stawrogin reluctantly accepts this offer and throws the money at the beggar. Later, during a conversation with Piotr about the most recent revolutionary meeting, Stawrogin fails to pay attention, sitting immobile on the chair. He tells Piotr about the demon that his wife of four years saw in him and tells Piotr about the planned murder. Piotr listens calmly and gives Stawrogin a letter from Lisa, in which she asks to meet with him. At the next meeting of the revolutionaries, Stawrogin declares that he does not want to be their leader any longer; Piotr and the others react with disbelief and dismay. During the violent discussions that follow, the revolutionaries present more and more outrageous arguments in favor of the revolutionary process. Stawrogin listens quietly to their excited ideas and then watches Piotr as he raises the possibility of all of them being denounced to the government. The shocked young people look at him in disbelief. When none of them replies and Szatow leaves, Stawrogin and Piotr stomp outside and talk angrily about Stawrogin's change of plans.

In further developments, we learn about Piotr's deception instigated by Stawrogin himself: He, the seemingly vociferous supporter of the revolution, denounces his friends, finally revealing himself as the spy and collaborator of the group. At the governor's office, he not only reveals to the governor that the revolutionary leaflets found in town belong to his own organization, Topor, but that he also supports the governor in his suppression of workers who come to the palace when the factories where they worked are closed down. In a dramatic scene, fliers are thrown at the workers while they stand silently with Szatow at their head, waiting for the governor to make an appearance. Officers on horses arrive and brutally disband the crowd. Piotr asks the governor to release Szatow, who, as a result, is the only person to leave the scene of the police beatings. This fact is not missed by the remaining workers. Szatow leaves the palace slowly, not looking at anybody. He goes to Wierchowienski where the security police carry out the search, and the two men engage in an intense discussion on the purposes of the revolution while the police look at Wierchowienski's books and notes. They are interrupted only by women screaming that there is a fire in the city.

On the way back to his flat, Staszow discovers that his wife Maria has returned from Switzerland. In this intense scene, we learn about the unreciprocated love of Staszow for his wife, who comes back to him only because she is forced to do so by her pregnancy and by her result-ant precarious condition. She talks angrily with Staszow, who looks at her as if she were a phantom. The ensuing scene in Staszow's flat shows the unhappy and embarrassed Maria and her husband, who is exhila-rated and ecstatic at her return. From the outset, though, Maria de-clares that she does not want to stay with Staszow any longer. She does not feel like his wife after such a long stay abroad, and has only come back to work for poor Russia. She looks around in disbelief at his poor abode. Suddenly, the pain in her stomach starts and she moves rest-lessly. Maria is about to give birth; Szatow runs out to get a midwife.

At the next meeting of the insurgents, Piotr behaves like a dictator, accusing the young men of starting the fire. He tells them that he knows everything about them and warns them that they will be denounced. When asked about the person behind the denunciation, he states that it will be Szatow; this final act of denunciation is abominable and trans-forms the revolutionary engagement of the young people into an exer-cise in fear and insanity. In the meantime, Lisa meets Stawrogin at his place, learns about the impending murder of Stawrogin's wife Maria and her brother, and leaves her lover in haste, disillusioned and silently despairing. On the way home she meets Wierchowienski, who tells her that he plans to leave Russia as well. Against the raging flames and flee-ing people, the old and ailing Wierchowienski and Lisa carry out a con-frontational discussion about the absurdity of life.

In the final sequence of the film, several events happen: after the murder, Piotr goes to see Kiryłow who, after a long conversation with Piotr, kills himself; Lisa bids farewell to the dying Wierchowienski on a boat; Stawrogin commits suicide; and all of the young insurgents are arrested with the exception of Piotr, who goes abroad to train new groups of young insurgents. The film ends with a scene presenting Staszow's former wife Maria and their teenage son, who shows his aggression by carelessly shooting a gun.

This ambitious adaptation of Dostoevsky's novel portrays passion-ately the atmosphere of prerevolutionary Russia. The country seems dirty, in a constant haze or fog, even in the daytime scenes. The general feeling of despair and agitation is very well depicted in the film's im-ages and music. From his personal notes in the Archives,[60] it seems that Wajda was preoccupied mainly with ways of presenting the violent na-ture of the revolution and of the "mad Russia" of that era. His intention was to portray the atmosphere of the time as unusual, intense, almost paranoid. He accomplished this task using several means. First, he presented the action as taking place in the autumn, against the backdrop of rain, fog, and darkened interiors and exteriors; second, he created shaky images using handheld cameras; and third, he enriched the film with disturbing music providing overtones of fear and despair.

In attempting to film this huge and complex novel, full of philosophical and historical deliberations and debates on good versus evil and the presence or absence of God, Wajda had to limit the diegetic material and to concentrate on certain aspects of the protagonists. This made viewing the film difficult for those viewers not familiar with Dostoevsky's novel; Zbigniew Bieńkowski and Andreas Kilb concur, both describing an incompatibility between text and film,[61] while Zdzisław Pietrasik criticizes Wajda for his poor casting (especially the non-Polish Omar Sharif as Wierchowienski) and for his lack of "the broad background, that social panorama of Russia in the middle of the last century which is portrayed in the novel. There is no history of the sickness, only its final stages[;] we see the effects, not the causes."[62]

The frames of the film could not confine the huge and complex novel and, as a result, the film narrative lacks in coherence and logic. Unlike Wajda's earlier film *Ashes,* which, despite its narrative and historical complexity, somehow flows smoothly through consecutive historical periods marked by convenient inter titles and by the main characters' development, *The Possessed* was not able to produce a similar feeling of consistency and psychological justification. In his attempt at presenting the atmosphere of prerevolutionary Russia and of Dostoevsky's novel, Wajda fails to clarify Stawrogin's change of mind about the revolution, his change of heart concerning Maria and Lisa, and his outlandish cynicism and distance. Similarly, while Szatow's problems seem clear, the conflict between Piotr and his father is shrouded in narrative and psychological mystery. The film seems to offer a series of concurrent comments on Dostoevsky's *Possessed*—on the theme of revolution, its feverishness and insanity; and on the themes of deceit, love, and father-son conflict. Sadly, not all of these comments work well in accordance with one another: some are left incomplete and unbalanced, leaving the spectator with the feeling of incompleteness and uncertainty.

In general, *The Possessed* did not attract much attention; this was due in part to the lack of clarity in its presentation of events, its inadequate or unconvincing performances, and its tortuous plot. The indecisive young revolutionaries were engaged in inconclusive plans that lead nowhere. Spectators could identify with none of them, nor could they identify with Stawrogin (unconvincingly played by Lambert Wilson) or with Staszow. The film veered between three or even four diverse, complicated plot lines, and it focused on the psychological states of the protagonists, whose intentions were not completely clear. While the presentation of the atmosphere of Russia seemed convincing and cine-matically beautiful, the portrayal of characters was not.

A few reviewers praised the film. Marcel Martin, for instance, points out that the film is "great and beautiful, evidence that Wajda has re-turned to the peak of his ambition and talent";[63] this statement is cor-roborated by Janina Kumaniecka, who considers Wajda's presentation of the revolution as true to historical fact and to the ideas of Dostoev-sky. Both Dostoevsky and Wajda suggest that "revolution is an oppor-tunity for the obsessed, the work and the result of thought speculations of the insane mind."[64]

The 1980s began with a series of films consolidating the strong posi-tion Wajda established in the 1970s and also continuing his earlier the-matic preoccupations: politics *(Man of Iron* and *Danton),* adaptations of great literary works *(The Possessed),* and World War II *(A Love in Ger-many* and *A Chronicle of Amorous Incidents).* However, while the 1970s was the time of feverish and successful film production, with one film after another in a rapid succession, the 1980s witnessed a period that culminated in the production of fewer and less spectacular films. Nev-ertheless, all the films produced in the 1980s are politically and socially important.

The film from this period having the greatest political might is *Man of Iron,* which put the Solidarity movement on the international map not only as a political occasion, but also as a cultural event. *Danton* con-firms Wajda's mastery in adapting Przybyszewska's play to the screen, cementing Wajda as a master of both theatrical and filmic discourses. *A Love in Germany* and *A Chronicle of Amorous Incidents,* on the other hand, both deal with issues of World War II in a meditative, almost nostalgic manner, no longer passionately attacking the war issues as his earlier war films did.

Although all of these films are well made and well executed as nar-ratives, not all of them are noteworthy in their visual aspects. Neither *Man of Iron* nor *A Love in Germany* is aesthetically captivating, with the former being widely defined as the film in which Wajda considerably loosened his cinematic discipline.[65] *Danton* and *A Chronicle of Amorous Incidents* each have a specific style, which makes each of them an aes-thetically unique film. *A Chronicle of Amorous Incidents* dazzles the spec-tator with a unique combination of images diffused by light and music. The diffused light creates a delicate halo around the faces of young lovers and makes the transition between life and death painless and ethereal while romanticizing the narrative and presenting it as a realm of nostalgia for past youth and love.

Danton's specific aesthetics, combining Jean Primorides's music and the muted colors of the revolution (red, blue, and white), which domi-nate the overall palette of the film, makes this film an exceptional artistic experience.[66] The film surprises the audience with its intensity of vision and perfectionism. While passionate and brimming with emotions, it nevertheless surprises the viewer with the attention paid to historical details in mise-en-scène and costume, and it overwhelms the spectator with its sophisticated color and music. It is a true work of art and/or a passionate political duel, depending on the reviewer. Still other critics, such as Marek Haltof, consider the film one of Wajda's greatest, despite the discrepancies in the presentation of historical facts. As in all of his other films, passion prevails, forcing the spectator to react to the presented events at the emotional, and not the intellectual level.

Based on my conversations with Wajda and from comments in his essays and media interviews, I would suggest that one of the main reasons for Wajda's diminished output in the 1980s is the change in his level of creative enthusiasm, caused by the defeat of the Solidarity movement and by Wojciech Jaruzelski's introduction of martial law. Deprived of his Unit X in 1983 and angry at the way in which recent political events had taken shape—the internment of Solidarity leaders; the closing of the Solidarity newspapers; and the closing down of cinemas and theaters—Wajda turned to working charitably with underground artists. This activity seemed more important to Wajda at that time than any large-scale filmmaking endeavors. After martial law ended, with new authorities at the helm of the Ministry of Culture, Wajda had to resort to the mundane process of applying for funds to finance his film projects even though in the past he had been able to get funds almost automatically.

❈ 6

GRANDE FINALE
Films of the Nineties

In the 1990s, Wajda nostalgically continues with World War II themes. In this period, he is more solemn than in his earlier films—as if he wanted to address the areas that had bothered him for years but that he felt he had not fully addressed before. One of the most interesting films produced in this period is *Korczak*, based on the true story of the Jewish doctor admired by Poles and Polish Jews alike, and who died in the Treblinka concentration camp with two hundred orphans in his charge. In *The Crowned-Eagle Ring*, Wajda presents young people taking political sides in the events of the Second World War, while in *Holy Week*, again, he concentrates on Jewish issues during World War II.

Nastasja and *Miss Nobody* are unusual detours into Japanese aesthetics and into the world of contemporary young people, respectively. *Nastasja* is an exciting experiment carried out by Wajda with the Japanese actor Tamasaburo Bando. This is one of the most original of Wajda's works and arguably his most provocative adaptation of a literary work (Fyodor Dostoevsky's *Idiot*). *Miss Nobody*, on the other hand, tells the story of three girls living in contemporary Poland, one of whom, Marysia, comes from a poor family; her social climb is similar to that of Mateusz Birkut in *Man of Marble*, but *Miss Nobody* lacks the power and honesty of its predecessor.

Wajda's most recent works—or at least the most recent I discuss in this book—*Mr. Thadeus* and *Revenge*, are based, respectively, on a long poem by Adam Mickiewicz and a play by Alexander Fredro. Together, they epitomize Wajda's dexterous choice of texts for film adaptations; his preoccupation with national and historical themes; his attention to historical detail; his deep understanding of the Polish national destiny; his meticulous approach in constructing mise-en-scène as a fascinating and visually complex space; his attention to detail; his skillful presentation of grandiose scenes; his subtle depiction of personal conflicts; and, finally, his mastery of narrative pace. These films constitute an appropriate conclusion to the book about the career of the greatest and most prolific Polish filmmaker.

Korczak (1990)

Korczak is set before and during World War II and begins with a radio broadcast delivered by Dr. Janusz Korczak, the renowned Jewish doctor and director of the orphanage for Jewish children on Krochmalna Street in Warszawa, who talks about his orphanage and about the sacrifices he and his staff make for the children in their care. After Korczak's talk, the director of the radio station politely persuades Korczak to stop broadcasting his show because of the difficult political situation for Jews and because of the rising anti-Semitic sentiments in Warszawa at that time. The film centers on Korczak himself, who epitomizes the plight of Jews amid the systematic Nazi extermination efforts; he is portrayed as an idealistic protector of children, one who sacrifices his own well-being, and later his life, to their fate. The film unfolds in a series of tableaux showing a saintly Korczak, whose life and deeds are illustrated much as the lives and deeds of recognized saints are often depicted in religious paintings and sculptures. In these tableaux, the focus is on the figure of Korczak, with other characters and the elements of mise-en-scène serving a disconcertingly, and at times discomfortingly supplementary role in the film.

The difficulty in watching this film lies in the discrepancy it reveals between the director's lofty assumptions before making the film and the film's images themselves, which seem to counteract his goals or, at the least, to afford additional and disturbing readings of the original plan. I would group my doubts concerning this disparity in the following areas: (1) Korczak as savior, saint, and father figure; (2) aesthetic solutions involving the representation of Korczak and the grotesque and the horror of the ghetto; and finally (3) the presentation of Poles as saviors. One of Wajda's foremost postulations for this film (as communicated by him in various interviews and private conversations in Kraków in 1999) was to present Korczak as a larger-than-life person who dies for the orphaned children. Most of the scenes in the film illustrate this assumption, in effect creating a monological portrait of the man, similar in its homogeneity to the statuesque portrayal of the heroic Maciek Tomczyk in *Man of Iron*. In one series of such scenes, Korczak takes the children to the river and plays serenely with them on the river bank. This tranquil scene is interrupted by Stefa Wilczyńska, his former colleague, who explains that war is coming and that something terrible may soon happen.

When the war does break out in 1939, Korczak is consistently presented not only as a charismatic man, such as when he calms the fearful children during the bombardment, but also as a patriot who helps injured Polish soldiers and risks his own life. At this point, Wajda makes the character a doubly heroic figure: both Jew and Polish patriot. Korczak identifies with the lost Polish cause by putting on "the uniform of the betrayed soldier," as he tells the young man who tries to convince him that he should take it off. (Themes of the Polish identity and Jewish identity coalesce strangely here as they did in the national dilemmas of Nina in *Landscape after Battle.*)

Korczak is also portrayed as a quintessential father figure. Later in the film, after 1940, in the ghetto where he is now forced to live with his young wards, Korczak organizes his group in the same way as on Krochmalna Street, creating a sense of stability and emotional safety for the traumatized children. With the help of Stefa, he takes care of them, pretending that everything is fine. In these idyllic scenes, he takes them in his arms when they are afraid of gunshots outside the windows; in other scenes, he obtains money from affluent Jews and uses it to buy food, which he carries laboriously from the shop in the ghetto. He takes the antisocial boy Szloma, whose mother is dying, into his care. After Szloma's medical examination, an older boy takes him around the orphanage. Shortly thereafter, Szloma tries to beat and kick the boy and steals a chocolate bar from another child's bed. However, in the process of socialization implemented by the orphanage's juvenile court, set up by the fatherly Korczak, Szloma turns into a good and obedient member/son of the orphanage community/family.

This theme of the father figure is carried over, once again, from Wajda's earlier films. The forgiving, understanding, and self-sacrificing father appears in many Wajda films, starting from *A Generation* and ending with *Revenge*. In *A Generation*, there is Sekuła; in *Ashes and Diamonds*, Konrad Szczuka, the benevolent enemy, who dies at the hands of Maciek Chełmicki, the surrogate son; in *Samson,* Malina; and so on. These characters are, on some level at least, altruistic and understanding; they protect, advise, chastise (when needed), explain the convolutions of history, and give final blessings. This idealized father, imagined and reimagined in so many of Wajda's films, emerges almost as if from the filmmaker's subconscious. In fact, I would suggest that this "fatherliness" theme goes even further, in that Wajda himself adopts the role of father—he who shows his "child," the Polish nation—the glories and the mistakes of the past, and, through the examples of such events, tries to educate Poles on how to handle difficult situations with dignity.

In his attempt to save the children, the idealized and highly moral Korczak is confronted with situations that bring his moral superiority into question. One of the most controversial scenes in the film shows Korczak with Szulc, a Jewish entrepreneur, who invites the doctor to have a drink at a restaurant and talks to him about business opportunities in the ghetto. The contrast between the poverty in the ghetto and the prosperity in the restaurant is shocking. When Korczak tells Szulc that the children in the orphanage are starving, the latter collects money for him from other affluent Jews in the restaurant. Suddenly, young members of the Fighting Jewish Organization barge in and denounce the entrepreneurs; they shoot at one of them and take Korczak away.

Quintessentially good and selfless, Korczak is sometimes portrayed glowing in a soft light, which makes him resemble "a figure based on Franciszek from Assisse, a Christian ascete canonized for the good deeds for the poor."[1] This device is particularly vivid in the scene on the riverbank and again in the film's final scene. By contrast, the reality of the occupation is grim and sad due to the overall dark aesthetics of the images. The action unfolds in dark interiors, and even when it takes place outside, the world seems hopelessly sad and grim. At the metaphoric level, no light of hope illuminates the horrific events in the film.

The only exception to this spiritual darkness is the scene depicting the German soldier quietly watching Korczak as the doctor waters his flowers: Still having faith in the superior nature of humanity, Korczak believes that the soldier does not shoot because he has not been ordered to do so. The two men look at each other quietly, the bright sun spreading a patina of normalcy across the situation. However, with the exception of this rare philosophical moment, the situation of ghetto life is grim and depressing. *Korczak* is an impossibly heartbreaking film, unlike *A Generation*, in which the horror of the ghetto is counterbalanced by the enthusiasm of the young boys who help Jewish insurgents and participate in the uprising themselves. In *Korczak*, Wajda presents the brutal truth of the ghetto without any romantic refitting. Up to the final scenes in the film, this grim aesthetics prevails, making the images heartbreaking in their explicitness.

The final sequences of the film show a very tired Korczak returning to the orphanage with food and money, but with very little hope. A newcomer and a refugee from a concentration camp in Latwia shouts that all of the Jews will be incinerated in concentration camps. Korczak, Stefa, and the other workers at the orphanage try to think of solutions. Will they let the children go free? Or will they accompany them on their way to the concentration camp? Korczak declares that they should learn how to live through defeat in the most beautiful way and decides to accompany his children on their way to the camp. During breakfast, the order of deportation comes. Korczak tells the children that they must go on a trip, so they have to take some of their belongings and go in an orderly fashion to the Umschlagplatz (Emporium). Quietly, under a green flag and a Jewish star, the children board the train amid the chaos and violence of forced deportation.

In the legendary final sequence, the last wagon separates itself from the remaining ones; when it stops, the door opens and the children jump out in slow motion, to disappear into the fog. The scene is idealistically beautiful, with a diffused light and romantic mist engulfing the children. After this scene, a caption appears with the statement that Korczak died with his children in Treblinka in 1942. Paradoxically, the scene also relieves the spectator from viewing the horror of Holocaust—here, specifically, the children's murder. By creating a romanticized version of such a well-known atrocity, Wajda situates the scene within the context of a general commentary on life and the sacrificial death of Korczak. The scene generates thoughts about sainthood, Korczak's later canonization, and his death, all as an escape from the Holocaust. As Philip Strick comments,

> Wajda's sudden sentimental epilogue brings the train to a halt and unleashes the children to misty freedom in tranquil countryside, joyously transfigured into legend before our eyes. Excusing us by this device from an intolerable finale of collective murder—and excusing himself the horror of staging it—Wajda pulls back from the brink over which the facts require his story to plunge and leaves us instead with a cunningly uninterrupted crusade.[2]

The scene at the end of the film produces a certain emotional relief to the unbearable bleakness of the whole film. Maybe there is some hope in death, to which Korczak leads the children peacefully. Death, perhaps, offers relief, calm, and the serene beauty of nature. Likewise, it brings the protagonists back full circle to the calm and serenity of the scenes in the beginning of the film. As in other films by Wajda, there is ideal symmetry in the construction of the whole film—from the world of normalcy in bright colors, through the hell of the Nazi occupation, and back again to normalcy: the world of diffused light and calm once again. On the other hand, this serenity in the presentation of the final scene aroused numerous unsympathetic reviews, some of which will be discussed herein.

The last issue worth examining in the film is its presentation of Poles as saviors. In this film, Poles are shown as generous helpers of Jews and even Korczak's potential saviors. For instance, Maryna Falska tries to save one Jewish girl by taking her home, and she wants to save Korczak himself by giving him a new set of documents that would allow him to avoid deportation. Other characters who are Poles also suggest another maneuver to save Korczak from imminent death: he could be declared unfit for the ghetto by the German doctors. However, Korczak refuses this stratagem completely. He responds that he is not concerned about his own life: The lives of his children are more important to him, and he is more than willing to share their fate. As if in response to earlier criticism of *Samson* and *The Promised Land*, Wajda insists on the presentation of the openly positive portrayal of "good" Poles who tried to save Korczak at any cost. With this film, he seems to mitigate the impact of the less positive portrayals of Poles in his earlier films. However, the overall positive presentation of Polish characters as good-hearted saviors, although decidedly idealistic, is followed by a truly polemical and honest *Holy Week*, in which Polish anti-Semitism raises its ugly head.

Although *Korczak* raises important issues and depicts them in striking black and white sequences, the film has flaws that viewers have found discomfiting. First, the depiction of Korczak is uniformly standardized throughout the whole film. The mythical doctor is overstated, stultified, and placed on a pedestal without any of the amusing distance given, for instance, to Mateusz Birkut in *Man of Marble*. Second, the film seems to apotheosize sacrificial and passive Jews who are, nonetheless, presented in a sentimental and monotonous way. According to foreign reviewers, the film raised explosive issues and provoked mixed feelings abroad. While some such critics were openly appreciative of Wajda's effort to portray the fate of Korczak, others were less than enthusiastic. Some considered the film stereotypically sentimental,[3] or even, as Sheila Johnston puts it, an "idolatrous" tribute paid to a Jewish doctor who offered no resistance to the Germans:

> Was, you can't help wondering, there really nothing more complex to Korczak than unadulterated goodness; and anyway, just how exemplary was his line of passive resistance? Near the end, the Jewish Combat Organisation, an underground resistance group critical of its peers for going like lambs to the slaughter, put that question: Korczak, they suggest, is guilty of reconciling his children to death.... But the point is circumnavigated, and the film wallows in his and the orphans' martyrdom without admitting that it might not have needed to end so.[4]

Most American reviews of the film written in the years 1990 and 1991 include similar critical remarks.[5]

However, other reviewers from papers such as the *Jewish Bulletin of Northern California* and the *New York Times* were sympathetic to Wajda and to his presentation of the Jewish people and their fate. They saw *Korczak* in a different way, as a film that continues important themes in Wajda's filmography, such as Jewish issues and World War II, in a most honest and compassionate way. Additionally, Wajda provides some sense of atonement and consolation to these Poles who did help Jews during World War II. Many people tried to help Korczak, arranging documents for him, negotiating his release with the Germans, and putting their own lives in danger for his sake. The role of Poles with respect to Jews in the film during World War II was acknowledged positively by many Polish reviewers.

Surprisingly, many French critics attacked Wajda furiously, even personally. This reaction was provoked largely by the controversial reaction of Claude Lanzmann, director of the film *Shoah* (1985), who accused Wajda of falsifying the truth about the history of the Shoah in order to cover up the participation of Poles in the crime. The debate—including the polemics of French journalists and various responses by Wajda, Agnieszka Holland, Claude Lanzmann, Ryszard Fijałkowski (Polish ambassador to France), and numerous representatives of Polish, German, and French cultural circles—is well documented in Wajda's archives[6] and is analyzed in detail by Terri Ginsberg.[7] The irony of this reception is especially poignant in view of the fact that the screenplay was based primarily on the writings of Korczak himself. Furthermore, screenwriter Agnieszka Holland, herself a woman of Jewish heritage, treated every scene in the film very carefully, being fully aware of the volatility of her subject. The preproduction notes for the film demonstrate how carefully the director negotiated every single scene with his screenwriter. It comes as no surprise, then, to learn that Wajda was horrified to read the condemnatory reviews of the French critics.

Of all the criticism directed against the film, the reaction against the final scene was especially intense. According to these critics, the final scene in Wajda's film, the children disappearing into the mist, was especially disturbing: "Under a flag with the star of David, the children and Dr. Korczak enter the sealed wagon singing. And then the doors swing open—a coda of a sleepy, disgusting dream on the edge of revisionism—and we see how the little victims, energetic and joyful, emerge in the slow-motion from the train of death. Treblinka as the salvation of murdered Jewish children."[8] Among the aforementioned critics, Claude Lanzmann and Daniele Heymann criticized the scene for its romantic, transhistorical treatment of the final day in the lives of the doomed children. They demanded an alternative, more realistic scene instead, one that would show what really happened to the children. In their opinion, the final scene was too gentle and symbolic, whereas a shot of the gas chambers would leave no doubt as to what had happened on that day. Ginsberg carries this argument to a higher aesthetic and critical ground, suggesting that "the phenomenological discourse overdetermining the hermeneutic structure of the film encourages an allegorical reception that may very well invoke anti-Semitism."[9] The most important problem of the film, according to her, is its histological focus in this scene and the histological portrayal of Korczak himself. Ginsberg suggests that we have in Korczak a kind of Judeo-Christian fusion that uses its sacrificial iconography for other purposes.[10]

The fate of Korczak and of the Jewish children is described and interpreted by a filmmaker informed by his own deeply entrenched, even if not overt, Catholic sensibilities. This ideological controversy of a Catholic filmmaker seeing salvation in the Jewish children's death, an element that many critics found profoundly disturbing, seems to lie at the basis of one of the cracks in the film, which reveals such complex cultural and social layers of interpretation that they warrant a separate essay on the reception of this film alone.[11] In short, the film produces contradictory ideological readings that, in their crisscrossing agendas and internal ambiguities, create tension and uncertainty as to the intentions of the filmmaker himself. Paired with demagogic aesthetics, the film imposes a specific reading of Korczak and of the reality in which he lived. Paradoxically, spectators resist this enforced presentation and react with a series of polemic readings in which they tried to negotiate the final meanings for themselves.

The Crowned-Eagle Ring a.k.a. *The Horse-Hair Ring* (1993)

Undaunted by the virulent discussion surrounding the film *Korczak*, Wajda turns to another contentious historical debate, this time the one surrounding the *end* of World War II. In this treatment of the war, Wajda nods nostalgically to one of his best films, *Ashes and Diamonds*. The film is based on the novel by Aleksander Ścibor-Rylski, written twenty years after World War II ended, and which Wajda planned to make into a film just after its publication. In 1965, however, the novel was too explosive and could not be made into a film in a Soviet-dominated country. Years later, after the change of the political system in Poland, the director turned to the book again.

The Crowned-Eagle Ring has to be seen in the context of two issues: historical and cinematic. First, the film deals with the fate of the members of Armia Krajowa (Home Army), and with their ideological and life choices, taking place just after the suppression of the Warszawa Uprising at the end of World War II. Cinematically, the film has to be seen in the context of Wajda's earlier film, *Ashes and Diamonds,* to which the director openly and self-reflexively refers in this film. An understanding of the historical subject of the Home Army is crucial to understanding the majority of war films made by Wajda, and especially important in the interpretation of this particular film.

The Home Army, to which Marcin, the main protagonist in the film belongs, was a major resistance group during World War II. Together with *bataliony chłopskie* (peasant batallions), they organized many resistance actions against Germans during the war. Over 400,000 strong, they also held "an overwhelming superiority over their communist-led rivals, who in the Gwardia Ludowa [People's Guard] and its successor, the Armia Ludowa [People's Army] never controlled more than 10,000 supporters."[12] The Home Army was linked directly to the government-in-exile in London, while the People's Army was directly subordinated to the communist Polish Workers' Party, with links to Moscow. However, it was the People's Army, not the Home Army, which was supported by the Soviets, the liberators of Poland from the Germans, and the new de facto rulers of Poland. After the war ended, the officers and soldiers of the Home Army were arrested and deported for trial; many were executed or sent to internment camps.[13] Some Home Army officers tried to accept the new situation in a stoic manner: one such case is described in the film. Marcin and Tartar represent two opposing ideological sides: Marcin is the Home Army officer, while Tartar, the former participant of the Warszawa Uprising, joins the Polish Workers' Party. Their cooperation ends bitterly for Marcin, who is deceived by the Soviet-backed rulers and treated as a pawn in their ideological struggle.

The Crowned-Eagle Ring begins with the Warszawa Uprising in 1944. Marcin, the young commander of a platoon, leads his soldiers into action. They shoot at advancing German tanks, run for cover, or shoot indiscriminately at the attackers. The quick pace of events, the seemingly inhuman advance of the tanks, and the destruction of buildings and people by the German enemy all contribute to the portrayal of the uprising as an idealistic, hopeless effort undertaken by young people who are unaware of their mortal danger and who risk their lives unnecessarily. Wajda's youths are enthusiastic daredevils carrying a Polish flag among the ruins, depicted in romantic, slow-motion tableaux that expose dramatically the uprising's beauty and, at the same time, its futility.

When the uprising ends abruptly, the young warriors emerge from various hiding places, approach the Germans resignedly, and leave their guns at the enemy's feet. However, Marcin and Wiśka hide their guns and escape with a group of other insurgents. Marcin commands everybody to take off their uniforms and armbands, for they must leave Warszawa soon: The Germans forced hundreds of the city's inhabitants to leave Warszawa, including the remaining insurgents who did not want to go to detention centers. Two events underline this moment of defeat. In the first one, Marcin takes off his partisan armband. The abandoning of the armband means a transition to the world of anonymity, a depressing prospect for the young people who fought for Poland under an ideological banner. This moment is further reinforced by his friend's giving up his "uprising name": Kostek, Marcin's friend and subordinate, renounces his assumed name and returns to his former name, Mietek; in doing so, he also renounces the idealism of the uprising itself. The defeat becomes even bitterer and more profound with these renunciations. Another of the young men who flees Warszawa is Tartar, who talks briefly with Marcin as they leave.

In a poignant scene in the ruins, where the former insurgents hide, Wiśka and Marcin declare their love for each other. She embraces the wounded Marcin and offers him a horse-hair ring in a gesture both dramatic and symbolic. The horse-hair ring provides the title to the film and a symbolic framework to the efforts of the Home Army, the members of which wore such rings. Simultaneously, the scene recalls the theme of love and war present already in *A Generation:* in this film, Wajda makes love a component of war, the horrors of which mix dramatically with the emotional complexities of the romantic scenario. The romantic scene is brutally disrupted by a Własow[14] soldier who abducts the half-dressed Wiśka. Both Marcin and Mietek try to defend her, but to no avail. Marcin is nearly killed and Mietek is shot in the arm. Wiśka goes with the soldier, rather than resisting, in order to save Marcin and the remaining insurgents. She looks back sadly at Marcin, but also at us, the film spectators, who witness one of the most appalling fragments of Polish history: the Własows, waiting for the end of the uprising, later collaborated with the Germans in the pacification of Warszawa and of the mercilessly brutalized Poles.

The following scenes take place at the hospital where Marcin is treated for his wounds. Marcin's former commander looks for the young man and explains that he has just returned from the East, where he was trained by the Soviets as a security agent. He is now looking for candidates for national security work in the Urząd Bezpieczeństwa (Security Office), the Polish equivalent of the Soviet NKWD (Narodnyi Komissariat Wnutriennych Dzieł, or Central Security Department), later the feared KGB.[15] Marcin declines the invitation. Amid these explanations, the Germans come looking for the remaining insurgents. Janina, Marcin's friend, comes with a wooden cart to take Marcin away from danger. Mrs. Choińska, the mother of a deceased insurgent called Dzidek, and Janina care lovingly for the wounded man, recalling the idealistic portrayal of women as sacrificial mother figures who tirelessly care for wounded soldiers, an image present in many art pieces (Polish and otherwise), especially in Artur Grottger's drawings.[16]

After recovering, Marcin tries to reorganize his former subordinates. He finds one of them behind a detention-center fence dealing in stolen or scavenged goods from the ruins, and another is seriously wounded in the hospital. At a certain point, Marcin, seeking contact with the present rulers of Poland, uses Tartar for this end. This particular moment is arguably the defining point of the film. Unlike Maciek Chełmicki, the Home Army soldier in *Ashes and Diamonds*, who dies at the end of the war, Marcin lives and wants to participate in the reconstruction of the new Poland no matter who is at its helm. He rationalizes this choice by explaining that he has three options for the future: oppose the invader, do nothing and go on living, or join the present rulers in order to contribute to Poland's future. Marcin, who feels responsible for the people from his old platoon and who wants to secure jobs and a political future for them, chooses the third option.

It is worth noting at this point that following the liberation of Poland by the Soviets, when peace was declared on 9 May 1945, all of Poland lay under Soviet control in the political and administrative sense:

> All existing local officials, from the mayor to the municipal caretaker, were unceremoniously replaced, often under the threat of charges of having collaborated with the Nazis. Peasants were invited at gunpoint to surrender their livestock and their food stores. Members of the Polish Resistance were given the choice between instant arrest, and service in one of the Soviet-sponsored formations. Anyone who showed the slightest

disinclination to obey immediately was written off as a war casualty. Once a liberated area had been processed in this manner, it was highly unlikely that anyone would be left who might undertake political enterprises of an independent character.[17]

The events leading to this situation are shown in the subsequent scenes. In January 1945, the Red Army enters Poland on its way to Berlin. The soldiers treat Poland as if it were their own land. Marcin watches the passing tanks with a mixture of awe and surprise, but Tartar fully accepts the invaders and even waves to them. Tartar is now a secretary of the PPR (Polish Workers' Army), a party organ supported by the Soviet Union, and he reluctantly listens to Marcin's pleas for himself and for his people. He replies that the PPR is not eager to support and hire the former members of the Home Army, which represents a different ideological position and is considered traitorous. However, when Tartar learns that Marcin has driving experience, a useful capability at the time, he hires him as his personal driver. Henceforth, Marcin participates in the work of the new Polish rulers. He witnesses the land partitioning and protects Tartar against acts of sabotage. When Marcin defends Tartar during an unexpected attack of saboteurs, the latter finally begins to trust him.

Marcin soon meets Kosior, the head of the Security Office at Tartar's department, who unceremoniously asks Marcin about his ties with various organizations. Kosior is straightforward and cynical in these questions, but he slowly accepts Marcin despite his being a former Home Army officer. Tartar asks him if he wants to keep working as his driver when the two young men hear the shouts of people being tortured at the security offices. Visibly moved, Tartar states that he does not approve of such methods. However, he also states derisively that it is not only guns that make a revolution, for sometimes people have to be sacrificed, as well—a contentious and highly debated issue in Polish history. Despite his new allegiances, Marcin tries to organize a meeting with his former Home Army subordinates, but only some of them arrive. Although his former compatriots no longer trust him, Marcin continues working with Kosior.

Soon, Kosior takes Marcin with him to a railway station. Soviet officers come to claim the building, behaving in a superior and dictatorial way. When one of them notices the horse-hair ring on Marcin's finger, he laughs cynically. Kosior understands this cynicism, for such a ring belongs only to members of the Home Army, who are sought out and persecuted by the Soviets. Kosior angrily takes the ring and cuts the crown from its top. Marcin acknowledges the damage sullenly but does not resist or complain. The cutting of the crown is symbolic of Marcin's personal downfall as a member of the Home Army and as a person. Older spectators of the film, particularly those who were active participants in the Warszawa Uprising, reacted to this scene with the ring in a highly emotional way, and several even wrote personal letters to Wajda. In one such letter, Jadwiga Sobol writes about the production method of horse-hair rings, and of their importance and symbolic significance for Home Army members.[18] This touching correspondence from an ordinary spectator attests to the validity of the themes presented by the director despite the time that had passed since the historical events took place.

The downfall and humiliation of the Home Army officers are further reinforced by one of the most disturbing sequences in the film, which takes place at the same railway station. Former members of the Home Army are led to trains bound for Siberia. When they enter the railway carts, though, they kneel and sing *"Bogurodzica"* (the oldest Polish religious song, and also the first Polish national anthem/war song). This futile but necessary act of defiance is shocking in its explicitness, and Marcin reacts with a shout. Of course, this particular scene is excessively baroque and has no reference to real documented events. However, Wajda creates the scene to stress the symbolic significance of the Home Army's downfall, thus elevating *The Crowned-Eagle Ring* to the level of general exegesis concerning the fate of Poland in general. A film ostensibly about double agents turns into a funereal song for the Polish quandary and its struggle for freedom.

Still naive in his attempt to find a new political way in postwar Poland, Marcin tries to organize a "good will" meeting between the PPR, the party in power, and the Home Army commanding staff. He talks to Home Army Major Steinert about his intentions, but the major warns Marcin that he may be a pawn in the political struggle between the Home Army and the Soviet-backed PPR, and that he should run for his life. When the suspicious Marcin spies on the activities of People's Army members in the nearby trees, he is ambushed by Kosior's people, thrown into a cold, wet cellar and, after several hours spent there, he is brought to Kosior for questioning. Kosior cynically presents to the bewildered Marcin the political status quo of Poland in 1945. He speaks about the real situation of Poland naively fought over, however bravely, by the members of the Home Army. The People's Army, supported and trained by the Soviets, is in the position of power at present. Behind this contingent of people stands the powerful Soviet Union with the ruthless Stalin at its helm. Thus, the members of the Home Army are forced to leave Poland or, if they do not want to be taken away to Siberia, to cooperate with the new rulers. When Marcin responds that Western countries will support Poland in its political struggle, Kosior shows him a newspaper with Winston Churchill's famous statement from the Jalta Conference in 1945. (According to this statement, Poland was to remain under the influence of the former Soviet Union as one of her satellites, not as an independent, freely governed country.) The political situation of Poland after 1945 had been decided once and, it seemed, for all.

When Marcin reports this conversation to Steinert, the latter realizes that Marcin has become the victim of a power game between the Home Army and the PPR, and he warns Marcin once again that he has to disappear. Instead, following Kosior's suggestion, Marcin proposes a meeting between the PPR and the commanders-in-chief of the Home Army in order to discuss the proposals for *vivus vivendi* for Poland. After the meeting, which ends on a positive note, the car is intercepted by the Soviets, however, and the Home Army officers are taken away. Unaware of these developments, Marcin and Janina sit in a bar and watch two young men repeat the famous "burning glasses" scene—and at the same bar—from *Ashes and Diamonds*. The remaking of this scene functions as a real and symbolic link to the earlier film.

This scene is remarkable in several ways: First, two temporal planes meet within the physical space of the one bar (Marcin and Janina meeting in 1958, and Maciek and Andrzej, Maciek's companion, meeting in 1945). Second, the two pairs of protagonists occupying the same space represent the same ideological perspectives, but from two different pragmatic approaches. Janina and Marcin have chosen to live and find a place for themselves in the postwar reality, while Maciek chose death. Finally, the two pairs frame the thirty-four-year span between the making of the two films, a time that marked the transformation of a young, romantic filmmaker into a mature and somewhat bitter master of cinema. Nonetheless, this reconstruction of the scene annoyed many spectators with its nostalgic and self-indulgent return to the director's own earlier (and superior) film, one that garnered him the respect and admiration of the whole world.

From this self-reflexive moment, the film moves back to the diegetic time of the film. A Home Army officer enters the bar and informs Marcin that the two senior Home Army officers are being interrogated at the Security Headquarters, and that all the other Home Army people who were at the meeting have been killed. The distraught Marcin finally realizes that he was only a tool in the ongoing political struggle: his only role was to facilitate the elimination of his own people. Back at the PPR headquarters, no one (including Tartar) wants to talk to him, Kosior seems to have disappeared, and Marcin is asked to sign a declaration: If he signs a statement that he will help eliminate the Polish Republic's enemies (i.e., his former friends and allies), he will be accepted as a member of the new regime. Marcin rejects the offer and is ordered to leave. He runs away and disappears among the ruins.

At their old meeting spot, Janina approaches him and tells him that she no longer wants to be involved with him, explaining that she has sensed the presence of Wisia with him all the time they were together. She then informs him that Wisia is upstairs. Marcin approaches Wisia and realizes that the young woman is only half alive, profoundly depressed and sad. He gives her the horse-hair ring back, but, seeing the absence of the ring's crown, she tosses it away. He turns away and, in a flashback, we see (presumably through Marcin's mind's eye) Wisia returning from the vicious encounter with the Własow soldier. In a gesture of final despair, Marcin takes the gun from under the stones in the ruins and shoots himself. Wisia is a silent witness to his death.

The Crowned-Eagle Ring is a tragic and acutely realistic depiction of the events at the end of World War II. Marcin is doubly deceived, a victim of history. On the one hand, he is deceived by those Western powers who had offered help to the Warszawa Uprising but did not keep their word; on the other, he is deceived by the new rulers of Poland, who use him as a pawn in their fight for absolute power. While Maciek in *Ashes and Diamonds* is an idealistic and heroic protagonist, never forfeiting his ideals, Marcin is a pitiful collaborator. Wajda himself considers the film a realistic interpretation of postwar events, less metaphoric than the symbolic interpretation of these events in *Ashes and Diamonds*.[19] Despite the political importance of the film's subject, both for the interpretation of the postwar past and of the time of the film's first screening, the film was not well received. To Poles, it seemed a faulty reinterpretation of *Ashes and Diamonds*. The film's idealistic warriors are supposed to kill their ideological enemies or die for the country, not collaborate with the new oppressors of Poland. The heroic Maciek had died, it seemed, only to be replaced by an undecided, opportunistic, and pitiful Marcin.

Major reviews of the film were mixed. Some reviewers (e.g., Jerzy Płażewski) considered the film one of the most important made by Wajda, but others (e.g., Andrzej Osęka) considered it a film full of pathos, with metaphors, symbols, and tableau-like sequences that simply do not correspond to real events. Osęka, especially critical of the film, concludes that Wajda has created an historical overview of the time after World War II, a time of moral choices, but the film seems artificial, without proper understanding of the matter of life, such as human behavior and speech.[20] Płażewski, on the other hand, considers the film an important contribution to the discussion of the postwar reality. He suggests that Wajda purposefully directs the audience's attention to the choices of Home Army members after the end of the war—that is, whether to collaborate with the Soviet occupier, die for the honor of Poland, or emigrate. While *Ashes and Diamonds* gave Maciek the heroic path, *The Crowned-Eagle Ring* once again embarked on a theme never before touched upon by any filmmaker. Wajda almost literally puts his hand in the fire, and in this sense the film is important.[21]

There was very little reaction to this film on the part of the general public, however. As Maria Kornatowska suggests, this was caused by "the war at the top" and "the infighting among the leaders" that had made Polish society turn away from politics.[22] Very persuasively, she also argues that this film, referring to "traditions and topics of Polish School[,] was created at the wrong moment, just like Juliusz Machulski's later *Squadron* (1995)...."[23] However, the film had an important political reading in the context of the current splintering of Solidarity in Poland. As Wajda comments,

> Indeed, for contemporary Polish artists, and especially for one who was involved and who supported Solidarity from its very beginnings, and who made films like my *Man of Iron* and *Man of Marble*, which in a way involved this entire movement, it's indeed sad to see how the myth of Solidarity collapses before our eyes, how former comrades split, and definitely there is a certain link [with the story of the *Crowned-Eagle Ring*].[24]

Nastasja (1994)

The next film made by Wajda is an artistic experiment closely involving Japanese actor and *onnagata* Tamasaburo Bando. It also introduces Wajda's fascination with Japanese culture, which manifested itself during the construction of the Manggha Center in Kraków. At the same time, the film manifests Wajda's interest in Fyodor Dostoevsky's works, which he adapted for the theater in many memorable plays. Wajda chose for his film the last chapter from *The Idiot*, which tells of the meeting between Prince Mishkin and Rogozin, just after Nastasja's murder by the latter. The history of the film, though, could make a fascinating film in itself. It was conceived as the result of a theatrical production of *Nastasja Filipovna* at the Stary Theater in Kraków in 1977. (The part of Rogozin was played by Jan Nowicki and Prince Myszkin by Jerzy Radziwiłowicz.) During one of the performances, a young woman stood up from the audience and declared that she was Nastasja. This event moved Wajda so much that for many years he thought about re-creating the same play with Nastasja present on the stage. This dream materialized only in Japan.

In 1981, the director visited Kyoto, where he saw Bando playing the part of *La Dame aux Camelias*. The fact that a man played the role of a woman perfectly inspired Wajda to create another version of the play with the help of this particular actor. In 1986, Wajda approached Bando and persuaded him to participate in his project. The outcome was the play *Nastasja*, which was performed in Japanese in Tokyo and Osaka. In this play, Bando plays the roles of both Myshkin and Nastasja. Later, Wajda invited Bando to Poland, to perform the same version of the play in Warszawa and in Kraków. The performance was sensationally successful, which prompted Wajda to produce the film version of the play. The film was shot in Warszawa, in the picturesque Pac Palace.[25]

The film starts with the scene in the church, in which Nastasja is about to marry Myshkin. Suddenly, she senses Rogozin staring at her; she turns her head and runs away with him to his carriage. A long shot of Nastasja reveals a beautiful woman dressed in a long, elaborate white dress and a wide-brimmed white hat. In the next sequence, we see Rogozin in his house. Later, Myshkin comes to inquire about his bride. From this initial scene, the whole film unfolds in the big vestibule-living room, in which the two protagonists carry out a dialogue about Nastasja. When Rogozin reveals that he has killed Nastasja, Myshkin goes into a state of shock. Rogozin picks up flowers from the windowsill with the purpose of adorning the body of Nastasja, but drops them on the floor on the way to the room where she lies. The two men begin to reminiscence about her when, on noticing a painting—Hans Holbein's *Body of the Dead Christ in the Tomb* (1521)—lying on the floor, Myshkin goes into an exalted monologue about God. The conversation between two men embraces the mystery of human existence, the relation of humanity to God, and the fight between good and evil.

The film does not follow any narrative chronology, but rather the logic of emotion and memory. In one manifestation of such logic, Myshkin is shown talking to the photo of Nastasja, looking at her lovingly and kissing her image. When Rogozin gives him Nastasja's earrings, Myshkin puts them on and slowly turns into Nastasja by means of earrings, a shawl, and his art, by the way he looks at Rogozin, and through the way he carries himself. When he turns into Nastasja, he puts on a light cream shawl, underlining the elements of idealism and innocence in his portrayal of an ideal woman. Rogozin admires this transformation, looking on in awe, and almost kneels in front of the woman he humbly and passionately adored. The dark passions of Rogozin and the innocent, idealistic love of Myshkin find their equivalents and/or representations in the aesthetic contrast of the clothes they wear. The earthly, erotic passion of Rogozin is expressed in his dark black clothes with reddish hues, while Myshkin's clothes are pale, ethereal, and elegant.

After all the extreme emotions that Myshkin experiences when he talks to Rogozin, he has an epileptic seizure and falls to the floor. Rogozin picks the prince up and cares for him tenderly, as if he were a child or a woman, suggesting a complex trajectory of feelings in Rogozin himself: Rogozin loved not only the woman, but also the bridegroom who was supposed to marry her. The film thus delves into the mysteries of human relationships, whereby it is not the love of the two men for Nastasja, but rather the tender relationship between the men themselves that becomes the focus of the film narrative. Upon recovering, Myshkin turns into Nastasja again. Fan in hand, in his talk with Rogozin he behaves as a proud, seductive lady who seduces and humiliates at the same time. Then he/she turns into Myshkin and back again, the number of transformations accelerating slightly. Under the bluish light and the haze of incense, taking place in various shot planes, the scene turns the relation between the men into a kind of emotional dance during which they exchange monologues about Nastasja, the painting, the nature of life and death, and the mystery of God.

The film ends with a quick series of scenes: the park to which Mysh-kin went after Nastasja fled the church; Rogozin's house just before Myshkin's arrival; and, finally, the unveiling of the final truth, the re-vealing of the "uncanny," the corpse of the dead woman herself. These scenes explain what really happened in an almost documentary fash-ion. In a moment of seeming telepathy, Myshkin wakes up suddenly on the park bench at the instant when Rogozin thrusts the knife into Nas-tasja's heart. In the last scene, Myshkin holds Rogozin in his arms and both of them rock silently while the light fades to darkness.

This film had an enthusiastic reception in Japan thanks to the ex-ceptional portrayal of the characters of Myshkin and Nastasja by Bando, and due to the fusion of the theatrical and the filmic.[26] At the same time, *Nastasja* is, as Kaori Shoji suggests,[27] a tribute from one artist (Wajda) to another (Bando) and "an eloquent puzzle that calls into question death, sin, [and] the eyes of God."[28] Andrea Hirsig, on the other hand, stresses the stylistic quality of the film, in which the art of Kabuki theater contributes to the highly stylized, dreamlike rendition of Dostoevsky's prose.[29] The film moves in theatrical scenes saturated with diffused white and yellow light. In fact, Alicja Helman considers the film a piece of cinematic theater that, due to the excellent photog-raphy of Paweł Edelman, has an oneiric quality.[30] *The Dreamy*

Thanks to Bando, Nastasja is eerily present at the scene of her own death, as if corroborating the argument that death is uncannily present in almost all of Wajda's films. Death, the immanent factor of nostalgia, influences the feelings of both Myshkin and Rogozin and turns the whole film into a nostalgic portrayal of an obsessive love that both unites and destroys the two men. The film is about the friendship of men, their love for each other, and their concern for one another's hurt feelings rather than for the woman who was the cause (and the victim) of their distress. Nastasja becomes the third party, at the same time a catalyst of this friendship but also its destroyer.

Holy Week (1995)

After his Japanese experiment, Wajda returns to the World War II trope once again. As if traumatized by war events in the past, events for which he feels personally and communally responsible, Wajda obsessively re-produces these moments of despair and shame. Born from his shame and disgust with Poles' general lack of response to the Jewish tragedy is the film *Holy Week*, which continues the themes of both *Samson* and *Korczak*. Here, Wajda reexamines Polish-Jewish relations in a more hon-est manner than in either *Samson* or *Korczak*. *Holy Week* deals openly and sincerely with the issue of Polish anti-Semitism.

The film begins with a scene showing a small number of Jewish peo-ple hiding in the woods, among them Irena Lilien and her father, Michał

Pawlicki. Suddenly, they see a large group of Jews being escorted by the Germans. Michał voluntarily joins them and is immediately attacked by the German officer. Irena hides deeper in among the trees. When everyone else leaves, Irena leaves her place of hiding and soon reaches the city of Warszawa. At the gate post, she poses as "Grabowska Irena"; when the Germans do not believe that her Polish papers are genuine, she produces a belt with precious stones to buy her way through. Walking in the streets of Warszawa, she passes the Warszawa ghetto, which is closely guarded by the Germans. Horrific scenes unfold before her eyes: Germans shooting at the ghetto inhabitants, houses burning, and people jumping out of windows. When a column of Jewish prisoners passes by, being led to the concentration camp, she learns from them that both her mother and her father are already dead.

Irena begins to search for a safe place to hide within the city. She reaches the house of Jan and Anna Malecki, near the ghetto, and begs them to give her lodging for a short time until she can get into the ghetto to be with her own people. Jan agrees to her request but worries constantly whether he has done the right thing in giving Irena shelter. Here, Wajda opens the quintessential hornet's nest when he describes Jan's fears and uncertainties: Afraid for the safety of his family, who can all be killed by the Germans if Irena is discovered at his home, he is forced to make a moral choice between granting Irena refuge and endangering the lives of his own family. To make the situation for Jan even more problematic, we learn that Anna is pregnant and that Jan's brother Julek is a member of the underground forces of the Home Army.

Although Jan finally brings Irena into his house, she is forced to remain in her room, waiting for an end to the horror. Nevertheless, the family does not exclude Irena from any conversations at the dinner table. It is here that a number of arguments between Pole and Jew take place. As if supplementing, countering, or perhaps responding to the criticism of the patient and suffering Jew in *Samson*, Wajda portrays Irena as an aggressive, argumentative, and determined woman; in fact, she declares that Jews will never forget Poles' lack of sensitivity to their tragic fate during World War II. The act of forgetting would mean also the loss of dignity. Soon, German soldiers appear near the house and Irena is forced to remain in her room. The Jewish ghetto is being "liquidated" (read: annihilated) on 20 April 1943. On learning this, Irena faints; upon waking, she realizes that she now has nowhere else to go and is completely dependent on Jan's and Anna's generosity.

Nearby, Jan and Anna talk about the events in the nearby ghetto and raise the question of Catholic responsibility for the mass murder committed by the Germans. They hear the shouts of the murdered people and, unable to bear the sound, decide to close the windows. This closing of the windows is a bitter commentary on the moral dilemma of the Maleckis, but also a commentary on Polish behavior in general—better to pretend not to hear the cries of the dying people, the film seems to say. In this candid presentation of the reaction of Poles to the horror of the extermination of the ghetto, Wajda plainly condemns non-Jewish Poles outright for their ethical abnegation and for their collusion with the Germans, however passive, in determining (or merely allowing) the fates of countless Jews.

The closing of the windows on the dying Jews is further reinforced by the openly anti-Semitic reaction of the Małecki's neighbors, the Piotrowskis, and particularly the vituperative house attendant Mrs. Piotrowski. The words and actions of the Piotrowskis represent the attitudes of the "simple Pole" toward Jews. In talking to Anna about the events in the ghetto, Mrs. Piotrowski scathingly states that there is no point in her own people dying for Jews. Suddenly, Mrs. Piotrowski and her husband notice Irena in the window of the Małeckis' apartment; unaware of those present in the yard, Irena has been trying to get some sun. She hides in panic when she notices them looking at her, but it is too late. The Piotrowskis acknowledge the presence of a mysterious guest in the Małeckis' apartment and guess that she must be a Jew. The resulting atmosphere of panic and dread is further reinforced by a scene depicting a conversation, in which a representative of *narodowcy* (radical nationalists, members of the Obóz Narodowo Radykalny or National Radical Organization)[31] argues that Poland should have no Jews and that the termination of Jews is a national priority. In the meantime, Mrs. Piotrowski, convinced that the Jewish woman puts the fate of the whole house at risk, denounces Małecki to a councilor who resides at the same house. When she returns to her home, though, Mrs. Piotrowski finds that her husband disagrees with her.

Józef Piotrowski's concern about Irena, however, reveals itself as entirely self-interested. Perceiving Irena as a stereotypically desirable Jewish woman, supposedly sexually accessible, he somehow manages to enter the Małeckis' apartment and get into Irena's room. During the attempted rape scene, the Jewish stereotype of a beautiful and sexually accessible woman is played out to the hilt. The simple, working-class Józef approaches Irena roughly and tries to force himself on her. After a short fight, he relents. When Józef leaves Irena's room, Mrs. Piotrowska accuses Irena of all the misfortunes in the house, including the fall of a little girl from the stairs. Ruthlessly, she enters Irena's room and throws her out, saying that she should go to the ghetto. Thrust out the front gate, Irena utters a momentous imprecation, wishing all Poles would be murdered in a manner similar to the Jews' deaths at the hands of the Germans.

This contentious scene is followed by another equally controversial scene, in which Anna goes to the church and kisses the figure of Christ on Good Friday. Meanwhile, Jan tries to find another place of shelter for Irena, but he is brutally killed by German agents in the vestibule of the prospective building. This scene is followed by Irena getting off the tram near the ghetto and passing several off-duty German soldiers at its entrance. Then, she disappears in the smoke rising from the burning ghetto. Wajda quite intentionally situates film's action during Holy Week, an important annual Catholic festive period, only to end it on Good Friday in the church. Hence, Poles' hypocrisy, despair, and shame are openly exposed in this final juxtaposition of scenes; on the same day, Irena condemns Poles for their treatment of her people. This parallelism of action is "an important narrative and ideological moment in the film."[32]

Once again, Wajda tries a controversial theme, one that he has dealt with many times before. As he has admitted in a private conversation, Wajda considers the Jewish theme one of the most difficult to handle. In his attempt to deal with such a sensitive issue, he wants to present Poles who "can look critically at themselves, which is the proof of intelligence, charity and conscience."[33] He seems to have no patience with self-denying Poles. No longer is he subliminally alluding to the Jewish question in the form of allusions or visual symbols as in *Samson.* This time, he condemns Poles directly for the lack of positive effort in saving the Jews. In plain images and brutally straightforward words, he calls to mind stereotypical comments about Jews, often associated with this racial group in the past: the Jew as "the other," "the problem," and the Jewish woman as beautiful, desirable, and sexually insatiable.

Some critics saw this film as an important example of "national self-criticism" or, alternately, as a form of morality play; they suggest that, in a self-critical manner, Wajda shows Polish society as "patriotic, antifascist but also deeply anti-semitic."[34] The concatenation of Christ's death with the deaths (one real and one perceived) of two main characters in the film raises the issues of Christian responsibility for the war atrocities and of Poles' response to them. In a deeply Catholic Poland, allowing for a senseless and brutal death of others meant the denial of Christian ideals. The scene in the church thus blatantly accuses Poles of hypocrisy and disregard for the fate of Jews. On the other hand, Tadeusz Sobolewski suggests that Wajda's provocation is not strong enough. After all, the fate of the many people behind the walls of the ghetto is not clearly shown, the Breughel-like depiction of the burning ghetto remains only a symbol of annihilation.

Similarly to Jerzy Andrzejewski, the author of the short story on which the film is based, Wajda faces the dilemma of being either morally condemnatory or brutally descriptive. Neither the author nor the filmmaker can choose sides in this moral conflict.[35] Both remain immobilized by the horrific historical situation they describe. In another publication, Sobolewski is even more critical of Wajda. He states that Wajda is too attached to Polish tradition and stereotypes to risk disturbing or questioning them. Rather, he argues, the filmmaker hides among them and idealizes them. Consequently, he protects Polish honor rather than questions it as a result of the events of World War II, and he leaves the volatile issue of Polish anti-Semitism untouched.[36] Nevertheless, Sobolewski, like Henning Bruns,[37] for instance, regards the film as an accurate depiction of war events. Sobolewski considers the film one of the last representatives of the Polish School in that it deals with World War II events in a provocative and conscientious way. Wajda glorifies life that has been condemned to death and presents fatalistically the heroism of its protagonists.[38] Stephen Holden agrees that the film is "a work of tragic realism that poses tough moral questions (and) a merciless examination of the behaviour of Poles living on the safe side of the ghetto."[39]

However, fascinated with the growth of capitalism in their own country and in changes in the surrounding European countries, most Poles expressed little interest in "old affairs" that were acknowledged by other Poles with a feeling of shame. This shame, related to the treatment of Jews during World War II, was little understood by younger Poles who withstood years of anti-Semitic indoctrination by their elders and did not really try to understand and relive the complex layers of guilt and shame related to the time of World War II. The Poland of the 1990s belongs to cinema as entertainment: Mafia films, comedies, and European and American films with contemporary content have filled the market to the brink, so audiences are no longer interested in settling scores with anybody or in analyzing their own collective responsibility. Compounding the weak reception of the film was the perception that the film was too reflective, verbalizing the doubts and feelings of shame and guilt, instead of playing them out cinematically.

Aesthetically, *Holy Week* represents the Polish School well since it was conventionally made; it unfolds slowly and presents events realistically and accurately—without, however, the aesthetic brilliance of *Ashes and Diamonds*. This later film is stylistically heavy and too unembellished. It does not allude gracefully to Poles' guilt, but brutally attacks them. This view is corroborated by several French critics, who considered the film mediocre, stylistically heavy (*Tribune juive*), and complicated and naïve (*Studio*) at the same time. A few others, though, such as Alain Riou and Eric Alexandre, consider *Holy Week* one of Wajda's greatest accomplishments, a great film dealing with volatile issues. In fact, the film raised emotions in France to such an extent that several symposia were organized in that country devoted to the problem of anti-Semitism in Poland.[40]

For his own part, Wajda considers *Holy Week* one of his most important films, which continues the theme presented in *Samson*, alluded to in *The Wedding* and in *Promised Land*, and fully portrayed in *Korczak*. After a careful reading of the script, Wajda decided to include the disparaging words uttered by Poles about Jews, repeated every day in many locations, but dismissed as "harmless" folklore in anecdotes, jokes, and innuendo that verbalize anti-Semitic prejudices even as laughter strips them of their virulent power.[41] Despite the fact that the film was a commercial failure, it remains an important contribution to the discussion of the Jewish question in Poland, a national nightmare not alleviated by the years of peace.

Miss Nobody (1996)

After the controversial *Holy Week,* Wajda chose to make a film about contemporary issues: *Miss Nobody,* based on a novel of the same title by Tomek Tryzna that was popular at the time. In this choice, Wajda had in mind young audiences whom he wanted to win over. The director's most recent films had not appealed to young people, from whose contemporary lives World War II was too far removed. It seems that Wajda wanted to address young people with his own "social issues" message. The film tells the story of three teenage friends, Marysia, Ewa, and Kasia, living in Wałbrzych, a middle-size town in south-western Poland in the 1990s. The credits appear against the background of a romanticized rural landscape, which, we soon realize, is an intentionally idyllic starting point.

Marysia comes from the country, but her parents rent an apartment in Wałbrzych with their daughter and three sons. Marysia starts at a new school in the big city and immediately experiences verbal abuse and humiliation from both teachers and other pupils. During the first such encounter (between Marysia and her physical education teacher), a fellow student, Kasia, also humiliated, flees tearfully. On leaving the classroom, Marysia notices Kasia at the fountain and approaches her. A friendship starts between the two girls; this friendship seems a blessed relief for Marysia, a naïve girl from the provinces who does not understand the cynical environment in which she is supposed to start a new life. Thus, Wajda contrasts the fundamentally superior life in the provinces with the corrupt life in the city, a contrast made even clearer as the film unfolds.

On their way home, Kasia enters the bookstore and, with the help of an unwilling Marysia, steals a book. Surprised and angry, Marysia prays silently. Here, Wajda is especially interested in the way Marysia has to negotiate her thorough religious upbringing with the new unexpected behaviors in her city-bred peers. When Kasia takes Marysia to her house, Marysia realizes with surprise that Kasia is the daughter of affluent parents, one of them a doctor. In this light, the theft of a book from the town bookstore takes a different perspective. Marysia tries to adapt to school life and to the strange, cynical behavior of students and teachers. To impress Kasia, she decides to cut her hair and put on a cynical face; she becomes arrogant in conversations with other children and with teachers as well. Although remaining under the "protection" of Kasia, however, she is still tormented by her other schoolmates. Marysia's behavior with her peers is counteracted by her inner conversations with God and with her parents at home. Her parents try to provide good-hearted support, but later laugh at their daughter when she wants to borrow her father's sweater to appear more fashionable at school.

Much of the film deals with the friendship between Kasia and Marysia. However, Marysia soon discovers other upsetting qualities in her friend. Kasia is aggressive and unpleasant, violent toward her schoolmates and arrogant with her teachers. When she is visited by the biology teacher at her home, she manipulates the woman into revealing her life situation to her so that the distraught woman begins to cry on her lap. At the same time, she winks cynically at Marysia, who hides behind the door in fear. As in similar situations, Marysia finds refuge in a silent prayer. After this episode, Kasia's behavior worsens rapidly: Marysia watches her imitate a mentally handicapped woman in the street and then sees Kasia fall on the floor suffering from a real epileptic seizure. Marysia helps the girl and decides to stay with her for the night.

That night, Marysia suffers from a strange hallucination: She dreams that she is attacked by a stranger. The following day, Kasia explains that it was her imagined brother, "Dziki" ("The Wild"), who attacked Marysia, and reveals her own loneliness; she has always been alone because her parents were always busy. Her father emigrated to France, while her mother worked all the time and never had time for her. After a mysterious walk in the woods during which the girls talk and try to exorcise Dziki, Marysia returns home. Her parents are unhappy that she did not return for the night; they do not listen to her explanations, but scold her. Later, her father whips her with a leather belt. The distressed Marysia wants to kill herself by leaping from the balcony of the high-rise, but her father takes her back to the apartment and tries to calm her. Marysia's friendship with Kasia ends with a troubling event reeking of witchcraft. Kasia takes Marysia to church and forces her to spit into the holy water basin; she explains that Marysia has to do it if she wants to know what hell looks like. The terrified Marysia does as she is told, and then she sees a strange face in the water. She immediately flees in terror from this sacrilege. Soaked with rain, she runs back home and enters the apartment shivering and crying. Her parents calm her with home remedies and put her to bed tenderly and lovingly.

The next girl whom Marysia befriends is Ewa, the daughter of two affluent businesspeople. This time, it is Marysia who is arrogant and cynical. Ewa takes Marysia to her home and introduces her parents, who apparently have no time for their daughter since they are always on their mobile phones. The girls go to Ewa's room, where Ewa dresses Marysia and tends to her needs. Marysia is thrilled by this care and pampering because she never got them from her own parents. When the girls fall asleep, Marysia again has a strange dream. In another scene with Ewa, the girls participate in a party for adults. Marysia is fascinated with Ewa's wealthy parents and dreams about her own parents being rich. She also acts abusively toward Ewa, terrorizing her and trying to show her superiority to her. Marysia's mother is quite upset with her daughter's cynicism, her new smoking habit, and her overall approach to life.

As with Kasia, however, Marysia discovers some cracks in her friendship with Ewa. For instance, Ewa does not take Marysia's suicide attempt seriously, and she is derogatory and cynical when the conversation turns to Kasia. In the meantime, Kasia wants to see Marysia to ask the girl's forgiveness. Eager to humiliate her former friend, Marysia refuses coldly. Later the relationship between Ewa and Marysia worsens rapidly when Ewa accuses Marysia of stealing a ring from her home. When Ewa and Marysia are invited to the countryside for a birthday party, they remain apart and do not try to communicate. When a storm breaks out, Marysia runs through the woods and comes across Kasia, who cries desperately because she has just learned of the death of her father.

Back in the city, ready to renew her friendship with Kasia, Marysia visits her at home. On the way, she meets a mail carrier who gives her a letter for Kasia from a music critic in Warszawa; Kasia, who is musically talented, has sent a CD of her music to the critic with the hope that he will help her release it. The critic now wants to see her. When Marysia enters Kasia's apartment, however, she overhears Ewa's voice in conversation with Kasia. The girls refer to Marysia as "Panna Nikt" (Miss Nobody), clearly mocking her. With a flash of insight, Marysia realizes that the two girls were close friends before and that she has only been a pawn in their struggle for dominance. Distressed and shocked, she tears up the music critic's letter and asks herself, "Is Miss Nikt really me?"

In a bold move characteristic of Wajda, the filmmaker moves the focus of the book from the one about girls reaching their emotional and sexual maturity to one about social and political maturity. The film deals with the process of maturity and the formation of identity. Wajda himself had very clear intentions when he was making the film:

> This is a film about growing in a literal sense—about growing to the time in which we are supposed to live, and about growing to be oneself. Everybody experiences a similar disillusionment when he faces real life. It happens many times at various times in one's life. The film shows it with great intensity and ends with a question mark: if Miss Nobody did everything to become a Miss Somebody and still remains nobody, what does she have to do again to become this somebody?[42]

The issue of social advancement, the move from the countryside to the town and the ideological shift from the deeply Catholic and rural identity to the cynical and cruel city identity, takes center stage. In her desire to become a "city girl," Marysia tries to please her friends by imitating their dress, behavior, and speech, the outcome of which is not always pleasant. Wajda participates in a discussion concerning the moral state of his country, which, in the move from socialism to capitalism, jeopardizes its dignity, ethical norms, and religion.

In this sense, this otherwise unexceptional film continues the themes of the School of Moral Concern in the exposure of social inequalities, the lack of scruples under capitalism, and the subsequent lack of care for the nation's children. *Miss Nobody* is not only a film with a universal message, but also a film that reflects on the present time of Poland. Despite the official political "freedom" in Poland at present, many people do not understand financial and class inequalities and remain distrustful and suspicious of them. In addressing these problems, Wajda had hoped for a more intense reaction from viewers. He naïvely thought that his openness and sincerity in the treatment of the problems of young people would be enough to guarantee the success of the film. Unfortunately, as many critics observed, *times have changed*—and the accepted norm for film themes, aesthetics, and filmmaking methods changed as well.

The general reception of the film was weak. Although most reviewers agree that the film contains important social and political messages, they suggest that a film about teenage girls is not the best vehicle for Wajda.[43] Wacław Świeżynski suggests that, although Wajda followed the plot of the novel *Miss Nobody* almost to the letter, he omitted some important "demonic" and "erotic" elements and, in this way, simplified the description of the feelings and experiences of the young women. In return for this sacrifice, Wajda produced "a readable metaphor of the state of the contemporary Pole, a morality play about betrayal and self-denial; he denied relativism and did not cross out hope."[44] Thus, as with his other films, Wajda himself dominated the film in the sense of producing a socially engaged dialogue with the public at large.

In some countries, Wajda's intentions were fully understood and the spectators responded to the director's postulations. For instance, Joanna Wiórkiewicz, reporting on the film from Berlinale, the International Film Festival in Berlin in 1997, noted that the festival audience fully identified with Wajda, the creator of this political dialogue, and rewarded the film with applause.[45] In Poland, however, Wajda was almost derided for the choice of theme and was questioned about his traditional filmmaking methods and about the narrow ideological (urban vs. rural) treatment of the novel's psychological and social richness. Tired of intense criticism of the film in Poland, Wajda quickly returned to the films he made best, nostalgic films about his country's past.

The last films to be discussed, *Mr. Thadeus* and *Revenge,* represent a specific trend of the past decade in Poland called "heritage cinema." As Ewa Mazierska proposes in her seminal essay "In the Land of Noble Knights and Mute Princesses: Polish Heritage Cinema," heritage films, generally based on well-known literary texts, tend to refer to the nation's past, presenting Polish nobility in an idealistic fashion.[46] In addition to *Mr. Thadeus* and *Revenge,* the films *Ogniem i mieczem (With Fire and Sword,* 1999), directed by Jerzy Hoffman; *Syzyfowe Prace (Sisyphean Labors,* 2000), directed by Paweł Komorowski; *Prezedwiosnie (Early Spring,* 2001), directed by Filip Bajon; and *Quo Vadis* (2001), directed by Jerzy Kawalerowicz all belong to this genre.[47] Each of these films provides and alternative, glowing portrayal of Poles and of their glorious past, and constitutes a sort of response to the difficult times in post-Communist Poland.

In Poland in the 1990s, disorder and uncertainty created economic and political chaos. Several quickly and unexpectedly changed governments, each introducing confusing fiscal policies, proved particularly challenging to the middle-aged and the elderly. Heritage films, then, referring to and glorifying the past, promised relief from everyday reality. In the production of Mr. Thadeus, Wajda wanted to "retreat from present-day Poland, which he finds deeply disappointing and disturbing, and to re-create the experience of belonging to one community or nation; an experience which, in his opinion, was destroyed after the introduction of martial law in Poland."[48]

These films must also be seen in the context of nostalgia, "the longing for return to an idealized 'home' or *nostos.*"[49] The preeminent quality of nostalgia in these films, though, seems to be death, whereby the past becomes an object lovingly portrayed—unchangeable, unchanging, more beautiful and ideal than the present simply because it is designed to contrast with it.

Mr. Thadeus (1999)

This film, an openly nostalgic encounter with the past, comes in the form of the adaptation of a long poem *Mr. Thadeus,* by Adam Mickiewicz. It is a work famous among Polish schoolchildren and adults alike, read in high schools across the nation and often a source of themes for graduation exams. The film is necessarily a highly condensed version of Mickiewicz's poem, which consists of twelve chapters and depicts a nobleman's life in Lithuania. The utopian story of Count Horeszko and Jacek Soplica is based on facts drawn from the endless squabbles of petty nobility in Poland. Told by Mickiewicz from the distanced position of an émigré writer, these squabbles turned into a beautiful, nostalgic tale, almost a fairy tale in its kindly and humorous description of Polish misdemeanors.

The most significant personae Wajda decided to include in the film are, in the romantic plot, Tadeusz, Zosia, Horeszko, and Telimena; and, in the intrigue plot, Horeszko and Soplica, members of the families whose conflict lies at the heart of "the last raid in Lithuania." Although the poem itself covers several concurrent life stories, Wajda decided to concentrate on these characters and on that of Reverend Robak (i.e., Jacek Soplica, played by Bogusław Linda), who, hidden from his own brother, Judge Soplica, under a priest's hood, prepares an uprising against the Russian oppressors in Lithuania. One of the reasons behind Wajda's decisions regarding which characters to include was his intent to make the film interesting to those who had never read the poem.

The actual production of the film was preceded by long preparation and research, during which time Wajda explained his intentions to interested critics and future audiences who waited impatiently for the realization of the famous poem on screen. Wajda was aware of how Poles would scrutinize the film for historical and literary inaccuracies. Hence, at the outset, he stated that he was interested not in close adherence to historical facts from the epoch, but rather in the creation of a work of art based on an awareness and knowledge of the epoch.[50] The film begins with a sequence presenting a group of Polish émigrés (among them is Adam Mickiewicz) gathering in Paris for a quiet meeting during which they reminisce and read poetry written by Mickiewicz himself. The poem is *Mr. Thadeus*, whose main protagonist, Tadeusz, a young nobleman, returns home from a long period at school.

In the subsequent sequence, we see the young man's return; Wajda shows Lithuania in the full morning sunlight on a beautiful summer day. The whole film, in fact, is shot in this romantic manner, with diffused light revealing the beauty of the country poor émigrés dream about. Tadeusz returns to the old manor in which he spent his childhood, recognizes the place, its furniture, and the various objects in the rooms. Suddenly, he looks through the window and sees a young girl, Zosia, who is only partly dressed. Zosia is a pupil and protégé of Telimena, Judge Soplica's sister, and now lives in the house. She flees immediately once she notices Tadeusz looking at her. In the old castle nearby, Horeszko, patriarch of the Horeszko family, converses with Gerwazy, who explains the essence of the conflict between the Soplica and Horeszko families and tries to convince Horeszko to reclaim the castle from the Soplicas. The count seems bored, however, and wants to return the castle to the Soplicas at the impending court proceedings. In later sequences, a new character is introduced: Robak, who is in reality Jacek Soplica. In the past, Jacek accidentally killed Esquire Carver Horeszko during a Russian attack on the castle and thus unintentionally started the whole chain of hostile events.

From the beginning of the film, Wajda introduces two major themes: that of the romance (or "love-triangle") between Tadeusz and Telimena and between Tadeusz and Zosia; and that of the ancient Horeszko-Soplica conflict. Against the background of these historical conflicts, Wajda presents a series of scenes portraying country life in Lithuania, which the expatriates in Paris miss (shown in the introductory, middle, and final sequences of the film). Among the activities are mushroom picking, a hunt, and slow evening dinners, all of which are portrayed by Wajda in the form of "slow motion" tableaux. The count romances Telimena, Tadeusz flirts with both Telimena and Zosia, and the noblemen discuss the qualities of rifles and drinks. Only Robak is concerned about Poland and with the country's liberation from the hands of its occupiers.

We see the invasion of the castle after Gerwazy has renewed the conflict over the evening dinner. Here Mickiewicz criticizes petty nobles for their egoism, selfishness, and cavalier manner, and for their eagerness to engage in senseless fights at any time. Only a few older, wiser noblemen like Maciek Królik-Bożeczka and Robak call for peace. In a self-reflexive moment of the film, Maciek addresses his criticism directly to the camera, as if berating the film's spectators. Here, Wajda clearly addresses contemporary audiences and politicians who consider the public good as their private domain and who engage in private battles instead of taking care of their country and its citizens. (During the 1990s, Poland was implicated in a series of financial and political scandals to which Wajda openly alludes, and that he criticizes, through Maciek's speech.)

The *zajazd* (invasion) ends with a great feast attended by Russian officers alarmed by the news of the battle. In a series of excellently executed sequences, Wajda shows his mass-scene forté: the scene of the battle between Polish noblemen and Russians, started by Tadeusz, who tries to protect Telimena from the advances of a Russian officer; and then Russian soldiers and officers fighting, drinking, and discussing Polish characteristics, highlighting their ambivalent attitude toward Poles. Some hate the land that they occupy as well as its people, but others have begun to love Poland and its rugged beauty and have no wish to harm anybody. In the final sequences of the film, Jacek Soplica, mortally wounded in battle with the Russians, confesses to his brother on his deathbed the nature of his disguise. Gerwazy explains the origin of the conflict between the Soplicas and the Horeszkos, and the war between Napolean and Russia is announced. The Napoleonic army crosses Lithuania on its way to Russia, Tadeusz proposes to Zosia, and Horeszko and Telimena dance together. Again, in a blend of personal and political, all of those in conflict dance together: The film ends with a grand polonaise in which all parties, including the Russian occupiers, participate.

The making of *Mr. Thadeus* was accompanied by an unprecedented press campaign during which every aspect of the poem was meticulously analyzed and compared with the film adaptation. Jerzy Armata discusses previous adaptations of the poem; Barbara Hollender analyzes every aspect of the film production,[51] including even the hairdos of the female protagonists; and Krzysztof Masłoń concentrates on the film's narrator, Gerwazy.[52] Interviews with Wajda himself or with Adek Drabiński, the assistant director, appear in *Gazeta Wyborcza*, *Kino*, and *Rzeczpospolita*. Readers of these magazines seem interested in every aspect of the film, from dialogues to visuals and music.[53]

The release of the film was a "national occasion,"[54] and spectators cried, laughed, and applauded every aspect of the film, from the actors to the military marches and the final polonaise. They treated the film as an occasion for the celebration of Polishness in Poland and abroad, and for uniting the Polish diaspora. Older spectators who had never gone to the cinema before crowded movie-houses everywhere, often turned out in their best. In such characters as Tadeusz, Zosia, Horeszko, and Notary, they recognized familiar figures they recalled from high school readings and from discussions at home and at work. For them, *Mr. Thadeus* was as much a refuge as that imaginary Lithuania was for those sad emigrants in Paris in 1834.

Mr. Thadeus was eagerly awaited by Poles for another reason, as well. Weary of the tumultuous 1990s, during which constant government struggles and uncertainty in both public and private spheres made lives difficult, they looked for the Poland of their dreams, a beautiful country in which all of their conflicts could be resolved and danced away in a polonaise. Poles identified with the utopian heroes of *Mr. Thadeus*, seeing themselves on the screen. From the safe distance of the audience, they could laugh at themselves and wonder at their follies, narrow-mindedness, egoism, stupidity, and emotional clumsiness. Seen by millions of Poles in Poland and abroad, this film provided some sense of closure to the political struggles that culminated in the change of the political system in Poland. In a sense, the film nostalgically portrays a Poland where human relations are more important than the dictates of any political system.

The film met with mixed critical reviews, however. Some reviewers acknowledged the fact that, since its premiere on 22 October 1999, the film was seen by over one million Poles in four weeks.[55] Audiences were openly touched and moved to tears. The premiere of the film was attended by the most accomplished artists and representatives of culture, academia, and business.[56] On the other hand, critics were dissatisfied with the film's theatricality, the predominance of spoken word over the visuals, and its general pomposity and lack of controversy.[57] Krzysztof Żurek openly criticized Wajda for the characters' one-dimensionality, for the lack of subtlety and sophistication in their presentation and the lack of drama in "national myths dressed in contemporary, technical garb."[58]

Other reviewers criticized the film for its lack of passion and feeling in favor of technical superiority and a polished rendering of scenes and characters. As Joanna Pawluśkiewicz notes, "the film lacks passion. There is no heart in this film. Everything is ideally balanced and without a grain of madness. Too pretty, too good, too clean and too clever....

The film is a cycle of masterly realized film etudes, shot and directed by the master. And I wanted to be moved to tears."[59] A similar opinion was expressed by Zbigniew Majchrowski in a panel discussion with Wojciech Owczarski and Zbigniew Zakiewicz, printed in *Dialog*.[60] Majchrowski complains that there is "too little of Wajda" in the film, too little of his passion and nonconformity. Poles got "a simplified *Pan Tadeusz*, reduced to the erotic and political intrigue and peppered with patriotic banality."

Yet political references, especially allusions to political elites, are clear in the film, both in the focus on Gerwazy and his story and in the passionate way the political discussions are carried out in the film. Zakiewicz proposes that the film is about Lepperism, about politicians like Andrzej Lepper: the ambitious, ruthless, and nonconformist individuals who do not shy away from blocking roads and violating Polish law to get where they want to go.[61] References to the contemporary *warchoł* (brawler) way of doing politics in Poland was also noted by Zdzisław Pietrasik, who pointed out that the nobles' council before the attack in the film clearly resembles the contemporary debates of Polish parliament.[62] On the other hand, Pietrasik criticizes Wajda for the frequent entries of Mickiewicz, both the narrator of the film and the author of the poem, which seemed to break the narrative consistency of the film.

In *Mr. Thadeus*, Wajda returns to the main themes of his career: history and politics. First, he devotes considerable attention to the plight of Robak, to whom the fight for Poland's independence is of prime importance. He also presents the relations between Poles and Russians in an open-minded way, thus avoiding and invalidating stereotypical and demonic portrayals of Russians as condescending and arrogant. However, unlike in his early films, Wajda presents the ideological and historical conflicts with a benevolent smile rather than with barely hidden anger masking his didacticism, as he did in his earlier films. History and politics are here observed and esteemed, not used passionately to foment a political argument. Wajda ends his demagogy with this film and instead takes pleasure in looking at every piece of history offered to him by the perceptive Mickiewicz. He turns each scene described by Mickiewicz into a piece of cinematic art, portraying both people and physical things as objects of nostalgia (e.g., in a certain memorable scene with coffee). Furthermore, he uses his theatrical talents, his aesthetic sensitivity, and his personal charm to influence his collaborators (actors and crew) to push for new heights and thus create a superb reading of the imaginary Poland that exists as a utopian world in the Polish subconscious. The magic dance based on Jacek Malczewski's famous painting *Zaklęty krąg (The Enchanted Circle)* turns from the bitter commentary on Poland's caricature of unity after the end of World War II in *Ashes and Diamonds* into a joyous hymn of love (the polonaise). The exuberant dance binds all Poles, their friends, and their enemies in one optimistic assembly of people dancing/working for the common purpose: Poland's prosperity and happiness. The "oneiric home" that Wajda shows in this film functions as an archetype of Polishness.[63]

Wajda objected strongly to all comments concerning his demagogic intentions in this film. He claimed that he thought about the adaptation of Mickiewicz's poem for a long time and often wondered which way to go. He resisted mythologization or parody and often wondered whether it would be possible to adapt *Mr. Thadeus* at all. He stated repeatedly that he was not interested in any references to contemporary history, but wanted only to show this story on the screen.[64] Nevertheless, the common assumption of Wajda's didactic intentions went almost undisputed. *Mr. Thadeus* was an undeniable confirmation of political wisdom and national goodwill on the part of the filmmaker in the context of Poland's effort to join the European Union (EU). In this interpretation of the film, Poles nobly join ranks with both enemies and friends to become a responsible and mature member of the EU.

Revenge (2002)

For one of his most recent films, Wajda chose to make an adaptation of Alexander Fredro's 1834 play *Revenge*, a well-known Polish comedy in which the characteristic vices of Poles—extreme individualism, barratry, distrustfulness, intractability, pugnacity, emotionalism, and the like—are exposed in a playful and intelligent manner. Fredro's play belongs to the canon of literary works taught in Polish high schools and is often produced in major Polish theaters. *Revenge* tells the story of two families living in the same castle, divided only by a collapsing wall. Both families, especially their older representatives, quarrel constantly and participate in all kinds of petty maneuvers, both sad and amusing. However, it is neither the conflict nor the shocking behavior on either side of the wall that is deplorable, but rather what the inhabitants say and how they say it. The play demonstrates Fredro's great wit: using the narrative as a pretext, he pokes fun at national pastimes in Poland and at Poles themselves.

After the phenomenal success of *Mr. Thadeus* (which, after 1989, was surpassed in popularity only by Jerzy Hoffman's *With Fire and Sword*), Wajda made *Revenge* not only, as some more skeptical reviewers suggest,[65] to have a financial and popular success similar to that of *Mr. Thadeus*, but also to continue the winning educational trend in his filmography. During press conferences both before and after the film, Wajda claimed that he wanted to make the satire in the film even sharper than that in the play and to bring the old play alive thanks to the visual abilities of the film medium.

Wajda chose the old, half-ruined castle of Ogrodzieniec as his film site. Its jagged walls serve as an ideal backdrop to the conflicts that, although realistic and universal, seem ridiculous and irrelevant in the context of a contemporary world that must unite for world peace. The modest set design, with only minimal adornment of the naked walls, costumes, and noble insignia such as coats of arms and family sables, functions as a mere signifier of the nobility and of the place and time of the film. The action takes place in winter, making the words of the play especially audible against the bleak landscape: The words written by Fredro almost two centuries ago stand out as a warning to the present generations of Poles. Moreover, the words are brilliantly delivered by an exceptional cast gathered by Wajda for the film, making the complex dialogue dazzle with humor and wit. Even the exquisite players of secondary roles, such as Daniel Olbrychski as Dyndalski, afford a veritable firecracker of verbal attacks and counterattacks filled with political and sexual innuendo.

Cześnik (Maciej) Raptusiewicz and his cousin Klara Raptusiewiczówna reside on one side of the wall, while Rejent Milczek (referred to as "Notary") and his son, Wacław, live on the other. These two families, or rather their older representatives, do not talk to each other and have been feuding for many years. Other characters residing in the castle are the widow Podstolina/Hanna and the swashbuckling braggart Papkin Józef, who is an impoverished captain of horse and an old acquaintance of Cześnik. The film starts with Papkin returning to the castle after an extended foray on the road. At the same time, Klara, Podstolina, and Cześnik return from a carriage ride. From subsequent scenes in the film, we learn that Klara and Wacław are in love with one another, and they try to spend time together—often through the wall—at every opportunity. On one occasion when they meet at the crumbling wall, however, Wacław's father, Notary, notices them; he decides to repair the wall and thus fill in all the holes through which the lovers might meet.

Cześnik, on the other side of the wall, wants to get rid of Notary altogether, and he uses Papkin for the negotiations. He also wants to draw upon the eloquent Papkin as his intermediary in another matter, though, for Cześnik wants to marry the aging but wealthy Podstolina, but does not know how to woo her himself. Papkin soon begins his "services" and addresses Podstolina with elaborate verbal overtures. Podstolina, however, thinks that Papkin flirts on his own behalf, so she responds with visible pleasure to the rhetoric of the younger man.

In the meantime, Notary repairs the wall, but Cześnik's people, Smigalski and Dyndalski, chase the workers away. In the scuffle, Wacław lets himself be captured by Papkin, and Notary writes a summons in the name of the supposedly injured workers. Fredro's criticism of barratry is readily apparent in Notary's long and elaborate letter, which actor Andrzej Seweryn underlines with his amusingly self-congratulatory reading of the letter in painstaking statements.

Shortly thereafter, Papkin presents Wacław to Cześnik as Notary's commissary (not his son) and asks for his safekeeping. Wacław tries to convince Cześnik that, instead of a fight, a mutual accord is more reasonable. Cześnik, brilliantly played by Janusz Gajos as a tough, demanding individual without much education or culture, stubbornly sticks to his decision, no matter how petty, ridiculous, or narrow-minded. This Cześnik is a familiar character to many Poles; he might stand for the cantankerous neighbor, the drunken and quarrelsome uncle at family gatherings, or the irresponsible politician, many of whom appeared in the Polish *seym* in post-Communist Poland. He is self-centered and egoistic—amusing, yet also pitiable and contemptible. Through Cześnik, Wajda is highly critical not only of the nobility that ultimately led Poland to its current state of political and social chaos, but also of his contemporaries who had quarreled in the government for many years in a similarly churlish way.

Wacław is held as a prisoner of war at Cześnik's home, but he is also given an assignment—to work as a private secretary for Podstolina. When he is introduced to her, Wacław realizes that Podstolina is in fact "Hanna," his long-forgotten former lover. Podstolina has not forgotten him, however, and tries to seduce Wacław once again. Wacław escapes the scene, however, and flees back to his father, Notary. Wacław explains that he loves Klara and wants to marry her despite their families' longstanding quarrels. His greedy father has other plans for him, unfortunately, and wants him to marry the wealthy Podstolina, quite against Wacław's will.

At the same time, Papkin is trying to seduce Klara (for himself) and bombards her with ardent speeches. He goes to Notary at the request of Cześnik, who wants to call Notary to duel for control of the castle, on the same day when Cześnik has planned to marry Podstolina. In the meantime, Podstolina and Notary concoct a marriage contract to entrap Wacław and thus to make *him* marry Podstolina (for the significant amount of money she would pay to the greedy Notary, Wacław's father). Papkin is shocked with this state of affairs and criticizes Podstolina for her decision to marry the young man. Finally, Papkin is thrown out of Notary's home and, in turn, tells Cześnik everything he has learned from Podstolina.

His pride offended, Cześnik devises a plan to abduct Wacław and to force him to marry Klara, unaware of the fact that the two young people have secretly been in love for some time. The abduction takes place, and the surprised Wacław learns from Cześnik that it is Klara he will finally marry, not Podstolina. Surprised and grateful at this turn of events, he thanks Cześnik, his abductor, and agrees to marry Klara in the chapel immediately. The film ends with a scene of reconciliation between the opponents Cześnik and Notary, preceded by several amusing moments of humor and a few surprising revelations.

First, Notary arrives in his hussar coat-of-arms, prepared to duel with Cześnik. Suddenly, he hears wedding music, and Wacław and Klara come to him to ask for his paternal blessing. Podstolina also appears, and, on seeing what has happened, tells everyone that she is poor and that her money in fact belongs to Klara. Happy at this news and eager to have a wealthy bride for his son, the greedy Notary quickly changes his attitude and blesses the young couple. At the same time, Notary reluctantly agrees to end the old feud between the two families, and the old war ends. Papkin bids farewell to everyone and the film ends with a theatrical drawing of the curtain.

The film *Revenge* is a skilful adaptation of a well-known play that appeals not only to those older spectators familiar with the playwright, but to younger audiences as well. The dialogue is presented flawlessly by the most prominent Polish actors of the time, who, while portraying these figures from the past, are able to imbue them with a sense of the present. In the figures of Cześnik and Notary, audiences recognize the familiar violent, passionate, and cantankerous characters presenting their arguments in the parliament or in local government debates. On one hand, the film rekindles a love for Fredro and his antics; it is amusing and light and provides good entertainment. On the other hand, Wajda's *Revenge* adds little to the interpretation of the play or its cantankerous characters: The film moves smoothly from one scene to the next, not missing a beat. In press conferences, Wajda often stated that he wanted *Revenge* to be a well-designed adaptation of a great Polish literary classic, similar to those great film adaptations of Shakespeare's plays.[66]

Predictably, the film pleased many spectators in Poland, yet angered others. Although some reviewers were surprised that Wajda decided to film such a well-known traditional play (saying things like, "It is a pity he wastes his talent on such old stuff"), most of them admired him for trying to reveal the most interesting aspects of the play.[67] Even those who were critical of the source material admit that "the play has a wealth of meanings, several levels of thinking and finesse of descriptions."[68]

Although the film is set in the eighteenth century, it nonetheless endorses a universal message espousing honesty and open-mindedness. It is a film that "makes fun of our national characteristics: barratry, buffoonery, lack of tolerance, and narrow-mindedness."[69] Justyna Kobus, however, states that the film is too mild and should promote a stronger political message. She suggests that Wajda should have used the play to communicate a vociferous attack on those in power. Thus, some spectators seemed disappointed with Wajda's amusing treatment of the play and accused him of an apolitical approach. As with *Mr. Thadeus*, the main criticism of the film is that, while made in a "correct" manner, skillfully adapted from the famous play, *Revenge* lacks the passion of Wajda's earlier films.

Other criticism concerns the casting of the protagonists, who were figures well known to Polish spectators. The portrayal of Cześnik was universally praised for its accuracy (and for its links with iconic contemporary figures), and for the fact that Wajda "imbued Cześnik with the contemporary spirit."[70] For instance, Bogdan Sobieszek states that Cześnik resembles contemporary politicians eager to raise arguments at any occasion. On the other hand, Papkin, played by the famous Roman Polański, did not appeal to some viewers. Piotr Kajewski complains that Papkin, who in the play was not only a proxy but also a colorful character in his own right ("half-clown, half-nobleman, scrounger, old stager"[71]) is instead a low-key, "mottled" old soldier in Wajda's *Revenge*, an unconvincing and timorous negotiator. Nevertheless, the largely colorful ensemble of characters amused spectators, many of whom knew the words of the play by heart. Poles could recognize themselves in Cześnik and in Notary, and in their constant musings about old conflicts. They admired the beautiful and spirited women and laughed at clumsy Papkin. This benign comedy is presented by Wajda with a smile of nostalgia and an awareness of the passage of time rather than with the ardency and passion of the earlier films.

For two reasons, *Revenge* is a much more meaningful part of Wajda's oeuvre than simply another adaptation of a literary work. First, Wajda is ironic and distanced in his version of the famous play, and, second, he is quite brave and open-minded in his portrayal of gender dynamics, certainly relative to his approach in earlier films. The irony and psychological distance from reality in the film are visible not only in the patchy treatment of the decorations, but also in the casting of two important characters in the play, Wacław and Papkin.

Wacław, the young suitor, is slightly surprised and detached when confronted by two strong and determined women, contemporary-looking Klara and strong-minded Podstolina/Hanna. He maneuvers carefully between the two women, somewhat startled by Klara's determination and passion and openly suspicious of Hanna's mature desire. Wacław's subdued masculinity is iterated further in the character of Papkin, a parody of the male adventurer, a problematic soldier with a questionable past, a self-centered negotiator and a ridiculous suitor. He is both laughed at and manipulated by both the clever Klara and the scheming Hanna.

These two women, Podstolina/Hanna and Klara, superbly played by Katarzyna Figura and Agata Buzek, respectively, are the best features of the film. They are strong, cynical, provocative (if need be), and manipulative; both know what they want and know how to get it. Their French costumes, exquisite (and excessive) makeup, and elaborate hairdos reinforce their exaggerated femininity, but also underlie their strength. This ironic and very contemporary interpretation of the two female characters might attest to Wajda's more open-minded perception of women, of female characters who can act as formidable opponents, not merely as passive observers of unfolding events.

At the same time, just as these fantastically clad and coiffured women seem to be somehow unreal, the whole story seems an unusual fairy tale. The action of the film, shot in a remote, half-fallen castle—only barely touched up by set designers to capture the sense of a lived-in space—and the aesthetic excess in the costumes and hairdos of the two women only reinforce this sense of distance from reality. Wajda, both playful and curiously detached, creates this simulacrum of theater and film, past and present, real and unreal, in a nostalgic farewell to Polish audiences.

In his most recent films, Wajda returns to the themes of World War II as if trying to relive, but also to reinterpret, the painful moments. In *The Crowned-Eagle Ring*, he replaces the idealistic protagonist from *Ashes and Diamonds* with a more realistic Marcin, as if trying to provide some justification for Poland's decisions made at the end of the war. In *Korczak* and *Holy Week*, he returns obsessively to Jewish questions, reliving the communal guilt of Poles. *Miss Nobody* attests to Wajda's social passions and attempts to influence young people with his social critique of the heartless 1990s. *Nastasja*, on the other hand, is testament to his fascination with Japan, theater, and Dostoevsky. Finally, both *Mr. Thadeus* and *Revenge* are nostalgic re-creations of the past, dear to Poles. This final chapter thus annotates almost all of the thematic concerns of Andrzej Wajda, tying them with the filmmaker's aesthetic traits, the abundance of which attests to his complex artistic background and to his directorial ambitions. The thematic concerns form an elaborate tapestry, the shape and look of which will be summarized in the conclusion.

❀ CONCLUSION

The exploration of Wajda's life and work has been quite a journey through the years of history: from the Middle Ages in *The Gates to Paradise*, through the eighteenth century in *Mr. Thadeus* and *Revenge*, to the 1990s in *Miss Nobody*. It has also been a journey through geographic Europe: Poland (in most of his films), Germany *(Pilate and Others* and *A Love in Germany)*, Siberia *(Siberian Lady Macbeth)*, France *(Danton)*, Lithuania *(Mr. Thadeus)*, and Russia *(The Possessed)*. These journeys involved many film protagonists, with their various passions, obsessions, social and political problems, and humor and despair. In a Bakhtinian fashion, all of these protagonists are heroes who question their own moral choices and actions, and who doubt their own existence in a deeply human, hesitant manner. They are internally dialogic and polemic with themselves and with the director himself, who expresses his own doubts through them.

However, the open-endedness of Fyodor Dostoevsky's *Underground Man* is not what Wajda procures for his heroes: Finally, all of the characters in his films define themselves through historical circumstances. Karol in *Promised Land*, Maciek in *Ashes and Diamonds*, Agnieszka in *Man of Marble*, and Danton in *Danton*, all of these characters' actions are historically determined. Only in Wajda's nostalgic or deeply personal films, such as *Everything for Sale* or *Hunting Flies*, do the hesitations of protagonists, their inner struggles with themselves, and their personal tragedies privilege their humanity over historical determinism and thus grant them an aura of fragility and poignancy. Wajda's heroes are the carriers of the filmmaker's thoughts and intentions.

Wajda's love for his country, his love of freedom, his awareness of difficult moral choices in specific historical circumstances, and his romantic tendencies in the presentation of love affairs are behind the protagonists' actions at every moment of their screen presence. Wajda's heroes are almost invariably wary interpreters of, or active participants in, the thematic aspects of his films. These thematic areas are as follows: First, the historical event of World War II. To date, twelve of his films have been devoted to this theme or have alluded indirectly to it: *A Generation, Kanal, Ashes and Diamonds, Lotna, Samson, Love at Twenty, Landscape after Battle, A Love in Germany, A Chronicle of Amorous Incidents, Korczak, The Crowned-Eagle Ring,* and *Holy Week.* The second area is his interest in pre-World War II Poland, particularly as that period forms Poland's contemporary national identity: *Ashes, The Wedding,* and *Promised Land.*

The third thematic area relates to the politics of postwar Poland and prompted the rise of the whole new film movement called the School of Moral Concern: *Man of Marble, Without Anesthetic, The Orchestra Conductor,* and *Man of Iron.* These films are openly political; they make people aware of the dismal social and political situation in Poland and prompt audiences to take action. Again, it is worth noting that many other films made by Wajda can also be called "political" although they do not directly address the political reality in Poland (Aesopian, they are political without direct authorial intention): *Innocent Sorcerers, Hunting Flies,* and *Danton.*

The fourth thematic area includes those films that deal with general aspects of life and death or with deeply personal feelings. In most of these films, Wajda seemingly prefers not to refer to himself. He tells his stories, while often expressing his own beliefs and desires, via his characters, only indirectly alluding to his own human condition. Films belonging to this group include *The Birchwood, The Shadow Line,* and *The Young Ladies of Wilko.* There is one film, however, which I include in this thematic section but which seems at first to resist this characterization. *Everything for Sale* is an unprecedented display of grief, mourning, and longing for the deceased actor Zbigniew Cybulski. Nevertheless, as if fearing to plainly demonstrate his own feelings, Wajda has Andrzej Łapicki play the part of the director in the film in such a distanced and cold way that he masks his own intense grief. In making this film, Wajda obviously wishes to demonstrate his grief, yet he also hides his true feelings and only alludes to them indirectly by allowing them in the performance of the other actors.

The fifth thematic group includes Wajda's attempts to adapt great literary works to the screen. Some of these adaptations were very successful, while others were not. One might argue here that almost all of Wajda's films (twenty-eight of them, in fact) are adaptations of renowned literary works. However, many of these are chosen because they raise issues relevant to the audiences at the time of their screening and were thus important for political or historical reasons, so I place them in a different thematic area. Among these literary adaptations, some are less effective than others: *Siberian Lady Macbeth, Gates to Paradise, The Possessed,* and *Miss Nobody.* For various reasons, these films did not arouse audiences' interest despite the fact that they raised important historical or social issues. *Pilate and Others* is an important aberration in this context because, while it raised crucial political and social issues in an exquisite adaptation experiment, it did not provoke as many political and artistic comments as, for instance, a similarly explosive *Man of Marble.*

Two films in this fifth group, however—*Mr. Thadeus* and *Revenge*—prove to be not only admirable adaptations, but also films that appeal strongly to Poles' national feelings. These remarkable heritage films constitute an apt commentary on Polish vices but also on their positive characteristics. They are beautifully made, appealing to Poles' need for national identification at the beginning of the twenty-first century. Lastly, there are two films in this thematic group that I would call "aesthetic experiments": *Roly Poly* and *Nastasja*. In these, Wajda experiments with both the form and the use of the actor. Based on well-known texts of Stanisław Lem and Fyodor Dostoevsky, respectively, these films attest to Wajda's courage in trying new approaches to film aesthetics.

All of Wajda's films, analyzed by decade, fall into these more or less unified groups. Wajda's best, most well-loved, and most critically appreciated films were created in two separate decades, the 1950s and the 1970s. Both decades were important for historical, political, and artistic reasons; as well, both periods were characterized by an explosion of talent in Polish art, in general. In this generous artistic context, Wajda's art flourished. The late 1950s was a time of enthusiastic growth in Poland, rebuilding after World War II and gaining prosperity under Socialism. It was also a time of the "straightening out of accounts" and of reconciliation with the recent past. The war films created by Wajda in the 1950s re-created the trauma of recent history and responded empathetically to Poles' grief and mourning.

The 1970s, on the other hand, were a decade of economic prosperity and cultural flexibility in Poland. Poles could enjoy relatively reasonable living conditions and could explore other aspects of life than merely economic ones. Films like *The Birchwood* and *The Young Ladies of Wilko* were widely admired for their artistic brilliance. The 1970s were also, however, a time of disillusionment with the political system, especially once Poles realized that they enjoyed prosperity only on bought time. The nation was debt-ridden, governed by corrupt party members. A tremendous dissatisfaction with the regime brought about the films of the School of Moral Concern, which stirred audiences with its seditious content and unorthodox style.

Those films produced in the 1960s, 1980s, and 1990s (with some outstanding exceptions) were less convincing in their authorial address. There are various reasons for this creative unevenness. Undoubtedly, historical circumstances, psychological or emotional difficulties, or uninteresting screenplays can account for some of them. Other reasons were revealed to me during my work in the archives, some communicated to me by the director himself during our private conversations in 1998 and 1999.

For instance, after 1981, Wajda's enthusiasm for making films as tools of political struggle and mature expression of thought underwent a bitter transformation. My belief is corroborated by Wajda's personal pronouncements in published interviews and articles of the period and since: In all of these sources, Wajda stresses the fact that the introduction of martial law in 1981 was damaging to his artistic career. Indeed, those films made after *Danton* no longer reveal the same authorial power or personal conviction as, for instance, his great works *Man of Marble* and *Promised Land.* The urgency and passion of political assertion gave way to the chilliness and sadness of disillusionment. This particular explanation seems to elucidate one of the reasons for Wajda's subsequent turn to nostalgia, the predominant theme of his films during the 1980s and 1990s.

In this nostalgic area, Wajda returns to the issues of World War II as if he believed he could say new and significant things that might shed additional light on the traumatic past. *A Love in Germany, A Chronicle of Amorous Incidents, Korczak, The Crowned-Eagle Ring,* and *Holy Week* all depict war themes in a nostalgic and nationally self-accusatory way. Poles in this era, however, are no longer interested in films like *Ashes and Diamonds:* The time for such films has passed, and Poles are interested more in the fate of post-Socialist Poland, in the rise of capitalism, and in their own individual fortunes than in the treatment of Poles by Germans during the war *(A Love in Germany),* the situation in Poland before the war *(A Chronicle of Amorous Incidents),* the fate of Jews during World War II *(Korczak* and *Holy Week),* or the historical situation of Poland after World War II *(The Crowned-Eagle Ring).* Nationalistic feelings of guilt give way to individualism and industriousness, while World War II becomes a thing of the past.

To be fair to the audiences of the 1990s, Wajda seems less convincing in his efforts to remind Poles of the past than in his early war films. One of the reasons lies in the films' aesthetics, which still resemble the now-outmoded aesthetics of the Polish School. Another reason is the lack of vitality in these film narratives, the lack of the remarkable energy that characterized earlier film texts; as well, there are a number of obvious miscalculations in structure and aesthetics in these films (e.g., *The Crowned-Eagle Ring* and *Holy Week*) and a general aura of sadness that permeates all of them with feelings of negativity and helplessness.

However, with the fate of Poland seeming to become more positive at the end of the 1990s, Wajda turns to heritage films to remind Poles of their glorious past, but also to unify them again. In these films, Wajda shows Poles in a positive light, but not without ignoring their negative characteristics such as egoism, selfishness, narrow-mindedness, and barratry. By using well-known school texts, Wajda reminds Poles that they are still a nation despite the internal and external (European) tendencies for globalization and diffusion of cultures. *Mr. Thadeus* and *Revenge,* both of them exceptional heritage films, unify Poles by addressing their national sensibilities and characteristics. Well received by Poles both in Poland and abroad, these two films once again confirmed Wajda's position as the national bard.

All of these thematic areas overlap, traversing the span of almost fifty years of artistic activity. Rarely appearing in more than one or two films in chronological succession, each theme is nevertheless consistently present in all of the films made by Wajda. With the exception of the early war films and the films of the School of Moral Concern, which were produced one after another, all of the other themes emerged and reemerged in particular decades. Overall, however, his concern for Poland and for its people prevails, binding the films into his highly nationalistic oeuvre.

One of the reasons for which Wajda should be remembered is his films' aesthetics, which is unique, modern, and unparalleled in its versatility. Called a "film painter," Wajda creates memorable visual tableaux, each composed like a painting. In these filmic paintings, every element of the frame is in its proper place, recalling the perfect centrality of Renaissance paintings, the "Golden Section," based on the idea of balance introduced by Rudolf Arnheim[1] as the main organizational principle of the image. The Golden Section rule postulates an absolute centrality of the image within the frame of the painting and, according to Herbert Zettl, can be applied to the discussion of other static images.[2] Whether following this rule consciously or subconsciously, Wajda creates carefully composed frames that, like paintings, are remembered as individual compositions.

There are many striking tableaux in Wajda's films. Among the best known of these are from *Ashes and Diamonds*, specifically the following three: (1) The opening scene with the protagonists Maciek and Andrzej waiting, guns visible, for the car bearing Szczuka; (2) the scene in the church with the figure of Christ hanging upside down; and later in the film (3) the scene of the two lovers on the bed, their faces turned upward. In *Lotna*, for example, these still images almost always involve the presentation of Lotna, the horse, and all of the activities related to the horse. The fetishization of the horse supersedes even the scenes of death involving people, with one significant exception—that of Officer Cadet Jerzy Grabowski being buried beneath a cherry tree by his young wife. Even here, though, the scene privileges the image of the tree above that of the dead officer.

These scenes are small paintings in stasis that can be admired on their own. I would argue that these exquisite images constitute a defining characteristic of the Polish School in general, of which *Ashes and Diamonds* is perhaps the most prominent representative. The aesthetic style of this movement is characterized by static images, slowly unfolding sequences, and the focus on the explication of political arguments, events, and human emotions. In my opinion, however, it is the quality of the images that adds to the school's greatness.

An example of such an image is the one in the ruined church in *Ashes and Diamonds* (see Fig. 1), which presents the scene in which Maciek and Krystyna talk about their future. The mise-en-scène is carefully planned, with the floor of the church covered in debris after the bombing; loose bricks lie in high piles, the floor of the church full of small craters and uneven surfaces. In the background, behind an interior arch, is a smaller second arch covered with wooden planks. In the extreme forefront, the wooden figure of Christ with a pronounced crown hangs upside down and looks slightly to the right. In the middle ground, Krystyna, on the left of the frame, and Maciek, on the right, talk calmly. Krystyna wears neat clothes and high heels while Maciek sits disheveled and half-crouching/half-leaning against a broken piece of a church pew. His face is angled toward Krystyna, who stands silently in a ruminative pose, eyes clearly on the ground. Both protagonists are serious, so engaged in their conversation that they seem almost unaware of their surroundings.

There is an ideal symmetry in the positioning of the protagonists on the opposite sides of the center line of the frame, with the figure of Christ taking center stage. The spectator acknowledges simultaneously the presence of the protagonists and of Christ, who seems almost to judge them silently. However, the Christ figure is also damaged, its left hand partly burned or destroyed, exacerbating the impression of destruction and hopelessness. Thus the figure of Christ also introduces a moment of disharmony, of unrest, into the ideally centered frame, as if comment-

Popiół i diament (Ashes and Diamonds), 1958
Zbigniew Cybulski (Maciek Chełmicki) and Ewa Krzyżewska (Krystyna)

ing on the state of affairs after World War II when, for a time, order and harmony disappeared altogether.

The three figures are placed in the context of receding space, expanding back into even more ruins and arches, which though initially open are finally closed tight with the arch covered by the wooden planks, sealing off the protagonists' chances for redemption and for a better life in the new Poland. The whole mise-en-scène is aesthetically dense or obfuscated, as well: Vertical and diagonal shadows crisscross the frame, further obliterating the clearly lit scene and introducing further elements of uncertainty and concealment into the frame.

In this carefully built frame, all of its elements are equally important. Together, the receding and complex background, the bricks, the mounds of earth, and the receding space form a site of destruction and disorder; in the middle ground, Maciek and Krystyna engage in an emotional dialogue, while, in the foreground, the figure of Christ addresses the spectator with its tragic inverted gaze and half-burned body. All these elements of the scene are additionally watched by a figure on the wall on the right of the frame, probably a life-size painting of one of the Polish queens of history. The complexity of this frame results in an emotional recognition for the spectator, but also in a moment of deep reflection on the irony of history, which, while claiming victory over the German occupier, destroys historical and religious traditions, and crushes order and stability in the newly liberated Poland. This thinly veiled criticism of the then new ruler of Poland, the Soviet Union, could not be pronounced in words by the filmmaker, but it is expressed in carefully crafted images that say much more than words.

We also witness this phenomenon in other films by Wajda, in which densely constructed images communicate complex culturally embedded messages. In Wajda's other films, static images sometimes constitute the film's overall grandeur in a consistent manner. These films in their entirety—*Siberian Lady Macbeth, The Birchwood, The Young Ladies of Wilko,* and *A Chronicle of Amorous Incidents* among them—reveal a consistent style that makes all of them complete artistic masterpieces wherein characters, mise-en-scene, lighting, and pace form an artistic unity.

In general, Wajda's films display a variety of complex issues in several intersections, such as *image and signified; image and sound; image and music;* and *image and political persuasion.* All of these intersections, and many others beyond these ones, require careful theoretical analysis that falls beyond the scope of this biography. However, I would like to conclude with the observation that Wajda incorporates the discourses of many Polish and non-Polish artists and reveals the influence of numerous cultural discourses and artistic and cultural Polish and World movements, all significantly contributing to the densification of his films. Among these are discourses of *Socialist Realism, Soviet silent cinema, documentary, classical painting, Polish Romanticism, Italian neo-Realism, Surreal-*

ism, Expressionism, Polish Romantic music, Polish theater, and *Hollywood cinema.*

Some discussion of these influences is present in the analysis of particular films within this book, while five influences in particular—*Eisenstein's montage, Socialist Realism, Polish Romanticism, Polish theater,* and *Hollywood cinema*—are discussed extensively in the fifth chapter of my first book on Wajda, *The Political Films of Andrzej Wajda.* It is also worth noting that other artistic influences have also been discussed at length by Tadeusz Miczka in his book *Artistic Inspirations in the Films and Television Productions of Andrzej Wajda.*

The reader has probably noticed that Wajda's films trigger an intense emotional response from me and from other reviewers as well. This observation prompts me to say, self-reflectively, that Wajda's films have such a general appeal, that they are so strongly commented upon in all corners of the globe (Japan and China are startling examples), because they convincingly express basic human emotions in real situations that are grounded in specific social conditions. There is something genuine in people torn by inner conflicts, in all the Macieks, Jasios, Staszeks, Agnieszkas, Karols, and Moryces. Basic human values like fairness, honesty, and honor, and feelings like love, hatred, despair, fear, and longing are vividly on display, reinforced by complex visuals, almost excessive acting, and elaborate music and sound.

We may argue ad infinitum as to whether this highly emotional content is delivered in an excessive, baroque, or kitschy way, yet Wajda's message remains clear and the presentation of his heroes in distress is highly convincing. Undoubtedly, the reception of Wajda's works depends on understanding Eastern European politics and culture; however, even without a knowledge of these nuances, spectators easily recognize the dilemmas of the protagonists in *Ashes and Diamonds, Man of Marble,* or *Promised Land,* the latter considered by many Polish critics to be the best Polish film ever made. Although I am often critical in my analysis of Wajda's films, I identify with several of his protagonists and understand their dilemmas profoundly. Agnieszka, Maciek, and the women from *The Young Ladies of Wilko* are particularly important to me. All of Wajda's characters, and the majority of the films that they inhabit, will remain with me for the rest of my days.

❀ NOTES

Introduction

1. The Manggha Center is Kraków's Japanese Center of Art and Technology, which opened on 30 November 1994. In the fall of 1987, when receiving the Kyoto Prize, Wajda proposed that the center be built. From that day on, as Etsuko Katano, the director of the Iwanami Hall, recalls, its proponents collected funds for building the center mostly in Tokyo and later throughout Japan. The fundraising lasted seven years; at the end, thanks to the help of 138,000 contributors and to the support of both the Polish and Japanese governments, the goal was reached. The Manggha Center has become a vital center of cultural exchange between Poland and Japan.

2. Wajda, *Podwójne spojrzenie* (Warszawa, 1998), 39–43.

3. Wajda, *Kino i reszta świata* (Kraków, 2000), 199.

4. Janina Falkowska, *The Political Films of Andrzej Wajda* (Oxford, 1996), 34–35.

5. Michel Foucault, "What Is an Author?" (Ithaca, 1977), 113–38.

Chapter One

1. Maria Dąbrowska (1889–1965) is the most prominent representative of social and psychological Realist prose. Her best-known book, *Noce i dnie* (*Nights and Days, 1933*), tells the life stories of several families of the intelligentsia and gentry.

2. Private letter from Andrzej Wajda to Janina Falkowska, 7 October 2001.

3. Jan Matejko (1838–93) is considered by Poles to be one of Poland's most prominent painters, specializing in historical paintings; he produced impressive, monumental compositions about historical events in Poland. Some of his most well-known works are *Kazanie Skargi* (*Skarga's Sermon*), *Bitwa pod Grunwaldem* (*Battle at Grunwald*), and *Hołd pruski* (*Prussian Tribute*).

Jacek Malczewski (1854–1929) is the most prominent representative of the Młoda Polska (Young Poland) movement in painting. He is especially known for his symbolic paintings such as *Cykl Zatrutej Studni* (*The Cycle of the Poisoned Well*). The influence of this painter is especially vivid in Wajda's *The Birchwood*.

Artur Grottger (1837–67) is the Romantic artist and painter who portrayed the perils of the *Powstanie styczniowe* (January Insurrection). His best-known works are *Warszawa I, Warszawa II, Polonia,* and *Lituania*.

Michał Elwiro Andriolli (1836–95) is the creator of highly romanticized drawings for Adam Mickiewicz's *Pan Tadeusz,* which served as the aesthetic basis for Wajda's film.

4. *Kalendarium,* whence comes much of Wajda's biography, is an elaborate typewritten calendar of the major events in Wajda's life, starting from his birth. Compiled by Wajda himself together with several collaborators, *Kalendarium* served as an excellent primary source for this book. At present, Wajda's *Kalendarium* is in the Andrzej Wajda Archives at the Manggha Center in Kraków.

5. According to the certificate issued by Dobrowolski, Wajda studied at his School of Drawing, Painting, and Sculpture from 1942 to 1946 *(Kalendarium).*

6. The Home Army (or National Army) was the clandestine Polish army that participated in numerous battles with the Germans and that also initiated the *Powstanie warszawskie* (Warszawa Uprising). The army was dissolved in 1945, but many of its officers continued covert activities after the "liberation" of Poland by the Soviets; they were also vehemently opposed to Soviet domination in Poland. References to the dilemmas and ideological choices of Home Army officers are depicted in both *Ashes and Diamonds* and *The Crowned-Eagle Ring.*

7. Andrzej Wróblewski (1927–57) was a friend of Wajda and a postwar painter whose powerful war-related paintings greatly influenced Wajda's own work.

8. Falkowska, *The Political Films of Andrzej Wajda* (Oxford, 1996), 57–58.

9. Norman Davies, *Heart of Europe* (Oxford, 1984), 6–10.

10. The following two books deal extensively with the history of the State Film School in Łódź:

Krzysztof Krubski et al., *Filmówka* (Warszawa, 1986); and

Lemann, Jolanta, ed. *Państwowa Wyższa Szkoła Filmowa Telewizyjna i Teatralna im. Leona Schillera w Łodzi 1948–1998* (Łódź, 1998).

11. *Kalendarium,* entry for 1950.

12. This film was finished only in 1955.

13. Wanda Wertenstein, *Wajda mówi o sobie* (Kraków, 1991), 9.

14. Marek Haltof, *Polish National Cinema* (New York, 2002), 74–75. See also note 26 in this chapter.

15. During this very busy time, Wajda was also going through divorce proceedings with Gabriela Obręba (see also note 25 in this chapter).

16. Maciej Karpiński, *The Theater of Andrzej Wajda* (Cambridge, 1989).

17. Wajda, *O polityce, o sztuce, o sobie* (Warszawa, 2000), 67.

18. Karpiński, *The Theater of Andrzej Wajda,* 23–24.

19. *Kino* is the most influential film monthly in Poland, and professors of Film Studies and distinguished film critics contribute regularly.

20. Wajda reluctantly provided information on his four wives, suggesting that his early marital experiences did not merit critical analysis (see private letter from Andrzej Wajda to Janina Falkowska, dated 7 October 2001). The following information is based on what the director himself wrote: Wajda married Gabriela Obręba, a student of the Kraków Academy of Fine Arts, in 1949 (she entered the academy in 1946, at the same time as Wajda). The ceremony took place in the Kraków Registry. They were divorced after ten years, on 19 August 1959. Gabriela died in 2000.

Zofia Zyczkowska, also a student of painting at the Warszawa Academy of Fine Arts, married Wajda on 19 December 1959 at the Registry in Warszawa. They were divorced after seven years, on 26 November 1966. Zofia died several years ago.

On 13 May 1967, Wajda married actress Beata Tyszkiewicz, with whom he has his only child, Karolina Wajda. Wajda and Beata were divorced on 28 July 1969.

Krystyna Zachwatowicz is the director's present wife. They were married at the Warszawa-Żoliborz Registry on 30 October 1975. Krystyna is also a graduate of the Academy of Fine Arts in Kraków, specializing in set design. She worked as a set designer at the famous Piwnica pod Baranami, and at present is a professor at two universities in Kraków: the Academy of Fine Arts and Państwowa Wyższa Szkoła Teatralna.

21. For Pec-Ślesicka's comments on her work with Wajda, see her interview with Małgorzata Dipont, "Jak się robi filmy—mówi Barbara Pec-Ślesicka, kierownik produkcji Zespołu X," in *Życie Warszawy* 176, dated 27 July 1978. Pec-Ślesicka remarks that Wajda tried to avoid employing women in his film crew until he met her.

22. In this year, Wajda also starts a series of conversations with Stanisław Janicki about his unrealized films. The purpose of these conversations was to coauthor a book called *Filmy Niezrealizowane*. As noted in *Kalendarium* (entry for 1969), the text of the book was printed in a monthly called *Film na Świecie*.

23. Unit X's film production (1972–83) is discussed in Wertenstein, *Zespół Filmowy X* (Warszawa 1991).

24. Other artists include Laco Adamik, Ryszard Bugajski, Jerzy Domaradzki, Feliks Falk, Janusz Kijowski, Marcel Łoziński, Radosław Piwowarski, Barbara Sass-Zdort, Janusz Zaorski, Tomasz Zygadło, and Andrzej Żuławski.

25. *Kalendarium*, entries for 1970–76.

26. Generally, the most important films of the School of Moral Concern, apart from Wajda's three contributions, are considered to be Krzysztof Zanussi's *Barwy ochronne* (*Camouflage*, 1977), *Constans* (*The Constant Factor*, 1980), *Kontrakt* (1980), and *Spirala* (*Spiral*, 1978); Feliks Falk's *Wodzirej* (*Top Dog*, 1978); Agnieszka Holland's *Aktorzy prowincjonalni* (*Provincial Actors*, 1979); and Krzysztof Kieślowski's *Amator* (*Camera Buff*, 1979). The production of *Camouflage* and *Man of Marble* in 1977 caused serious perturbations in party circles: the vice-minister of culture was demoted, his place filled by Janusz Wilhelmi, one of the most repressive party *apparatchiks*. Thanks to Wilhelmi's intervention, production on Andrzej Żuławski's famous science-fiction film *Na srebrnym globie* was stopped and the distribution of *Wodzirej* was forbidden. Wilhelmi died in an airline accident only a year after his appointment, and control over the production and distribution of films relaxed somewhat.

Lawrence Wechsler suggests that the trend of Moral Concern was later continued by other prominent filmmakers until as late as the 1980s. He also suggests the inclusion of other films than the ones mentioned here. He calls the nine films he discusses in his article the "Banned Films," "the films of suppressed visions." They are Antoni Krauze's *Prognoza pogody* (*The Weather Forecast*, 1982); Agnieszka Holland's *Kobieta samotna* (*A Woman Alone*, 1988); Krzysztof Kieślowski's *Przypadek* (*Blind Chance*, 1987); Janusz Zaorski's *Matka królów* (*Mother of Kings*, 1987); Jerzy Domaradzki's *Wielki bieg* (*The Big Run*, 1987); Feliks Falk's *Był jazz* (*There Was Jazz*, 1984); Piotr Szulkin's *Wojna Światów* (*War of the Worlds*, 2000); and Ryszard Bugajski's *Przesłuchanie* (*Interrogation*, 1989). All of these films attest to Wechsler's assertion that "culture in Poland has invariably stood for more, in degree and kind, than a heritage of works in which artists related 'the adventures of their souls.' It has always been a meeting place of social, historical, civic and moral debate." Wechsler, "Banned Films," *Cineaste* 13, no. 3 (1984), 11–13.

To these films, Bolesław Michałek also adds Janusz Kijowski's *Kung-fu* (1980), produced by Unit X. Michałek, "Lokalny Film, Prowincjonalna Krytyka. Rozmowa z Bolesławem Michałkiem, krytykiem filmowym, kierownikiem literackim Zespołu X" *Kierunki* 14, no. 5 (May 5, 1981).

27. Komitet Obrony Robotników (The Workers' Defense Committee), an underground dissident organization, was active from 1976 to 1981. Adam Michnik and Jacek Kuroń were its leaders.

28. Nina Darnton, "Poland's Man of Films," *New York Times Magazine* (1981), 141.

29. Andrzej Chodakowski and Andrzej Zajączkowski, *Robotnicy 1980 (The Workers '80,* 1981).

30. Wajda, *Moje Notatki z Historii.* Akson Studio + Kanał Plus, 1996. This series of programs consists of five parts: (1) Jeszcze nie zginęła, (2) Miedzy wojnami, (3) Życie na niby; (4) Wiedzieliśmy czego od nas chcą, and (5) Oni budowali nasze szczęście. In these films, Wajda personally describes some of the more important historical issues he has presented in his films.

31. Private letter no. 2 (Andrzej Wajda to Janina Falkowska), 7 October 2001. According to this letter, the momentous meetings with Wałęsa include the participation in the Komitet Doradczy Lecha Wałęsy in 1984, the funeral of Jerzy Popiełuszko in the same year, the meeting with Wałęsa on the occasion of the release of interned Solidarity activists in 1986, and the preparation of the Miodowicz-Wałęsa debate for Polish television.

32. Komitet Ocalenia Kinematografii was founded in the early months of 1981. Its purpose, among other things, was to ensure the financial viability of the film industry in Poland and to cut industry ties to state financial support, which was mostly politically motivated. Wajda foresaw self-sufficiency and self-financing of the film industry, and these projections were fully realized after Solidarity came to power in 1989.

For further discussion of Komitet Ocalenia Kinematografii, see Krzysztof Kłopotowski, "Uzupełniam swój życiorys," *Tygodnik Solidarność* no. 2 (April 1981), 14.

33. *Kalendarium,* entry for 1980.

34. Such libelous articles appeared, for example, in *Barwy,* a rightist weekly publication supported by the organization known as Grunwald. (See *Kalendarium* entries for 1980–81.)

35. This is the anniversary of one of the first anti-Socialist demonstrations in Poland (*Kalendarium,* 1981).

36. Falkowska, *Dialogism in the Films of Andrzej Wajda,* 64–67.

37. *Fakty* 19 (14 May 1983).

38. Barbara Hollender, "Andrzej Wajda—Dowódca i Poeta" (Warszawa, 1995), 240.

39. *Kalendarium,* entry for 1986.

40. Private letter from Lech Wałęsa to Andrzej Wajda, dated 4 September 1988.

41. The first democratic government led by Tadeusz Mazowiecki was elected in 1989. For further explanation, see *Mała Encyklopedia PWN* (Warszawa: Wydawnictwo Naukowe PWN, 1999), 758.

42. Falkowska and Haltof, *The New Polish Cinema* (Trowbridge, 2003).

43. Maria Kornatowska, "Polish Cinema," *Cineaste* 19, no. 4 (1993): 47.
44. Ibid., 48–49.
45. Pat Dowell, "The Man Who Put Poland on the Post War Map of Cinema," *Cineaste* 19, no. 4 (1993): 52.
46. Ibid., 53.

Chapter Two

1. Tadeusz Kubiak is a Polish poet specializing in moody lyrics about ordinary people, although he also creates satiric poems and children's poems.
2. "Nie ma żelaznego scenariusza filmu dokumentalnego" in Andrzej Wajda, "Eksplikacja reżyserska filmu *Ceramika Iłżecka*." Andrzej Wajda Archives.
3. Notes on *A Generation*. Andrzej Wajda Archives. Original text: Czego się nauczyłem w Szkole na Targowej? To dobre pytanie. Zależy jak na to spojrzeć. Jeśli od strony wykładów i ćwiczeń szkolnych, to niewiele. Nie zaznajomiono nas praktycznie ani z zasadami inscenizacji, ani techniką reżyserowania aktorów. Dużo mówiło się ale dość ogólnie o sztuce filmowej, ale ja warsztat reżysera zobaczyłem na praktyce u Forda, no i tyle co się sam naciąłem robiąc moje trzy nieudane etiudy (które zresztą, ilekroć wracałem do szkoły jako wykładowca studenci pokazywali mi zawsze zręcznie wtykając pomiędzy swoje prace, które byłem zobowiązany obejrzeć). Ale w tych właśnie nieudanych etiudach była dla mnie cała wartość Szkoły Filmowej w Łódzi. Nie tylko zrozumiałem, ale odcierpiałem moje błędy w tych filmikach, przez lata wracałem do nich, żeby dać sobie dokładną i prawdziwą odpowiedź, jak to powinno być zrobione.
4. Haltof, *Polish National Cinema* (New York, 2002), 73–109.
5. Ibid., 74.
6. Ibid., 74–76.
7. Dennis de Nitto and William Herman, *Film and the Critical Eye* (New York, 1975), 364.
8. See, for instance, Mirosław Derecki, "Wajda niepokorny. Rozmowa z prof. Aleksandrem Jackiewiczem," *Kamena* 13 (21 June 1981).
9. Wajda, *Double Vision* (New York, 1989).
10. I have held several conversations with Wajda (between 1998 and 2000 in particular) that helped clarify some bibliographical issues.
11. Letter from the rector of the Łódź Film School to Andrzej Wajda, dated 19 January 1954. Andrzej Wajda Archives.
12. The Gwardia Ludowa (People's Guard) was a clandestine military organization of the Polish Workers' Party and operated in the years 1942–43. The organization fought using sabotage and clandestine operations against German police and their communication lines. In 1944, it was renamed Armia Ludowa (People's Army). For other details, see *Mała Encyklopedia* (1999), 278.
13. Płażewski et al., eds., *Wajda Films I* (Warszawa, 1996), 35.
14. For interesting suggestions on this issue, see the following book: Ewa Mazierska and Elżbieta Ostrowska, *Women in Polish Cinema* (New York, 2006).
15. Poland went through three partitions of its territory by Russia, Prussia, and Austria. The first partition took place in 1772, the second in 1793 (without

Austria's participation), and the third in 1795. These partitions had a great influence on the rise of nationalistic feelings in Poles. The play *Dziady* (*Forefathers' Eve*, 1832) was written by Adam Mickiewicz (1798–55), an accomplished representative of Polish Romanticism, the most famous of Polish poets, and a die-hard proponent of liberation ideals.

16. Stanisław Grzelecki, *"Pokolenie," Życie Warszawy* 27 (1 Feb 1955).

17. Ibid.

18. This relation between love, politics, and the gender politics they embrace has been discussed in Elżbieta Ostrowska, "Dangerous Liaisons: Wajda's Discourse of Sex, Love and Nation," *The Cinema of Andrzej Wajda. The Art of Irony and Defiance* (London, 2003), 46–63.

19. Derek Hill, "Young Polish Anarchists," *Tribune* (24 Jun 1960).

20. Płażewski et al., *Wajda Films I*, 32.

21. Ibid., 31–36.

22. The most famous postwar films dealing with the themes of war are Leonard Buczkowski's *Zakazane piosenki* (*Forbidden Songs*, 1947), Wanda Jakubowska's *Ostatni etap* (*The Last Stage*, 1948), and *Ulica graniczna* (*Border Street*, 1949).

23. Roman Polański, *Roman* (Warszawa, 1989), 87–89.

24. The committee met on 8 July 1953. The following participants were present: President Albrecht; Citizens Czeszko, Gromb, Starski, Toeplitz, and Żywulska; and the director Karpowski. Excerpts from the discussion are presented in Płażewski et al., *Wajda Films I*, 31–32.

25. Płażewski et al., *Wajda Films I*, 31.

26. Andrzej Wajda Archives.

27. Płażewski et al., *Wajda Films I*, 37.

28. Grzelecki, *Życie Warszawy* 27 (Warszawa, 1955). Original text:
W wielu scenach filmu uderza właśnie owa intensywność widzenia, wzmocniona jeszcze kontrastowym montażem. Montaż, oparty na nagłych przejściach, jest jednym ze środków filmowych, służących wydobyciu atmosfery okupacyjnych dni, kiedy nagłość wydarzeń zaskakiwała ludzi, kiedy tak wiele spraw rozstrzygało się w krótkich, pełnych napięcia chwilach, kiedy sytuacja nieustannej walki każdy róg ulicy czyniła progiem nieznanego.

29. Hill, "Young Polish Anarchists."

30. Adam Ważyk, "Opinia dla Komisji Scenariuszowej" (Warszawa, 1953). Andrzej Wajda Archives.

31. Polański, *Roman*, 87–89.

32. Jerzy Wilmański, "Cztery Pokolenia," *Odgłosy* 41 (14 Oct 1973).

33. Płażewski et al., *Wajda Films I*, 10.

34. Ibid., 49.

35. Original text: *"po co się krwawiło, żeby jak szczury …"* ("why did we have to bleed like this when we escape like rats, after all …").

36. Ryszard Bugajski et al., "Stulecie kina: świadectwo wieku czy zbiór mitów?" *Więź*. Sierpień 8, no. 442 (1995): 19. Original text:
W filmie *Kanał* nie mogłem pokazać, że po drugiej stronie Wisły stoją radzieckie wojska, kiedy na tym brzegu dogorywa powstanie. Wystarczyło jednak, że doprowadziłem moich bohaterów do wylotu Kanału, z którego patrzyli na drugi brzeg. Publiczność wiedziała już co mam jej do powiedzenia, porozumiewaliśmy się bez słów, symbolicznym, magicznym prawie językiem.

37. Płażewski et al., *Wajda Films I*, 47.

38. Ibid., 45.

39. For other awards the film received, consult the filmography.

40. On the romantic tradition in Wajda's films, see Maria Janion, "Wajda I wartości," *Odnawianie znaczeń* (Kraków, 1980), 112–19; "Egzystencja ludzi i duchów. Rodowód filmowej wyobraźni Andrzeja Wajdy," *Projekt krytyki fantazmatycznej* (Warszawa, 1991), 110–19; "Jeruzalem Słoneczna i Zaklęty Krąg," *Płacz generała* (Warszawa, 1998), 261–71; and Andrzej Kotliński, "Kawaleria Wajdy," *Filmowy Świat Andrzeja Wajdy* (Kraków, 2003), 119–39.

41. Płażewski et al., *Wajda Films I*, 49.

42. Władysław Bartoszewski, *Stolica* (Warszawa, 1957).

43. Bolesław Michałek, *Teatr i Film* (Warszawa, 1957).

44. Płażewski, "Sukces polskiego filmu w Cannes. Korespondencja własna," *Teatr i Film* no. 1 (1957): 12.

45. The members of the Commission were Tadeusz Konwicki, Jerzy Kawalerowicz, Wilhelm Mach, Jerzy Stefan Stawiński, and Jerzy Zarzycki (as reported in *Wajda Films I* 45).

46. Płażewski et al., *Wajda Films I*, 47.

47. Jean de Boroncelli, *Le Monde* (10 May 1957).

48. Wolfgang Ebert, *Die Zeit* (1 Aug 1958).

49. Bosley Crowther, *New York Times* (10 May 1961).

50. *Cahiers du Cinema* (June 1957).

51. The following quotation sheds more light on this issue: "A nation is a spiritual principle, the outcome of the profound complication of history; it is a spiritual family not a group determined by the shape of the earth.... Two things, which in truth are but one, constitute this soul or spiritual principle. One lies in the past, one in the present. One is the possession in common of a rich legacy of memories; the other is present-day consent, the desire to live together, the will to perpetuate the value of the heritage that one has received in an undivided form." Ernest Renan, "What is a nation?" *Nation and Narration* (London, 1990), 18–19.

52. Renan, "What is a nation?" 19.

53. Wajda, "Moje notatki z historii," *Kwartalnik Filmowy*, no. 15–16 (Fall–Winter 1996/1997): 7–21. Original text:

Aby dalej życ, trzeba zapomnieć, a żeby zapomnieć, trzeba utrwalić nasze doświadczenia, nasze przeżycia, całą przeszłość, która pozostała za nami. Losy chłopców z Kanału, Tadeusza z Krajobrazu po bitwie, Marcina z Pierścionka z orłem w koronie, a także Maćka Chełmickiego z Popiołu i Diamentu, mogły być moim udziałem. Po prostu miałem więcej szczęścia. Przypadek sprawił, że nie znalazłem się w ich sytuacji, więc moim obowiązkiem było na miarę mojego talentu, moich zdolności i moich możliwości opowiedzieć o ich losach.

54. Beata Sowińska, "Jerzy Andrzejewski o *Popiele i diamencie.*" *Stolica* 8, no. 43 (1958): 18. Original text:

Zamiar ekranizacji mojej powieści zrodził się już dawno, bo w latach 1948– 49. Myśleli wówczas o zrobieniu filmu Erwin Axer oraz Antonioni Bohdziewicz. Z różnych przyczyn plany te nie doszły do skutku. Jesienią roku ubiegłego przyszedł do mnie Wajda z koncepcją zrobienia z Popiołu i Diamentu scenariusza filmowego. Zasiedliśmy razem do pisania w Oborach. Praca pochłonęła z górą miesiąc. Zdecydowalismy się na ograniczenie pewnych wątków powieści, jak również na zamknięcie całości filmu w 24-ch godzinach, starając się w ten sposób uzyskać klasyczną jedność czasu.

55. The Armia Krajowa (Home Army) was a military organization started in 1939, the purpose of which was to fight the German enemy in concert with other military organizations of the Polish armed forces. It answered to the Polish government on emigration in London. After the end of the war, on 19 January 1945, the Home Army was dissolved, but some of its members continued their fight for independence, a fact referred to in the film *Ashes and Diamonds* (*Mała Encyklopedia PWN* 46).

56. For other comments see De Nitto and Herman, "*Ashes and Diamonds*," 365.

57. Ibid., 363–67.

58. Marek Hendrykowski, "Styl i kompozycja *Popiołu i diamentu* Andrzeja Wajdy," *Analizy i interpretacje* (Katowice, 1984), 72–92, 75. Original text: "w dramacie historii *nolens volens* uczestniczą wszyscy."

59. Maciek's famous comments on his dark glasses are, respectively, "pamiątka nieodwzajemnionej miłości do ojczyzny" and "za długo spacerowałem po kanałach."

60. This translation of the poem comes from De Nitto and Herman, "*Ashes and Diamonds*," 384. Original text:

Coraz to z ciebie, jako z drzazgi smolnej.
Wokoło lecą szmaty zapalone
Gorejąc nie wiesz, czy stawasz się wolny,
Czy to, co twoje, ma być zatracone?
Czy popiół tylko zostanie i zamęt
Co idzie w przepaść z burzą?–
Czy zostanie
Na dnie popiołu gwiaździsty dyjament,
Wiekuistego zwycięstwa zaranie . . . .

61. Haltof, *Polish National Cinema*, 87–88.

62. De Nitto and Herman, "*Ashes and Diamonds*," 367.

63. Hendrykowski, "Styl i kompozycja *Popiołu i diamentu* Andrzeja Wajdy." As Hendrykowski comments, the subplot of Marek Szczuka, absent in the original novel by Andrzejewski, was considered by some critics to be *niepotrzebne naddanie* (an unnecessary addition).

64. For other comments on the father-son relation in the film, see Paul Coates, "Forms of the Polish Intellectual's Self-Criticism: Revisiting *Ashes and Diamonds* with Andrzejewski and Wajda," *Canadian Slavonic Papers* 38, nos. 3–4 (1996): 287–303.

65. Hendrykowski, "Realizm i symbolizm *Popiołu i diamentu* Andrzeja Wajdy," *Kino* 1 (1972): 25–27.

66. Hendrykowski, "Styl i kompozycja *Popiołu i diamentu* Andrzeja Wajdy," 88. Original text:

Opowiadając na nowo historię Maćka Chełmickiego, nadał jej Wajda wymiar niepowtarzalnie konkretny i zarazem mityczny. Uobecnienie ekranowe ludzkiego dramatu, który przez lata poprzednie pozostawał dla naszego kina tematem tabu, dokonało się w kształcie zdumiewającym i rewelacyjnym. Wtargnięcie w sferę mitu nie było bynajmniej reżyserowi potrzebne po to, by uzyskać wydźwięk patetyczny, lecz po to, aby pomnożonym przez wiele tysięcy przypadków biografiom ludzi takich, jak Maciek przywrócić nareszcie właściwy im wymiar tragiczny, do którego odebrano im przedtem prawo.

67. Ibid., 75. Original text: *"chwyt maksymalnego zagęszczenia i nasycenia czasu oraz przestrzeni filmowej."*

68. Conversation with Wajda in 2000.

69. Wajda, *Double Vision*, 74. Original text:
coś' nieuchwytnego pomiędzy dwiękiem i obrazem, co stanowi duszę filmu. Owszem, można wyciąć z *Popiołu i Diamentu* te czy inne słowa, ale nie można ocenzurować gry Zbyszka Cybulskiego; a przecież w jego sposobie zachowania tkwiło to 'coś,' co w owych czasach było polityczną nieprzyzwoitością: wolność chłopca w ciemnych okularach wobec narzuconej rzeczywistości.

70. The People's Army was composed of regular conscripts, usually representatives of lower classes in Poland who were trained by the Red Army in the former Soviet Union in the years 1941–45 (*Mała Encyklopedia* PWN 46–47).

71. "Protokół z dyskusji nad filmem pt. 'Popiół i Diament.'" (Protocol from the discussion of the film *Ashes and Diamonds*) 12 July 1958. Andrzej Wajda Archives.

72. Private letter written by Wajda. Andrzej Wajda Archives.

73. Płażewski et al., *Wajda Films I*, 70.

74. Derecki, "Wajda niepokorny." Original text:
Nawet mentor Wajdy, Aleksander Ford proponował mi sojusz w zwalczaniu "szkoły polskiej." Robił to z pozycji jeszcze stalinowskich; w dużej mierze chodziło o *Popiół i diament*—że zbyt "narodowy," zbyt "patriotyczny." Siły w kręgu partii z którymi się identyfikował Ford, były wówczas jeszcze tak wpływowe, że *Popiołu i diamentu* nigdy nie wystawiono na żadnym festiwalu filmowym do konkursu. Więcej: ówczesny dyrektor Naczelnego Zarządu Kinematografii, Jerzy Lewiński, który dopuścił, żeby *Popiół i diament* został pokazany poza konkursem na festiwalu w Wenecji, podobno przypłacił tę decyzję utratą stanowiska.

75. Płażewski et al., *Wajda Films I*, 70–71.

76. Ibid., 70–75.

77. Hendrykowski, "Realizm i symbolizm *Popiołu i diamentu* Andrzeja Wajdy," 27. Original text:
Niektórzy spośród krytyków byli po prostu wystarczająco leniwi, żeby przypisywać Wajdzie skłonność do "manierycznej barokowości" oraz "pustej ornamentyki," ale nie dość pracowici, by zadać sobie trud odszukania sensu w tym, co uznali za bezsensowne—i nie dość odważni, by przyznać, że nie potrafią go odkryć tam, gdzie ozdoba i znaczenie wynikają z siebie nawzajem.

78. *Kalendarium.*

79. The short story "Lotna" is taken from Wojciech Żukrowski's *Selection of Short Stories* (Warszawa, 1972).

80. On the discussion of the uhlan charge, see Kotliński, "Kawaleria Wajdy," 119–39.

81. "Wojenko, wojenko" is a sad song about the fate of soldiers during a military conflict: *"Wojenko, wojenko, cóżes ty za pani, że za tobą idą, że za tobą idą chłopcy*

malowani." ("War, war, what a lady you are. Handsome men always follow you.")

82. Artur Grottger (1837–67) produced well-known romantic paintings and drawings that glorified the January Insurrection (1863–64) in Poland.

83. Anna Rozicka, *"Lotna*-tekst zredukowany," *Film i kontekst* (Wrocław, 1988), 137.

84. Ibid., 138.

85. Alicja Helman, "Sarmata na płonącej żyrafie," *Ekran* 42 (1959).

86. On the cult of cavalry in prewar Poland, see Chris Caes, "Catastrophic Spectacles: Historical Trauma and the Masculine Subject in *Lotna,*" *The Cinema of Andrzej Wajda: The Art of Irony and Defiance* (London, 2003), 116–31.

87. Krzysztof Teodor Toeplitz, "Podzwonne kawaleryjskiej Polski," *Świat* (18 Oct 1959): 17.

88. Stanisław Grzelecki, "Poezja rekwizytów," *Życie Warszawy* (8 Oct 1959): 4.

89. Stanisław Ozimek, "Prosto do nieba czwórkami szli," *Film* 41 (11 Oct 1959).

90. Zygmunt Kałużyński, "Koszmar kawaleryjski czyli koniec Polski szlacheckiej," *Polityka* 43 (24 Oct 1959).

91. Andrzej Kijowski, "Jak powstaje szmira," *Przegląd Kulturalny* 44 (1959).

92. Andrzej Werner, *Polskie, arcypolskie....* (London, 1987). Quoted by Chris Caes in his unpublished paper "Modernity, Masculinity and Spectacle," presented at the international conference "Filmowe i teatralne światy Andrzeja Wajdy" at the Łódz University in Poland in 2001.

93. Ibid.

94. Marcel Martin, *Cinéma* 65 (Apr 1965).

95. Guy Gauthier, *Image et Son* (Oct 1965).

96. The Board of Cinema (Zarząd Kinematografii) was part of the Polish Ministry of Culture.

97. Letter to Prezes Zarządu Kinematografii, Minister Tadeusz Zaorski, dated 20 July 1959. Andrzej Wajda Archives.

98. Wajda's private notes on *Lotna*. Andrzej Wajda Archives.

99. Wajda, *Podwójne spojrzenie* (Warszawa, 1998), 41.

100. Zbigniew Kałużyński, "Koszmar kawaleryjski czyli koniec Polski Szlacheckiej," *Polityka* 43 (24 Oct 1959).

101. Caes, "Modernity, Masculinity and Spectacle."

Chapter Three

1. Skolimowski, a young up-and-coming boxer at the time, later became a well-known director himself. Skolimowski was also a poet and the youngest member of the Polish Writers' Union.

2. Jerzy Andrzejewski, "Znów po latach zapragnąłem powrócić do odległych cieni . . . ." (Andrzej Wajda Archives—letter to Andrzej Wajda).

3. Ibid. Original text:

Mieli wówczas: on, plutonowy podchorąży Hektor z batalionu "Zośka"— lat osiemnaście, ona, łączniczka Ewa z "Parasola"—rok może nawet dwa mniej, więc w kształtach najpierwszej młodości błądzą oboje u skraju zapomnienia, już tylko jako zanikające cienie zatrzymani i utrwaleni w czasie, na którym szczęk gwałtownych oręży wycisnął szczególnie dramatyczne piętno.

4. Komisja Ocen Scenariuszy, 28 April 1959. Present at the meeting were Minister Zaorski and Citizens Andrzejewski, Adler, Arct, Bratny, Goldberg, Hager, Karpowski, Konwicki, Lewiński, Pollak, Skowroński, Ścibor-Rylski, Skolimowski, and Starski. Andrzej Wajda Archives.

5. Komisja Ocen Scenariuszy. Original text: "Chodziłoby o to, żeby ten utwór coś wniósł do naszego życia, to jest dramat maskowania czy braku uczuć i na ten temat mamy prawo zrobić film i mamy prawo coś powiedzieć. To jest film, który te idee realizuje, pokazuje to w sposob moralny i zapewniam, że problem ten w takiej formie znajdzie się na ekranie." Andrzej Wajda Archives.

6. Płażewski et al., *Wajda Films I*, 102. Both comments come from the letter sent to Wajda by the Department of Pastoral Assistance in Warszawa after the film's premiere. The letter is dated 7 January 1961. Andrzej Wajda Archives.

7. Ibid., 103.

8. Robert Vas, *Sight and Sound* (London, 1961–62).

9. Płażewski et al., *Wajda Films I*, 103–4.

10. Kazimierz Brandys, *Samson* (Warszawa, 1960).

11. Michał Mirski, "Bronię Prawdy Samsona," *Polityka* 48 (Dec 1961), credits these attacks to the representatives of the Obóz Narodowo Radykalny (ONR) (National Radical Organization), a right-wing organization that started its activities in 1934, which was officially dissolved later that year by the authorities, and which then acted illegally afterwards (*Encyclopedia PWN*, Warszawa, 544). Composed of young men, mainly university students, the ONR advocated the "national purity" of Poland.

12. Norman Davies, *A History of Poland* (New York, 1982), 418.

13. Mirski, "Bronię Prawdy Samsona."

14. Ibid.

15. Based on the original letter from Kazimierz Brandys to Wajda, Warszawa, 23 October 1961. Andrzej Wajda Archives.

16. Georges Sadoul, *Les Lettres Françaises* (Paris, 1964).

17. Miron Czernienko, *Andrzej Wajda* (Moskwa, 1965).

18. Maria Oleksiewicz, Samson [rubryka: Dzisiejszy program] *Żołnierz Polski* 39. Warszawa (24 Sep 1961).

19. Plażewski, "Zbyt piękne, by było prawdziwe," *Przegląd Kulturalny* 473. Warszawa (21 Sep 1961).

20. Płażewski et al., *Wajda Films I*, 110.

21. Czernienko, *Andrzej Wajda*.

22. Klaus Eder, *Andrzej Wajda* (Munich, 1980).

23. Zdzisław Beryt, "Samotność Samsona," *Gazeta Poznańska*. Poznań (2 Sep 1961).

24. Płażewski et al., *Wajda Films I*, 125.

25. Ibid., 126.

26. Richard Roud, *Sight and Sound* (London, 1962).

27. Gene Moskovitz, *Variety*. New York (20 May 1964).

28. Józef Hen, "Prawoslawny Andrzej Wajda," *Film* 15, Warszawa (12 Apr 1964).

29. Andrzej Zakrzewski, "Wajda i jasny," *Tygodnik Kulturalny* 13. Warszawa (29 Mar 1964).

30. Płażewski et al., *Wajda Films I*, 126.

31. Yves Boisset, *Cinéma 62*. Paris (Jul–Aug 1962).

32. Płażewski et al., *Wajda Films I*, 143.

33. Ibid., 152.

34. Ibid., 143.

35. Andrzej Żuławski, "Jak opowiedziec te historie?" *Film* 34. Warszawa (16 Aug 1964).

36. Andrzej Kijowski, "O *Popiolach*," *Ekran* 43. Warszawa (24 Oct 1965); and Rafał Marszałek, "Nasi klasycy," *Współczesność* 21. Warszawa (20 Oct 1965).

37. Stefan Morawski, "Kto ma rację?" *Ekran* 48. Warszawa (28 Nov 1965).

38. Stefan Żółkiewski, "Wokół *Popiołów*. Poezja i pasja spoleczna," *Film* 42. Warszawa (17 Oct 1965).

39. Płażewski et al., *Wajda Films I*, 155–56.

40. Ibid.

41. Urs Jenny, *Süddeutsche Zeitung*. Munich (7 May 1966).

42. Peter W. Jansen, *Filmkritik*. Frankfurt u/M (Jun 1967).

43. Beata Sowińska, "Jerzy Andrzejewski o *Popiele i diamencie*," *Stolica* 8, no. 43 (1958): 18. Original text:

myślimy o (następnym scenariuszu) razem z Wajdą. Piszę obecnie książke pod tytułem "Bramy raju." Jest to powieść historyczna, dziejąca się w początkach 13 wieku, kiedy to załamały się wyprawy krzyżowe. Bohaterami są tu dzieci francuskie, które udały się na krucjatę do Ziemi Świętej. Co zafascynowało mnie głównie?—Niezmienność ludzkich uczuć i tęsknot w tym wypadku kilkunastoletnich dzieci, tęsknot, które w zetknięciu z rzeczywistoscią doznają klęski.

44. Płażewski et al., *Wajda Films I*, 162.

45. Ibid., 164.

46. Robert Benayoun, *Le Point*. Paris (5 Nov 1979).

47. Claude Michel Cluny, *Cinéma 79*. Paris (Dec 1979).

48. Bolesław Michałek, *The Cinema of Andrzej Wajda* (London, 1973).

49. That is, his body is only partially his own. A percentage of his body now "belongs" to another victim of the crash, while other parts are composed of various different fragments, each with its separate (deceased) owner.

50. Płażewski et al., *Wajda Films I*, 176.

51. Krzysztof Teodor Toeplitz, "Wajda Redivivus," *Film Quarterly* 23, no. 2 (Winter 1969–70): 37–41.

52. Ibid., 39.

53. Louis Marcorelles, *Le Monde*, Paris (13 Mar 1971). (Andrzej Wajda Archives)

54. Philip Strick, *Monthly Film Bulletin*. London (Feb 1969). (Andrzej Wajda Archives)

55. Krzysztof Mętrak, "'Ja na sprzedaż," *Film* 6. Warszawa (9 Feb 1969); Zygmunt Kałużynski, "Rozterki artystow," *Polityka* 4. Warszawa (25 Jan 1969); Joanna Guze, "Portret wlasny artysty z czasów dojrzałości," *Film* 5. Warszawa (2 Feb 1969).

56. Penelope Houston, *The Spectator*. London (21 Jun 1969).

57. Toeplitz, "Wajda Redivivus," 39–40. Also, see this article on the comparison between Konwicki's *Salto* and *Everything for Sale*, especially in its discussion of Zbigniew Cybulski's performance.

58. Davies, *Heart of Europe* (Oxford, 1984), 11.

59. The apartment had to be "arranged," not purchased. There was a scarcity of accommodation in Poland, so it was usually not money but connections with authorities in charge that could assure a person of the purchase.

60. The Palace of Culture in Warszawa was a huge building in the center of the city, built after World War II in the Social Realist style. The building is a symbol of Communist Poland, but also an object of jokes for whole generations of Poles.

61. On the emasculation of men and the syndrome of "Mother Poland," see Ewa Mazierska and Elżbieta Ostrowska, *Women in Polish Cinema* (New York, 2006).

62. Płażewski, "Dwa ramiona huśtawki," *Kino* 9. Warszawa (Sep 1969); Andrzej Werner, *Film*. Warszawa (17 Aug 1969).

63. Toeplitz, "Prowokacja Andrzeja Wajdy," *Kultura*. Warszawa (31 Aug 1969); Klaus Eder, *Andrzej Wajda* (Munich, 1980).

64. Mateusz Werner, qtd. in Płażewski et al., *Wajda Films I*, 209.

65. Piotr Borowiec, "Kariera senatora Wajdy," *Gazeta* 38 (1994): 38. Original text: "Każda niemal replika jest albo dwuznaczna, albo zupełnie pozbawiona logicznego sensu, ale fabuła filmu pokierowana jest znakomicie—rezultatem jest miażdżąca krytyka snobizmu niektórych środowisk pseudo-intelektualnych, a także bardzo celna parodia pewnej swoiście polskiej formy matriarchatu (gdzie żona ze ścierką twardo trzyma męża pod pantoflem)."

66. Toeplitz, "Wajda Redivivus," *Film Quarterly* 23, no. 2 (1969–70), 41.

67. Ibid., 40.

68. See Mazierska and Ostrowska, *Women in Polish Cinema*; Maria Malatyńska, "Poziomkowa polana," *Życie Literackie* (Kraków, 1986), 81–90.

Chapter Four

1. Płażewski et al., *Wajda Films I*, 215.

2. Stanisław Malczewski's symbolic and romantic paintings belong to the canonic representations of Polish culture and sensibility. In most of his paintings, Malczewski presents peasant women as symbolic representations of love, death, freedom, and so forth. This link between femininity, peasant roots, and high art is, among other things, what makes Malczewski so quintessentially Polish. This aspect of Polishness especially fascinated Wajda, who in this sense referred to Malczewski in many other films, such as *The Wedding*. For an in-depth analysis of the influence of art on Wajda's films, see Tadeusz Miczka, *Inspiracje plastyczne w twórczości filmowej i telewizyjnej Andrzeja Wajdy* (Katowice, 1987).

3. Jerzy Niesiobędzki, *Rozmowy istotne* (Gdańsk: Wydawnictwo Morskie, 1983), 28.

4. Etienne Lalou, *Le Figaro*. Paris (9 Feb 1978).

5. Jarosław Iwaszkiewicz, *Eros i Tanatos* (Warszawa, 1970).

6. André Cornand, *Image et Son*. Paris (Feb 1978).

7. Robert Chazal, *France-Soir*. Paris (1 Feb 1978).

8. Angelo Signorelli, *Cineforum*. Venice (Apr 1979).

9. Niesiobędzki, *Rozmowy istotne*, 28.

10. Melchior Wańkowicz, *Kultura*. Warszawa (4 Oct 1970).

11. Toeplitz, "Krajobraz po bitwie," *Miesięcznik Literacki* 7 (July 1970).

12. Waldemar Chołodowski, "Filmowa podróż do kresu pewnej moralności," *Tygodnik Kulturalny* 35 (30 Aug 1970); Alicja Helman, "Nasz wielki temat," *Fakty i Mysli* 16 (1970).

13. John Pym, *Monthly Film Bulletin.* London (Jan 1977).

14. Private letter of Agnieszka Osiecka to Andrzej Wajda. Płażewski et al., *Wajda Films I,* 239.

15. Dario Zanelli, *Il Resto Di Carlino.* Bologna (15 Mar 1970).

16. *La stampa.* Turin (18 Jul 1980).

17. Rob Baker, *Soho Weekly News.* New York (16 Feb 1978).

18. Alicja Helman, "Nasz wielki temat."

19. Davies, *God's Playground* (New York, 1982), 626.

20. Ibid., 626–33.

21. Zbigniew Kustosik, "Piłat w hitlerowskiej Kongresshalle. Andrzej Wajda mówi *Kurierowi* o realizacji filmu kręconego z udziałem polskich aktorów w RFN," *Kurier Polski* (14 Sep 1971).

22. Wanda Wertenstein, "Wariacje na znany temat: wywiad z Andrzejem Wajdą," *Kino* 3 (Mar 1975): 2–10.

23. Płażewski et al., *Wajda Films I,* 259.

24. Wertenstein, "Wariacje na znany temat," 8.

25. Anonymous letter to the Prime Minister, Piotr Jaroszewicz, dated 1 February 1975. Andrzej Wajda Archives.

26. Płażewski et al., *Wajda Films I,* 259.

27. Ibid., 260.

28. Eder, *Andrzej Wajda* (Munich, 1980).

29. Ugo Buzzolan, *La Stampa.* Turin (18 Oct 1980).

30. Kałużynski, "O Wajdzie bez znieczulenia," *Polityka* 49 (9 Dec 1978).

31. On the correspondences between the play and the film, see Elżbieta Wysińska, "Filmowa rzeczywistość *Wesela,*" *Film* (18 Feb 1973), 8–11.

32. For a theoretical analysis of the play and the film, see Janusz Plisiecki, "Analiza i interpretacja filmu *Wesele* Andrzeja Wajdy," *Studia Filmoznawcze* (Wrocław, 1997), 125–33.

33. Film Polski/Export and Import of Films brochure. Andrzej Wajda Archives.

34. Wernyhora, a legendary Cossack from Zaporoże who lived in the eighteenth century, was the author of mystical forecasts about the fate of Poland. Zawisza (Czarny) was a famous knight, a symbol of dignity and chivalric virtues, of the fifteenth century; he fought in the Battle of Grunwald. Stańczyk was a royal clown at the court of Zygmunt August II, the last of the Jagiellonian kings.

35. On the use of the art of painting in *Wesele,* see Toeplitz, "'Wesele' jak najdalej od kolorowej bajki," *Miesięcznik Literacki* 1 (Jan 1973), 74–77.

36. Ibid., 75.

37. *Chocholy* (straw men) are piles of hay usually set by peasants after harvest. They resemble human beings in shape.

38. For a more meticulous explanation on the specific situation of the peasantry during Poland's partition, see Jadwiga Łużyńska Dorobowa, "Filmowa wizja świadomości społeczno-narodowej chłopów w okresie zaborów," *Wieś i Rolnictwo* 2, no. 55 (1987), 88–104.

39. Original words taken from the play *The Wedding.*

40. Szela was the leader of the peasants in 1846 during the largest uprising in Galicia. He fought against the oppression of his people by their own rulers, a situation that lasted for several centuries in Poland.

41. Kałużynski, "'Wesele' czekało na kino," *Polityka* 3 (20 Jan 1973), 9.

42. Coates, "Revolutionary Spirits: *The Wedding* of Wajda and Wyspiański," *Literature/Film Quarterly* 20, no. 2 (1992), 127–32.

43. Toeplitz, "'Wesele,'" 74.

44. Kałużynski, "Dramat bezsiły, czy komedia złudzeń," *Polityka* 9 (3 Feb 1973).

45. Jarosław Iwaszkiewicz, private letter to Wajda, dated 12 January 1973.

46. Plisiecki, "Analiza i interpretacja filmu *Wesele* Andrzeja Wajdy," 132.

47. Gilles Jacob, "L'Express," Paris (14 Jan 1974); Louis Chauvet, "Le Figaro," Paris (12 Jan 1974).

48. Robert Chazal, "France-Soir," Paris (12 Jan 1974).

49. Jacques Siclier, "Le Monde," Paris (15 Jan 1974); Robert Nenayoun, "Le Point" (7 Jan 1974).

50. Francois Maurin, "L'Humanite," Paris (12 Jan 1974); Jean Loup Pasek, *CINEMA* 74, no. 184 (Feb 1974).

51. Caryn James, "Land of Promise," *New York Times Film Reviews* (5 Feb 1988).

52. Maria Marszałek, "Rozmowa z Andrzejem Wajdą," *Literatura* (2 Oct 1975): 1–2.

53. Bożena Krzywobłocka, "Ziemia obiecana dla filmowców"; a copy of the essay was sent to Ekran, Warszawa (1975). Andrzej Wajda Archives.

54. Anna Pyszny, "Adaptacja filmowa *Ziemi obiecanej* Władysława Reymonta," (Wrocław, 1978), 63.

55. Michał Komar, "'Ziemia obiecana' Andrzeja Wajdy," *Dialog* 2 (Feb 1975), 117–22.

56. Pyszny, "Adaptacja filmowa *Ziemi obiecanej* Władysława Reymonta," 64–67.

57. Ibid., 68.

58. Ibid.

59. Daniel Talbot, of New Yorker films, in a letter to Andrzej Wajda dated 14 October 1977. Andrzej Wajda Archives.

60. James, "Land of Promise."

61. A conversation with Wajda in Kraków, 2000.

62. Kałużynski, "Czarna Łódź Kolorowa," *Polityka* 8 (22 Nov 1975), 8.

63. Toeplitz, "Zachwyty i obawy," *Miesięcznik Literacki* 3 (Mar 1975), 92.

64. Andrzej Markowski, "*Smuga cienia* na ekranie," *Polska* 4, no. 260 (1976), 7.

65. Ibid., 23.

66. Piotr Kajewski "Impas i poryw" *Odra* 11, no. 189 (Nov 1976).

67. Markowski, "*Smuga cienia* na ekranie," 7.

68. Juliet McLauchlan, "'Smuga Cienia' Andrzeja Wajdy," *Literatura* 36 (Sep 1976), 6.

69. Ibid., 8.

70. Aleksander Jackiewicz, "'Smuga cienia'—poszukiwanie innego języka," *Kino* 127, no. 11 (Sep 1976), 19.

71. Janina Falkowska, *The Political Films of Andrzej Wajda* (Providence, 1996), 67–79.

72. Haltof, *Polish National Cinema*, 147.

73. See note 26 in chapter 1.

74. Maureen Turim, "Remembering and Deconstructing: The Historical Flashback in Man of Marble and Man of Iron," *The Cinema of Andrzej Wajda* (London, 2003), 93–102.

75. Aleksei Grigorevich Stakhanov was a Soviet coal miner in the Donets basin whose team increased its daily output sevenfold by an improved division of labor (1935). A Stakhanovite is a worker who reaches the highest efficiency in his work and who, by constantly raising his qualifications and exceeding quotas, is always first in the Socialist competition. See Słownik Wyrazów Obcych, Państwowy Instytut Wydawniczy, 1959, 619; Falkowska, *The Political Films of Andrzej Wajda*, chap. 2, note 16; Geoffrey Fox, "Men of Wajda," *Film Criticism* 6, no. 1 (1981), 3–9, note 3.

76. *Man of Marble* is full of multiple ironies, which function as additional glossia in the film. The film directs the spectator to the question of humor in Eastern Europe, its dialogic relation to the influences from the West, and its derisive quality. For instance, the last scene in *Man of Marble* suggests the following questions: Is Wajda mocking Hollywood or does the mockery fall short? Are the ironies all under control or are they implied by a sarcastic spectator conscious of Western snobbery? Sadly, the answers to these interesting questions fall beyond the scope of this book. The problem of humor in Eastern Europe requires a detailed analysis of the cultural and literary glossia that contribute to its qualities.

77. Falkowska, *Political Films of Andrzej Wajda*, 67–79.

78. Bolesław Hołdys quotes Krzysztof Kłopotowski's speech, presented at Jagiellonian University in Kraków on 13 October 1980, at the conference "Young Polish Cinema," reprinted in *Powiększenie. Students' Film Monthly* (Apr 1981), 45–51.

79. For the division of the films into scenes and sequences, see Falkowska, *Political Films of Andrzej Wajda*, Appendix I.

80. The fragments shown during the projection in the projection room are in fact fragments of the excised footage from Burski's films.

81. Birkut worked with two other workers as part of a three-man team: One of them gave him the bricks to be laid and the other gave him the mortar. Birkut's aim was to lay the bricks as fast as he could. After World War II, the country had to be rebuilt. There was no other way to force the workers into undertaking such an enormous task with poor pay and insufficient food without starting a huge propaganda machine based on the workers' competition. The more the worker worked, the more bricks he laid, the more respect he supposedly earned from his coworkers, and the more privileges from the party authorities.

82. During the Stalinist regime, the workers were slowly though reluctantly getting used to the spectacles organized by the party. The anger and awe on seeing officials from the higher echelons of the party slowly gave place to inertia and indifferent attendance at party meetings and festivities. In the years of Gierek (1970–80), the years in which the film was produced and also Agnieszka's time in the film,

> the Party's reputation for honesty, fairness and morality slumped. It became known by a word of mouth that Party and Government officials at the national, regional and local levels were taking advantage of the relaxed moral climate; they were feathering their own nests and using their positions and influence to do favours for their relatives and friends. Corruption increased, and a new class of privileged Party people emerged. Elitism among the higher echelons of the Party bred an arrogant attitude toward the people and a disdain for their concerns. The links between

the Party hierarchy and the masses, especially the industrial workers, became rusty with disuse. Nicholas G. Andrews, *Poland 1980–81* (Washington DC, 1985), 22.

83. For instance, W. Wierzewski, "Nowe filmy polskie. Czas teraźniejszy, czas miniony," *Kultura* 53 (4 Mar 1977), 8.

84. The presence of the Social Realism discourse in Wajda's films is especially vivid in *Man of Marble* and *Man of Iron*.

85. Czesław Miłosz, *The Captive Mind* (New York, 1981), 239.

86. A similar kind of jargon was generally used on TV and on the radio, the (in)famous *propaganda sukcesu* (success propaganda), when the reality presented in the media was only colorful, never black or gray. In this particular sequence, Wajda introduces the historical discourse characterized by this style, which reached its height in the late 1970s.

87. As Paul Coates notes, this idealistic presentation of the industrial landscape in *Man of Marble* could be compared with the industrial sublime of *Promised Land*, another film by Wajda that shows the process of industrialization, this time in nineteenth-century Łódź. Private conversation with Prof. Paul Coates, McGill University, April 1992.

88. Dan Georgakas and Lenny Rubenstein, *The Cineaste Interviews* (Chicago, 1983), 323.

89. Godzic Wiesław, "Political Metaphor—*Man of Marble* by Andrzej Wajda" (Katowice, 1984), 119.

90. Michał Głowiński, "Fabryczne dymy i kwitnąca czeremcha," *Kino* 5 (1991), 28.

91. On a different interpretation of Burski's role, see Tadeusz Lubelski, "'He Speaks to Us'" (London, 2003), 30–45.

92. Jan Dawson, "Man of Marble," *Sight and Sound* (Autumn 1979), 260.

93. David Thomson, "Orson Welles and *Citizen Kane*" (Montreal, 1990), 35.

94. Ibid., 40.

95. Ibid.

96. Płażewski et al., *Wajda Films II*, 77–85.

97. Micciche, qtd. in ibid., 82.

98. Płażewski, qtd. in ibid., 81.

99. Krzysztof Kłopotowski, "Życie i śmierć Mateusza Birkuta," *Literatura* 453, Warszawa (23 Oct 1980).

100. Płażewski et al., *Wajda Films II*, 82–85.

101. Falkowska, *The Political Films of Andrzej Wajda*, 56-67.

102. Vincent Canby, "Film: Failed Marriage in Postwar Poland," *New York Times* (9 Oct 1979).

103. Kałużynski, "O Wajdzie bez znieczulenia," *Polityka* 49 (9 Dec 1978); Janusz Zatorski, "Gorączka sumienia," *Kierunki* 51 (17 Dec 1978); and Zbigniew Kłaczyński, "Przypadki reportera," *Film* 1 (7 Jan 1979).

104. Kłaczyński, "O Wajdzie bez znieczulenia."

105. Zatorski, "Gorączka sumienia."

106. Andrzej Kuśniewicz et al., "Bez znieczulenia," *Kultura* 33 (31 Dec 1978).

107. Charity Scribner, *Requiem for Communism* (Cambridge, 2003), 64.

108. Ewa Lachnit, "Andrzej Wajda—Portret." (Film prod. Fundacja dla Uniwersytetu *Jagiellońskiego* 1989. Excerpt from soundtrack.) *Kino* 275, no. 24 (1990): 20–22. Original text:

A one grają wolno, ponieważ one nigdzie się nie śpieszą, bo ich życie jest inne, ich egzystencje, oczekiwanie. To jest właśnie ten czas o którym mówiłem. Ja nie mam czasu, bo ja maluję ten czas o którym mówiłem. Ja nie mam czasu, bo ja maluję coś co jest w innym rytmie, szybkim, to jak ja mam się przenieść w inny czas, i co? Patrzeć, że one tak leżą na tej trawie, patrzą i nic z tego nie wynika, i to jest właśnie temat filmu.

109. Piotr Lis, "Niektóre aspekty związków filmowo-literackich na podstawie *Panien z Wilka* Andrzeja Wajdy," *Krąg Historii i Literatury* (1987), 88–89.

110. Andrzej Wajda, "O filmowaniu prozy Iwaszkiewicza," *Dialog: Miesięcznik* 25, no. 1 (1980), 92–97.

111. On other developments in Poland and Polish cinema, see Haltof, *Polish National Cinema*, 146–56.

112. The persuasive acting of Krystyna Janda and Andrzej Seweryn may have been reinforced by the real divorce of these two actors, which immediately preceded the making of this film.

113. Sauro Borelli, "Entuzjazm w Berlinie dla ostatniego filmu Wajdy," *L'Unita* (29 Feb 1980).

114. Kłopotowski, "Nic świętego," *Literatura* (24 Apr 1980), 9.

115. Maria Malatyńska, "Bez szansy," *Życie Literackie* 1479, 5–6.

116. Toeplitz, "Dyrygent," *Kultura*, Warszawa (6 Apr 1980).

117. Andrzej Lipiński, "Wytworne nieudanie," *Ekran* 17, Warszawa (24 Apr 1980).

118. Nicholas Wapshott, "Andrzej Wajda Wields the Baton," *Times* (22 Nov 1980), 42.

119. Pedro Crespo, *Cinestudio*, Madrid (9 Sep 1980).

120. Jean-Pierre Le Pavec, *Cinema*, Paris (1980).

Chapter Five

1. For a detailed description of this historical situation, see Davies, *God's Playground*, 625–33.

2. According to Małgorzata Szpakowska, "Prawdy i nieporozumienia," *Kino* (1983), 9–12, the following materials were used in *Man of Iron:* materials from Polska Kronika Filmowa (Polish Film Chronicle); materials from Telewizja RFN (German Television); fragments of the films *Sierpień* (August), by Ireneusz Engler and Leon Kotowski, and *Robotnicy '80* (August '80), by Andrzej Chodakowski and Andrzej Zajączkowski.

3. Mariusz Muszkat, "Laury niezasuszone," *Tygodnik Solidarność* 14 (21 Aug 1981).

4. Czesław Dondziłło, "Bez ochronnych barw," *Film* 34 (23 Aug 1981), 3–5.

5. Jerzy Surdykowski, "Żelazem po marmurze," *Życie Literackie* 154 (3 Sep 1981), 5.

6. Ibid.

7. This interpretation is questioned openly by Paul Coates, who postulates that a more complex discursive situation is present in *Man of Marble*. In fact, unquestionably, what is open to debate in *Man of Marble* is the question of the filmmakers' relation to "them" (e.g., Burski). However, "they" are clearly "bad

guys" as well. (Private conversations with Prof. Paul Coates, McGill University, Montreal, April 1992.)

8. Szpakowska, "Prawdy i nieporozumienia," 10.

9. Paweł Jędrzejewski, "Wajda na linie," *Ekran* 35 (30 Aug 1981).

10. Kłopotowski, *"Człowiek z żelaza.* Kontrowersje: Odpowiadam na zarzuty," *Tygodnik Solidarność* 14 (6 Nov 1981).

11. Gilbert Adair, "Blue Movie: *Danton," Sight and Sound* 52, no. 4 (1983), 284.

12. Andrzej Walicki, *Philosophy and the Romantic Nationalism,* 243.

13. Coates suggests that this scene is worse less because of its iconography and more because of the workers' shy "this is our solidarity" statement. The spectator might have been annoyed by a timid flag-waving in this scene, which also reiterates the potency of the discourse of Solidarity. (Private conversation with Prof. Paul Coates, McGill University, Montreal, April 1992.)

14. Vincent Canby, "Act of Bravery. *Man of Iron," New York Times Film Reviews* (12 Oct 1981), C14–3.

15. Tadeusz Szyma, "Człowiek z żelaza," *Tygodnik Powszechny* 28 (12 Jul 1981).

16. Haltof, *Polish National Cinema,* 158.

17. The declaration crafted in 1789 is used in a symbolic sense in the film. Wajda introduces the film and ends it with the famous words, as if reminding spectators what the revolution was all about—the rights of citizens.

18. Wajda denies that his film refers to the Poland of the 1980s, saying that that argument is *"niemiłym uproszczeniem. Jeśli miałoby się szukać analogii historycznych, należałoby je odnieść do zupełnie innej epoki"* ("an unpleasant simplification. If we were to look for an analogy, we would have to refer it to a completely different epoch"). See M. Ostrowski, "Danton czy Robespierre?" *Polityka* (5 Feb 1983). On the other hand, such denials by the filmmaker could themselves be political in nature—that is, to allow him to continue making films in Poland in the 1980s.

19. Ireneusz Łęczek, *"Danton," Trybuna Robotnicza* 39 (16 Feb 1983).

20. This remark, together with an insightful analysis of the role played by Robespierre in the French Revolution, was presented by Prof. Jan Baszkiewicz in an interview conducted by Krzysztof Kreutzinger for a popular Polish weekly *Film,* dated 10 April 1983.

21. David Sterritt, *"Danton," Christian Science Monitor* (10 Jun 1983).

22. Ibid.

23. Philip Strick, *"Danton," Monthly Film Bulletin* 9 (1983), 242.

24. I refer here to the scene at the beginning of the film in which a little boy is forced to learn by rote the dictates of the Declaration of the Rights of Man and the Citizen. The discourse of the historical past reminds the spectator of the political discourse of every totalitarian society, whether French or Polish, where the regime was trying to educate whole generations of young people to change their mentality and their understanding of reality and history. The time of Stalinism with its ideological impositions, and the time of martial law in Poland when the autonomous powers of university rectors and academic bodies were reduced and the party tightened its supervision over academic research institutions, immediately came to the Polish spectator's mind.

25. Marcel Ophuls, "The Provocation and Interrogation of Andrzej Wajda on the Matter of *Danton* as Performed by Marcel Ophuls," *American Film* 9, no. 1 (1983).

26. As Wajda himself admits in the *Cineaste* interview, neither of these features ought to imbue Wajda with enthusiasm for revolution—his declared Socialism, however, ought to have done so.

27. Ophuls, "Provocation and Interrogation of Andrzej Wajda," 25.

28. Ibid., 94.

29. Jan Sajdak, "Dwaj adwokaci przed sądem historii," *Odra* (1 May 1983).

30. Anne Chaussebourg, "Un etrieten avec M. Louis Mermaz—La revolution n'est pas a l'ordre du jour en France," *Croix* (7 Jan 1983).

31. Laurent Dispot, "L'Histoire escamotée," *Matin* (7 Jan 1983).

32. For further analysis of Przybyszewska's *Danton Affair* and Wajda's theatrical production based on this drama, see Maciej Karpiński, *The Theatre of Andrzej Wajda* (Cambridge, 1989).

33. Ibid., 34–57.

34. Ibid., 49.

35. Ibid., 53.

36. Strick, "*Danton*," 242.

37. Ibid.

38. In this acknowledgment of the importance of sound and music for the interpretation of film messages, Wajda seems to have acknowledged Eisenstein's revolutionary statement concerning this issue, articulated in 1928. In "Sound and Image," a manifesto published on 5 August 1928, Eisenstein, Pudovkin, and Alexandrov correctly predicted,

> Only the use of sound as counterpoint to visual montage offers new possibilities to developing and perfecting montage. The first experiments with sound must be directed toward its "noncoincidence" with visual images. Only this method can produce the feeling we seek, the feeling which, with time, will lead to the creation of new orchestral counterpoint of image-vision and image-sound.

Qtd. by David A. Cook in *A History of Narrative Film* (New York: Norton, 1990), 281.

39. Haltof, *Polish National Cinema*, 167.

40. Płażewski, "Żeby nigdy więcej," *Kino* 2 (1984), 42–43.

41. Film Crew creates agitation in the Village (Filmleute sorgen fuer Unruhe im Dorf) *Stuttgarter Zeitung* (18 May 1983).

42. Tadeusz Szyma, "Miłość w Niemczech," *Tygodnik Powszechny* (29 Jan 1984).

43. Marcin Kowalski, "Miłość nieodwzajemniona," *Trybuna Ludu* 271 (15 Nov 1983), 5.

44. *New York Times* (9 Nov 1984).

45. Kevin Farrington, "*A Love in Germany*," *Cineaste* 14, no. 2 (1985), 18–21.

46. Rodo Fruendt, "Insanity Is the Rule (Der Irrsinn ist die Regel). Andrzej Wajda's Disputed Film Based on Hochhuth's Book *Eine Liebe in Deutschland*," *Sueddeutsche Zeitung* (6 Dec 1983).

47. Angelika Kaps, "Question of Responsibility (Frage nach Verantwortung). Wajda films Hochhuth's *Eine Liebe in Deutschland*," *Tagesspiegel* (1 May 1983).

48. Farrington, "*A Love in Germany*," 20.

49. Rex Reed, "*Love in Germany* is *Force Sans Finesse*," *New York Post* (9 Nov 1984).

50. Szyma, "Miłość w Niemczech," *Tygodnik Powszechny* (29 Jan 1984), 8.

51. Ostrowska, "Dangerous Liaisons," 46–63.

52. Malatyńska, "Poziomkowa polana," 81–90.

53. Tadeusz Szyma, "Kronika wypadków miłosnych," *Tygodnik Powszechny* (4 Jan 1987). This view is shared by Janusz Wróblewski in "Pamięć wyzwolona," *Kino* 2 (1987), 8–11.

54. Szyma, "Kronika wypadków miłosnych."

55. Kazimierz Młynarz, "Duch żywego człowieka," *Kultura* 5 (4 Feb 1987).

56. Maciej Pawlicki, "Tam, gdzie rosły poziomki," *Tygodnik Kulturalny* (18 Jan 1987).

57. Szyma, "Kronika wypadków miłosnych."

58. Młynarz, "Duch żywego człowieka."

59. Pawlicki, "Tam, gdzie rosły poziomki."

60. Andrzej Wajda Archives.

61. Zbigniew Bieńkowski and Andreas Kilb, qtd. in *Wajda Films II,* 227.

62. Zdzisław Pietrasik, qtd. in *Wajda Films II,* 227.

63. Marcel Martin, *La Revue du Cinema,* Paris (Feb 1988).

64. Janina Kumaniecka, qtd. in *Wajda Films II,* 226.

65. For a highly critical analysis of *Man of Iron* and *Man of Marble* in this respect, see Scribner, *Requiem for Communism,* 45–63.

66. Falkowska, *Political Films of Andrzej Wajda,* 156–61.

Chapter Six

1. See also Terri Ginsberg, *Święty Korczak z Warszawy, Filmowy Świat Andrzeja Wajdy* (Kraków, 2003), 344.

2. Strick, *"Korczak," Monthly Film Bulletin* (Nov 1990), 324.

3. Tim Pulleine, *"Korczak," Guardian* (25 Oct 1990).

4. Sheila Johnston, "Passive Resistance and Active Service," *Daily Telegraph* (25 Oct 1990).

5. Some of the most scathing comments are republished in *Wajda Films II,* 242–47.

6. Ibid., and Andrzej Wajda Archives.

7. Ginsberg, *Święty Korczak z Warszawy,* 337–57.

8. Danièle Heymann, "L'homme de rêve et l'homme de plomb," *Monde* (13–14 May 1990), 10.

9. Ginsberg, *Święty Korczak z Warszawy,* 341.

10. Ibid., 356.

11. Ibid.

12. Davies, *God's Playground,* 466.

13. Ibid., 466–75.

14. Wlasow soldiers fought under the command of the Soviet general, Andriej Wlasow, who joined the Germans and organized the Soviet Liberation Organization (ROD) at the side of German occupiers. He was taken prisoner by Americans after World War II ended, deported to the Soviet Union, and sentenced to death.

15. Davies, *God's Playground,* 471.

16. Ostrowska, "Dangerous Liaisons," 46–63.

17. Davies, *God's Playground,* 471.

18. Private letter of Jadwiga Sobol, dated 23 May 1992. Andrzej Wajda Archives.

19. Wajda, "W obronie tradycji przed przemocą systemu," *Kino* 9 (1994), 4.

20. Andrzej Osęka, "Symbol wbrew prawdzie," *Gazeta Wyborcza* 221 (12 Sep 1993), 10.

21. Płażewski, "Z włosia czy z orłem w koronie?" *Wyborcza* 221 (21 Sep 1993), 11.

22. Kornatowska, "Polish Cinema," 49.

23. Ibid., 45, 49–50.

24. Dowell, "The Man Who Put Poland on the Post-War Map of Cinema," 53.

25. This history of the film is told by Wajda in *Wajda Films II*, 271–74.

26. Jan Kłossowicz, "Dostojewski, Wajda I Tamasaburo Bando," *L'Express. Spotkania* 17 (1993): 44–45.

27. Kaori Shoji, "Bando Has It Both Ways in *Nastasja*," *Japan Times* (28 Oct 1994).

28. Ibid.

29. Andrea Hirsig, "Onnagata Tamasaburo Triumphs as Dostoevsky's Femme Fatale," *Mainichi Daily News* (15 Apr 1994), 9.

30. Alicja Helman, "Filmowy Teatr Andrzeja Wajdy," *Tygodnik Powszechny* 50 (1994).

31. See note 11, chapter 3.

32. Adam Michnik and Tadeusz Sobolewski, "From Our Side of the Wall," *Gazeta Wyborcza* 10–11 (Jun 1995), 14–15.

33. Ibid., 14.

34. Marek Rapacki, "Awantura o Wajdę," *Gazeta Wyborcza* (18 Jun 1996), 1.

35. Tadeusz Sobolewski, "Lęk przestrzeni," *Gazeta Wyborcza* (26 Feb 1996), 4.

36. Sobolewski, "Biedni Polacy," *Kino* (Nov 1995): 17–41.

37. Henning Bruns, "Alle Bilder lugen," *Berliner Zeitung* (21 Feb 1996).

38. Sobolewski, "Biedni Polacy," 41.

39. Stephen Holden, "On How to Suffer and the Reasons," *New York Times* (25 Jan 1996), 19.

40. Marek Rapacki, "Awantura o Wajdę," *Gazeta Wyborcza* (18 Jun 1996), 1.

41. Michnik and Sobolewski, "From Our Side of the Wall," 14–15.

42. For instance, see Jan Schulz-Ojala, "Hinfort, Boses!" *Tagesspiegel* (24 Feb 1997).

43. Wacław Świeżyński, "Panna Nikt," *Gazeta Telewizyjna* 20–27 (Feb 1998), 4.

44. Joanna Wiórkiewicz "Andrzej Wajda w Berlinie," *Samo życie* 5, no. 21 (May 1997), 8.

45. Ibid.

46. Ewa Mazierska, "In the Land of Noble Knights and Mute Princesses: Polish Heritage Cinema," *Historical Journal of Film, Radio and Television* 21, no. 2 (2001), 167–82.

47. Ibid., 167.

48. Ibid., 168.

49. Charity Scribner, *Requiem for Communism* (Cambridge, 2003).

50. Jerzy Armata, "Do trzech razy sztuka czyli 'Pan Tadeusz' w kinematografie" *Gazeta Krakowska. Dodatek Nadzwyczajny Gazety w Krakowie* (7 Jul 1998).

51. Barbara Hollender, "Zajazd w kinie," *Rzeczpospolita* (26 Jul 1998), 8–13.

52. Krzysztof Masłoń, "Gerwazy Lustrator," *Rzeczpospolita* (26 Jul 1998), 9–12.

53. Jacek Szczerba, "Wygrałem na loterii—spotkałem dwie różne osobowości i chyba zyskałem więcej niż oni—mówi Adek Drabiński o Jerzym Hoffmanie i Andrzeju Wajdzie," *Gazeta Wyborcza* (13 Nov 1998); Jerzy Wójcik, "Najtrudniejsze z moich przedsięwzięć. Rozmowa z Andrejem Wajdą o ekranizacji *Pana Tadeusza*" *Rzeczpospolita* 120 (4980) W3, Warszawa (23–24 May 1998); and Zdzisław Pietrasik, "Polonez być musi. Rozmowa z Andrzejem Wajdą, nie tylko o *Panu Tadeuszu*," *Kino* 5 (1998), 48–50.

54. Kałużynski and Tomasz Raczek, "Aria na ściśniętym gardle," *Wprost* 47 (Nov 1999), 118–19.

55. Ibid., 119.

56. Ibid.

57. Raczek, "Litania do *Pana Tadeusza*," *Wprost* 44 (31 Oct 1999), 76.

58. Krzysztof Żurek, "*Pan Tadeusz*," *Przekrój* 45 (1999).

59. Joanna Pawluśkiewicz, "Sucha chusteczka," *Kino* 2 (2000), 28.

60. Wojciech Owczarski et al., "Soplicowo na sprzedaż?" *Dialog* 2 (2000), 108–18.

61. Ibid., 111.

62. Zdzisław Pietrasik, "*Pan Tadeusz*: To już ostatni taki film polski. Horror w zaścianku," *Polityka* 43 (23 Oct 1999), 17–18.

63. Owczarski et al., "Soplicowo na sprzedaż?" 108–9.

64. These comments arose during my conversations with the director in the year 2000 and in his numerous TV statements.

65. Justyna Kobus, "*Zemsta* Wajdy," *Wprost* 40 (6 Oct 2002), 118–19.

66. Ibid.

67. Piotr Wojciechowski, "Co widać w lustrze hrabiego Fredry?" *Przekrój* 40 (2002), 58; Bogdan Sobieszek, "*Zemsta*," *Film* 11 (Nov 2002), 92.

68. Ibid.

69. Kobus, "*Zemsta* Wajdy," 118.

70. Sobieszek, "*Zemsta*," 92.

71. Piotr Kajewski, "Urojenia żartem i serio," *Odra* 12 (2002), 89.

Conclusion

1. Rudolf Arnheim, *Toward a Psychology of Art* (Berkeley, 1966), 45.

2. Herbert Zettl, *Sight, Sound, Motion* (Belmont, 1999), 122–24.

❀ BIBLIOGRAPHY

1. Archival Sources

All archival sources come from the Andrzej Wajda Archives at the Manggha Center in Kraków.

2. General

Anderson, Benedict. *Imagined Communities: Reflections on the Origin and Spread of Nationalism.* London: Verso, 1983.

Andrews, Nicholas G. *Poland 1980–81. Solidarity vs The Party.* Washington DC: National Defense UP, 1985.

Andrzejewski, Jerzy. *Ashes and Diamonds.* Trans. D. J. Welsh. London: Weidenfeld, 1962.

———. *Popiół i diament.* Warszawa: Państwowy Instytut Wydawniczy, 1970.

———. *Wielki Tydzień.* Warszawa: Czytelnik, 1993.

Arnheim, Rudolf. *Toward a Psychology of Art.* Berkeley: U of California P, 1966.

Ascherson, Neal. *The Polish August.* New York: Viking, 1981.

Ash, Timothy Garton. *The Polish Revolution.* London: Granta, 1983.

Bakhtin, Mikhail. *Problems of Dostoevsky's Poetics.* Ed. and trans. Caryl Emerson. Minneapolis: U of Minneapolis P, 1984.

———. *Speech Genres and Other Late Essays.* Eds. Caryl Emerson and Michael Holquist. Trans. V.W. McGee. Austin: U of Texas P, 1986.

———. *The Dialogic Imagination: Four Essays.* Ed. M. Holquist. Trans. C. Emerson and M. Holquist. Austin: U of Texas P, 1981.

Balski, Grzegorz, ed. *Directory of Eastern European Film-Makers and Films.* Westport: Greenwood, 1992.

Bhabha, Homi K. *Nation and Narration.* Ed. London and New York: Routledge, 1990.

Borowski, Tadeusz. *Wspomnienia, wiersze, opowiadania.* Warszawa: Państwowy Instytut Wydawniczy, 1977.

Brady, Leo, and Morris Dickstein. *Great Film Directors. A Critical Anthology.* New York: Oxford UP, 1978.

Brandys, Kazimierz. *Samson, Antygona.* Warszawa: Czytelnik, 1962.

Branigan, Edward, R. *Point of View in the Cinema.* Berlin: Mouton, 1984.

Bren, Frank. *World Cinema I: Poland.* London: Flicks, 1986.

Bugajski, Ryszard, J. Bolewski, T. Lubieński, Bolesław Michałek, D. Michałowska, M. Skwarnicki, J. Turowicz, A. Wajda, and Piotr Wojciechowski. "Stulecie kina: świadectwo wieku czy zbiór mitów?" *Więź.* Sierpień 8, no. 442 (1995): 17–30.

Bulhakov, Mikhail. *The Master and Margarita*. Trans. M. Ginsburg. New York: Grove, 1967.

Ciechowicz, Jan, and Tadeusz Szczepański, eds. *Zbigniew Cybulski. Aktor XX wieku*. Gdańsk: U of Gdańsk P, 1997.

Coates, Paul. *The Story of the Lost Reflection*. London: Verso, 1985.

———. *The Red and the White: The Cinema of People's Poland*. London: Wallflower, 2005.

Cook, David A. *A History of Narrative Film*. New York: Norton, 1990.

Davies, Norman. *A History of Poland. God's Playground*. New York: Columbia UP, 1982.

———. *Heart of Europe. A Short History of Poland*. Oxford: Clarendon, 1984.

De Nitto, Denis, and William Herman. *Film and the Critical Eye*. New York: Macmillan, 1975.

Dondziłło, Czesław. "Bez ochronnych barw." *Film* no. 34 (Aug 23, 1981): 3–5.

———. *Młode kino polskie lat siedemdziesiątych*. Warszawa: Młodzieżowa Agencja Wydawnicza, 1985.

Dorobowa, Jadwiga Łużynska. "Filmowa wizja świadomości społeczno-narodowej chłopów w okresie zaborów." *Wieś i Rolnictwo* 2, no. 55 (1987): 88–104.

Falkowska, Janina, and Marek Haltof, eds. *The New Polish Cinema. Industry, Genres, Auteurs*. Trowbridge, England: Flicks, 2003.

Foucault, Michel. *Power/Knowledge*. Ed. Colin Gordon. New York: Pantheon, 1980.

———. "What Is an Author?" *Language, Counter-Memory, Practice: Selected Essays and Interviews*. Trans. D. Bouchard and S. Simon. Ithaca: Cornell UP, 1977. 113–38.

Freund, Elizabeth. *The Return of the Reader. Reader-Response Criticism*. London: Methuen, 1987.

Friedman, Lester. "The Necessity of Confrontation Cinema: Peter Watkins Interviewed." *Literature/Film Quarterly* 11, no. 4 (1983): 237–48.

Furhammar, Leif, and Folke Isaksson. *Politics and Film*. Trans. K. French. New York: Praeger, 1971.

Georgakas, Dan, and Lenny Rubenstein. *The Cineaste Interviews. On the Art and Politics of Cinema*. Chicago: Lake View, 1983.

Gieysztor, Aleksander. *History of Poland*. Warszawa: PWN, 1979.

Goldfarb, Jeffrey C. *On Cultural Freedom. An Exploration of Public Life in Poland and America*. Chicago: U of Chicago P, 1982.

Goulding, Daniel, ed. *Post New Wave Cinema in the Soviet Union and Eastern Europe*. Bloomington: Indiana UP, 1989.

Haltof, Marek. "A Fistful of Dollars: Polish Cinema after 1989 Freedom Shock." *Film Quarterly* 48, no. 3 (1995): 15–25.

———. *Polish National Cinema*, New York: Berghahn, 2002.

Hames, Peter, ed. *24 Frames: Central Europe*. London: Wallflower, 2004.

Helman, Alicja, and Tadeusz Miczka, eds. *Analyses and Interpretations. Polish Film*. Katowice: Wydawnictwo Uniwersytetu Śląskiego, 1984.

Hendrykowska, Małgorzata, ed. *Widziane po latach. Analizy i interpretacje filmu polskiego*. Poznań: Wydawnictwo Poznańskiego Towarzystwa Przyjaciół Nauk, 2000.

Hjort, Mette, and Scott Mackenzie, eds. *Cinema and Nation*. London: Routledge, 2000.

Holland, Agnieszka. *Korczak*. Warszawa: Wydawnictwa Artystyczne i Filmowe, 1991.

Insdorf, Annette. *Indelible Shadows: Film and the Holocaust*. Cambridge: Cambridge UP, 1989.

Iwaszkiewicz, Jarosław. *Eros i Tanatos: Proza Jarosława Iwaszkiewicza*. Warszawa: Czytelnik, 1970.

Jankun-Dopartowa, Mariola. "Prawdy żywe kina polskiego lat osiemdziesiątych." *Konkurs* 1 (1990): 40–50.

Jankun-Dopartowa, Mariola, and Mirosław Przylipiak, eds. *Człowiek z ekranu: z antropologii postaci filmowej*. Kraków: Arcana, 1996.

Kłopotowski, Krzysztof. "Uzupełniam swój życiorys." *Tygodnik Solidarność* 2 (Apr 1981).

Kornatowska, Maria. "Polish Cinema." *Cineaste* 19, no. 4 (1993): 47–50.

Kracauer, Siegfried. *From Caligari to Hitler. A Psychological History of the German Film*. New Jersey: Princeton UP, 1947.

Krubski, Krzysztof, Marek Miller, Zofia Turowska, and Waldemar Wiśniewski. *Filmówka. Powieść o Łódzkiej Szkole Filmowej*. Warszawa: Tenten, 1986.

Lemann, Jolanta, ed. *Państwowa Wyższa Szkoła Filmowa Telewizyjna i Teatralna im. Leona Schillera w Łodzi 1948–1998. Księga Jubileuszowa*. Łódź: Państwowa Wyższa Szkoła Filmowa Telewizyjna i Teatralna, 1998.

Lewandowski, Jan F. *100 filmów polskich*. Katowice: Videograf II, 1997.

Liehm, Mira, and Antonin J. *The Most Important Art: Soviet and Eastern European Film After 1945*. Berkeley: U of California P, 1977.

Lubelski, Tadeusz. *Strategie autorskie w polskim filmie fabularnym lat 1945–1961*. Kraków: Jagiellonian UP, 1992.

———. "Wzlot i upadek wspólnoty, czyli kino polskie 1975–1995." *Kino* 31, no. 356 (1997): 17–20.

MacBean, James Roy. *Film and Revolution*. Bloomington: Indiana UP, 1975.

Mała Encyclopedia PWN A–Z, Warszawa: Wydawnictwo Naukowe PWN, 1999.

Marsh, Rosalind. *Images of Dictatorship. Portraits of Stalin in Literature*. London: Routledge, 1989.

Marszałek, Rafał, ed. *Historia filmu polskiego 1962–1967*. Vol. 5. Warszawa: Wydawnictwa Artystyczne i Filmowe, 1985.

———. *Historia filmu polskiego 1968–1972*. Vol. 6. Warszawa: Wydawnictwa Artystyczne i Filmowe, 1994.

Marx, Karl. *Collected Works*. Vol. 5. New York: International, 1976.

Mast, Gerald. "Film History and Film Histories." *Quarterly Review of Film Studies* 1, no. 3 (1976): 297–314.

———. *A Short History of the Movies*. New York: Pegasus, 1971.

Maynard, Richard. *Propaganda on Film. A Nation at War*. Rochelle Park: Hayden, 1975.

Mazierska, Ewa. "In the Land of Noble Knights and Mute Princesses: Polish Heritage Cinema." *Historical Journal of Film, Radio and Television* 21, no. 2 (2001): 167–82.

Mazierska, Ewa, and Elżbieta Ostrowska. *Women in Polish Cinema*. New York: Berghahn, 2006.

Metz, Christian. *Language and Cinema*. The Hague: Mouton, 1974.

———. *Film Language. A Semiotics of the Cinema*. Trans. Michael Taylor. New York: Oxford UP, 1974.

Michałek, Bolesław. "Lokalny Film, Prowincjonalna Krytyka. Rozmowa z Bolesławem Michałkiem, krytykiem filmowym, kierownikiem literackim Zespołu X." *Kierunki* 14, no. 5 (May 1981).

Michałek, Bolesław, and Frank Turaj. *Le Cinéma polonais.* Paris: Pompidou, 1992.

———. *The Modern Cinema of Poland.* Bloomington: Indiana UP, 1988.

Michnik, Adam, and Tadeusz Sobolewski. "From our side of the wall." *Gazeta Wyborcza* 10–11 (Jun 1995): 15.

Miczka, Tadeusz, ed., with Alina Madej. *Syndrom konformizmu? Kino polskie lat sześćdziesiątych.* Katowice: Wydawnictwo Uniwersytetu Śląskiego, 1994.

Miłosz, Czesław. *The Captive Mind.* New York: Vintage, 1981.

Nichols, Bill. "Critical Approaches to Film Then and Now." *Cineaste* 5, no. 2 (1972): 8–14.

———. *Ideology and the Image.* Bloomington: Indiana UP, 1981.

Nurczyńska-Fidelska, Ewelina, and Bronisława Stolarska, eds. *"Szkoła polska"— powroty.* Łódź: Wydawnictwo Uniwersytetu Łódzkiego, 1998.

Nurczyńska-Fidelska, Ewelina, and Zbigniew Batko, eds. *Polish Cinema in Ten Takes.* Łódź: Łódzkie Towarzystwo Naukowe: 1995. *[Bulletin de la Société des Sciences et des Lettres de Łódź, Vol. 45; Série: Recherches sur les arts].*

Obcych, Słownik Wyrazów. Warszawa: Państwowy Instytut Wydawniczy, 1959.

Ostrowska, Elżbieta. "Filmic Representations of the 'Polish Mother' in Post-Second World War Polish Cinema." *European Journal of Women's Studies* 5 (1998): 419–35.

Paul, David W., ed. *Politics, Art and Commitment in the East European Cinema.* London: Macmillan, 1983.

Petrie, Graham, and Ruth Dwyer. *Before the Wall Came Down: Soviet and East European Filmmakers in the West.* New York: UP of America, 1990.

Polan, Dana. "The Text between Monologue and Dialogue." *Poetics Today* 4, no. 1 (1983): 145–52.

Polański, Roman. *Roman.* Warszawa: Polonia, 1989.

Ponzio, Augusto. "The Relation of Otherness in Bakhtin, Blanchot, Lévinas." *Recherches Sémiotiques* 7, no. 1 (1987): 1–18.

Propp, Vladimir. *Morphology of the Folktale.* Austin: U of Texas P, 1968.

Renan, Ernest. "What Is a Nation?" *Nation and Narration.* Ed. Homi K. Bhabba. London: Routledge, 1990. 6–21.

Scribner, Charity. *Requiem for Communism,* Cambridge: MIT Press, 2003.

Ścibor-Rylski, Aleksander. *Człowiek z marmuru.* Warszawa: Wydawnictwa Artystyczne i Filmowe, 1988.

Ścibor-Rylski, Aleksander. *Pierścionek z końskiego włosia. Powieść,* do druku podał i opatrzył posłowiem Tadeusz Drewnowski, Warszawa: Fundacja "Kultura 90," 1991.

Stam, Robert. "Bakhtinian Translinguistics: A Postscriptum." *The Cinematic Text. Methods and Approaches,* ed. Barton R. Palmer. New York: AMS, 1989. 343–51.

———. *Reflexivity in Film and Literature. From Don Quixote to Jean-Luc Godard.* Irvington: Columbia UP, 1991.

———. *Subversive Pleasures. Bakhtin, Cultural Criticism and Film.* Baltimore: Johns Hopkins UP, 1989.

Szanto, George, H. *Theatre and Propaganda.* Austin: U of Texas P, 1978.

Taras, Ray. *Poland. Socialist State, Rebellious Nation.* Boulder: Westview, 1986.

Thomson, David. "Orson Welles and *Citizen Kane*." *Art as Film*. Ed. Paul Coates. Montreal: P.S. Presse, 1990. 35.

Todorov, Tzvetan. *Genres in Discourse*. Trans. Catherine Porter. Cambridge: Cambridge UP, 1990.

Turaj, Frank. "Poland: The Cinema of Moral Concern." *Post New Wave Cinema in the Soviet Union and Eastern Europe*. Ed. Daniel J. Goulding. Bloomington: Indiana UP, 1989. 143–71.

Turim, Maureen. "Remembering and Deconstructing: The Historical Flashback in *Man of Marble* and *Man of Iron*." *The Cinema of Andrzej Wajda. The Art of Irony and Defiance*. Eds. John Orr and Elżbieta Ostrowska. London: Wallflower, 2003. 93–102.

Volosinov, Valentin Nikolaevich. *Marxism and the Philosophy of Language*. Trans. Ladislav Matejka and I. R. Titunik. New York: Seminar, 1973.

Walicki, Andrzej. *Philosophy and Romantic Nationalism: The Case of Poland*. Oxford: Clarendon, 1982.

Wechsler, Lawrence. "Banned Films." *Cineaste* 13, no. 3 (1984): 11–13.

White, Hayden. *Metahistory. The Historical Imagination in Nineteenth-Century Europe*. Baltimore: Johns Hopkins UP, 1973.

———. *Theories of History. Papers Read at a Clark Library Seminar, March 6, 1976*. Los Angeles: U of California P, 1978.

———. *Tropics of Discourse. Essays in Cultural Criticism*. Baltimore: Johns Hopkins UP, 1978.

Wierzewski, W. "Nowe filmy polskie. Czas teraźniejszy, czas miniony." *Kultura* 53 (4 Mar 1977): 8.

Williams, Raymond. *Marxism and Literature*. Oxford: Oxford UP, 1977.

Włodarczyk, Wojciech. *Socrealizm. Sztuka polska w latach 1950–1954*. Kraków: Wydawnictwo Literackie, 1991.

Zettl, Herbert. *Sight, Sound, Motion. Applied Media Aesthetics*. Belmont: Wordsworth, 1999.

Żukrowski, Wojciech. *Lotna*. Warszawa: Książka i Wiedza, 1969.

3. Books on Wajda

Czernienko, Miron. *Andrzej Wajda*. Moskva: Iskusstvo, 1965.

Dostojewski—teatr sumienia. Trzy inscenizacje Andrzeja Wajdy w Teatrze Starym w Krakowie: Biesy, Nastazja Filipowa, Zbrodnia i Kara, scenariusze-komentarze opracował Maciej Karpiński, Warszawa: Pax, 1989.

Eder, Klaus. *Andrzej Wajda*. Munich: Claus Hanser, 1980.

Falkowska, Janina. *The Political Films of Andrzej Wajda: Dialogism in "Man of Marble," "Man of Iron," and "Danton."* Providence: Berghahn, 1996.

Film na Świecie 329–33 (May-Jun 1986). Issue devoted to unrealized films of Andrzej Wajda.

Ginsberg, Terri. *Święty Korczak z Warszawy, Filmowy Świat Andrzeja Wajdy*. Eds. Ewelina Nurczyńska-Fidelska and Piotr Sitarski. Kraków: Universitas, 2003. 337–57.

Karpiński, Maciej. *The Theatre of Andrzej Wajda*. Cambridge: Cambridge UP, 1989.

Kornatowska, Maria. *Wodzireje i amatorzy.* Warszawa: Wydawnictwa Artystyczne i Filmowe, 1990.

Kwartalnik Filmowy 15–16 (1996–97). Issue devoted to Andrzej Wajda.

Michałek, Bolesław. *The Cinema of Andrzej Wajda.* London: Tantivy, 1973.

Miczka, Tadeusz. *Inspiracje plastyczne w twórczości filmowej i telewizyjnej Andrzeja Wajdy.* Katowice: U of Silesia P, 1987.

Mruklik, Barbara. *Andrzej Wajda.* Warszawa: Wydawnictwa Artystyczne i Filmowe, 1969.

Nurczyńska-Fidelska, Ewelina. *Polska klasyka literacka według Andrzeja Wajdy.* Katowice: Śląsk, 1998.

Nurczyńska-Fidelska, Ewelina, and Piotr Sitarski, eds. *Filmowy i teatralny świat Andrzeja Wajdy.* Kraków: Wydawnictwo Uniwersytetu Łódzkiego, 2003.

Orr, John, and Elżbieta Ostrowska, eds. *The Cinema of Andrzej Wajda: The Art of Irony and Defiance.* London: Wallflower, 2003.

Płażewski, Jerzy, Grzegorz Balski, and Jan Słodowski. *Wajda Films.* Vols. 1–2. Trans. Jolanta Kozak, Ewa Krasińska, Michael J. Oczko, and Elżbieta Petrajtis. Warszawa: Wydawnictwa Artystyczne i Filmowe, 1996.

Trinon, Hadelin. *Andrzej Wajda.* Paris: Seghers, 1964.

Wertenstein, Wanda. *Wajda mówi o sobie. Wywiady i teksty.* Kraków: Wydawnictwo Literackie, 1991.

———. *Zespół filmowy X.* Warszawa: Wydawnictwo "Officina," 1991.

4. Articles on/about Films, and Interviews Regarding Wajda

Adair, Gilbert. "Blue Movie: *Danton.*" *Sight and Sound* 52, no. 4 (1983): 284.

Bickley, Daniel. "The Cinema of Moral Dissent: A Report from the Gdańsk Film Festival." *Cineaste* 11, no. 1 (1980–81): 10–15.

Bickley, Daniel, and Lenny Rubenstein. "Between the Permissible and the Impermissible: An Interview with Andrzej Wajda." *Cineaste* 11, no. 1 (1980–81): 2–9, 49.

Biró, Yvette. "*Landscape after Battle:* Films from 'the Other Europe.'" *Daedalus* 119, no. 1 (1990): 161–82.

Borelli, Sauro. "Entuzjazm w Berlinie dla ostatniego filmu Wajdy. Tak umiera mistrz." *L'Unita* (29 Feb 1980).

Borowiec, Piotr. "Kariera senatora Wajdy." *Gazeta* 38 (1994): 38.

Bukoski, Anthony. "Wajda's *Kanał* and Mrożek's *Tango.*" *Literature/Film Quarterly* 20, no. 2 (1992): 133–37.

Caes, C[hris] J. "Catastrophic Spectacles: Historical Trauma and the Masculine Subject in *Lotna.*" *The Cinema of Andrzej Wajda: The Art of Irony and Defiance.* Eds. John Orr and Elżbieta Ostrowska. London: Wallflower, 2003. 116–31.

Canby, Vincent. "Act of Bravery. *Man of Iron.*" *The New York Times Film Reviews* (12 Oct 1981): C14–3.

———. "Film: Failed Marriage in Postwar Poland." *New York Times* (9 Oct 1979).

Chyb, Dariusz. "Inspiracje malarskie w filmach Andrzeja Wajdy." *Kwartalnik Filmowy* 15–16 (1996): 144–86.

Coates, Paul. "Forms of the Polish Intellectual's Self-Criticism: Revisiting *Ashes and Diamonds* with Andrzejewski and Wajda." *Canadian Slavonic Papers* 38, nos. 3–4 (1996): 287–303.

————. "Man of Marble." *24 Frames: Central Europe.* Ed. Peter Hames. London: Wallflower, 2004.

————. "Notes on Polish Cinema, Nationalism and Wajda's *Holy Week*." *Cinema and Nation.* Eds. Mette Hjort and Scott MacKenzie. London: Routledge, 2000. 189–202.

————. "Observing the Observer: Andrzej Wajda's *Holy Week* (1995)." *Canadian Slavonic Papers* 42, nos. 1–2 (2000): 25–33.

————. "Revolutionary Spirits: *The Wedding* of Wajda and Wyspiański." *Literature/Film Quarterly* 20, no. 2 (1992): 127–32.

————. "Wajda's Imagination of Disaster: War Trauma, Surrealism and Kitsch." *The Cinema of Andrzej Wajda: The Art of Irony and Defiance.* Eds. John Orr and Elżbieta Ostrowska. London: Wallflower, 2003. 15–29.

————. "Walls and Frontiers: Polish Cinema's Portrayal of Polish-Jewish Relations." *Polin: Studies in Polish Jewry* 10 (1997): 221–46.

Cowie, Peter. "Wajda Redux." *Sight and Sound* 49, no. 1 (1979–80): 32–34.

Darnton, Nina. "Poland's Man of Films." *New York Times Magazine* (11 Oct 1981): 141.

Dawson, Jan. "Man of Marble." *Sight and Sound* (Autumn 1979): 260.

De Nitto, Dennis, and William Herman. *"Ashes and Diamonds." Film and the Critical Eye.* New York: Macmillan, 1975. 362–95.

Derecki, Mirosław. "Wajda niepokorny. Rozmowa z prof. Aleksandrem Jackiewiczem." *Kamena* 13 (21 Jun 1981).

Dispot, Laurent. "L'Histoire escamotée." *Matin* (7 Jan 1983).

Dowell, Pat. "The Man Who Put Poland on the Post War Map of Cinema." *Cineaste* 19, no. 4 (1993): 52.

Eagle, Herbert. "Andrzej Wajda: Film, Language, and the Artist's Truth." *Cross Currents: A Yearbook of Central European Culture* 1 (1982): 339–53.

————. "Wajda's *Danton*." *Cross Currents: A Yearbook of Central European Culture* 3 (1984): 361–73.

Falkowska, Janina. "A Case of Mixed Identities: The Representation of Women in Post-Socialist Polish Films." *Canadian Woman Studies* 16, no. 1 (1995): 35–37.

————. "'The Political' in the Films of Andrzej Wajda and Krzysztof Kieślowski." *Cinema Journal* 34, no. 2 (1995): 37–50.

Farrington, Kevin. *"A Love in Germany." Cineaste* 14, no. 2 (1985): 18–21.

Fox, Geoffrey. "Men of Wajda." *Film Criticism* 6, no. 1 (1981): 3–9.

Friedman, Régine-Mihal. "Violence du sacrifice et sacrifice de la violence dans *Danton* de Andrzej Wajda." *Athanor: Rivista d'Arte, Letteratura, Semiotica, Filosofia* 2 (1991): 126–36.

Fruendt, Rodo. "Insanity Is the Rule (Der Irrsinn ist die Regel). Andrzej Wajda's Disputed Film Based on Hochhuth's Book *Eine Liebe in Deutschland*." *Sueddeutsche Zeitung* (6 Dec 1983).

Ginsberg, Terri. "Święty Korczak z Warszawy." Eds. Ewelina Nurczyńska-Fidelska and Piotr Sitarski. *Filmowy i teatralny świat Andrzeja Wajdy.* Kraków: Wydawnictwo Uniwersytetu Łódzkiego, 2003. 337–357.

Głowiński, Michał. "Fabryczne dymy i kwitnąca czeremcha." *Kino* 5 (1991): 28.

Godzic, Wiesław. "A Political Metaphor—or *Man of Marble* by Andrzej Wajda." *Analyses and Interpretations. Polish Film.* Eds. Alicja Helman and Tadeusz Miczka. Katowice: Uniwersytet Śląski, 1984. 106–119.

Gow, Gordon. "Cult Movies: *Ashes and Diamonds.*" *Films and Filming* 23, no. 6 (1977): 22–25.

Grzelecki, Stanisław. "*Pokolenie.*" *Życie Warszawy* 27 (1 Feb 1955).

———. "Review of *Lotna.*" *Życie Warszawy* (8 Oct 1959).

Haltof, Marek. "The Representation of Stalinism in Polish Cinema." *Canadian Slavonic Papers* 42, nos. 1–2 (2000): 47–61.

Helman, Alicja. "Filmowy Teatr Andrzeja Wajdy." *Tygodnik Powszechny* 50 (1994).

———. "Sarmata na płonącej żyrafie." *Ekran* 42 (1959).

———. "The Masters Are Tired." *Canadian Slavonic Papers* 42, nos. 1–2 (2000): 99–111.

Hendrykowski, Marek. "Polska szkoła filmowa jako formacja artystyczna." *Kwartalnik filmowy* 17 (Spring): 120–30.

———. "Realizm i symbolizm *Popiołu i diamentu* Andrzeja Wajdy." *Kino* 1 (1972): 25–27.

———. "Styl i kompozycja *Popiołu i diamentu* Andrzeja Wajdy." *Analizy i interpretacje. Film polski.* Eds. Alicja Helman and Tadeusz Miczka. Katowice: Wydawnictwo Uniwersytetu Śląskiego, 1984. 72–91.

———. "Uśmiech Stalina, czyli jak polubić socrealizm." *Kwartalnik filmowy* 41–42 (Spring-Summer): 65–89.

Hirsig, Andrea. "Onnagata Tamasaburo triumphs as Dostoevsky's femme fatale." *Mainichi Daily News* (15 Apr 1994): 9.

Holden, Stephen. "On How to Suffer and the Reasons." *New York Times* (25 Jan 1996): 19.

Hollender, Barbara. "Andrzej Wajda—Dowódca i Poeta." *Gwiazdy w Zbliżeniu. Portrety Aktorów i Reżyserów Polskich.* Ed. Jacek Lutomski. Warszawa: Presspublica, 1995. 237–43.

———. "Zajazd w kinie." *Rzeczpospolita* (26 Jul 1998): 8–13.

"Interview with *Wieczór Andrzeja Wajdy.*" Polish broadcast: Canal+ (26 Apr 1997).

Jackiewicz, Aleksander. "'Smuga cienia'—poszukiwanie innego języka." *Kino* 127, no. 11 (Sep 1976): 19.

Janion, Maria. "Egzystencja ludzi i duchów. Rodowód filmowej wyobraźni Andrzeja Wajdy." *Projekt krytyki fantazmatycznej. Szkice o egzystencjach ludzi i duchów.* Warszawa: Wydawnictwo PEN 1991. 110–19.

———. "Jeruzalem Słoneczna i Zaklęty Krąg." *Płacz generała. Eseje o wojnie.* Warszawa: 1998. 261–71.

———. "Wajda i wartości." *Odnawianie znaczeń.* Kraków: Wydawnictwo Literackie, 1980. 112–19.

Jędrzejewski, Paweł. "Wajda na linie." *Ekran* 35 (30 Aug 1981).

Kajewski, Piotr. "Urojenia żartem i serio." *Odra* 12 (2002): 88–89.

Kałużynski, Zygmunt. "Czarna Łódź Kolorowa." *Polityka* 8 (22 Nov 1975): 8.

———. "Dramat bezsiły, czy komedia złudzeń." *Polityka* 9 (3 Feb 1973).

———. "O Wajdzie bez znieczulenia." *Polityka* 49 (9 Dec 1978).

———. "'Wesele' czekało na kino." *Polityka* 3 (20 Jan 1973): 9.

Kałużynski, Zygmunt, and Tomasz Raczek. "Aria na ściśniętym gardle." *Wprost* 47 (Nov 1999): 118.

Kaps, Angelika. "Question of Responsibility (Frage nach Verantwortung). Wajda films Hochhuth's *Eine Liebe in Deutschland.*" *Tagesspiegel* (1 May 1983).

Kłopotowski, Krzysztof. "*Człowiek z żelaza.* Kontrowersje: Odpowiadam na zarzuty." *Tygodnik Solidarność* 14 (6 Nov 1981).

——. "Nic świętego." *Literatura* (24 Apr 1980): 9.

Kłossowicz, Jan. "Dostojewski, Wajda i Tamasaburo Bando." *L'Express. Spotkania* 17 (1993): 44–45.

Kobus, Justyna. "*Zemsta* Wajdy. *Zemsta* Andrzeja Wajdy to nieprzeciętnie kosztowny przeciętny teatr telewizji." *Wprost* 40 (6 Oct 2002): 118–19.

Komar, Michał. "'Ziemia obiecana' Andrzeja Wajdy." *Dialog* 2 (Feb 1975): 117–22.

Kotliński, Andrzej. "Kawaleria Wajdy." *Filmowy Świat Andrzeja Wajdy*. Eds. Ewelina Nurczyńska-Fidelska and Piotr Sitarski. Kraków: Universitas, 2003. 119–39.

Kowalski, Marcin. "Miłość nieodwzajemniona." *Trybuna Ludu* 271 (15 Nov 1983): 5.

Kustosik, Zbigniew. "Piłat w hitlerowskiej Kongresshalle. Andrzej Wajda mówi *Kurierowi* o realizacji filmu kręconego z udziałem polskich aktorów w RFN." *Kurier Polski* (14 Sep 1971).

Kuśniewicz, Andrzej, Rafał Marszałek, Anna Tatarkiewicz, Janusz Tazbir, and Krzysztof Teodor Toeplitz. "Bez znieczulenia." *Kultura* 33 (31 Dec 1978).

Lachnit, Ewa. "Andrzej Wajda—Portret." (Film prod. Fundacja dla Uniwersytetu *Jagiellońskiego* 1989. Excerpt from soundtrack.) *Kino* 275, no. 24 (1990): 20–22.

Łęczek, Ireneusz. "*Danton*. Rewolucja francuska według Wajdy." *Trybuna Robotnicza* 39 (16 Feb 1983).

Lewis, Clifford, and Carroll Britch. "Andrzej Wajda's War Trilogy: A Retrospective." *Film Criticism* 10, no. 3 (1986): 22–35.

Lis, Piotr. "Niektóre aspekty związków filmowo-literackich na podstawie *Panien z Wilka* Andrzeja Wajdy." *Krąg Historii i Literatury* (1987): 83–97.

Long, Kristi S. "Man of Iron: Representing and Shaping Historical Consciousness through Film: A Polish Case." *Journal of Popular Culture* 30, no. 1 (1996): 163–71.

Lothe, Jakob. "Andrzej Wajda's Adaptation of Conrad's *The Shadow Line*." *Conrad and Poland*. Eds. Alex Kurczaba and S. Boulder. New York: Distributed by Columbia UP, 1996. 217–32.

Lubelski, Tadeusz. "'He Speaks To Us': The Author in *Everything for Sale, Man of Marble* and *Pan Tadeusz*." *The Cinema of Andrzej Wajda: The Art of Irony and Defiance*. Eds. John Orr and Elżbieta Ostrowska. London: Wallflower, 2003. 30–45.

——. "Popiół i diament." *Kino* 9 (1992): 20–23, 44–46.

——. "Stara nowa 'Ziemia obiecana.'" *Kino* 9 (2000): 4–5, 61.

——. "Wajda. Portret mistrza w kilku odsłonach." Wrocław: Wydawnictwo Dolnośląskie, 2006.

Malatyńska, Maria. "Bez szansy." *Życie Literackie* 22 (1980): 5–6.

——. "Poziomkowa polana." *Życie Literackie*. Kraków: Młodzieżowa Agencja Wydawnicza (28 Dec 1986): 81–90.

Markowski, Andrzej. "Smuga cienia na ekranie." *Polska* 4, no. 260 (1976): 7.

Masłoń, Krzysztof. "Gerwazy Lustrator." *Rzeczpospolita* (26 Jul 1998): 9–12.

Mazierska, Ewa. "Non-Jewish Jews, Good Poles and Historical Truth in the Films of Andrzej Wajda." *Historical Journal of Film, Radio and Television* 20, no. 2 (2000): 213–26.

——. "The Exclusive Pleasures of Being a Second Generation Intelligent: Representation of Social Class in the Films of Andrzej Wajda." *Canadian Slavonic Papers* 44, nos. 3–4 (2002): 233–49.

McLauchlan, Juliet. "'Smuga Cienia' Andrzeja Wajdy." *Literatura* 36 (Sep 1976): 6–8.

Miczka, Tadeusz. "Literature, Painting, and Film: Wajda's Adaptation of *The Shadow-Line*." *Conrad on Film*. Ed. Gene M. Moore. Cambridge: Cambridge UP, 1997. 135–50.

Mirski, Michał. "Bronię Prawdy Samsona." *Polityka* 48, vol. 2, no. 12 (1961).

Młynarz, Kazimierz. "Duch żywego człowieka." *Kultura* 5 (4 Feb 1987).

Muszkat, Mariusz. "Laury niezasuszone." *Tygodnik Solidarność* 14 (21 Aug 1981).

Nurczyńska-Fidelska, Ewelina. "Andrzej Wajda's Vision of *The Promised Land*." *The Cinema of Andrzej Wajda: The Art of Irony and Defiance*. Eds. John Orr and Elżbieta Ostrowska. London: Wallflower, 2003. 146–59.

———. "Romanticism and History. A Sketch of the Creative Output of Andrzej Wajda." Eds. Ewelina Nurczyńska-Fidelska and Zbigniew Batko. *Polish Cinema in Ten Takes*. Łódź: Łódzkie Towarzystwo Naukowe, 1995. 7–19.

Ophuls, Marcel. "The Provocation and Interrogation of Andrzej Wajda on the Matter of *Danton* as Performed by Marcel Ophuls." *American Film* 9, no. 1 (1983): 24–28, 30, 93–95, 98.

Osęka, Andrzej. "Symbol wbrew prawdzie." *Gazeta Wyborcza* 221 (21 Sep 1993): 10.

Ostrowska, Elżbieta. "Dangerous Liaisons: Wajda's Discourse of Sex, Love and Nation." Eds. John Orr and Elżbieta Ostrowska. *The Cinema of Andrzej Wajda. The art of irony and defiance*. London: Wallflower, 2003. 46–63.

Ostrowski, M. "Danton czy Robespierre?" *Polityka* (5 Feb 1983).

Owczarski, Wojciech, Zbigniew Majchrowski, and Zbigniew Żakiewicz. "Soplicowo na sprzedaż?" *Dialog* 2 (2000): 108–18.

Paul, David. "Andrzej Wajda's War Trilogy." *Cineaste* 20, no. 4 (1994): 52–54.

Pawlicki, Maciej. "Tam, gdzie rosły poziomki." *Tygodnik Kulturalny* (18 Jan 1987).

Pawluśkiewicz, Joanna. "Sucha chusteczka." *Kino* 2 (2000): 28.

Pec-Ślesicka, Barbara. "Jak się robi filmy—mówi Barbara Pec-Ślesicka, kierownik produkcji Zespołu X." *Życie Warszawy* 176 (27 Jul 1978).

Pietrasik, Zdzisław. "*Pan Tadeusz*: To już ostatni taki film polski. Horror w zaścianku." *Polityka* 43 (23 Oct 1999): 17–18.

———. "Polonez musi być. Rozmowa z Andrzejem Wajdą, nie tylko o *Panu Tadeuszu*." *Kino* 5 (1998): 48–50.

Płażewski, Jerzy. "Sukces polskiego filmu w Cannes. Korespondencja własna." *Teatr i Film* 57, no. 1 (1957): 12–13.

———. "Z włosia czy z orłem w koronie?" *Wyborcza* 221 (21 Sep 1993): 11.

———. "Żeby nigdy więcej." *Kino* 2 (1984): 42–43.

Plisiecki, Janusz. "Analiza i interpretacja filmu *Wesele* Andrzeja Wajdy." *Studia Filmoznawcze* 18. Ed. Sławomir Bobowski. Wrocław: Wydawnictwo Uniwersytetu Wrocławskiego, 1997. 125–33.

Pyszny, Anna. "Adaptacja filmowa *Ziemi obiecanej* Władysława Reymonta." *Film a Literatura*. Wrocław: Dolnośląskie Towarzystwo Społeczno-Kulturalne, 1978. 63–77.

Raczek, Tomasz. "Litania do *Pana Tadeusza*." *Wprost* 44 (31 Oct 1999): 76.

Reed, Rex. "*Love in Germany* is force sans finesse." *New York Post* (9 Nov 1984).

Rickey, Carrie. "*Man of Iron*." *Village Voice* (Sep 23–29, 1981).

Rozicka, Anna. "*Lotna*-tekst zredukowany." *Film i kontekst*. Eds. Danuta Palczewska and Zbigniew Benedyktowicz. Wrocław: Ossolineum, 1988. 129–48.

Rubenstein, Lenny. "A Love in Germany: An Interview with Andrzej Wajda." *Cineaste* 14, no. 2 (1985): 19–20.

———. "*Danton.*" *Cineaste* 9, no. 1 (1983): 36–37.

———. "*The Orchestra Conductor.*" *Cineaste* 10, no. 4 (1980): 11–12.

Ruciński, Krzysztof. "Two Men Against History." *Kinoeye* 3, no. 3 (2003).

Sajdak, Jan. "Dwaj adwokaci przed sądem historii." *Odra* (1 May 1983).

Saniewski, Wiesław. "Kino polskie lat siedemdziesiątych. Dyskusja redakcyjna." *Film Na Świecie* 9 (1979).

Shoji, Kaori. "Bando Has It Both Ways in *Nastasja.*" *Japan Times* (28 Oct 1994).

Sobieszek, Bogdan. "*Zemsta.*" *Film* 11 (Nov 2002): 92.

Sobolewski, Tadeusz. "Biedni Polacy." *Kino* 11 (1995): 17–41.

Sowińska, Beata. "Jerzy Andrzejewski o *Popiele i diamencie.*" *Stolica* 8, no. 43 (1958): 18.

Sterritt, David. "*Danton.*" *Christian Science Monitor* (10 Jun 1983).

Strick, Philip. "*Danton.*" *Monthly Film Bulletin* 9 (1983): 242.

———. "*Korczak.*" *Monthly Film Bulletin* 11 (1990): 324.

Surdykowski, Jerzy. "Żelazem po marmurze." *Życie Literackie* 154 (3 Sep 1981).

Świeżynski, Wacław. "*Panna Nikt.*" *Gazeta Telewizyjna* 20–27 (Feb 1998): 4.

Szpakowska, Małgorzata. "Prawdy i nieporozumienia." *Kino* (1983): 9–12.

Szporer, Michael. "Andrzej Wajda's Reign of Terror: *Danton's* Polish Ambiance." *Film Quarterly* 37, no. 2 (1983–84): 27–33.

———. "Woman of Marble. An Interview with Krystyna Janda." *Cineaste* 18, no. 3 (1991): 12–16.

Szyma, Tadeusz. "Człowiek z żelaza." *Tygodnik Powszechny* 28 (12 Jul 1981).

———. "Kronika wypadków miłosnych." *Tygodnik Powszechny* (4 Jan 1987).

———. "Miłość w Niemczech." *Tygodnik Powszechny* (29 Jan 1984): 8.

Todorov, Tzvetan, and Robert Julian. "The Wajda Problem." *Salmagundi* 92 (1991): 29–35.

Toeplitz, Krzysztof Teodor. "Review of *Lotna.*" *Świat* (18 Oct 1959).

———. "Wajda Redivivus." *Film Quarterly* 23, no. 2 (Winter 1969–70): 37–41.

———. "'Wesele' jak najdalej od kolorowej bajki." *Miesięcznik Literacki* 1 (Jan 1973): 74–77.

———. "Zachwyty i obawy." *Miesięcznik Literacki* 3 (Mar 1975): 92.

Trbic, Boris. "*A Generation* and *Kanał.*" *Senses of Cinema: An Online Film Journal Devoted to the Serious and Eclectic Discussion of Cinema* 14 (2001).

Turim, Maureen. "Remembering and Deconstructing: The Historical Flashback in Man of Marble and Man of Iron" Eds. John Orr and Elżbieta Ostrowska. *The Cinema of Andrzej Wajda. The Art of Irony and Defiance.* London: Wallflower, 2003. 93–102.

Twórczość Andrzeja Wajdy. *Kwartalnik Filmowy* 15–16 (1996–97).

Wapshott, Nicholas. "Andrzej Wajda Wields the Baton." *Times* (22 Nov 1980): 42.

Wertenstein, Wanda. "Wariacje na znany temat: wywiad z Andrzejem Wajdą." *Kino* (March 1975): 2–10.

Wiórkiewicz Joanna. "Andrzej Wajda w Berlinie. W poszukiwaniu wspólnego dla Europy języka." *Samo życie* 5, no. 21 (May 1997): 8.

Wojciechowski, Piotr. "Co widać; w lustrze hrabiego Fredry?" *Przekrój* 40 (2002): 58.

Wokół scenariusza do filmu *Kanał* Andrzeja Wajdy: Protokół z posiedzenia Komisji Ocen Filmów i Scenariuszy w dniu 24 I 56." *Iluzjon* 41: 45–49.

Woroszylski, Wiktor. "'Jestem' Janusza Korczaka i Andrzeja Wajdy." *Kino* 8 (1990): 1–5.

——. "Pierścionek ze znakiem pytania." *Kino* 4 (1993): 11.

Wróblewski, Janusz. "Pamięć wyzwolona." *Kino* 2 (1987): 8–11.

Wysińska, Elżbieta. "Filmowa rzeczywistość *Wesela*." *Film* (18 Feb 1973): 8–11.

Żuławski, Andrzej. "The Ashes Diary (5): How to Tell This Story?" *Film* (16 Aug 1964).

Żwinogrodzka, Wanda. "Spopielony diament: Nieprawy mit." *Dialog: Miesięcznik Poświęcony Dramaturgii Współczesnej: Teatralnej, Filmowej, Radiowej, Telewizyjnej* 41, nos. 5–6 (1996): 136–47.

6. Books and Articles Written by Wajda

Andrzej Wajda. O polityce, o sztuce, o sobie. Warszawa: Prószyński and S-ka, 2000.

——. *Double Vision. My Life in Film.* New York: Holt, 1989.

——. *Kino i reszta świata.* Kraków: Wydawnictwo Znak, 2000.

——. "Kogo posłać do kąta?" *Kino* 7 (1975): 2–9.

——. "List Polskiej Federacji DKF do Sejmowej Komisji Kultury i Sztuki." *Kino* 1 (1981): 18.

——. "Moje notatki z historii." *Kwartalnik Filmowy,* nos. 15–16 (Fall-Winter 1996–97): 7–21.

——. "O filmowaniu prozy Iwaszkiewicza." *Dialog: Miesięcznik* 25, no. 1 (1980): 92–97.

——. "On Staging *The Possessed*." *Polish Perspectives* 17, no. 4 (1974): 67.

——. "Reżyser filmowy i świat współczesny. Andrzej Wajda w rozmowie z Romanem Polańskim." *Kino* 2 (1972): 31–36.

——. "Spotkałem wielu ludzi." *Kino* 4 (1991): 4–9.

——. "The Artist's Responsibility." *Politics, Art and Commitment in Eastern European Cinema.* Ed. David W. Paul. London: Macmillan, 1983. 293–97.

——. "The Katowice Regional TV Programme Is on the Air." *OIRT Radio Television* 38, no. 6 (1988): 13–17.

——. *Three Films [Ashes and Diamonds, Kanał, A Generation].* London: Lorrimer, 1984.

——. "W obronie tradycji przed przemocą systemu." *Kino* 9 (1994): 4, 21–22.

——. "Wajda's Censored Speech." *Cineaste* 13, no. 3 (1984): 13.

Wajda, Andrzej, and Stanisław Janicki. "Marzenia są ciekawsze: film o nie zrealizowanych projektach Andrzeja Wajdy." *Kino* 4 (1999): 24–29.

Wajda, Andrzej, and Tadeusz Lubelski. "Dlaczego filmuję *Pana Tadeusza*. O potrzebie samoograniczenia." *Kino* 5 (1988): 4–9.

※ FILMOGRAPHY

Pokolenie (A Generation), 1955 ✓

Director: Andrzej Wajda.
Screenplay: Bohdan Czeszko, (based on his novel, *Pokolenie*).
Director of Cinematography: Jerzy Lipman.
Music: Composed and conducted by Andrzej Markowski, performed by the Warszawa Philharmonic Orchestra.
Production Designer: Roman Mann.
Set Decoration: Jerzy Skrzepiński, Józef Galewski.
Costume Designer: Jerzy Szeski.
Makeup: Zdzisław Papierz.
Sound: Józef Koprowicz.
Editing: Czesław Raniszewski.
Assistant Directors: Kazimierz Kutz, Konrad Nałęcki.
Camera Operator: Stefan Matyjaszkiewicz.
Assistant Camera Operator: Czesław Grabowski.
Production Manager: Ignacy Taub.
Artistic Consultant: Aleksander Ford.
Cast: Tadeusz Łomnicki (Stach), Urszula Modrzyńska (Dorota), Tadeusz Janczar (Jasio Krone), Roman Polański (Mundek), Ryszard Kotas (Jacek), Janusz Paluszkiewicz (Sekuła), Zbigniew Cybulski (Kostka), Ludwik Benoit (Grzesio), Jerzy Krasowski, Zofia Czerwińska, Stanisław Milski, Tadeusz Fijewski, Juliusz Roland, Kazimierz Wichniarz, August Kowalczyk, Hanna Skarżanka, Cezary Julski, Zygmunt Zintel, and others.
Production: Wytwórnia Filmów Fabularnych 2 in Wrocław, 1954.
Premiere: 26 January 1955, Warszawa.
Awards: 3rd Grade National Award.

Kanał (Kanal), 1957 ✓

Director: Andrzej Wajda.
Screenplay: Jerzy Stefan Stawiński, (based on his novel, *Kanał*).
Director of Cinematography: Jerzy Lipman.
Music: Jan Krenz.
Sound: Józef Bartczak.
Production Designer: Roman Mann.
Interiors Designer: Leonard Mokicz.
Costume Designer: Jerzy Szeski.
Makeup: Halina Sieńska.

Editing: Halina Nawrocka.
Camera Operator: Jerzy Wójcik.
Assistant Directors: Janusz Morgenstern, Kazimierz Kutz.
Assistant Camera Operators: Andrzej Gronau, Czesław Grabowski.
Assistant Designers: Roman Wołyniec, Halina Krzyżanowska.
Makeup Assistant: Halina Turant.
Editing Assistant: Aurelia Rut.
Production Manager: Stanisław Adler.
Cast: Wieńczysław Gliński (Lt. Zadra), Teresa Iżewska (Stokrotka), Tadeusz
    Janczar (Korab), Emil Karewicz (Mądry), Władysław Sheybal (Composer),
    Stanisław Mikulski (Smukły), Teresa Berezowska (Halinka), Tadeusz
    Gwiazdowski (Kula), Adam Pawlikowski (German Officer), Zofia Lindorf,
    Jan Englert, Janina Jabłonowska, Maria Kretz, Kazimierz Dejunowicz,
    Zdzisław Leśniak, Maciej Maciejewski, and students of PWSTiF in Łódź.
Production: ZAF "Kadr" in WFF 1 in Łódz, 1956.
Premiere: 20 April 1957, Warszawa.
Awards: Jury's Special "Silver Palm" Award at 10th International Film
    Festival in Cannes, 1957; Gold Medal at the IFF of the International Youth
    and Student Festival, Moscow, 1957; Honorary Mention diploma at the IFF
    in Ibadan, 1961; Brasilian Film Critics' Distinction at Rio de Janeiro, 1961;
    Film magazine Readers' Award ("Golden Duck") for 1957.

Popiół i diament (Ashes and Diamonds), 1958 √

Director: Andrzej Wajda.
Screenplay: Jerzy Andrzejewski (based on his novel) and Andrzej Wajda.
Director of Cinematography: Jerzy Wójcik.
Second Director: Janusz Morgenstern.
Music: Jan Krenz and Michał Kleofas Ogiński (Polonaise), performed by the
    Rythmic Quintet of Polish Radio, Wrocław, conducted by Filip Nowak.
Sound: Bogdan Bieńkowski.
Production Design: Roman Mann.
Costume Design: Katarzyna Chodorowicz.
Makeup: Halina Sieńska, Halina Turant, Halina Zając.
Editing: Halina Nawrocka.
Camera Operator: Krzysztof Winiewicz.
Assistant Directors: Andrzej Wróbel, Anita Janeczkowa, Jan Włodarczyk.
Assistant Camera Operators: Wiesław Zdort, Zygmunt Krusznicki, Jerzy
    Szurowski, Bogdan Myśliński.
Assistant Set Designers: Leszek Wajda, Jarosław Świtoniak, Marian Kowaliński.
Assistant Editor: Irena Choryńska.
Production Assistants: Zygmunt Wójcik, Michał Sosiński.
Production Manager: Stanisław Adler.
Cast: Zbigniew Cybulski (Maciek Chełmicki), Ewa Krzyżewska (Krystyna),
    Wacław Zastrzeżyński (Konrad Szczuka), Adam Pawlikowski (Andrzej),
    Bogumił Kobiela (Drewnowski), Jan Ciecierski (Porter), Stanisław Milski
    (Pieniążek), Artur Młodnicki (Kotowicz), Halina Kwiatkowska (Mrs
    Staniewicz), Ignacy Machowski (Maj. Waga), Zbigniew Skowroński

(Słomka), Barbara Krafftówna (Stefka), Irena Orzecka (Grandmother
Jurgiełuszka), Aleksander Sewruk (Świecki), and Józef Pieracki,
Mieczysław Łoza, Tadeusz Kalinowski, Zofia Czerwińska, Grażyna
Staniszewska and others.
Production: ZAF "Kadr" at WFF 1 in Łódz and WFF 2 in Wrocław.
Premiere: 3 October 1958, Warszawa.
Awards: FIPRESCI Award at the 20th IFF in Venice, 1959; Canadian
Federation of Film Associations Award at the 3rd IFF in Vancouver, 1960;
Crystal Star Award of the French Film Academy for Ewa Krzyżewska,
1960; Diploma of Merit in Ibadan, 1961; American producer D.O.
Selznick's "Silver Laurel" Award for 1962; West German Film Critics'
Award for 1962; Czechoslovakian Film Critics' Award for 1965; *Film*
magazine Readers' Award ("Golden Duck") for 1958.

Lotna (Lotna), 1959

Director: Andrzej Wajda.
Screenplay: Wojciech Żukrowski (based on his short novel, *Lotna*) and
Andrzej Wajda.
Director of Cinematography: Jerzy Lipman.
Second Director: Janusz Morgenstern.
Music: Tadeusz Baird, performed by the National Philharmonic Orchestra in
Warszawa, conducted by Witold Rowicki.
Sound: Leszek Wronko.
Set Design: Roman Wołyniec.
Costume Design: Lidia Gryś, Jan Banucha.
Makeup: Stefan Szczepański, Roman Baszkiewicz.
Editing: Janina Niedźwiedzka, Lena Deptuła.
Military Consultant: Col. Karol Rómmel.
Camera Operator: Andrzej Gronau.
Assistant Director: Sylwester Chęciński.
Assistant Camera Operators: Czesław Grabowski, Antoni Nurzyński.
Assistant Set Designers: Halina Krzyżanowska, Leonard Mokicz, Marian
Kowaliński, A. Wejman.
Production Manager: Stanisław Adler.
Cast: Jerzy Pichelski (Capt. Chodakiewicz), Adam Pawlikowski (Lt. Wodnicki),
Jerzy Moes (Off. Cad. Jerzy Grabowski), Mieczysław Łoza (Sgt. Mjr.
Latoń), Bożena Kurowska (Ewa), Karol Rómmel (Priest), Roman Polański,
Wiesław Gołas, Tadeusz Somogi, Artur Młodnicki, Bronisław Dardziński,
Henryk Hunko, Tadeusz Kosudarski, Irena Małkiewicz, and others.
Production: ZRF "Kadr" at WFF 1 in Łódz, and WFF 2 in Wrocław, 1959.
Premiere: 27 September 1959, Zielona Góra.

Niewinni czarodzieje (Innocent Sorcerers), 1960

Director: Andrzej Wajda.
Screenplay: Jerzy Andrzejewski, Jerzy Skolimowski.

Director of Cinematography: Krzysztof Winiewicz.
Music: Krzysztof Trzciński-Komeda.
Vocals: Sława Przybylska.
Sound: Leszek Wronko, L. Księżak.
Makeup: Zdzisław Papierz.
Editing: Wiesława Otocka, Aurelia Rut.
Camera Operator: Wiesław Zdort.
Assistant Directors: Paweł Komorowski, Urszula Orczykowska, J. Karwowski.
Assistant Camera Operator: Tadeusz Jaworski.
Production Assistants: Romuald Hajnberg, Arkadiusz Orłowski.
Production Manager: Stanisław Adler.
Cast: Tadeusz Łomnicki (Bazyli / Andrzej), Krystyna Stypułkowska (Pelagia /
   Magda), Wanda Koczewska (Mirka), Zbigniew Cybulski (Edmund),
   Roman Polański (Polo), Krzysztof Trzciński-Komeda (Komeda), Kalina
   Jędrusik-Dygatowa (Journalist), Teresa Szmigielówna (Nurse), Jerzy
   Skolimowski (Boxing Champion), Andrzej Nowakowski, and others.
Production: ZRF "Kadr" at WFF in Łódz, 1960.
Premiere: 17 December 1960, Warszawa.
Awards: Diploma of Merit at 15th IFF in Edinburgh, 1961.

Samson (Samson), 1961

Director: Andrzej Wajda.
Screenplay: Kazimierz Brandys (based on his novel, *Samson*) and Andrzej Wajda.
Director of Cinematography: Jerzy Wójcik.
Music: Tadeusz Baird, performed by the National Philharmonic Orchestra,
   conducted by Stanisław Wisłocki.
Sound: Józef Bartczak.
Production Designer: Leszek Wajda.
Interior Set Decorations: Leonard Mokicz.
Set Decoration: Stefan Filipiak.
Costume Designers: Jan Banucha, Wiesława Chojkowska.
Makeup: Mirosław Jakubowski.
Editing: Janina Niedźwiecka.
Camera Operator: Wiesław Zdort.
Assistant Directors: Andrzej Żuławski, Zygmunt Hubner, Daniel Szylit,
   Barbara Zdort, Urszula Orczykowska.
Assistant Camera Operator: Czesław Grabowski.
Assistant Decorator: Halina Krzyżanowska.
Makeup Assistants: Jan Płażewski, Krystyna Chmielewska.
Editing Assistant: Maria Mastalińska.
Production Assistants: Zdzisław Mrozowicz, Ardadiusz Orłowski, Ryszard
   Jesionowski, Teresa Olszewska.
Lights: Aleksy Krywsza.
Photos: Jerzy Woźniak.
Production Manager: Stanisław Daniel.
Cast: Serge Merlin (Jakub Gold "Samson"), Alina Janowska (Lucyna),
   Elżbieta Kępińska (Kazia), Tadeusz Bartosik (Pankrat), Władysław

Kowalski (Fiałka), Jan Ciecierski (Mr. Malina), Beata Tyszkiewicz (Stasia), Irena Netto (Mother), with Roman Polański, Jan Ibel, Ryszard Ronczewski, Bogumił Antczak, and others.
Production: ZRF "Kadr" and ZRF "Drog" at WFF 1, Łódz, 1961.
Premiere: 11 November 1961, Warszawa.

Sibirska Leidi Makbet/Powiatowa Lady Makbet (Siberian Lady Macbeth a.k.a. [Fury Is a Woman]), 1962

Director: Andrzej Wajda.
Screenplay: Sveta Lukić, (based on a short story by Nikolai Leskov).
Director of Cinematography: Aleksandar Sekulović.
Music: Dušan Radić, based on motives from Dmitri Shostakovitch's opera *Katerina Izmailova*, performed by the Lublana Philharmonic Orchestra, conducted by Oskar Danon.
Sound: Vladimir Dodik.
Production Designer: Miomir Denić.
Costume Designer: Mira Glisić.
Editing: Milanka Nanović.
Production Manager: Milenko Stanković.
Cast: Olivera Marković (Katerina Izmailova), Ljuba Tadić (Sergei), Miodrag Lazarević (Zinovy Izmailov Nikiticz), Branka Petrić (Aunt), Ingrid Lotarijus (Sonietka), with Spela Rozin, Kapitalina Erić, and others.
Production: Avala Film in Belgrade, 1961.
Premiere: 22 January 1962, Belgrade (world premiere); Polish premiere, 1964.
Awards: 9th Annual Pula Festival of Yugoslav Films, 1962: awards for Cinematography by Aleksandar Sekulović and for best female role played by Olivera Marković.

Miłość dwudziestolatków (Love at Twenty), 1962

Director: Andrzej Wajda.
Screenplay: Jerzy Stefan Stawiński.
Director of Cinematography: Jerzy Lipman.
Composer: Jerzy Matuszkiewicz.
Costume Designers: Ewa Starowieyska and Jerzy Sieński.
Editing: Halina Nawrocka.
Assistant Director: Andrzej Żuławski.
Production Manager: Barbara Pec-Ślesicka.
Cast: Barbara Kwiatkowska-Lass (Basia), Zbigniew Cybulski (Zbyszek), Władysław Kowalski (Władek), and others.
Production: ZRF "Kamera," 1962.
Premiere: 22 June 1962. Berlin (world premiere); Polish premiere, 1965.
Note: The remaining episodes that comprise *Love at Twenty* were directed by Francois Truffaut, Renzo Rossellini, Marcel Ophuls, and Shintaro Ishihara. The film was jointly produced by Ulysses-Unitec (Paris), Cinesecolo (Rome), Toho-Yowa (Tokyo), Beta (Munich), and ZRF "Kamera" (Warszawa).

Popioły (Ashes), 1965 √

Director: Andrzej Wajda.
Screenplay: Aleksander Ścibor-Rylski, (based on the novel by Stefan Żeromski, *Ashes*).
Director of Cinematography: Jerzy Lipman.
Second Director: Andrzej Żuławski.
Music: Andrzej Markowski, performed by the National Philharmonic Orchestra, conducted by the composer.
Sound: Jan Czerwiński and Jerzy Neugebauer.
Production Designer: Anatol Radzinowicz.
Costume Designers: Ewa Starowieyska and Jerzy Szeski.
Interior Set Decoration: Marek Iwaszkiewicz.
Makeup: Tadeusz Schessler, Mieczysław Pośmiechowicz, and Kirył Trojanow.
Camera Operators: Andrzej Kostenko, Franciszek Kądziołka, and Zbigniew Raplewski.
Editing: Halina Nawrocka.
Assistant Directors: Andrzej Brzozowski, Halina Lachowicz, Włodzimierz Olszewski.
Assistant Camera Operators: Jerzy Białek and Stanisław Matuszewski.
Assistant Designers: Maria Zalewska, Ireneusz Salański, Andrzej Płocki, and Ignacy Gaworkiewicz.
Assistant Costume Designers: Maria Kobierska, Danuta Polis.
Sound Assistant: Józef Tomporek.
Editing Assistant: Anna Rubińska.
Production Assistants: Stanisław Moroszkiewicz, Helena Nowicka, Mieczysław Adler, Henryk Szlachet, Lechosław Szuttenbach.
Consultants: Zbigniew Michalski (battles), Karol Lindner (uniforms), Aleksander Czerwiński (weapons), Andrzej Banach (manners), Janina Jarzynówna (dance), Andrzej Osadziński and Kazimierz Stawiński (horseback riding), Zbigniew Prus-Niewiadomski (vehicles).
Production Managers: Włodzimierz Śliwiński and Konstanty Lewkowicz.
Cast: Daniel Olbrychski (Rafał Olbromski), Pola Raksa (Helena de With), Bogusław Kierc (Krzysztof Cedro), Beata Tyszkiewicz (Princess Elżbieta Ginutułtówna), Piotr Wysocki (Prince Gintułt), Józef Duriasz (Capt. Piotr, Rafał's brother), Władysław Hańcza (Rafał's Father), Jadwiga Andrzejewska (Rafał's Mother), Stanisław Zaczyk (Prince Józef Poniatowski), Jan Świderski (Gen. Sokolnicki), Jan Nowicki (Captain Wyganowski), Jan Koecher (De With), Janusz Zakrzeński (Napoleon), Barbara Wrzesińska (Zofka, Rafał's sister), Zbigniew Sawan (Count Cedro), Zofia Saretok (Helena's Aunt), Józef Nalberczak, Adam Mularczyk, Arkadiusz Bazak, Andrzej Kozak, Stanisław Mikulski, Alicja Boniuszko, Jerzy Kaczmarek, Adam Królikiewicz, Krzysztof Litwin, Irena Olszewska, Ryszard Pietruski, Jerzy Przybylski, Bogusław Sochnacki, Janusz Sykutera, Tomasz Zaliwski, and others.
Production: ZRF "Rytm" at WFF in Łódź, 1965.
Premiere: 25 September 1965, Warszawa.
Awards: *Film* magazine "Golden Duck" Readers' Award for 1965.

Bramy Raju (The Gates to Paradise), 1968

Director: Andrzej Wajda.
Screenplay: Andrzej Wajda and Jerzy Andrzejewski (based on his novel *The Gates to Paradise*).
English Dialogue: Donald Howard.
Director of Cinematography: Mieczysław Jahoda.
Music: Ward Swingle.
Costume Designer: Ewa Starowieyska.
Editing: Derek Twist.
Assistant Director: Władysław Sheybal.
Producer: Sam Waynberg.
Cast: Lionel Stander (Monk), Ferdy Mayne (Count Ludovic, Narrator), Jenny Agutter (Maud), Mathieu Carriere (Alexis), John Ferdyce (Jacob), Pauline Challoner (Blanche), Denis Gilmore (Robert), and others.
Production: Jointex Film, London, and Avala Film in Belgrade, 1967.
Premiere: First shown 23 June 1968 at the IFF in West Berlin. World premiere in London, England, 18 January 1971. Not shown in Poland.

Przekładaniec (Roly Poly), 1968 / *Layer Cake*

Director: Andrzej Wajda.
Screenplay: Stanisław Lem, (based on his short story).
Director of Cinematography: Wiesław Zdort.
Music: Andrzej Markowski.
Sound: Wiesława Dembińska.
Production Designer: Teresa Barska.
Interior Set Decorations: Maciej Putowski.
Costume Designers: Barbara Hoff and Teresa Tryburska.
Makeup: Krystyna Chmielewska.
Editing: Halina Prugar.
Camera Operator: Andrzej Ramlau.
Assistant Directors: Andrzej Piotrowski, Włodzimierz Kamiński.
Assistant Camera Operator: Józef Bakalarski.
Assistant Designer: Wiesław Orłowski.
Makeup Assistant: Jolanta Mijal.
Editing Assistant: Grażyna Kociniak.
Production Manager: Barbara Pec-Ślesicka.
Cast: Bogumił Kobiela (Richard Fox and Thomas Fox), Ryszard Filipski (Lawyer), Anna Prucnal (Fox's Wife), Jerzy Zelnik (Dr. Burton), Piotr Wysocki (Dr. Benglow), Tadeusz Pluciński (False Priest), Wojciech Rajewski (The Man with the Dog), Marek Kobiela, Gerard Wilk, Ewa Gąsowska, Marta Przyborzanka, Barbara Mikielska, Elżbieta Nowacka, Barbara Biernacka, and the music group "Niebiesko-Czarni".
Production: ZRF "Kamera" for Polish Television at WFD, Warszawa, 1968.
Premiere: 17 August 1968, on Polish television.
Awards: "Golden Screen" (1968) by the film weekly *Ekran*; Radio and Television Committee awards for the director and the writer.

Wszystko na sprzedaż (Everything for Sale), 1969

Director: Andrzej Wajda.
Screenplay: Andrzej Wajda.
Director of Cinematography: Witold Sobociński.
Music: Composed and conducted by Andrzej Korzyński, performed by the orchestra and by the "Trubadurzy" band.
Sound: Wiesława Dembińska.
Production Designer: Wiesław Śniadecki.
Costumes: Katarzyna Chodorowicz.
Makeup: Jadwiga Świętosławska and Anna Adamek.
Editing: Halina Prugar.
Camera Operator: Maciej Kijowski.
Assistant Directors: Andrzej Piotrowski, Andrzej Kostenko, Krystyna Grochowicz.
Assistant Camera Operators: Bohdan Borewicz, Lech Zielaskowski, Aleksy Krywsza.
Assistant Designers: Mariusz Kowalski, Hanna and Gabriel Rechowicz.
Editing Assistant: Grażyna Pliszczyńska.
Production Assistants: Tadeusz Szarski, Bogusław Kozakiewicz, Danuta Iwanowska.
Production Manager: Barbara Pec-Ślesicka.
Cast: Andrzej Łapicki (Andrzej, Film Director), Beata Tyszkiewicz (Beata, Andrzej's Wife), Elżbieta Czyżewska (Ela, the Actor's Wife), Daniel Olbrychski (Daniel), Małgorzata Potocka (Mała), Witold Holz (Witek, Assistant Director), Bogumił Kobiela (Bobek), Franciszek Starowieyski, Irena Laskowska, Tadeusz Kalinowski, Wiesław Dymny, Witold Dederko, Andrzej Kostenko, Wanda Warska, Adam Pawlikowski, Józef Fuchs, Wojciech Solarz, with T. Baljon, J. Domański, B. Ejmont, K. Fus, A. Gawroński, W. Hoffman, I. Harasymowicz, B. Jarosz, M. Kalenik, J. Karaszkiewicz, B. Lyakowski, E. Nowacka, R. Ostałowski, L. Pietraszak, A. Piotrowski, J. Turowicz, and others.
Produced: ZRF "Kamera" at WFD in Warszawa; and WFF in Łódz, 1968.
Premiere: 25 January, 1969, Warszawa.
Awards: Syrenka Warszawska ("Warszawa Mermaid") by the Film Critics' Club of the Polish Journalists' Association (SDP), 1969.

Polowanie na muchy (Hunting Flies), 1969

Director: Andrzej Wajda.
Screenplay: Janusz Głowacki, (based on his short story, *Hunting Flies*).
Director of Cinematography: Zygmunt Samosiuk.
Music: Andrezj Korzyński, executed by the Polish radio Orchestra, directed by the composer; the "Trubadurzy" band with Andrzej Nebeski's group.
Sound: Wiesława Dembińska.
Production Designer: Teresa Barska.
Interior Set Designer: Maciej Putowski.
Costume Designer: Renata Własow.

Makeup: Halina Turant-Ber.
Script: Krystyna Grochowicz.
Editing: Halina Prugar.
Camera Operator: Wacław Dybowski.
Assistant Directors: Jan Budkiewicz, Daniel Olbrychski.
Assistant Camera Operators: Tadeusz Janczak, Eugeniusz Maciaszek.
Assistant Decorator: Wacław Jasinowski.
Assistant Makeup Artist: Krystyna Leszczyńska.
Assistant Mixers: Ryszard Skibinski, Stanisław Malazek.
Assistant Editors: Andrzej Dziewicki, Grażyna Pliszczyńska.
Production Assistants: Janina Krassowska, Andrzej Kotkowski, Tadeusz
  Drewno.
Production Manager: Barbara Pec-Ślesicka.
Cast: Małgorzata Braunek (Irena), Zygmunt Malanowicz (Włodek), Ewa
  Skarżanka (Włodek's Wife, Hanka), Hanna Skarżanka (Włodek's Mother-
  in-law), Józef Pieracki (Włodek's Father-in-law), Daniel Olbrychski
  ("Castaway"), Irena Laskowska (Journalist), Marek Grechuta, Irena
  Dziedzic, Leszek Krogosz, Jacek Fedorowicz, Artur Litwiński, Witold
  Dederko, Stefan Friedman, Marek Perepeczko, Julia Bratny, Leon
  Bukowiecki, Antonina Girycz, Jerzy Kaczmarek, Jerzy Karaszkiewicz,
  Andrzej Krasicki, Tomasz Lengren, Jolanta Lothe, Wanda Lothe-
  Stanisławska, Ludwik Pak, Ryszard Pietruski, Ryszard Pracz, Jerzy
  Próchnicki, Kazimiera Utrata, Mieczysław Waskowski, and the "Bliscy
  płaczu" group (R. Poznakowski, S. Kowalewski, K. Krawczyk and M.
  Lichtman).
Produced: PRF "Zespoły Filmowe" at WFD in Warszawa in Łódz, 1969.
Premiere: 21 May 1969 at the IFF in Cannes.

Brzezina (The Birchwood), 1970

Director: Andrzej Wajda.
Screenplay: Jarosław Iwaszkiewicz, (based on his short story, *The Birchwood*).
Director of Cinematography: Zygmunt Samosiuk.
Music: Andrzej Korzyński, preformed by an orchestra conducted by Jan
  Pruszak.
Piano: Janusz Sent.
Vocals: Łucja Prus.
Music Consultant: Anna Grabowska.
Sound: Wiesława Dembińska.
Production Designer: Maciej Putowski.
Costume Designer: Renata Własow.
Makeup: Mirosław Jakubowski.
Editing: Halina Prugar.
Second Director: Jan Budkiewicz.
Camera Operator: Edward Kłosiński.
Assistant Directors: Andrzej Kotkowski, Krystyna Grochowicz.
Assistant Camera Operator: Franciszek Lokaj, Mieczysław Kozaczyk.
Assistant Designers: Wacław Jesionowski and Wojciech Filipowicz.

Makeup Assistant: Anna Adamek.
Sound Assistant: Kazimierz Kucharski.
Editing Assistant: Irena Jasińska.
Production Assistants: Janina Krassowska, Janusz Szela.
Production Manager: Barbara Pec-Ślesicka.
Cast: Daniel Olbrychski (Bolesław), Emilia Krakowska (Malina), Olgierd
    Łukaszewicz (Stanisław), Marek Perepeczko (Michał), Jan Domański
    (Janek), Danuta Wodyńska (Katarzyna), Elżbieta Zolek (Ola), Mieczysław
    Stoor, Jerzy Próchnicki, Andrzej Kotkowski, Jerzy Oblamski, Alina
    Szpakówna and Irena Skwierczyńska.
Production: PRF "Zespoły Filmowe" TOR Film Unit for Polish television.
    Made at WFD in Warszawa and WFF in Łódz, 1970.
Premiere: 10 November 1970, Warszawa.
Awards: FIPRESCI Award at the International Film and Television Fair
    (MIFED) in Milan, 1970; Gold Medal for "creative directing" for Andrzej
    Wajda, and the award for the male role of Daniel Olbrychski at 7th IFF in
    Moscow, 1971; "Golden Seal" at 7th IFF Cineteca Italiana in Milan, 1975.

Krajobraz po bitwie (Landscape after Battle), 1970

Director: Andrzej Wajda.
Screenplay: Andrzej Brzozowski and Andrzej Wajda, (based on a novel by
    Tadeusz Borowski).
Director of Cinematography: Zygmunt Samosiuk.
Music: Antonio Vivaldi *(The Four Seasons)*, Fryderyk Chopin *(Polonaise in A
    major)* and Zygmunt Konieczny, performed by the Polish Radio Orchestra
    conducted by Stefan Rachoń. Vocals by Ewa Demarczyk. Gypsy ballad
    sung by Robert Michaj.
Sound: Wiesława Dembińska.
Production Designer: Jerzy Szeski, Renata Własow.
Choreography: Marek Gołębiowski.
Editing: Halina Prugar.
Assistant Director: Andrzej Brzozowski.
Production Assistants: Janina Krassowska, Janusz Szela, Wiesława
    Dyksińska, Zbigniew Ronert.
Production Manager: Barbara Pec-Ślesicka.
Cast: Daniel Olbrychski (Tadeusz), Stanisława Celińska (Nina), Tadeusz
    Janczar (Karol), Mieczysław Stoor (Ensign), Zygmunt Malanowicz (Priest),
    Leszek Drogosz (Tolek), Aleksander Bardini (Professor), Stefan Friedmann
    (Gypsy), Jerzy Zelnik (American Camp Commander), Anna German
    (American Woman), Andrzej Piszczatowski (Sentry), Bohdan Tomaszewski
    (Polish Liaison Officer), Małgorzata Braunek (German Woman on bicycle),
    Józef Pitorak (Bishop), Andrzej Beksiński (Priest), Alina Szpakówna
    (German Woman), Józef Harasiewicz (Foreman), Wojciech Lewandowski
    (Major), Leonard Mokicz (Colonel), Małgorzata Leśniewska (Prisoner),
    Jerzy Oblamski, Jerzy Bekker, Witold Holz, Jerzy Próchnicki, Kazimierz
    Rowiński (Prisoners), Tomasz Lengren, Stanisław Michalski, Oskar Dewitz

(American Soldiers) with Agnieszka Fittkau, Jerzy Gaździński-Łapiński, Herman Lercher, Leszek Kowalski, Konrad Wawrzyniak and others.
Production: PRF "Zespoły Filmowe" Film Unit "Wektor," 1970.
Premiere: 14 May 1970 at the IFF in Cannes (world premiere). Polish premiere: 8 September 1970, Warszawa.
Awards: *Film* magazine "Golden Duck," 1970; "Warszawa Siren" Award of the Film Critics' Club of the SDP, 1971; "Golden Globe" at the 3rd IFF Cineteca Italiana in Milan, 1971; First Prize at the 5th IFF in Colombo, 1972.

Piłat i inni (Pilate and Others), 1972

Director: Andrzej Wajda.
Screenplay: Andrzej Wajda, (based on a novel by Mihail Bulhakov, *The Master and Margaret*).
Director of Cinematography: Igor Luther.
Music: Johann Sebastian Bach (chorales from the *St. Matthew Passion*).
Sound: Ludwig Gebhardt.
Production Designer: Andrzej Wajda.
Costume Designers: Andrzej Wajda, Günther Lüdecke.
Props: Jürgen Weitkunat, Anton Kirchner.
Makeup: Ludwig Ziegler.
Lighting: Klaus Buchner.
"Script-Girl": Dörte Gens.
Editing: Joanna Rojewska.
Assistant Director: Helga Asenbaum.
Assistant Editor: Waltraut Wischniewski.
Production Assistants: Gunther Henel, Jiži Kaska.
Text Editor: Heinrich Carle.
Dubbing: Konrad von Molo.
Production Manager: Klaus Michael Kühn.
Cast: Wojciech Pszoniak (Joshua Ha-Nocri), Jan Kreczmar (Pilate), Daniel Olbrychski (Matthew), Andrzej Łapicki (Afranius), Marek Perepeczko (the Centurion Mark "Death Rat"), Władysław Sheybal (Caiphas), Jerzy Zelnik (Judas), Peter M. Hollmann, Hans Schulze, Günther Meissner, Walter Ladengast, Erwin Adolf Leitner, and others. German voices: O.E. Hasse, Rüdiger Bahr, Jürgen Claussen, Hans Michael Rehberg, Herbert Weikert.
Production: Zweites Deutsches Fernsehen, Mainz (West Germany), 1971.
Premiere: 29 March 1972 on TV-ZDF, West Germany. Polish premiere, January 1975.
Awards: West German TV "Bambi" Award, 1972.

Wesele (The Wedding), 1973

Director: Andrzej Wajda.
Screenplay: Andrzej Kijowski, (based on the play by Stanisław Wyspiański).
Cinematography: Witold Sobociński.

Music: Stanisław Radwan, Eugeniusz Rudnik (Experimental Studio of the
Polish Radio).
Sound: Wiesława Dembińska.
Scenography: Tadeusz Wybult.
Interior Set Decoration: Maciej Putowski.
Costumes: Krystyna Zachwatowicz.
Makeup: Halina Ber, Irena Czerwińska.
Second Director: Andrzej Kotkowski.
Editing: Halina Prugar.
Photos: Renata Pajchel.
Camera Operator: Sławomir Idziak.
Script: Magda Stelmaszczyk.
Assistant Directors: Krzysztof Bukowski, Witold Holz.
Assistant Camera Operators: Jan Mogilnicki, Piotr Jaszczuk.
Scenographer's Assistants: Felicja Błaszyńska, Piotr Dudziński.
Second Production Manager: Tadeusz Drewno.
Production Manager: Barbara Pec-Ślesicka.
Cast: Daniel Olbrychski (Bridegroom), Ewa Ziętek (Bride), Małgorzata
Lorentowicz (Councilor's Wife), Barbara Wrzesińska (Maryna), Andrzej
Łapicki (Poet), Wojciech Pszoniak (Journalist and Stańczyk), Marek
Perepeczko (Jasiek), Maja Komorowska-Tyszkiewicz (Rachela), Franciszek
Pieczka (Czepiec), Marek Walczewski (Host), Emilia Krakowska (Marysia),
Gabriela Kwasz (Zosia), Maria Konwicka (Haneczka), Iza Olszewska
(Hostess), Andrzej Szczepkowski (Nose), Mieczysław Czechowicz (Priest),
Kazimierz Opaliński (Father), Bożena Dykiel (Kasia), Mieczysław Stoor
(Wojtek), Janusz Bukowski (Kasper), Leszek Piskorz (Staszek), Ania
Góralska (Isia), Artur Młodnicki (Wernyhora), Olgierd Łukaszewicz
(Phantom), Czesław Wołłejko (Hetman), Wirgiliusz Gryń (Ghost-Szela),
Czesław Niemen (Chochol's Voice), and the folk groups "Kamionka" from
Łysa Góra, "Koronka" from Bobowa, and "Opocznianka" from Opoczno.
Production: PRF "Zespoły Filmowe," Zespół Filmowy "X" group at WFD in
Warszawa, 1972.
Premiere: 8 January 1973, Kraków.
Awards: "Silver Shell" award at 21st IFF in San Sebastian, 1973; Grand Prix
"Golden Grape" for the best Polish film of 1972/73 at 5th Lubuskie Film
Summer, 1973; "Golden Camera" award from *Film* magazine, 1973.

Ziemia obiecana (Promised Land), 1975

Director: Andrzej Wajda.
Screenplay: Andrzej Wajda, (based on a novel by Władysław Reymont,
Promised Land).
Cinematography: Witold Sobociński, Edward Kłosiński, Wacław Dybowski.
Second Directors: Andrzej Kotkowski and Jerzy Domaradzki.
Music: Wojciech Kilar, performed by the Great Orchestra of Polish Radio and
Television, conducted by Konrad Bryzek. Ballad "Promised Land," by
Zygmunt Konieczny and Jonasz Kofta.
Music Consultant: Anna Grabowska.

Sound: Krysztof Wodziński, Leszek Wronko.
Scenography: Tadeusz Kosarewicz.
Set Design: Maciej Putowski, Maria Osiecka-Kuminek.
Costumes: Barbara Ptak, Danuta Kowner.
Makeup: Halina Ber.
Editing: Halina Prugar, Zofia Dwornik.
Consultants: Chief Conservator of Łódz Andrzej Szram, Małgorzata
    Laurentowicz, Jerzy Walczak, Andrzej Byszewski, Czesław Dziumowicz,
    Angelika Wegner, Włodzimierz Kryński.
Camera Operator: Janusz Kaliciński.
Photos: Renata Pajchel.
Director's Assistants: Krystyna Grochowicz, Jerzy Obłamski, Michał
    Ratyński.
Camera Operator's Assistants: Jan Górski, Jan Wiaderkiewicz.
Scenographer's Assistants: Piotr Dudziński, Andrzej Haliński, Adam
    Kopczyński.
Costume Designer Assistants: Alicja Karolak, Janina Tur-Kiryłow.
Makeup Assistants: Anna Adamek, Alicja Kozłowska, Jolanta Sołtysik.
Sound Assistants: Andrzej Hanzl, J. Szczeciński, J. Tomporek.
Editing Assistants: Jadwiga Ignatczenko, Anna Rubińska.
Production Manager Assistants: Anna Kłobukowska, Elżbieta Kozłowska,
    Jerzy Szebesta, Waldemar Król, Barbara Pietrakowska.
Second Production Managers: Janina Krassowska and Kazimierz Sioma.
Production Manager: Barbara Pec-Ślesicka.
Cast: Daniel Olbrychski (Karol Borowiecki), Wojciech Pszoniak (Moryc Welt),
    Andrzej Seweryn (Maks Baum), Anna Nehrebecka (Anka), Tadeusz
    Białoszczyński (Karol's Father), Franciszek Pieczka (Muller), Bożena
    Dykiel (Mada Muller), Danuta Wodyńska (Mrs. Muller), Marian Glinka
    (Wilhelm Muller), Andrzej Szalawski (Bucholc), Jadwiga Andrzejewska
    (Mrs. Bucholc), Kalina Jędrusik (Mrs. Lucy Zucker), Jerzy Nowak
    (Zucker), Stanisław Igar (Grunspan), Kazimierz Opaliński (Maks's Father),
    Andrzej Łapicki (Trawiński), Zbigniew Zapasiewicz (Kessler), Piotr
    Fronczewski (Horn), Wojciech Siemion (Wilczek), Jerzy Zelnik (Stein),
    Włodzimierz Boruciński (Halpern), Marek Walczewski (Bum-Bum),
    Bogusław Sochnacki (Grossgluck), Bohdana Majda (Mrs. Grossgluck),
    Teodor Gendera (Endelman), Aleksander Dzwonkowski (Priest),
    Kazimierz Wichniarz (Zajaczkowski), Zdzisław Kuźniar (Kaczmarek), Jan
    P. Kruk (Servant Mateusz), Jerzy Obłamski (Malinowski), Zofia
    Gryglaszewska (Mrs. Malinowska), Grażyna Michalska (Zośka
    Malinowska), Maciej Goraj (Adam Malinowski), Lidia Korsakówna
    (Widow), Emilia Krakowska (Gitla), Kazimierz Kaczor (Kipman), Jerzy
    Przybylski (Bucholc's Doctor), Mieczysław Waśkowski (Bucholc's
    Servant), Alicja Sobieraj (Anka's Servant), Janina Grzegorczyk (Mrs.
    Socha), Krzysztof Majchrzak (Socha), Janina Tur-Kiryłow (Singer), Ryszard
    Bronowicz (Singer), Witold Dederko (Old Dyer), Tomasz Lengren
    (Foreman), Jerzy Braszka (Engineer), Antoni Byszewski (Coachman), Józef
    Lodyński (Leon), Zofia Wilczyńska (Mrs. Grunspan), Lena Wilczyńska
    (Mrs. Endelman), Andrzej Wohl (Clerk), and others.
Production: PRF "Zespoły Filmowe," Zespół "X" group at WFF in Łódz, 1974.

Premiere: 21 February 1975, Warszawa.

Awards: Złote Lwy Gdańskie ("Gdańsk Golden Lions") at the 2nd Festival of Polish Feature Films in Gdańsk, 1975 (ex aequo), plus awards for W. Pszoniak, W. Kilar, and for scenography; Film Critics' Club of Association of Polish Journalists' "Warszawa Mermaid" award; "Złote Grono" award at Lubuskie Film Summer, 1975; Minister of Culture's Award for Andrzej Wajda, 1975; Golden Medal at 9th IFF in Moscow, 1975; nominated for Oscar in 1976; also, seven awards at international film festivals, including Golden Hugo at 11th IFF in Chicago, 1975; Grand Prix at 21st IFF in Valladolid, 1976; First Prize at 18th IFF in Cartagena (Columbia), 1978; First Prize at 19th IFF in Avellino, 1978.

Smuga cienia (The Shadow Line), 1976

Director: Andrzej Wajda.

Screenplay: Bolesław Sulik and Andrzej Wajda, (based on a short story "The Shadow Line" by Joseph Conrad).

Director of Cinematography: Witold Sobociński.

Music: Wojciech Kilar, performed by the Great Orchestra of Polish Radio and Television, conducted by Konrad Bryzek and Lech Brański performed by an orchestra conducted by the composer.

Music Consultant: Anna Grabowska.

Sound: Wiesława Dembińska, Jadwiga Malinowska.

Sceneography: Teresa Barska and Allan Starski.

Interior Set Design: Maria Osiecka-Kuminek.

Costumes: Krystyna Zachwatowicz, Wiesława Krop-Konopelska.

Makeup: Halina Ber, Anna Adamek.

Director's Co-Workers: Michael Darlow, Zorika Zarzycka.

Camera Operator: Andrzej Jaroszewicz.

Editing: David Naden, Mieczysława Kalisz.

Literary Consultant: Zdzisław Najder.

Photos: Renata Pajchel.

Assistant Directors: Zbigniew Kamiński, Krystyna Grochowicz, Magdalena Stelmaszczyk.

Assistant Camera Operator: Bogdan Borewicz.

Scenographer's Assistants: Janusz Pol, Maciej Morski.

Production Assistants: Andrzej Smulski, Alina Kłobukowska, Elżbieta Kozłowska, Waldemar Król, Andrzej Swat, Janusz Dziumowicz. Production cooperation on behalf of Thames Television: Jack Dawison, Udi Eichler, Mike Fash, Allan James, Mimi Kommins, Sandy Macrae, Robin Parker, Marylin Vince, Vicky Woolfson, Path Worth.

Thames Television Producer: Jolyon Wimhurst. Production Supervisor on behalf of Bulgaria, Mikolaj Welew.

Production Manager: Barbara Pec-Ślesicka.

Cast: Marek Kondrat (Joseph Conrad), Graham Lines (Burns), Tom Wilkinson (Ransome), Bernard Archard (Capt. Ellis), John Bennett (Host of the Club), Martin Wyldeck (Capt. Giles), Richard Bartlett (Doctor), Piotr Cieślak (First Officer), Zygmunt Hubner (Capt. "Vidara"), Eugeniusz

Priwieziencew (Frenchy), Gordan Richardson (Harbour Doctor), Stanisław Tym (Jacobus), Jerzy Zelnik (Secretary of the Captain's Office), Peter Cartwright, Geoffrey Collins, Geoffrey Hinsliff, John Quentin, Jeffrey Wickham, Marian Czyżewski, Stefan Friedmann, Piotr Garlicki, Tadeusz Jastrzębowski, Krzysztof Kumor, Zygmunt Maciejewski, Tomasz Mościcki, Adam Perzyk, Radosław Piwowarski, Igo Sawin, Maciej Staniewicz, and others.
Production: PRF "Zespoły Filmowe," Zespół "X," and Thames Television (London) at WFD in Warszawa, 1976.
Premiere: 1 July 1976, British TV (ITV); 6 September 1976, Warszawa.
Awards: Main award (II) at the 3rd Festival of Polish Feature Films in Gdańsk, 1976; award at the International Week of Maritime Films in Cartagena (Spain), 1979.

Człowiek z marmuru (Man of Marble), 1977

Director: Andrzej Wajda.
Screenplay: Aleksander Ścibor-Rylski.
Director of Cinematography: Edward Kłosiński.
Second Directors: Krystyna Grochowicz and Witold Holz.
Music: Andrzej Korzyński, performed by the "Ali Babki" group and instrument team, conducted by the composer.
Vocals: Jerzy Gert, Zdzisław Gozdawa, Alfred Gradstein, Andrzej Nowikow, Franciszek Pałka, Kazimierz Serocki, Wacław Stępień, Tadeusz Sygietyński, Władysław Szpilman; performed by the Polish Army Choir and Orchestra, the Folk Dance and Song Group "Mazowsze," and the Czejanda Choir.
Sound: Piotr Zawadzki.
Music Consultant: Małgorzata Jaworska.
Scenography: Allan Starski, Wojciech Majda.
Interior Set Design: Maria Osiecka-Kuminek.
Costumes: Lidia Rzeszewska, Wiesława Krop-Konopelska.
Makeup: Anna Adamek.
Camera Operator: Jacek Łomnicki.
Script: Magdalena Stelmaszczyk.
Editing: Halina Prugar.
Photos: Renata Pajchel.
Assistant Director: Leszek Tarnowski.
Assistant Camera Operators: Jan Ossowski, Jerzy Tomczuk.
Assistant Set Designer: Maria Lubelska.
Makeup Assistant: Iwona Kamińska.
Editing Assistant: Maria Kalicińska.
Assistant Producers: Elżbieta Kozłowska, Janusz Dziumowicz, Waldemar Król.
Second Production Managers: Alina Kłobukowska, Andrzej Smulski.
Production Manager: Barbara Pec-Ślesicka.
Cast: Jerzy Radziwiłowicz (Mateusz Birkut/Maciek), Krystyna Janda (Agnieszka), Tadeusz Łomnicki and Jacek Łomnicki (Film Director Burski), Michał Tarkowski (Wincenty Witek), Piotr Cieślak (Michalak), Wiesław Wójcik (Party Secretary Jodła), Krystyna Zachwatowicz (Hanka Tomczyk),

Magda Teresa Wójcik (Editor), Bogusław Sobczuk (TV Editor), Leonard Zajączkowski (Cameraman), Jacek Domański (Sound Engineer), Irena Laskowska (Museum Clerk), Zdzisław Kozień (Agnieszka's Father), Wiesław Drzewicz (Owner of Ostoja), Kazimierz Kaczor (Secret Police Colonel), Ewa Ziętek (Secretary), Grzegorz Skurski (Driver and Light Engineer), Jerzy Moniak (Witek's Deputy), Elżbieta Borkowska, Edmund Karwański, Henryk Łapiński, Irena Oberska, Zbigniew Płoszaj, Juliusz Roland, Maciej Rayzacher, Dorota Stalińska, Zdzisław Szymborski, Mariusz Swigoń, Krystyna Wolańska, Andrzej Wykretowicz, and others.
Commentary Voices: Mieczysław Grabka and Andrzej Seweryn.
Production: PRF "Zespoły Filmowe," Zespół "X" at WFD in Warszawa, 1976.
Premiere: February 25 1977, Warszawa.
Awards: FIPRESCI award at 31st IFF in Cannes, 1978; main award plus award for Jerzy Radziwiłowicz at 9th FEST in Belgrade, 1979; award for Jerzy Radziwiłowicz at 6th IFF in Brussels, 1979; special critics' award at 20th IFF in Cartagena (Columbia), 1980.
Note: The film used archival materials of the Polish Newsreel, as well as works by J. Bocheński, St. R. Dobrowolski, J. Ficowski, E. Fiszer, J. Gałkowski, A. Kłobukowska, H. Kołaczkowska, M. Lebkowski, T. Urgacz.

Bez znieczulenia (Without Anesthetic aka Rough Treatment), 1978

Director: Andrzej Wajda.
Screenplay: Agnieszka Holland and Andrzej Wajda.
Cooperation: Witold Zaleski.
Director of Cinematography: Edward Kłosiński.
Music: Jerzy Derfel, Wojciech Młynarski.
Sound: Piotr Zawadzki.
Scenography: Allan Starski.
Set Design: Maria Osiecka-Kuminek.
Costumes: Wiesława Starska.
Makeup: Halina Ber.
Camera Operator: Janusz Kaliciński.
Photos: Renata Pajchel.
Editing: Halina Prugar.
Assistant Directors: Krystyna Grochowicz, Krzysztof Tchórzewski, Jolanta Jedynak.
Assistant Camera Operators: Jan Ossowski, Jerzy Tomczuk.
Scenographer's Assistants: Maria Lubelska-Chorłowska, Magdalena Dipont.
Costume Designer's Assistant: Anna Włodarczyk.
Makeup Assistant: Grażyna Dąbrowska.
Sound Assistants: Małgorzata Lewandowska, Tadeusz Wosiński.
Editing Assistant: Maria Kalicińska.
Production Assistants: Alina Kłobukowska, Małgorzata Pakuła, Bożena Michalska, Tomasz Bek.
TV Sequences: Mariusz Walter, Tomasz Dębiński, Gabriela Miłobędzka, Henryk Babulewicz.
Production Manager: Barbara Pec-Ślesicka.

Cast: Zbigniew Zapasiewicz (Jerzy Michałowski), Ewa Dałkowska (Ewa Michałowska), Andrzej Seweryn (Jacek Rościszewski), Krystyna Janda (Agata), Emilia Krakowska (Wanda, the Dentist), Roman Wilhelmi (Broński), Kazimierz Kaczor (Editor in Chief), Iga Mayr (Ewa's Mother), Aleksandra Jasieńska (Oleńka), Marta Salinger (Gapcia), Stefania Iwińska (Nursemaid), Halina Golanko (Ewa's Sister), Jerzy Stuhr (Ewa's Attorney), Magda Teresa Wójcik (Michałowski's Attorney), Danuta Balicka-Satanowska (Judge), Jolanta Kozak-Sutowicz (Assistant to the Dentist), Zygmunt Kęstowicz (Assistant Editor), Tadeusz Andrzejewski, Teodor Gandera, Zbigniew Grusznic, Jerzy Kałucki, Waldemar Kapitułka, Krzysztof Kiersznowski, Hanna Kulina, Michał Kula, Wanda Lothe-Stanisławska, Maciej Maciejewski, Stanisław Michalski, Andrzej Mrowiec, Izabela Olejnik, Witold Pyrkosz, Bogdan Szymkowski, Tomasz Stockinger, Bogusław Sobczuk, Jerzy Radziwiłowicz, Grzegorz Wons, Wojciech Wysocki, Krystyna Wolańska, and others.
Production: PRF "Zespoły Filmowe," Zespół "X" Group at the WFD in Warszawa, 1978.
Premiere: 27 November 1978, Warszawa.
Awards: Grand Prix (ex aequo) at the 5th Polish Feature Films Festival in Gdańsk, 1978; "Warszawa Mermaid" of the Critics' Club of the Association of Polish Journalists, 1979; the Ecumenical Jury Award at the IFF in Cannes, 1979.

Panny z Wilka (The Young Ladies of Wilko), 1979

Director: Andrzej Wajda.
Screenplay: Zbigniew Kamiński, (based on a short story by Jarosław Iwaszkiewicz).
Cinematography: Edward Kłosiński.
Music: *First Violin Concerto* by Karol Szymanowski.
Music Consultant: Anna Grabowska.
Sound: Piotr Zawadzki.
Set Design: Allan Starski.
Interior Set Design: Maria Osiecka-Kuminek.
Costume Designer: Wiesława Starska.
Makeup: Anna Włodarczyk, Grażyna Dąbrowska.
Camera Operators: Janusz Kaliciński, Ireneusz Hartowicz.
Photos: Renata Pajchel.
Editing: Halina Prugar.
Assistant Directors: Krystyna Grochowicz, Magdalena Holland, Marek Netzel, Jolanta Jedynak.
Assistant Designer: Maria Lubelska-Chrołowska.
Production Assistants: Alina Kłobukowska, Henryk Włoch, Tomasz Bek, Maciej Skalski, Jolanta Jarzecka, Wanda Helbert, Elżbieta Kotynia.
Production Manager: Barbara Pec-Ślesicka.
French Producer: Tony Molière.
Cast: Daniel Olbrychski (Wiktor Ruben), Anna Seniuk (Julcia), Maja Komorowska (Jola), Stanisława Celińska (Zosia), Krystyna Zachwatowicz

(Kazia), Christine Pascal (Tunia), Zbigniew Zapasiewicz (Julcia's Husband), Zofia Jaroszewska (Wiktor's Aunt), Tadeusz Białoszczyński (Wiktor's Uncle), Andrzej Łapicki (Doctor), Paul Dutron (Jola's Husband), Joanna Poraska (Mother), Kazimierz Orzechowski (Priest), Krystyna Wolańska, Jolanta Kozak-Sutowicz, Andrzej Szenajch, Witold Kałuski, Barbara Stępniakówna, Andrzej Grzybowski, Filip Jasieński, Anna Wachnicka, Małgorzata Wachnicka, and others.

Production: PRF "Zespoły Filmowe," Zespół "X" Group, and Pierson Production; Les Films Moliere (Paris) at WFD in Warszawa, 1979.

Premiere: 4 September 1979, Warszawa.

Awards: Special award at the 6th Polish Feature Films Festival in Gdańsk, 1979, plus awards for set and interior design for Allan Starski and Maria Osiecka-Kuminek. Oscar nomination, 1980.

Dyrygent (The Orchestra Conductor), 1980 √

Director: Andrzej Wajda.

Screenplay: Anrzej Kijowski.

Director of Cinematography: Sławomir Idziak.

Music: *Fifth Symphony* by Ludwig van Beethoven, performed by the Great Orchestra of Polish Radio and Television, conducted by Stanisław Wisłocki.

Music Consultant: Małgorzata Jaworska.

Sound: Piotr Zawadzki.

Scenography: Allan Starski.

Interior Set Design: Maria Osiecka-Kuminek.

Costumes: Wiesława Starska.

Makeup: Anna Adamek.

Camera Operator: Piotr Kwiatkowski.

Photos: Renata Pajchel.

Editing: Halina Prugar.

Assistant Directors: Jakub Ruciński, Andrzej Kazanecki, Jolanta Jedynak.

Assistant Camera Operators: Bogdan Stankiewicz, Jerzy Tomczuk.

Scenographer's Assistants: Maria Lubelska, Joanna Lelanow.

Production Assistants: Alina Kłobukowska, Tomasz Bek, Maciej Skalski, Jolanta Jarzecka, Wanda Helbert.

Production Manager: Barbara Pec-Ślesicka.

Cast: Sir John Gielgud (John Lasocki), Krystyna Janda (Marta), Andrzej Seweryn (Adam Pietryk, Marta's Husband), Jan Ciecierski (Marta's Father), Marysia Seweryn (Marta and Adam's Daughter), Józef Fryźlewicz (Voivod), Janusz Gajos (Warszawa Dygnitary), Mary Ann Krasiński (Marta's American Friend), Anna Łopatowska (Anna), Mavis Walker (Lillian, Lasocki's Wife) and Tadeusz Czachowski, Marek Dąbrowski, Stanisław Górka, Jerzy Kleyn, Elżbieta Strzałkowska, Jerzy Schmidt, Wojciech Wysocki, Stanisław Zatłoka; and members of the Polish Army Symphony Orchestra.

Production: PRF "Zespoły Filmowe," Zespół "X" group at WFD in Warszawa, 1979.

Premiere: 27 February 1980, at IFF of West Berlin (world premiere). Polish premiere, 24 March 1980, Warszawa.

Awards: "Silver Bear" for the best male part to Andrzej Seweryn at the IFF in West Berlin, 1980; "Golden Seal" at the Belgrade FEST in 1981.

Człowiek z Żelaza (Man of Iron), 1981

Director: Andrzej Wajda.
Screenplay: Aleksander Ścibor-Rylski.
Director of Cinematography: Edward Kłosiński.
Music: Andrzej Korzyński, performed by an orchestra conducted by the composer.
Music Consultant: Małgorzata Przedpelska.
Music Registration: Sławomir Wesołowski, Mariusz Zabrodzki.
Sound: Piotr Zawadzki.
Production Designer: Allan Starski.
Interior Set Decoration: Magdalena Dipont.
Costumes: Wiesława Starska.
Makeup: Anna Adamek.
Second Director: Krystyna Grochowicz.
Second Production Designer: Maria Chrołowska.
Camera Operator: Janusz Kaliciński.
Editing: Halina Prugar.
Photos: Renata Pajchel.
Assistant Directors: Andrzej Chodakowski, Stanisław Kałużynski, Łukasz Zieliński.
Assistant Camera Operators: Jan Ossowski, Krzysztof Ciesielski, Mieczysław Kozaczyk.
Assistant Production Designer: Maria Lelanow.
Editing Assistants: Wanda Walerowicz, Danuta Leśniewska.
Production Assistants: Maciej Skalski, Iwona Ziółkowska, Henryk Włoch, Iwona Kłapińska, Wanda Helbert, Jacek Górnowicz.
Second Production Managers: Alina Kłobukowska, Maciej Wojtulewicz.
Production Manager: Barbara Pec-Ślesicka.
Cast: Jerzy Radziwiłowicz (Maciej Tomczyk), Krystyna Janda (Agnieszka, Maciej's Wife), Marian Opania (Winkiel), Andrzej Seweryn (Capt. Wirski), Irena Byrska (Hulewicz's Mother), Wiesława Kosmalska (Anna Hulewicz), Krzysztof Janczar (Kryska), Bogusław Sobczuk (TV Journalist), Bogusław Linda (Radio Technician), Franciszek Trzeciak (Badecki), Józef Tesarz (Boss), Janusz Gajos (First Representative), and others. Guest stars: Lech Wałęsa, Anna Walentynowicz, Stanisław J. Borowczak, Zbigniew Lis, Teodor Kudła.
Production: PRF "Zespoły Filmowe," Zespół "X" group at WFD in Warszawa, 1981.
Premiere: 2 May 1981 at IFF in Cannes (world premiere). Polish premiere, 27 July 1981, Warszawa.
Awards: "Golden Palm" and the Ecumenical Jury's Award at 34th IFF in Cannes, 1981; British Film Critic's Award at The London Film Festival, 1981; Oscar nomination 1982.

Danton (Danton), 1983 ✓

Director: Andrzej Wajda.
Screenplay: Jean-Claude Carriere, (based on the play by Stanisława Przybyszewska, *Danton's Case*).
Cooperation: Andrzej Wajda, Agnieszka Holland, Bolesław Michałek, Jacek Gąsiorowski.
Cinematography: Igor Luther.
Music: Jean Prodromides, performed by the National Philharmony Orchestra conducted by Jan Pruszak and by Warszawa Music Society's Choir conducted by Maciej Jaśkiewicz.
Scenography: Allan Starski.
Set Design: Maria Osiecka-Kuminek.
Costumes Designer: Yvonne Sassinot de Nesle.
Costumes: Anne le Laugardiere, Wiesława Starska, Krystyna Zachwatowicz.
Sound: Jean-Pierre Ruh, Dominique Hennequin, Piotr Zawadzki.
Makeup and Hair-Dressers: Jackie Reynal, Jacques Michel, Anna Adamek, Iwona Kamińska.
Script: Krystyna Grochowicz, Elsa Chabrol.
Casting: Marie-Christine Lafosse, Henri Laurent.
Costumes Execution: Tirelli-Rzym.
Historical Consultants: Profs Jan Baszkiewicz and Stefan Meller.
Documentary Research: Herve Grandsarte.
Editing: Halina Prugar-Ketling.
Assistant Directors: Hugues de Laugardiere, Michał Lisowski.
Scenographer's Assistant: Gilles Vaster.
Interior Set Decorator's Assistant: Jacques Flamand.
Production Assistant: Patrick Bordier.
Production Manager: Alain Depardieu.
Gaumont's Production Supervisor: Emmanuel Schlumberger.
"X" Group's Production Supervisor: Barbara Pec-Ślesicka.
Les Films du Losange's Production Supervisor: Margaret Menegoz.
Cast: Gerard Depardieu (Danton), Wojciech Pszoniak (Robespierre), Anne Alvaro (Eleonore Duplay), Rolande Blanche (Lacroix), Patrice Chereau (Camille Desmoulins), Emmanuelle Debever (Louison Danton), Krzysztof Globisz (Amar), Roland Guttman (Herman), Gerard Hardy (Tallien), Tadeusz Huk (Couthon), Stephane Jobert (Panis), Marian Kociniak (Lindet), Marek Kondrat (Barere de Vieuzac), Bogusław Linda (Saint-Just), Alain Mace (Heron), Bernard Maitre (Legendre), Lucien Melki (Fabre d'Eglantine), Serge Merlin (Philippeaux), Erwin Nowiaszak (Collot d'Herbois), Leonard Pietraszak (Carnot), Roger Planchon (Fouquier Tinville), Angel Sedgwick (Brother Eleonore), Andrzej Seweryn (Bourdon), Franciszek Starowieyski (David), Jerzy Trela (Billaud-Varenne), Anne-Marie Vennel (Woman from a Queue), Jacques Villeret (Westermann), Angela Winkler (Lucille Desmoulins), Jean-Loup Wolff (Herault de Sechelles), Czesław Wołłejko (Vadier), Wladimir Yordanoff (Guard's Commander), Małgorzata Zajączkowska (Maid-Servant), Szymon Zaleski (Lebas).
Coproduction: Gaumont, TF 1 Films Production, SFPC, TM with the participation of French Ministry of Culture and Film Polski.

Production: Les Films du Losange, Paris, and Zespół "X" group, Warszawa, 1982.
Premiere: 7 January 1983, Paris; 31 January 1983, Warszawa.
Awards: Louis-Delluc's award for Best French Film, 1982; "Cesar 83" award for Andrzej Wajda's direction.

Eine Liebe in Deutschland (A Love in Germany), 1983

Director: Andrzej Wajda.
Screenplay: Bolesław Michałek, Agnieszka Holland and Andrzej Wajda, (based on a novel by Rolf Hochhuth).
Cinematography: Igor Luther.
Scenography: Allan Starski.
Costumes: Ingrid Zöre, Krystyna Zachwatowicz.
Music: Michel Legrand.
Editing: Halina Prugar-Ketling.
Production Manager: Peter Hahne.
Producer: Arthur Brauner.
Coproducer: Emmanuel Schlumberger.
Cast: Hanna Schygulla (Paulina), Marie-Christine Barrault (Marie Wyler), Armin Müller-Stahl (Mayer), Elisabeth Trissenar (Elisabeth Schinittgens), Piotr Łysak (Stanisław Zasada), Daniel Olbrychski (Wiktorczyk), Gérard Désarthe, Bernard Wicki, Otto Sander, and others.
Production: Gaumont TF1/FP Stand'Art, CCC Film Kunst France, FRG 1983.
Premiere: Paris and Berlin, 1983. Shown in Poland on TV in 1990.

Kronika wypadków miłosnych (A Chronicle of Amorous Incidents), 1986

Director: Andrzej Wajda.
Screenplay: Andrzej Wajda, (based on a novel by Tadeusz Konwicki).
Cinematography: Edward Kłosiński.
Music: Wojciech Kilar.
Scenography: Janusz Sosnowski.
Costumes: Lidia Rzeszewska.
Editing: Halina Prugar-Ketling.
Production Manager: Barbara Pec-Ślesicka.
Cast: Paulina Młynarska (Alina), Piotr Wawrzyńczak (Witek), Bernardetta Machała (Greta), Dariusz Dobkowski (Engel), Tadeusz Konwicki (Stranger), Jarosław Gruda (Lowa), Tadeusz Łomnicki (Rev. Baum), Krystyna Zachwatowicz (Witek's Mother), Joanna Szczepkowska (Cecylia), Gabriela Kownacka (Olimpia), Bohdana Majda (Cecylia and Olimpia's Mother), Adrianna Godlewska (Alina's Mother), Leonard Pietraszak (Alina's Father), Andrzej Krasiński (Bishop), and others.
Production: PRF "Zespoły Filmowe" Zespół "Perspektywa," Warszawa, 1985.
Premiere: 24 November 1986, Warszawa.

Biesy (The Possessed), 1988

Director: Andrzej Wajda.
Screenplay: Jean-Claude Carriere in cooperation with Andrzej Wajda, Agnieszka
   Holland, Edward Żebrowski (based on a novel by Fyodor Dostoevsky).
Dialogues: Jean-Claude Carrière.
Cinematography: Witold Adamek.
Music: Zygmunt Konieczny.
Sound: Piotr Zawadzki.
Scenography: Allan Starski.
Costumes: Krystyna Zachwatowicz and Jolanta Jackowska.
Editing: Halina Prugar-Ketling.
Casting: Marie-Christine Lafosse.
Assistant Directors: Krystyna Grochowicz, Romain Goupil, Michał Lisowski,
   Piotr Hanuszkiewicz, Jan Dąbrowski, Paweł Wierkowski.
Assistant Camera Operators: Piotr Jaszczuk, Jan Ossowski, François Paumard.
Editing Assistants: Alicja Torbus-Wosińska, Anita Wandzel.
Scenographer's Assistants: Barbara Nowak, Barbara Komosińska, Ignacy
   Łodziński, Herve Grandsarte, Regis des Places, Marc Denize.
Photos: Renata Pajchel.
Production Manager: Barbara Pec-Ślesicka.
Cast: Isabelle Huppert (Maria Szatow), Jutta Lampe (Maria Liebiadkina),
   Philippine Leroy Beaulieu (Liza), Bernard Blier (Governor), Jean-Phillipe
   Ecoffey (Piotr Wierchowienski), Laurent Malet (Kiryłow), Jerzy
   Radziwiłowicz (Szatow), Omar Sharif (Stiepan Wierchowienski), Lambert
   Wilson (Mikolaj Stawrogin), Phillippe Chambon (Szigalew), Jean-Quentin
   Chatelain (Wirginski), Remi Martin (Erkel), Serge Spira (Fiedka), Wladimir
   Yordanoff (Lebiadkin), Zbigniew Zamachowski (Liamszyn), Piotr
   Machalica (Maurycy), Bożena Dykiel (Wirginska), Krzysztof Kumor
   (Adjutant), Witold Skaruch (Governor's Secretary), Tadeusz Łomnicki
   (Capt.), Wojciech Zagórski (Monk), Jerzy Klesyk (Seminarian), Tadeusz
   Włudarski (Coachman), Bogusz Bilewski (Police Commander), Ryszard
   Bromowicz (Servant), Jarosław Kopaczewski, Czesław Mroczek,
   Eugeniusz Kamiński, Józef Kalita, Klemens Mielczarek, Ryszard Jabłoński
   (Workers), Paweł Szczęsny, Jacek Bursztynowicz, Grzegorz Wons,
   Stanisław Górka (Plotters), Alina Świdowska (Wirginski's Sister), Beata
   Niedzielska (Student), Helena Kowalczyk (Maid).
Production: Gaumont Films (Films A2); Margaret Menegoz, Les Films du
   Losange, Paris, 1985.
Premiere: March 1988, Paris. Shown in Poland on TV, 1 July 1988, as *Shatov
   and the Demons.*

Korczak (Korczak), 1990

Director: Andrzej Wajda.
Screenplay: Agnieszka Holland.
Director of Cinematography: Robby Müller.
Scenography: Allan Starski.
Costumes: Wiesława Starska, Małgorzata Stefaniak.

Music: Wojciech Kilar, performed by the Great Orchestra of Polish Radio and Television in Katowice, conducted by Antoni Wit. Jewish song arranged by Wojciech Kaleta, performed by Nina Gajewska.

Sound: Janusz Rosół.

Special Effects: Bogdan Nowak.

Military Uniforms: Jan Rutkiewicz.

Editing: Ewa Smal.

Makeup: Ewa Symko-Marczewska, Jolanta Pruszyńska.

Second Directors: Krystyna Grochowicz, Paweł Wierkowski.

Assistant Camera Operator: Jakub Wdowicki.

Scenographer's Assistants: Ewa Skoczkowska, Marek Burgemajster, Robert Czesak, Grzegorz Piątkowski.

Assistant Directors: Andrzej Kotkowski, Ami Drozd.

Script: Małgorzata Zdziarska.

Set Design: Anna Kowarska, Magdalena Dipont.

Photos: Renata Pajchel.

Editors: David Thompson (BBC), Willi Segler (ZDF).

Production Organisers: Marek Składanowski, Robert Lipiński, Teresa Maleszewska.

Production: Regina Ziegler, Janusz Morgenstern.

Production Supervisor: Wolfgang Handtke.

Production Manager: Barbara Pec-Ślesicka.

Cast: Wojciech Pszoniak (Dr. Korczak), Ewa Dałkowska (Stefa Wilczyńska), Teresa Budzisz-Krzyżanowska (Maryna Falska), Marzena Trybła (Esterka), Piotr Kozłowski (Heniek), Zbigniew Zamachowski (Szulc), Jan Peszek (Bauer), Aleksander Bardini (Adam Czerniakow), Wojciech Klata (Szloma), Krystyna Zachwatowicz (Szloma's Mother) and Jerzy Zass, Michał Staszczak, Agnieszka Kruk, Karolina Czernicka, Maria Weymayr, Anna Mucha, Adam Siemion (children) and Marek Bargiełowski, Maria Chwalibóg, Andrzej Kopiczyński, Robert Atzorn, Janusz Bukowski, Stanisława Celińska, Edgar Hoppe, Barnhard Howe, Ewa Isajewicz-Telega, Piotr Kazimierski, Grzegorz Klien, Zygmunt Kęstowicz, Agnieszka Kumor, Olaf Lubaszenko, Katarzyna Łaniewska, Alicja Migulanka, Włodzimierz Press, Jan Prochyra, Danuta Szaflarska, Aniela Świderska-Pawlik, Zbigniew Suszyński, Tomasz Traczyński, Jerzy Walczak, Maciej Winkler, Jacek Wójcicki, and others.

Stuntmen: Janusz Chlebowski, Robert Brzeziński, Józef Szczepański, Ryszard Janikowski.

Studio: Wytwórnia Filmów Dokumentalnych i Fabularnych – Warszawa. Geyer Werke – Berlin. Film Studio "Perspektywa" – Regina Ziegler Filmproduction – Telmar Film International – Erato Films – ZDF – BBC Films.

Premiere: 6 May 1990, Kraków.

Pierścionek z orłem w koronie (The Crowned-Eagle Ring [a.k.a. The Horse-Hair Ring]), 1993

Director: Andrzej Wajda.

Screenplay: Andrzej Wajda, Maciej Karpiński, Andrzej Kotkowski, (based on a novel by Aleksander Ścibor-Rylski *Pierścionek z końskiego włosia* [The Horsehair Ring]).

Cinematography: Dariusz Kuc.
Set Design: Allan Starski.
Interior Set Design: Anna Kowarska.
Costumes: Małgorzata Stefaniak, Wiesława Starska.
Music: Zbigniew Górny.
Sound: Małgorzata Lewandowska, Andrzej Bohdanowicz.
Editing: Ewa Smal.
Photos: Renata Pajchel.
Production Manager: Barbara Pec-Ślesicka.
Cast: Rafał Królikowski (Marcin), Agnieszka Wagner (Wiśka), Adrianna
    Biedrzyńska (Janina), Maria Chwalibóg (Liaison Officer), Jadwiga
    Jankowska-Cieślak (Mrs. Choińska), Cezary Pazura (Kosior), Mirosław
    Baka (Tartar), Piotr Bajor (Steinert, Home Army Maj.), Tomasz Konieczny,
    Jerzy Trela, Jerzy Kamas, and others.
Production: Film Studio "Perspektywa," Heritage Films, Cine Elektra,
    Regina Ziegler Filmproduction, Erato Films.
Premiere: 21 November 1992, Polish Feature Films Festival in Gdynia.

Nastasja (Nastasja), 1994

Director: Andrzej Wajda.
Screenplay: Andrzej Wajda. From the stage adaptation of *The Idiot* by Fyodor
    Dostoevsky by Andrzej Wajda and Maciej Karpiński.
Cinematography: Paweł Edelman.
Scenography and Costumes: Krystyna Zachwatowicz.
Japanese Translation: Masao Yonekawa.
Japanese Adaptation: Masafumi Soito.
Sound: Małgorzata Lewandowska.
Cast: Tamasaburo Bando (Prince Mishkin/Natasha Filipovna), Toshiyuki
    Nagashima (Rogozin).
Production: Say-To Workshop (Tokyo), Heritage Films Ltd. (Warszawa).
Premiere: 29 November 1994, on the opening day of the Japanese Artistic
    and Technical Center, Manggha Center, in Kraków.

Wielki Tydzień; (Holy Week), 1995

Director: Andrzej Wajda.
Screenplay: Andrzej Wajda, (based on a short story by Jerzy Andrzejewski).
Cinematography: Wit Dąbal.
Scenography: Allan Starski.
Costumes: Wiesława Starska, Andrzej Szenajch.
Interior Set Design: Ewa Braun.
Music: G. F. Narholz, F. Ullmann, S. Burtson, O. Siebien, R. Baumgartner,
    J. Clero, V. Borek.
Sound: Krzysztof Grabowski.
Editing: Wanda Zeman.

Assistant Directors: M. Magdalena Szwarcbart, Ewa Brodzka, Joanna Lambert.
Assistant Camera Operators: Jan Górski, Zbigniew Szukała.
Scenographer's Assistants: Ewa Rojek, Robert Czesak, Grzegorz Piątkowski, Waldemar Weiss.
Sound Assistants: Witold Popkiewicz, Jacek Szatański.
Editing Assistant: Małgorzata Orłowska.
Photos: Renata Pajchel.
Assistant Producers: Grażyna Kozłowska, Jan Janik.
Producer: Lew Rywin.
Production Manager: Michał Szczerbiec.
Cast: Beata Fudalej (Irena Lilien), Wojciech Malajkat (Jan Małecki), Wojtek Pszoniak (Zamojski), Magdalena Warzecha (Anna Malecka), Jakub Przebindowski (Julek Malecki), Bożena Dykiel (Mrs. Piotrowska), Cezary Pazura (Mr. Józef Piotrowski), Agnieszka Kotulanka (Karski's Wife), Artur Barciś (Zaleski), Krzysztof Stroiński (Osipowicz), Michał Pawlicki (Irena's Father), Maria Seweryn (Miss Marta), Tomasz Preniasz-Struś (Władek), Andrzej Szenajch (the Guard), Radek Pazura, Norbert Rakowski, Agnieszka Buczek, Andrzej Brzeski, Ewa Kolasińska, Dawid Wójcik, Maria Skowron, Agnieszka Mirowska-Tomaszewska, Paweł Iwanicki, Maciek Syta, Krzyś Stanczykiewicz, and others.
Production: Heritage Films, Polish Television and Film Production Agency, Canal Plus, WFDiF, Warszawa 1995.
Premiere: 6 November 1995 at the Polish Feature Films Festival in Gdynia; and 20 February 1996 at the International Feature Films Festival in Berlin.

Panna Nikt (Miss Nobody), 1996

Director: Andrzej Wajda.
Screenplay: Radosław Piwowarski, (based on the novel *Miss Nobody,* by Tomek Tryzna).
Cinematography: Krzysztof Ptak.
Set Design: Janusz Sosnowski.
Costumes: Małgorzata Stefaniak.
Interior Set Decoration: Wiesława Chojkowska.
Sound: Piotr Zawadzki.
Editing: Wanda Zeman.
Second Director: Krystyna Grochowicz.
Assistant Directors: Wojciech Klata, Anna Kiliańska.
Assistant Camera Operator: Jacek Januszyk.
Set Designer Assistant: Krzysztof Stefankiewicz.
Photos: Renata Pajchel.
Assistant Production Manager: Robert Lipiński.
Production Manager: Barbara Pec-Ślesicka.
Cast: Anna Wielgucka (Marysia), Anna Mucha (Kasia), Anna Powierza (Ewa), Stanisława Celińska (Marysia's Mother), Janga Jan Tomaszewski (Marysia's Father), Małgorzata Pieczyńska (Kasia's Mother), Małgorzata Potocka (Ewa's Mother), Leszek Teleszyński (Ewa's Father), Anna

Romantowska (Instructor), Anna Chudzikiewicz (Polish Language
Teacher), Elżbieta Karkoszka (Art Teacher), Małgorzata Hajewska (Mad
woman), Adam Siemion (Tadzio), and others.
Production: Film Studio "Perspektywa," Janusz Morgenstern, Polish
Television, 1995/96.
Premiere: 25 October 1996.

Pan Tadeusz (Mr. Thadeus), 1999

Director: Andrzej Wajda.
Screenplay: Andrzej Wajda, Jan Nowina Zarzycki, Piotr Wereśniak (based on
the long poem *Pan Tadeusz* by Adam Mickiewicz).
Cinematography: Paweł Edelman.
Music: Wojciech Kilar. Recorded in the Concert Hall of the Great Symphonic
Orchestra of the Polish Radio, Katowice.
Assistant Director: Adek Drabiński.
Second Directors: Marek Brodzki, Ewa Brodzka.
Assistant Directors: Marcin Szczerbic, Karolina Wajda, Ilona Braciak, Michel
Lisowski.
Producer: Lew Rywin.
Cast: Bogusław Linda (Soplica Jacek [Rev. Robak]), Daniel Olbrychski
(Gerwazy), Grażyna Szapołowska (Telimena), Andrzej Seweryn (Judge),
Marek Kondrat (Count/Hrabia), Krzysztof Kolberger (Adam Mickiewicz),
Siergiej Szakurow (Rykow), Jerzy Bińczycki (Maciej Królik-Rózeczka),
Alicja Bachleda-Curuś (Zosia), Michał Żebrowski (Soplica Tadeusz (pan
Tadeusz)), Jerzy Trela (Podkomorzy), Jerzy Grałek (Wojski), Marian
Kociniak (Protazy), Piotr Gąsowski (Rejent), Andrzej Hudziak (Asesor),
Władysław Kowalski (Jankiel), Krzysztof Globisz (major Płut), Cezary
Kosiński (Bartek Brzytewka), Marek Perepeczko (Maciej Chrzciciel), Piotr
Cyrwus (Maciej Konewka), Wojciech Alaborski (Buchman), Stefan Szmidt
(Bartek Prusak), Lech Dyblik (Szlachcic), Adam Wolańczyk (Skołuba),
Henryk Baranowski (Napoleon Bonaparte), Krzysztof Kołbasiuk
(Dąbrowski Jan Henryk), Józef Fryźlewicz (Kniaziewicz Karol Otto),
Andrzej Łapicki (Ksiądz), Mieczysław Kalenik (Stolnik), Grażyna
Barszczewska (Stolnikowa), Dorota Naruszewicz (Ewa Stolnikówna),
Maria (Mariola) Mamona (Podkomorzyna), Ewa Konstancja Bułhak
(Panna Podkomorzanka), Zuzanna Lipiec (Panna Podkomorzanka), and
others.
Production: Heritage Films, Canal+ Polska, Les Films du Losagne, Le Studio
Canal+, Wizja TV, Telewizja Polska, Vision Film Production, Komitet
Kinematografii, Agencja Produkcji Filmowej, Państwowe Instytucje
Filmowe (Apollo Film, Kraków; Film Art, Poznań; Max Film, Warszawa;
Neptun Film, Gdańsk; Odra Film, Wrocław; Silesia Film, Katowice,
Poland, France.
Premiere: 22 October 1999.
Awards: "Diamond Ticket" from the Polish Cinema Association for the
highest grossing film, 1999; "Polish Eagles" for best Cinematography, best
scenography, best music, and best director, 2000.

Zemsta (Revenge), 2002

Director: Andrzej Wajda.
Screenplay: Andrzej Wajda (based on an adaptation of a play *Revenge* by Alexander Fredro).
Cinematography: Paweł Edelman.
Director's Cooperator: Marek Brodzki.
Second Director: Ewa Brodzka.
Assistant Directors: Anna Kaplińska, Michał Piłat, Miron Bilski, Magdalena Daniel, Jan Kwieciński.
Camera Operator: Marek Rajca.
Scenography: Tadeusz Kosarewicz, Magdalena Dipont.
Interior Set Decoration: Wiesława Chojkowska.
Costumes: Krystyna Zachwatowicz, Magdalena Biedrzycka.
Music: Wojciech Kilar, performed by the National Philharmonic Chamber Orchestra in Warszawa, conducted by Antoni Wit.
Production Manager: Kamil Przełęcki.
Cast: Roman Polański (Papkin Józef), Janusz Gajos (Cześnik [Maciej] Raptusiewicz), Andrzej Seweryn (Notary Milczek), Katarzyna Figura (Podstolina Hanna), Daniel Olbrychski (Dyndalski, Cześnik's Steward), Agata Buzek (Klara Raptusiewiczówna, Cześnik's Niece), Rafał Królikowski (Wacław Milczek, Notary's Son), Lech Dyblik (Śmigalski, Cześnik's Steward), and others.
Production: Arka Film, Vision Film Production, Telewizja Polska.
Premiere: 30 September 2002.
Awards: "Polish Eagle" for best director, 2003.

❀ Andrzej Wajda—Selected Prizes

Order of the Banner of Labor (second class), Poland, 1975

Minister of Culture and Art (first class), Poland, 1975

Premio David di Donatello—Luchino Visconti, Italy, 1978

Order of Kirill and Methodus (first class), Bulgaria 1978

Cesar Award, France, 1982

Oficier, Legion d'Honneur, France, 1982

Felix—European film Award for Lifetime Achievement, 1990

Order of Rising Sun, Japan, 1995.

Super Wiktor '99 for Lifetime Achievement, Poland, 2000.

Oscar for Lifetime Achievement, United States, 2000.

Doctor Honoris Causa

American University in Washington, United States (1981)

Bologna University, Italy (1988)

Jagiellonian University in Cracow (1989)

🏵 INDEX

Pokolenie (A Generation), 1955
Tadeusz Łomnicki (Stach), Urszula Modrzyńska (Dorota), Tadeusz Janczar
(Jasio Krone), Roman Polański (Mundek) and Ryszard Kotas (Jacek)

Kanal (Kanał), 1957
Teresa Iżewska (Stokrotka), Tadeusz Janczar (Korab) and Władysław Sheybal
(Composer)

Popiół i Diament (Ashes and Diamonds), 1958
Zbigniew Cybulski (Maciek)

Lotna (Lotna), 1959
A horserider attacking the German tank

Niewinni czarodzieje (Innocent Sorceres), 1960
Tadeusz Łomnicki (Bazyli/Andrzej) and Teresa Szmigielówna (Nurse)

Samson (Samson), 1961

Popioly (Ashes), 1965
Daniel Olbrychski (Rafał Olbromski) and Piotr Wysocki (Prince Gintułt)
among Masons

Wszystko na sprzedaż (Everything for Sale), 1969
Beata Tyszkiewicz (Beata, Andrzej's Wife) with her child.

Wszystko na sprzedaż (Everything for Sale), 1969
Beata Tyszkiewicz (Beata, Andrzej's Wife), Elżbieta Czyżewska (Ela, the Actor's Wife) and Małgorzata Potocka (Mała).

Polowanie na muchy (Hunting Flies), 1969
Małgorzata Braunek (Irena) and Hanna Skarżanka (Włodek's Mother-in-law)

Brzezina (The Birchwood), 1970
Daniel Olbrychski (Bolesław) and Elżbieta Zolek (Ola).

Krajobraz po bitwie (Landscape after Battle), 1970
Daniel Olbrychski (Tadeusz) and Stanisława Celińska (Nina)

Wesele (The Wedding), 1973
Daniel Olbrychski (Bridegroom) and Ewa Ziętek (Bride)

Wesele (The Wedding), 1973
Daniel Olbrychski (Bridegroom), Ewa Ziętek (Bride) and Andrzej Łapicki
(Poet).

Ziemia Obiecana (Promised Land), 1975
Daniel Olbrychski (Karol Borowiecki), Wojciech Pszoniak (Moryc Welt), and
Andrzej Seweryn (Maks Baum)

Ziemia Obiecana (Promised Land), 1975
Workers on their way to the factory in Łódź

Smuga cienia (The Shadow Line), 1976
Marek Kondrat (Joseph Conrad) and his crew

Człowiek z marmuru (Man of Marble), 1977
Krystyna Janda (Agnieszka) and Bogusław Sobczuk (TV Editor)

Człowiek z marmuru (Man of Marble), 1977
Jerzy Radziwiłowicz (Mateusz Birkut/Maciek) and Michał Tarkowski
(Wincenty Witek) surrounded by workers.

**Panny z Wilka (The Young
Ladies of Wilko), 1979**
Anna Seniuk (Julcia) and
Maja Komorowska (Jola)

**Panny z Wilka (The
Young Ladies of
Wilko), 1979**
Daniel Olbrychski
(Wiktor Ruben)

Dyrygent (The Orchestra Conductor), 1980
Sir John Gielgud (John Lasocki) and Krystyna Janda (Marta)

Człowiek z żelaza (Man of Iron), 1981
Jerzy Radziwiłowicz (Maciej Tomczyk) and Krystyna Janda (Agnieszka, Maciej's Wife)

Człowiek z żelaza (Man of Iron), 1981
Marian Opania (Winkiel) and Bogusław Linda (Radio Technician)

Danton (Danton), 1983
Gerard Depardieu (Danton)

Kronika wypadków miłosnych (Chronicle of Amorous Incidents), 1986
Paulina Młynarska (Alina) and Piotr Wawrzyńczak (Witek)

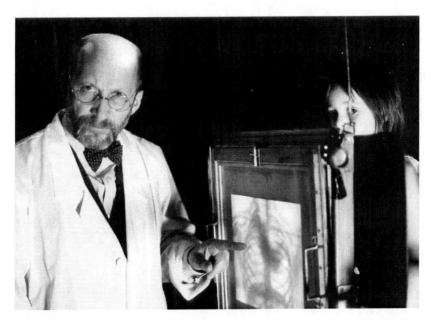

Korczak (Korczak), 1990
Wojciech Pszoniak (Dr. Korczak)

Pierścionek z orłem w koronie (The Crowned-Eagle Ring [a.k.a. The Horse-Hair Ring]), 1993
Rafał Królikowski (Marcin) and Cezary Pazura (Kosior)

Wielki Tydzień (Holy Week), 1995
Beata Fudalej (Irena Lilien), Wojciech Malajkat (Jan Małecki), Magdalena
Warzecha (Anna Malecka) and Jakub Przebindowski (Julek Małecki)